MW00994720

Objectivity and the Parochial

Objectivity and the Parochial

Charles Travis

OXFORD
UNIVERSITY PRESS

OXFORD
UNIVERSITY PRESS

Great Clarendon Street, Oxford OX2 6DP

Oxford University Press is a department of the University of Oxford.
It furthers the University's objective of excellence in research, scholarship,
and education by publishing worldwide in

Oxford New York

Auckland Cape Town Dar es Salaam Hong Kong Karachi
Kuala Lumpur Madrid Melbourne Mexico City Nairobi
New Delhi Shanghai Taipei Toronto

With offices in

Argentina Austria Brazil Chile Czech Republic France Greece
Guatemala Hungary Italy Japan Poland Portugal Singapore
South Korea Switzerland Thailand Turkey Ukraine Vietnam

Oxford is a registered trade mark of Oxford University Press
in the UK and in certain other countries

Published in the United States
by Oxford University Press Inc., New York

British Library Cataloguing in Publication Data

Data available

Library of Congress Cataloging in Publication Data

Data available

Typeset by SPI Publisher Services, Pondicherry, India
Printed in Great Britain
on acid-free paper by
MPG Books Group, Bodmin and King's Lynn

ISBN 978-0-19-959621-8

1 3 5 7 9 10 8 6 4 2

To the memory of my uncle, Herman Travis. One who knew him would find him throughout my work and throughout my way with life. Where there is good in either, I hold him responsible.

Provenance

Versions of the essays collected here first appeared, or will appear, as follows:

'What Laws of Logic Say': *Hilary Putnam: Pragmatism and Realism*, U. Zeglin and J. Conant, eds., Routledge Series in Twentieth Century Philosophy, London: Routledge, 2001, pp. 188–208.

'Frege's Target': *Logic, Thought and Language* (Royal Institute of Philosophy Lectures), Cambridge: Cambridge University Press, 2002, pp. 341–379. Reprinted by courtesy of the Royal Institute of Philosophy.

'The Twilight of Empiricism': *Proceedings of the Aristotelian Society*, vol. 104, part III (February 2004), pp. 245–270. Reprinted by courtesy of the Editor of the Aristotelian Society: © 2004.

'Psychologism': *The Oxford Handbook of Philosophy of Language*, Ernest LePore and Barry Smith, eds., Oxford: Oxford University Press, 2006, pp. 103–126. Reprinted by kind permission of the Press.

'Morally Alien Thought': *What Determines Content*, Tomas Marvan, ed., Newcastle: Cambridge Scholars Press, 2006, pp. 243–270. Reprinted by kind permission of the Press.

'To Represent As So': *Wittgenstein's Enduring Arguments*, D. Levy and E. Zamuner, eds., London: Routledge, 2008, pp. 4–29. Reprinted with kind permission of Taylor and Francis Books.

'The Proposition's Progress': *The Oxford Handbook on Wittgenstein*, Marie McGinn, ed., Oxford: Oxford University Press, forthcoming. Printed by kind permission of the Press.

'Truth and Merit': *New Essays on the Philosophy of J. L. Austin*, Martin Gustafson and Richard Sørli, eds., Oxford: Oxford University Press, forthcoming. Printed by kind permission of the Press.

'The Shape of the Conceptual': *Putnam At 80*, M. Baghramian, ed., Oxford: Oxford University Press, forthcoming. Printed by kind permission of the Press.

'Thought's Social Nature': *The European Journal of Philosophy*, forthcoming. Reprinted by kind permission of the journal, and of Wiley-Blackwell, publishers.

'Faust's Way': (forthcoming as 'Du Côté de Chez Faust' in a collection edited by Jean-Phillipe Narboux and Emmanuel Bermon).

Contents

Introduction

This seems to abolish logic; but does not.
(*Philosophical Investigations* §242)

1. The Parochial

We have the capacity to think about the world: to translate its impingement on us into making it bear for *us* in determinate ways on how to treat it (on what the thing to do would be). Rain spattering my face, I can think that my legs are getting soaked, or that I will probably catch cold, or that of the 36 plans, running for cover is the best. The idea continues: if thinking about the world is what we *can* do, thus draws on *capacities*, then surely there must be something in our constitution which *enables* it. What is thus enabled is, in Frege's terms, our 'presenting particular cases to consciousness as falling under given generalities' (1882, *Kernsatz* 4)—presenting things as we find them to ourselves as *a* case of things being such-and-such way there is for them to be, as one among an indefinite variety of particular cases that would so count. Enabling would then be, inter alia, equipping us with generalities under which to bring things.

If what so equips us is found in our constitution as the particular sort of being that we are, then we *are* equipped just as a being of that sort would be—of *that* sort. So, it seems, there might be other sorts: different constitutions, perhaps, different equipment. So, it seems, we are, or can only see that we are, thinkers *of a particular sort*, our thought of a particular form. Those generalities under which we bring things have a *particular* shape, where, for all we can see, there might be others, supplied by other constitutions with which a thinker *could* be equipped.

I will refer to as 'parochial' any form, or shape, of some being's thought which is not required simply by the demand of being a thinker as such, so that there is room for there to be *thinkers* whose thought lacked that feature—so to any form of thought for which there might be others. So, too, any feature of those generalities under which we are equipped to bring things (present things to ourselves) which might be absent from the stock of generalities under which some other sort of thinker is equipped to bring things will be parochial in the present sense.

There is always the optimistic view: our minds *equip* us with means for thinking about the world, for organizing it into a picture. But then, equally, there is the pessimistic one: our minds *saddle* us with what *pretend to be* ways of thinking of the world. So they strike us. They *would*, after all: that is what it is to be saddled with them. Might they not, though, fail to be what they pretend? If we really are equipped to think about the world, then each way we might thus think things would decide, of what the world provides for us to think that way, what is, and what is not, a case of things so being. Given the world there is to think about, might it not be, at least sometimes, perhaps always, that what we *take*—and *could* take—to decide this, really fails to do so: that that parochial design which equips us to *acknowledge* such issues as decided when we would, which thus *seems* to put generalities within our reach, really *blocks* us from seeing what is so? If there are many ways for a mind to be organized, might ours not need to be organized differently if we are genuinely to think about the world? Might not our verdicts as to which ways things are, really reflect, not those verdicts which the world itself dictates, but merely the dictates of that design we happen to be saddled with—a certain sensibility, rather than a certain *sense* for how things are? (Here, in germ, is an idea of how the parochial might threaten to abolish logic.)

A thought is of *things* being a certain way—a way it presents to consciousness as among the ways things are. Here 'things' bears its catholic reading: do not ask *which* things. Some component in a thought might represent *a* thing as a certain way there is for *something* to be. Its generality is also a scheme for partitioning the world: there are those things whose being as they are *is* their falling under that generality, and there are those things whose being as they are is *not* that. The worry here is that there may be bad schemes: the world resists partition in such terms. Not that it is yet clear what it would be for a scheme to be bad in this sense, or when one might be. But nor (despite historical attempts, to be mentioned below) is it to be ruled out that there might be such a thing.

We are equipped, or so it seems to us, with generalities in terms of which to think—following Frege, generalities under which for us to present particular cases to ourselves as falling. To be so equipped, the idea is, is to be equipped to recognize what would count as falling, or not falling, under each such generality—when a particular case would be such as so to fall, or not fall. But there are two senses of 'recognize', marked in German by 'anerkennen' and 'erkennen'—acknowledging (or accrediting), versus taking in a fact. The worry so far is: acknowledging (or accrediting) what we are prepared to as what counts as falling under some (supposed) generality may be recognition (*Erkennung*) of nothing, for we may be prepared to acknowledge where there *is* no fact to be recognized. I raised this worry in a global form: perhaps we are prepared to acknowledge things as what would count as falling under some supposed generality where there is no fact that this is so, because (the world being unfriendly to our form of thought) this supposed generality simply fails to decide when a particular case would, and when it would not, so fall; in this sense it is no real generality at all. What purports to be a way of deciding what falls under it fails to decide the cases the world we inhabit in fact provides, or even, given its grounding in that world, fails to be a coherent way of deciding *any* particular case.

This is one form a perceived threat of a gap between *Anerkennung* and *Erkennung* may take. Kant worried about the possibility of such a gap, at least enough to ask for a 'validation' of those generalities with which we are equipped—some proof that they *do* apply to our world, at the very least that they do decide the particular cases we might encounter. Kant suggests what I think has proved a more gripping, and persistent, way of portraying such a threatened gap. The idea is: if the generalities our minds make available to us for thought are genuine (in the above sense), then they are governed by certain principles involving them, which are, thus, *true*. 'Every event has a cause' would be a stab at such a principle. At the very least, and at the level of principles of greatest scope, any generality would be subject to the laws of logic. Excepting logic for the moment, Kant's idea was that, still, whether such principles *are* true depends on how the world is (where 'the world' is that of which we judge in deploying these generalities: that on which the *truth* of our judgements turns). For him, that the world is thus obliging is something that needs to be shown. (Essay 9 is the fullest discussion here of this form of the worry.)

With this portrayal of the threat, we can link Kant to an earlier tradition (Leibniz). If the generalities available to us for thought are governed by given principles, as per above, then, one might think, having them available for our thinking requires knowing, or being equipped to recognize the truth of, those principles. For example (Leibniz) it would require knowing the laws of logic. So our design equips us for such knowledge. But then the worry is how this can possibly *be* knowledge (or, in any case, whether it is). Suppose that our design merely equipped us to be unshakeably convinced of these principles. That would not be knowledge, even if we happened to be right. And with what right could we claim to be right, once we realized this? Perhaps still worse, how can we allow the parochial such a role without allowing the *truth* of these principles to depend on our design? Which, where those principles are laws of logic, it would seem, really must abolish that subject altogether (as Frege constantly insisted).

There is still another way of seeing the threat posed by a gap between a preparedness for *Anerkennung* and an *ability* for *Erkennung*. This threat can also be felt in still another way. To be equipped by design with a preparedness for *Anerkennung* is to be equipped with a certain sensibility; to have inclinations to respond to particular cases in particular ways. By contrast, the truth of a *judgement* is meant to turn only on how things *are*, independent of any inclination *any* thinker might have to respond to things so being in one way or another. But now, it can easily come to seem (it *has* often enough come to seem to some) that, with a parochial design in play, the correctness of our (would-be) judgements must be decided, in part, by the nature of our inclinations, or sensibilities, in which case it can be no true *correctness*, of the kind judgement aspires to, at all. Thus it is that the parochial can seem to destroy judgement, and so logic, in the very attempt to provide means for its exercise. (Essays 2, 4, 6, and 10 focus on this form of worry.)

Barry Stroud, in a series of highly interesting essays (e.g. 1984, 1994, 1999, 2000), has argued a thesis which I construe this way: *if* Kant is right that there is the problem he thinks there is—or an intelligible project of providing the proof he tries to give—then there is no answer to the question how we can know that *our* stock of generalities is right for thinking of the world. For all we can ever know, it is not. I think there is much to say for Stroud's view, put in this conditional form. So it had better turn out that Kant is *not* right as to what the problem is (which is not to say that there is *no* problem).

One attempt at avoiding Kant's problem is traditional empiricism. In one sense this is anachronistic, though the allure of this way with things is so strong that, I think, empiricism still thrives among us. Cast in present terms, the aim of empiricism is to deny the parochial any role in making thoughts available to us, or at least to limit that role to the minimum, so that, at least very nearly, it is the world itself, and nothing else, which makes generalities available to us in terms of which to think. To discover the need for a parochial capacity in the recognition of some domain of supposed facts is, for the empiricist, just to discover that there is really no such domain of *fact* at all. It should be obvious that the world *could not* perform the role assigned it here. And yet such is the pull of empiricism that it has not been. Essays 2 and 3 here each work towards showing why empiricism is hopeless.

2. Man the Measure

One alternative to empiricism is this idea: the parochial could not be held responsible for providing us only with pseudo-thought (or thoughts) insofar as *our* (purported) way of thinking about the world was the *only* way, the only thing thought could be: the only thing that would be *thinking*; the only way to be a thinker. In whatever respects this is true of our thought, our thought is not parochial. Even if it took some parochial design to make this available to us, what the design furnished would not be parochial. Donald Davidson, as I read him, had an idea roughly along these lines (see, e.g. 1974). Unfortunately there is no real discussion of Davidson in these essays—a failing which I still hope to make up for elsewhere. But this idea faces two grave problems—so grave that I doubt that any version which might dissolve the problem could be right. One problem is this. Suppose that it is true that there is no such thing as *another* form of thought. If you are a thinker, no matter of what species, or on what planet, you are saddled with *our* form, in whatever way we can make sense of thought, or ours, as having forms. Does that remove the problem? The problem was: if there are various forms of thought, what shows that we have a *good* one (if we do)? But suppose that there is at most one, if any, way of thinking of the world. Why think that *that* must be a good one? Any problems about the world *fitting* the categories imposed by a given way of thinking, if there are many ways, seem to remain if there is at most one. There is still the worry, if there *ever* was one: why suppose our 'thinking' actually is *thinking*. To echo Stroud, if it were not, how could we ever discover this? Would the 'thinking' we were still saddled with not be an insuperable obstacle to seeing this?

There surely *are* understandings of 'way' on which there is only one way of *thinking* about the world (if thinking is, in Frege's terms, presenting it as falling under generalities under which (or their negations) things *might* fall). To be thinking at all, for example, one must satisfy whatever is required for the objectivity of thought. That is a way of thinking, on *some* understanding of 'way'. On it, for example, one must take postures towards the world which he sees as *thrust* on him, not by psychological or physical, but by *rational* force. To judge that the salt is on the table is, per se, to see oneself as, given the world's impingement on him, having nothing else to think on that score: thinking otherwise would not be pursuing the goal, truth, hence not judging. We do not *choose* to judge. Does the fact that we think in the only way there is to think, on this understanding of 'way', help with the problem? The problem was that whatever capacities, or functions, of mind saddle us with thinking as we do might saddle us with mere illusions of judging, where it seems blindingly clear to us that judging is what we are doing. *That* problem (if it ever was one) is certainly not dissolved by there being only one form of thought in the sense just scouted. What other sense for 'way' *might* dissolve the problem?

The second problem is that such an idea wears on its face the appearance of legislation: we would not *call* something 'thought' unless it were of such-and-such form. We can, of course, decide to speak in that way. But it is not obvious how this could be anything more than a mere decision. It would be another matter if anything not of such-and-such form simply did not fit the concept *thinking*. But where this might even seem to undermine the problem it is highly unlikely to be true. The concept *thinking*, like any, is made of many strands. Its applying to something or not is a matter of the interplay of (indefinitely) many factors. So any (here relevant) claim of the form, 'It would not be (we would not call it, it would not count as) *thinking* unless such-and-such' is liable either to lie on shaky ground, or to be merely a claim about nomenclature.

Descartes, in the *Discours de la Méthode* (Descartes, 1637), proposed that there is something about us, as thinkers, which distinguishes us from mere brutes. It lies in our creativity in problem-solving and in our ability to converse. Thinkers, the idea is, have a certain distinctive versatility and plasticity in their dealings with the world which mere brutes, and mere machines, lack. That idea survives any mistakes Descartes may have made as to who the *mere* brutes, and mere machines, are. It is one central strand in the idea of thinking. Now suppose that Martians, or dolphins, in fact exhibit just that sort of creativity which Descartes had in mind (or, anyway, should have had in mind). But suppose that, for some reason or other, they are not what we would *call* thinkers. To fantasize, suppose that Martians present the world to their consciousness as tied together by relations of shmausation, rather than relations of causation, and that (implausibly) it turns out to be part of what we mean by 'think' that we would not call it thinking unless you thought in terms of causation. So Martians are not thinkers in the meaning of the act. So what? Such would be what I am calling a merely terminological point.

There is still something to be said for what I am branding here (in unscholarly fashion) a Davidsonian approach. I cannot, of course, *credit* anyone (Martian or not) with thinking that such-and-such, unless that such-and-such is something I myself might think. Saying that someone thinks that 'flamistan shrdlu', no understanding of *flamistan shrdlu* having been provided, is saying nothing. Suppose we add to this that we could not count a being as a thinker unless *we* could credit it with thinking things. Suppose we could argue from that to: a being could not *count* as a thinker unless *we* could credit it with thoughts. Then if Martians are thinkers, we can credit them with thoughts, hence ones *we* can think, *modus tollens* allowed.

Where does this thought get us? What do we do in crediting a thinker with judging such-and-such? To judge something is to hold a posture towards the world—to see, picture, it in a particular way. Each thinker holds *his* posture towards the world—pictures it as he does. To say him to judge, for example,

that the salt is on the table is to begin on decomposing his posture into elements,
particular postures there are for one to hold. One discerns a shape in his picture
of the world, one liable also to be discernible in the pictures of other thinkers. It
goes with other shapes towards forming *his* picture. With enough such other
shapes, it may go, in our hands, towards forming a picture of his picture. Now
the idea is: if a Martian is a thinker, we must be able to decompose his posture
towards the world as we decompose our own: to discern, or carve out, shapes in
it which are among the shapes one might find in the thinking of one of us—thus
to form a picture of *his* thinking. There is some plausibility in this.

Wittgenstein wrote,

Let us imagine that the people in a country engaged in usual human activities and, with
this, use what appears to be an articulate language. When we observe their doings, they
are comprehensible, seem logical. But when we try to learn their language, we find this
impossible. With them there is no regular connection between what they say, the
sounds, and their activities; though these sounds are not superfluous; if, for example, we
gag one of them, this has the same sorts of consequences as for us; without these sounds,
their activities fall into confusion . . .

Should we say that these people have a language; orders, notices, and so forth? There
is insufficient regularity here for what we call 'language'.

(*Investigations* §207)

Wittgenstein imagines people of whom we could never say that, for example
they just expressed the thought that the soup was getting cold. One might move
from this to that we could never (justifiedly) say of one of them that he *thinks*
the soup is getting cold. So, if the Davidsonian idea just scouted is right, these
people would not meet the requirements for counting as thinkers. This would
make Wittgenstein right in saying that they would not count as having a
language. (Since, if they *do* have a language, then they pass Descartes' tests.)
But *is* Wittgenstein right about this?

As a preliminary I condense a line in Frege. (One can find it less condensed in
some of the essays here, e.g. 7, 9.) Central to Frege's approach to logic, he tells
us, was to start from truth (hence judging), then to move immediately to whole
thoughts, decomposable as needed. He does not, he insists, begin with concepts
as building blocks and construct thoughts out of them. (See Frege 1919a.) It is a
consequence of this approach that, as he also insists repeatedly, a thought
is decomposable in many ways—decompos*able*, not intrinsically such as to
decompose precisely *thus*—to be one particular structuring of one set of constituents. (See 1882a, 1892b, 1919b.) Frege reminds us, 'One must not forget
that different sentences can express the same thought' (1892b: 199). When one
expresses a thought in words—in what Frege calls an *Aussage* (a particular

predication of things of things)—one decomposes it in some one way. One thus presents it under one of its identities—in one of the ways it may be viewed. If Wittgenstein's people (call them Martians) ever express thoughts, these are always presented in ways in which they cannot be presented to *us*. *We* cannot so decompose them. This does not show that Martians do not express thoughts, or even ones we might also express. Perhaps—though it follows from nothing supposed so far—we could never have sufficient grounds for ascribing to a Martian the thinking of any given thought presented in a way we *could* present one. This would make Martians *very* alien. It need not show that they fail Descartes' tests. So it *need* not show they do not think.

3. The Conceptual

Leaving Davidson's idea here for the moment, I turn to reason why it is intrinsic to thought to be parochial. For this I first need a distinction, at least inspired by Frege, which plays a central role in at least the last half of the essays here. I call it the conceptual-nonconceptual distinction. It is central to most of the essays here. It begins from this thought of Frege's:

> A thought always contains something by means of which it reaches beyond the particular case to present this to consciousness as falling under some given generality.
>
> (1882b: *Kernsatz* 4)

Any thought is, *of* a way *for* things to be (again, 'things' on catholic reading), that things are that way. It represents things *being* such-and-such way, thus representing things *to be* that way. If the thought is true, it is so in just one of indefinitely many ways for it to be true. If it is true that Sid is slurping soup, this could be true whether the soup is chicken or mushroom, whether he does so in the company of Pia or not, whether she also slurps or not, etc., ad infinitum. The generality of the thought—generality of that sort intrinsic to *any* thought, not just general ones as opposed to singular ones, etc.—consists in this multiplicity of ways for it to be true, or, since its generality is that of the way things are according to it, in the multiplicity of ways there are for things to instance that ways for things to be. What has that sort of generality, I will say, belongs to (is a bit of) *the conceptual*. It has, as I will say, a *reach*, by which it reaches some range of (in Frege's term) particular cases. For it to have the reach it does is for it to reach just those particular cases which it does, or would. On the other side of the distinction I have in mind lie particular cases. I will say little about them for the moment except that they are the sort of thing to instance bits of the conceptual (to be a case of things (or of something) being such-and-such way), and not the sort of thing themselves to be instanced by anything. For example, Sid slurping soup (read as *things being such that Sid is slurping soup*) is a way for things to be: things being as they now are is, as it happens, a case of things being that way (since, as it happens, Sid is now slurping soup).

Frege speaks of an object *falling under* a concept as 'the fundamental logical relation, to which all other logical relations reduce' (1892–1895, 128). Similarly, here, what I am calling *instancing* is the fundamental relation between the conceptual and the nonconceptual. *Logical* relations, such as entailment, hold within the domain of the conceptual. They do not hold between bits of the nonconceptual, nor between the nonconceptual and the conceptual. So, in particular, if logical inference provides the model for deriving one thing from another, then there is no such thing as *deriving* from some bit of the conceptual— some rule or principle, say—that such-and-such bit of the conceptual is instanced by such-and-such particular case. Let us dwell for a moment on what this means.

Suppose someone were to ask *why* Sid slurping soup (that way *for* things to be, such that he is doing this) reaches as it does, or what *makes* it do so. A perfectly good answer to that question would be: nothing does. It is intrinsic to that way for things to be to reach precisely as it does. You would not be talking about *that* way for things to be unless you were talking about a way for things to be with just that reach, which is to say: in specifying, or mentioning, a way for things to be we have done no less than fixing its reach. This is the truth in this idea: one may interpret an assertion in taking it to be the expression of this or that thought, but one cannot interpret a thought. An *assertion* might reach in this way or that, depending on whether it expressed this thought or that, but where we take it to have expressed some given thought, we cannot then take that *thought* to reach in this way or that, depending on some further factor. Such is part of the role of the notion of a thought in our talk about the representing that thinkers do. I will return to that idea.

But if nothing makes a given bit of the conceptual reach in this way or that, then *nothing* does. In particular, no relations between bits of the conceptual *make* any given bit of the conceptual reach in *any* way rather than any other— though identifying various relata as what reaches *thus* may, in virtue of the supposed relations, require taking some further relatum to be what reaches *so*. So if one asked what *makes* the notion *someone slurping soup* reach just where it does, it would be pure myth, or fantasy, to answer that that notion is governed by a certain rule, where a particular case is one of someone slurping soup just in case it satisfies the rule. (Though, for all this, there *might* be a rule, citing which on an occasion is then a way of explaining to someone *where* this notion reaches.) For a rule is a bit of the conceptual, and there is then the question when something would be a case of a particular case satisfying it. What we would have is an exact parallel of a homunculus explanation in psychology: the homunculus pushes the button and makes us recognize the contents of the bowl as soup, but how does the homunculus know when to push the button? (Again, this is not to rule out answering more mundane questions, such as 'Given what soup usually is, why call *this* soup?', by citing links *being soup* bears to other bits of the conceptual—against a background in which the relation of the conceptual to the nonconceptual is in general unproblematic.)

Suppose we now raise the following question. When you, or I, mention *slurping soup*, for example, as what someone is now doing, how can it be that we *mention* a bit of the conceptual which reaches in some definite particular way? Or how can we have some given bit of the conceptual in mind? (One could ask how *that someone is slurping soup* can be what we are thinking in holding the whole postures we do towards the world. But it will simplify matters here to think of the linguistic case.) Or, if you think that if we did mention *slurping soup*, then there is no *further* question as to how our mentioning reaches as it does, then how can anyone ever *mention* slurping soup?

There is something which can at least appear to make this question hard. Suppose that Pia now says to Sid, 'Would you please stop slurping your soup?' If there is something determinate she has asked him to do, then she has mentioned a way for someone to be, namely, such that he is now slurping soup, as a way Sid is now supposed to be. If she has done that, then she has mentioned what reaches in a particular way to particular cases. Now consider Sid, tomorrow, engaged in being just as he will be tomorrow—say, at lunchtime. *Ceteris paribus*, that way Pia thus mentioned either reaches, or counter-reaches, that particular case. That is, either Sid's being as he then will be is a case of someone slurping soup, or it will be a case of him not. But the thought, of that particular case, that just *that* (Sid's being in just *that* condition which he then will be in) is a case of someone slurping soup is not one now available for Pia to think at all. Just as there are (I suppose) many waiters in Bucharest of whom Pia cannot now think, '*He's* rude', so there are many particular cases (such as the one just mentioned) of which Pia cannot now think, '*That's* a case of things being the way I have in mind in asking Sid to please stop instancing someone being that way.' The reason is the same in both cases: lack of acquaintance. Having never been to Bucharest, there are ever so many waiters there of whose existence Pia is yet unaware, and thus of whom she cannot think that *they* are rude. Having never yet been impinged on by the world as it will be tomorrow at lunchtime, there is a particular case of whose existence Pia is not yet aware, hence of which she cannot now think that *that* is someone slurping soup. She may know, or have good reason to think, that Sid will be *some* way or other tomorrow at lunch, so that there will be such a thing as the way he will then be, and she may speculate that, whatever else that will instance, it will no doubt instance someone slurping soup—just as she may now hold a view about Bucharest that, whoever the waiters there may be, they are no doubt all rude. But this is another matter. Thus the difficulty. How can Pia *now* mention a way for someone to be—for example such that he is slurping soup—which, in fact, reaches (or counter-reaches) to particular cases she cannot now think of, or get in mind, at all? What makes the way she mentions one which, despite that handicap, does so reach?

It is tempting to answer this question by mentioning something else Pia *can* now have in mind. It is just here that one may be tempted to the myth mentioned above. The idea would be that what Pia *can* now have in mind is, as Frege once termed it (Frege, 1904), a 'law of association' (*Gesetz der Zuordnung*—some rule, or principle, which assigns particular cases when they arise either the status of instancing someone being the relevant way (the one she has in mind), or as *not* so instancing this (*ceteris paribus* if you like)). But this is clearly a homunculus explanation. It simply raises the further question how she can have in mind a *rule* which so reaches. And we are off on our regress. (Thus later Wittgenstein's constant fascination with the question how one can wish for something which is not even there yet, and other variations on that theme.) Let us draw the general moral. For Pia to have some way for things (or for something) to be in mind is for her to relate to some given bit of the conceptual—to which, no doubt, it is intrinsic to reach just *so*. If the question is how she can get into such a relation, the answer cannot lie in appeal to any further bit of the conceptual. No such bit, regardless of its relations to that bit of the conceptual she does have in mind, and regardless of its reach to the nonconceptual, could possibly provide the explanation needed here.

If it is intrinsic to each bit of the conceptual to reach just as it does, and a bad question what makes it so reach, there remains the problem how *our* representing (in thought and deed) reach as they do. How do *we* manage to represent particular cases as falling under particular generalities? There is a hint of an answer in this. Suppose Pia says to Sid, 'Please stop slurping your soup.' Suppose that Pia and Sid are prepared (or equipped) to agree nearly enough on when Sid would have done what she asked—of given particular cases, whether they would count as this. Then, at first approximation, Pia's communicative aims—bracketing questions of how Sid reacts to the request (e.g. whether he complies)—are achieved. In matters of saying what she wanted to, she has reached all the success she could reasonably wish. So, too, if Sid reacts in producing a particular case which both would agree is his stopping slurping, in the meaning of the act, then Pia will have achieved all the success *she* aims at of that particular sort which is distinctive of requests—all the success *in re* compliance which she could have wished. Which, at first approximation, would just *be* her request being complied with. Change from request to assertion, and the relevant success would be truth, where it is the role of the content of an assertion—the thought expressed—to be the measure of when truth was achieved. So if Pia had said, 'Sid, you are slurping your soup (again)', then the same sort of agreement, if it existed, would (again at first approximation) play the same role in fixing when truth would have been achieved.

The requisite agreement between Pia and Sid here would extend to (for them) novel cases, for example to Sid's doing just that which he will be doing the next day at noon. This is just to stress that what is involved here is not some set of actual reactions, but rather capacities (in some sense of the term). What is needed for the sort of success Pia would aim at in her request is a sort of shared capacity for acknowledgement, a sense for what to acknowledge when it comes to particular cases instancing, or not, the relevant generality, if you like, a shared sensibility. So, on the approximate story so far, it is shared sensibilities which fix what content, so what reach, our representings have. There is no *further* adjudicator, or measure, of their content—for example of what it would *really* be for one of our assertions to be true.

I have said that all this is at first approximation. What has been left out is the possibility that Pia, or Sid, or both, may be cranky, or recalcitrant, in the face of one case or another—that Sid, changing his manner of taking soup, will insist, ad infinitum, that what he is now doing is *not* slurping, where Pia is equally adamant that it is. The remedy for that is to insist that if Pia did say something (in this case, request something), then what she said is, in principle, understandable to *one*, where the thing about *one* is: for any specifiable ones, *one* might be another. That is if Pia has requested something, then indefinitely many thinkers (including ones yet to be made) *might* succeed in understanding what it was. For any given particular case, this might be novel for indefinitely many of these, and (so) these might be recognizable as understanders independently of what they make of it. What fixes the reach of Pia's representing is, thus (if it exists), a shared sensibility (sense for acknowledgement) among some such extendible community of thinkers.

4. The Parochial and Reach

Thus, in rough outline, a simple story of representing by given thinkers. To some it will seem, to be blunt, all too mired in the human, the quotidian. The response is: given what is *intrinsic* to the conceptual, there is no coherent rival story, or none any less mired in the quotidian. Useless, for example, to appeal to rules *governing* Pia's words, and to which, in using them, she implicitly subscribes. Indeed, one might well think, the mire of the quotidian—our *conduct* of our lives—is at the root of those ideas on which the conceptual is built, such notions as Sinn, or *thought*, something from which these notions may, usefully, abstract away, but ties to which can never be completely severed. (Essay 11 explores the nature of such ties.) The idea of agreement *among* thinkers may strike some as incidental. What is then called for is a private language argument, as supplied elegantly by Frege (1918: 67–69), and, again, more elaborately, by Wittgenstein (1953: 243–308).

Wittgenstein suggests the story I have just told in *Investigations* §242:

Understandings by means of language consist, not just in agreement in definitions, but (strange as this may sound) in agreement in judgements.

Agreement in judgements is agreement in judgements, of particular cases, that these are, or are not, ones of things being what was to be understood to be spoken of. The understanding that language would achieve if rightly taken is the understanding it *bears*—its content as used to achieve understanding. The remark is followed with what I have taken as the motto of this introduction. It is worth noting that the very next paragraph in the *Investigations*, §243, begins Wittgenstein's discussion of private language. Elsewhere (2006, chapter 5) I have suggested that one main reason for this is to spell out the idea that there is really no alternative to agreement in the role assigned it here in fixing the content of our representings: that agreement is *not* incidental to the case—thus counteracting the idea that it is somehow strange, or 'touchy-feely', to appeal to this as Wittgenstein does (and I just have), or that this role for agreement could possibly abolish logic. As Frege insisted, thoughts are essentially social, that is, shareable (see essays 6, 10). (So, incidentally, the idea that, as it has sometimes been put, the 'origin of all content' might lie in the relations of some supposed vehicles of thought inside the head to the environment around them is, in the end, incoherent.)

If the reach of our representings (at least in language) is fixed by agreement—by shared capacities for acknowledgement, shared sensibilities, as per above, then the parochial *permeates* our thinking—even if not quite all the way to (in some sense) the highest levels of its generality, at least nearly enough all thinking about the world we inhabit. (For discussion of such relative generality see essays 7, 9.) For take any given such sensibility—say, a capacity for acknowledging particular cases as instancing, or not, what *we* mention when we mention slurping soup. Lacking just that sensibility could not disqualify a being from being a thinker *überhaupt*. Nor would having a rival sensibility—say, one for what instances *shmurping* soup, where the reach of shmurping *largely*, but not entirely, overlaps with that of slurping, but deviates at points. Nor could it be illogical, or contradictory, for some group of thinkers to have, or be able to get, shmurping, but not slurping, in mind. Logic's confines are the conceptual. The differences here envisioned between one form of thought and another concern only perceptions of relations between the conceptual and the nonconceptual. Such differences may well mean that those envisioned different thinkers from us would have their eyes open to different regions of the conceptual than those to which ours are open. But for all that, such different beings might be as adept as we are at making the world bear on how they are to treat it. Relating the nonconceptual they encounter to bits of the conceptual within their sight, and navigating their way around that region of the conceptual within their view *might* make them as adept at dealing with the world as we are. By Descartes' tests *such* beings would be thinkers. Not that the world *is* inhabited by thinkers with other forms of thought, but that, given the role of agreement in any thinker's thought, our form of thought can only be regarded as *a* form among others.

To mention some bit of the conceptual in the ways we typically do it, is already to fix a reach for it. Such is an intrinsic part of what we are to be taken to have mentioned. Where, and insofar as, such is so, there is no *further* role for sensibility in fixing whether what we mentioned reaches *here* or *there*. That role has already been played. Fix a thought as that which Pia expressed in saying Sid to slurp soup, and what *that* thought reaches (what would instance things being as it represents them) cannot depend *further* on what anyone would take it to. Any such dependence has been played out in the fixing. But if I speak of a way for things to be—say, such that Sid is slurping soup—what does *that* reach to? Well, what did I thus speak of? Only agreement could decide that. In this way, that region of the conceptual which is available to us in thought is stamped with our shared sensibilities. There is no other way of mentioning anything which has the sort of reach it is intrinsic to the conceptual to have. That our thought is parochial—is one form among many—is just a consequence of this. It remains to say just what this means. One might *even* wonder whether it leaves *anything* for thought to be.

5. Decomposition and Agreement's Scope

What, then, of the Davidsonian idea? Its core was: we could not regard any being as a thinker if we could not (rationally, justifiedly) ascribe it thoughts—say (or take) it to think (judge) that things are thus and so, and we could not ascribe it thoughts except in ascribing it thoughts that *we* could think. That last point, at least, should be uncontroversial. What of the rest? Well, in ascribing a thought to a being—in taking it to think that such-and-such—we carve out from its whole posture (way of standing) towards the world one particular element. We, so to speak, begin on a decomposition of that posture. In *saying* a being to think that such-and-such, we, similarly, articulate some thought into elements. We *say* this by means of an *Aussage*—some given structured predicating of things of things. We structure the thought in a particular way. In each case, we articulate, or carve (on any given occasion for doing this) in just one of the ways that such articulation can be done. (Again Frege's point: whole thoughts come first; the same thought might be expressed in many different sentences.) The conceptual at our disposal is thus manifest in the bits of the conceptual we draw on in arriving at the articulations, or decompositions, that we do. Now, by the idea which I am here calling Davidsonian, we would arrive at the limits of forms of thought if we came upon a being, as adept as it may seem to be at Descartes' tests, for which we could not do this. Let us for the moment leave it moot whether such a being, thus defeating *our* capacities, might, for all that be a thinker.

The two sorts of decomposing just mentioned draw on our conceptual capacities, so *our* form of thought in a very special way. It is (at least) hard to imagine engaging in them in anything like the way we do without language. And what we do while so engaged can be very specially revealing of what the structure of our form of thought—insofar as it *is* a particular form, and has a particular structure—is. This suggests another way to view the issue. Consider, again, the Martians, with their Martian form of thought—one as alien from ours as a form could be. Still, if they are thinkers at all, and if thought is essentially social in the minimal sense just given, then, though we may be no good at decomposing either the thought of a Martian thinker, or the thoughts of Martian thinkers, the Martians can, at least, decompose each others' thought, and thoughts, for each of those two mentioned tasks of decomposition. The means they thus deploy will *identify* their form of thought just as the means we deploy identifies ours. And we must suppose they have such means. If their means *were* ours, or near enough to that, then we could, in principle, understand them, in a way in which, by hypothesis we cannot. If thought is parochial in the way just suggested, then at least what it is to be a thinker—that very way for something to be—seems not, as such, to require that this condition be satisfied. We can make that much sense of their means of decomposition, so their form of thought, being so fundamentally different from ours. Given Frege's idea that a thought is decomposable in many ways, our respective means for decomposing might *even* be mutually unintelligible, in the sense just scouted, while it remained so that anything thinkable at all is thinkable by us. Or at least if not, that would be for reasons beyond anything yet in view. This calls into question Wittgenstein's idea that those incorrigibly baffling creatures he mentions could not be regarded, by us, at least, as thinkers, or at least as language users, at all. I have just *raised* issues, not settled them. I mean only to indicate that unfolding the significance of the parochial will take more than the means so far in view; that the parochial is, after all, *interesting*.

So thinking (if there *is* any, one might be tempted to add) is an *essentially* parochial phenomenon. Our initial spectres thus return. Is the form *our* would-be thought takes adequate to the world we in fact inhabit? If so, what assurance can we have of this? And does it have that objectivity which is the hallmark of real thinking (taking) something to be so? Does its would-be truth turn *simply* on how things *are*, independent of our so taking them? Or does whether things are as we represent them turn, in part, at least, on our responses to them—what we are inclined, or designed, to feel or say, confronted with the world? Does the parochial contribute merely to *how* we represent things to be? Or must its attempts to do that ineluctably taint when things would count as *thus* represented? The phenomena of occasion-sensitivity *can*, in fact, make it difficult to see the answer here. They need to be unpacked carefully. (I have attempted that unpacking in essays 8, 11 here, also elsewhere.)

6. Frames for Representing

For defusing the worry in its first form one more familiar tactic needs mentioning. Wittgenstein tried it in *Tractatus* 6.32–6.361. He soon abandoned it. His version adapts an idea of Frege's. *If* thought is parochial, then, for Frege, logic must, anyway, be a special case. Laws of logic (for Frege the unfolding of the concept *truth*) are, to begin with, among the most general truths there are. One can read this as meaning: they are not special cases of more general laws. So, for one thing: they are not specifically about any particular sort of thing—about some one sort, that is, as opposed to any other—not about electrons, quarks, puddings, for example, or, in a sense, even about *thoughts* in any way they are not equally about anything else. So, the idea is, their truth is *absolutely* not liable to turn *in any way* on how things are, where there is even room for such a thing as their having been, or being, otherwise. (Here see essays 7, 9.) So their truth is not *hostage* to anything.

What does their truth turn on? The rough idea is: a law of logic reflects the most general structure of thought as such—of *the* domain of thoughts, or any closed under logic's ways of forming thoughts from others. For the law to be true is for that (or any such) domain to have the structure it reflects. Since the truth of the law is hostage to nothing, *this* structure would structure any such domain, thus, the idea is, for any given form of thinker, the domain of all thoughts available to him. With this we reach limits to the parochial: thought is, as a rule, parochial perhaps, but *not* in its most general structure.

I postpone logic. What is of present interest is Wittgenstein's Tractarian adaptation of this idea. His idea, in brief, is that what Frege holds of thought in general is true of the most general structure of *special* domains of discourse, at least wherever there can be a theory—an unfolding of *some* concept—which correctly assigns a most general structure to that domain. The guiding image for this idea is that of a net, or mesh. One might also use the image of a coordinate system for a space (for example, a system with an origin between my eyes, an axis through my retinas, another axis through the origin and perpendicular to it). If we wanted to describe a graffito on a wall, we might (whether in thought or deed) place a mesh over the wall. We could then describe each cell in the mesh by assigning it a colour—the aim being to assign it the colour which occupied the most of that cell. The description of all the cells jointly would then be a description of the wall. Up to a point (but only up to a point) we might make the description more exact by making the cells smaller. Our description could be true or false, depending on what colours we ascribed to what cells. But the shapes of the cells—say, hexagonal or square—have nothing to do with the correctness of our description. They are just not part of what we are describing, not something of which our description might be true or false. They determine what form our description takes (since there is one bit of it for each cell). But *they* do not aim at any correctness which is liable to turn on how *what* we describe is. So, the idea is, *they*, or their shape, is not liable to turn out to be wrong if the world is uncooperative. They aspire to no correctness which might be hostage to anything. Or so the idea goes.

Now the idea is: just as the shape of the mesh, or its cells, imposes a particular structure on the descriptions we give of the wall with the graffito, so, too, some particular domain of discourse may be governed by most general laws which impose on it a shape, but only as the mesh imposes shape. Thus, *their* correctness (truth) is no more hostage to how things in fact are than the mesh's correctness is. (There is already a telling disanalogy here. Whereas the cells in the mesh are not hostage to the world for any success at all like truth—they *aim* for none— laws of the sort Wittgenstein has in mind here, like Frege's laws of logic, *do* aim for truth.) The rather unfortunate example Wittgenstein chose to illustrate this idea was Newtonian physics. His proposal was: the laws of Newtonian me- chanics reflect the most general form of a system of description for capturing the particulars of the world's mechanics. So, whereas 'The moon has momentum M' might very well be true or false, the law that force equals mass times acceleration, like the shape of the mesh above, says *nothing* about the way the world is, so is *hostage* to nothing as to how it is.

Wittgenstein thus proposes a response to Kant. Those most general propositions which, on Kant's view, would have to be true if our form of thought had application to the world, just like propositions about the mesh we hold over the graffito, do not describe the world at all. They merely reflect the structure of that mesh which we happen to lay over it, in terms of which we then describe it. So their truth is *in no way* hostage to how the world proves to be. Kant is thus mistaken to think either that they need, or that they admit, of validation of any sort, so of the sort a 'deduction of the categories' was meant to provide. So, for example (Wittgenstein's) within Newtonian mechanics we describe the world in assigning bodies momenta, but merely reflect the structure of the mesh we thus lay over it in saying momentum to equal mass times velocity. In the same spirit,

If there were a law of causation it would have to take the following form: 'There are laws of nature.' But this can't be said. It shows itself.

(1922: 6.36)

If the parochial, in gracing us with that form of thought which is ours, stamps no more form on it than is captured by such propositions, it is entirely benign. That parochial which shapes Martian thought might, true enough, stamp it with a different form. But such differences arise only within what is, anyway, an area of entirely free choice.

This Tractarian idea starts from an important truth. It might be nice if it were right. But it is not, or not if read so as to render the parochial benign—as Wittgenstein himself was soon enough to see. Even our thought's most general forms (if such there be) are not quite as proof from being hostage to the world as Wittgenstein makes out here—a lesson of physics which, while undeniable, led twentieth-century philosophy down more than its share of garden paths. Hilary Putnam showed the right way of reading physics' lessons, and, accordingly, of responding to what worried Kant. (Here see essay 9.)

7. What Minds Might Shape

This region of the *Tractatus* may yet harbour truth. Its general form is as follows. Judging (in Frege's sense) is bringing a particular case under some given generality. So long (or insofar) as a form in thought (or in our thought) merely works to fix under which generalities we bring particular cases, it poses no threat to the aspirations of genuine judgement as to how things stand. There is, on the one hand, the *way* things are, and then, on the other, various ways *for* things to be. The *way* things are might articulate into various ranges of *ways* things are (each a way for things to be). But it might do that in many alternative ways. (Again Frege's idea of multiple decomposability of thoughts, here showing its metaphysical side.) Some ways may be more illuminating, or useful, than others. But, among these, so far as truth is concerned, it is free choice.

This idea guided later Wittgenstein's conception of engaging with the world in thought. It might also guide a conception of the objectivity of judgement. (Here see essay 4.) Very roughly, the objectivity of judgement requires that whether the particular case one brings under some generality in so judging in fact *falls under* that generality depends only on what the generality is, and on how the particular case is. Any thinker's thought is shaped by what is parochial in *it*. Ours is. So is the Martian's. For a given thinker, the parochial thus makes some given region of the *conceptual* accessible. It thereby shapes that given thinker's thought. This is not to shape whatever nonconceptual there is to instance, or not, any given item in that region. It shapes the *thinker's* thought by making only certain shapes within the conceptual available to him. But we *need* not think of this as shaping any particular item to be found in the conceptual. The parochial selects for us ways for us to represent things to be. That need not be for it to operate on any given such way so as to decide when things would be like *that*. One *could* say correctly: 'The parochial shapes *what would count as* things being such that F (though not *whether* things being as they are *is* things being F—something decided just by *how* things are). But this can just mean: the parochial fixes what it is we mention, *what* one speaks of, in speaking of F—how talk of 'being F' is to be understood. It need not be seen as deciding, of what we in fact speak of, how that reaches. All of this can be seen as no more than grammar.

This idea guides this whole collection. Again, the *Tractatus* provides a cautionary note. One can say: *insofar* as a form of thought *merely* shapes (as per above) the generalities under which we bring things, its correctness is *hostage* to nothing. But, as driven home by Putnam, it is another thing to say, correctly, or to see, of any given form of thought that that is all it does, and (virtually) never correct to say that there could be no such thing as it doing more. The world may *teach* us whether that is all it does or not, or, preliminary to that, what it might be for it to be doing more.

8. Containing the Parochial

Can our thought claim that objectivity which marks judgement? Consider Sid eating his soup at lunch tomorrow. Does his being as (or doing what) he then is, fall under the generality, *someone slurping soup*? There are, to be sure, two distinct questions here. It is one thing to ask whether his being as he then is *counts as* a case of *someone slurping soup*—whether *that* is such that Sid counts as being it. Here our capacity for acknowledgement, and for agreement, comes into play. It is, prima facie, another question whether Sid is slurping his soup. It may be agreed all around that if *he* is producing those noises (in the expected normal way), then he *is* slurping; if not, not. There may still remain the question where those noises are coming from and how. (Compare the (in)famous 'whoopee cushion'.) Those whose disagreement as to whether Sid is slurping turns on such matters may be disagreeing on objective matter of fact, though if they continued to disagree after arbitrarily much awareness of how it was that Sid was on that occasion, then they would disagree (inter alia) as to what slurping is—and though there may be variation across occasions for saying so in just when they would count as having the one sort of dispute, and when as having the other.

So those who disagree as to whether Sid is slurping may disagree as to how Sid is, or, of his being as he is, whether *that* is someone slurping. These are intelligibly different sorts of disagreement. The first is to be resolved by further revelation as to how he is. The second, if that is all it is, is not resolvable at all, or, if so, only insofar as it is a matter of what *one* (those of us who can get slurping in mind) would count as slurping. These are different *types* of disagreement. But are actual disagreements always exclusively of the one type or the other? To caricature the situation: if thinkers like us would be inclined to acknowledge what Sid is doing now as a case of someone slurping, is that sure to have nothing to do with how antipathetic thinkers like us would find him today, or how sympathetic tomorrow (after he had brought Pia those flowers)? How certain can it really be that our sensibilities are *merely* shaping our stock of generalities under which particular cases are to be brought, and not also shaping our propensity to acknowledge the truth of particular judgements which bring one or another particular case under some such generality? How can we be sure that agreement, in the role assigned it in linking us to given stretches of the conceptual, does not, ineluctably, spill over so as to infect, and thus destroy, the *truth*, or falsity, of our would-be judgements, does not reduce them to mere expressions of our preferences our inclinations in giving names to things? Here I merely remark: the fact that we can be *mistaken* as to whether our acknowledgement is tainted by such things as finding Sid antipathetic, hardly shows that it is *ineluctably* so. If anything, the idea of a mistake here suggests the contrary.

For Sextus, to *judge* that a chariot is bearing down on one is to engage in a disrecommended form of intellectual activity. But to *say* that a chariot is bearing down, and act accordingly, is fine, so long as what you say carries only the force,

'This is how things strike me'. There is an inevitable worry that such apparent refraining from judging is just a sham. That is one way in which the distinction between judging and merely expressing feelings might collapse. The threat here is in the reverse direction. If it is agreement that decides what would count as someone slurping soup, might not all our posturing as judgers, in the serious disputes we pretend to have, be no more than sham-judging? Might we not be, through and through, impostors? That worry, even if only vaguely felt, is occasion to ask more pointedly just what the hallmark objectivity of judgement is really meant to be (the topic of essay 4). As usual, it pays to start from Frege.

Frege insists (1893, 1918) that if something is true, then it is so regardless of anyone's attitude towards its being so, or even of whether anyone has any attitude towards its so being. 'Just as a planet has been in interaction with other planets before anyone has seen it', he tells us, so a truth is true before anyone has discovered it (1918: 69). Judging is a posture whose goal is truth. The above begins on what is objective in that posture. How might it be elaborated? Today (such is progress) most people believe that the planets antedate *any* thinking (at least in our region of the universe). So, too, for the truth of a judgement. Independent of any one making it, it is a true posture *for one* to hold. To *judge* thus and so, Frege tells us, is to acknowledge its truth. To state it is to announce such acknowledgement (1918: 62). It would not be a fact that many now realize that the planets antedate thinkers unless many took a certain attitude towards things being as they are. So, unlike the fact that the planets do antedate thinkers, this last fact would not have been a fact no matter what anyone thought. For all that, it would still be a fact no matter what anyone thought as to its being so. This points to the kind of independence of thinkers that the objectivity of judgement consists in.

9. Points of Agreement

In 1918 Frege introduces the above idea of the autonomy of truth (from us) in conjunction with another: the intrinsically social nature of thought (see essays 8, 10): anything any given thinker might think, *one* might think: anything thinkable by *anyone* may be disputed, investigated, agreed or disagreed on, by many (or any, another). There is, Frege insists (and elegantly argues) no such thing as a *private* thought. With, but only with, that as background, the following might capture the autonomy of truth from us: for anything there is to judge, anyone judges it truly just in case *anyone* who judged it would thereby judge truly. (Here see essay 4.) So if that most people think that the planets antedate thinking is something one might *judge*, then it matters not *who* judges it (if anyone), or under what conditions, rather, anyone who so judged would judge truly (if it is true), or falsely (if it is false).

This idea has the character of a regulative principle. I mean by that roughly the following: nothing in it decides *when* two people would be judging the same thing. Following Frege (though perhaps not where he himself intended), one would suspect that there may be no unique answer to that question, but that different ones would be correct as given on different occasions. Nor does anything in the principle tell us where there *is* something to judge, except that we may coherently suppose there is only where we would also suppose (coherently) that anyone who judged it would be correct just in case everyone who judged it would be. So, to take another example from Frege, if a patient complains to his doctor that he is in pain, so far, that *might* be just a *kvetch*. If there is such a thing as someone being in pain, then there is the case where the patient is in pain, and the case where he is not. If so, then, by the above, *that* the patient is in pain is something many may think. So the patient, his doctor, and some extra consultant may all agree in thinking that the patient is in pain. They may all think that very same thing; so far, at least, remaining on the same page. In which case, by the principle, either all thus think truly, or all thus think falsely. Nothing in this forces our hand as to whether there is such a thing as someone being in pain, or when the doctor and that extra consultant *would* be thinking the very same thing of the patient.

Perhaps, then, the *hallmark* of judgement's objectivity is just that if we do count a posture as one of judging, or something as a potential object of judging, we are thereby bound to treat it according to the above principles. (To grasp what judgement is, one may still need a *sense* for when to call something that, but not one the workings of which are given by the dictates of some further principles.) Such was Wittgenstein's idea in *Philosophical Grammar* (§§79–80), and, again in *Philosophical Investigations* (§§136–137). As he put it in *Investigations*,

It looks as if . . . the explanation—a proposition is that which could be true or false—determines what a proposition is in saying: What fits the concept 'true', or what the concept 'true' fits, is a proposition. So it is as if we had a concept of true and false with whose help we could determine what is, and what is not, a proposition. What *engages* with the concept of truth (like a gear), *that* is a proposition.

But this is a bad picture. . . . [T]he proposition that only a *proposition* can be true can only say that we only predicate 'true' and 'false' of what we call a proposition.

. . .

To say that check did not fit our concept of a pawn would mean that a game in which pawns were checked, in which, say, the one who lost his pawn lost—that such a game would be uninteresting, or stupid, or complicated, or some such thing.

(§136)

It is a fact of our form of thought—of our standing towards the world in the ways we do—that we *do* treat certain things as objects of judgement, as obtaining, or not, with that objectivity which marks judgement. We *do* take there to be such a thing as someone being in pain, or choking, or having that peculiar itch at the back of his throat which honeydew melon can cause. To do that is, per se, to treat certain attitudes as acknowledging what would, and would not, count as someone slurping, or feeling pangs of sciatica, or feeling the effects of honeydew; and other things as attitudes as to *how*, say, Sid is in being as he is—whether or not, for example in such-and-such way, where that would, in fact, count as someone slurping.

What would it be for us to be *wrong* in regarding something as an object of *judgement*? Wittgenstein answered this above. Perhaps it turns out to be too stupid, or complicated, or embarrassing, to suppose that there are some champagnes which have undertones of brioche on the palate, and others which do not. There is no more than such considerations to identify the *correct* place to draw the distinction between the objective and the not. This reading of Frege is philosophically interesting. Undeniably, from Hume on (and no doubt before), much ink has been spilled on trying to *argue* that, say, it *cannot* be *true* that it is better to marry than to burn—not on the perhaps reasonable grounds (if so things are) that, on due reflection, there is really nothing to choose between these fates, but on grounds of some alleged inaptitude for judgement of any proposition (or any within some relevant class) invoking the notion *better than*. So, in a way, Wittgenstein's Tractarian intuition was on the right track. That Sid is slurping is something of which to *judge*—something either true or false— (on those occasions, in those circumstances, in which it is that) is just, so to speak, a 'grammatical' fact, that is, a fact about the structure of *our* thinking— pending the world's proving to us that, for some reason (stupidity, complexity) it cannot be so regarded (by us).

The conceptual is autonomous. When we think something to be so, we connect to some bit of it which reaches just where it does, independent of *anything* else (except, perhaps, that there be those cases to reach to). It is just that the parochial is needed to forge any such connection. And, in any given case of such a connection, there is no access (at least for us—I bracket Martians) to where what we thus connect to reaches, except via exercise of those parochial capacities which forged the connection to begin with. Nor at second level (again bracketing Martians) is there any access to where such a connection has been forged, except by more of the same. There is an understandable inclination to think that objectivity *must* come to more than that. But there is nothing else for us coherently to think it to come to. Wittgenstein's unfolding of Frege's idea points us in this direction. What *may* remain is to remove anxieties provoked, most often, by inattention to the details of our means of representing those connections the parochial forges, and what we are thus connected to.

10. The Idea of Logical Competence

There remains that special case: logic. It is harder (to say the least) to identify any parochial character in those notions of which logical laws are built. It is, again, harder (again to say the least) to identify any way in which a law of logic is hostage to things being (or not being) as they are rather than otherwise. The role of a law of logic, one might well think, is precisely not to be so hostage. The problem is to understand that remark properly. Here I have much less to say than I wish I did. But I can at least point to a few ideas which I think will be important in trying to understand the role of logic better.

One might begin with Leibniz. Leibniz saw fundamental laws of logic as guiding our thinking about the world—as propositions we appeal to in our thinking, hence must grasp (so acknowledge as true) if we are to think at all. One who did not grasp these laws, he holds, could not *learn* at all. Hence, he also held, knowing them must be innate. Given the relation he saw between 'ideas', or concepts, and principles, I think we can say what must be innate to be the idea of truth and the idea of identity. (See Leibniz: 1753.) Innate knowledge; hence knowledge by design; hence knowledge which is the work of the parochial. But if there is really *no* learning without recognizing logic's laws, then logic *cannot* be parochial. On the one hand, if we need to *recognize* laws of logic to judge, or to engage in active thinking, then, it seems, knowledge of them must be innate, so the work of the parochial. On the other hand, if logic's laws describe (or reflect) the most general structure of a system to which *any* thought belongs, there can be nothing parochial in their recognition.

Perhaps the point can be finessed: *knowledge* of logic must be conferred on any thinker by *some* design—his design as the sort of thinker he is—but this need only state a condition on parochial design resulting in a *thinker*. However parochial a form of thought may be, the idea is, there is at least *a* shape it takes (somehow) which would be shared by *any* form of thought. In Frege's terms, there are, perhaps, different sorts of minds, but there is also *the* mind. (See 1918: 74.)

Can the parochial be thus domesticated? Wittgenstein worried about this in his progression from the 1936 *Philosophical Grammar* (1974) to *Philosophical Investigations* (1953) (on which see essay 7). In the *Grammar* he tried out the idea that it is for a language to say what inferential moves are possible within it, what, expressed in it, might be true, or could not be otherwise, and so on. One might see that idea as inspired by the idea of systems of representation expressed in *Tractatus* 6.32–6.34. One way to cast that idea is: a language is answerable to no prescriptions from outside it by which it might be right or wrong in what it thus lays down for operating within it. To stress, this is meant to go for *a* language—one among many—not *the* language. As he quickly saw, such a view is, at best, not *quite* satisfactory. For we cannot make sense of a language (correctly) prescribing just *anything* in such matters. As he puts it,

So does it depend entirely on our grammar what will be called (logically) possible, what not—namely, just what it permits?—But that is surely arbitrary!—*Is* it arbitrary?—It is not just any sentence-like picture that we can do something with, not every technique has an application in our lives.

(1953: §520)

So now, it seems, if grammar is not to be the final word on what is possible, what not—if it is not entirely up to a system for representing things to decide this for itself—then further arbitration can only be in terms of *us*, in terms of what *we*—I and my fellow thinkers, with whom I can share thoughts—are prepared to *recognize* as possible; to *anerkennen*, where *Anerkennung*, in such cases, is just to be *Erkennung*. At which point the parochial appears again as what seems the final arbiter.

There is a familiar oscillation here. On the one hand, while one can make logical errors, commit fallacies, in one's thought, there is no such thing as thinking *counter* to the laws of logic—thinking in a way such that some such fallacy would not *be* a fallacy. Nothing could count as that. Nothing could count as a *thought*, while also counting as not governed by logic's laws. So it seems things must be. But what *does* count as a thought? And by *what* laws must anything which so counts be governed? A thought, for present purposes, is something there is for one to think. There is what we could recognize as such a thing. It may be that there are certain laws such that we could not acknowledge this of anything, without at the same time treating it as governed by them. For there to be no such *thing* as thinking counter to these laws can require, it seems, no more than this. For there is no more *to* require. (Of course, this does not rule out our friends, the Martians, who (following Descartes) recognizably *think* things, though *we* cannot identify those things. The things *they* think may then simply fall without the scope of those laws *we* recognize as governing all *we* can recognize as a thought.)

We are thus pressed, once again, into recognizing a role for the parochial. What this oscillation shows, I think, is that its two poles reflect two different, but legitimate, perspectives on ourselves. The problem is to see each pole properly for what it is, and in proper relation to the other. Essays 10 and 11 are first steps towards that goal.

11. How Logic Speaks

But to see what it would be for a law of logic to be inviolable, in the sense in which, at the one pole of the oscillation, it shows up as such, one needs to attend carefully to what it is that such a law says, or just how it applies to the things there are for us to think, and to express. For Frege, laws of logic prescribe, for any thinker, how one must think to reach the goal, truth (1897: 139). They reflect the most general inferential structure of *a* system of thoughts within which they are themselves elements, and to which *any* thought belongs. What they reflect are inferential paths through that system. It is in accordance with this conception that Frege conceived *Begriffschrift* as a language. A very special purpose one to be sure. *Just* the thing for the purposes of certain special forms of discourse; not in general just the thing for our purposes in communicating in daily life. He suggests, in one image, that *Begriffschrift* stands to, say German, as a microscope to the eye: the eye can do so much more than a microscope, but for some purposes only a microscope will do. Or, again, *Begriffschrift* stands to German as a tool to the hand: the tool is rigid, and hence cannot do all the things which the malleable hand can; but sometimes rigidity is just what you need.

Perhaps it is misleading to view *Begriffschrift* in this way. A language, such as German, has a stock of devices, each for saying things to be some particular way. Those devices speak of things being that way; are dedicated to use for speaking of that. There is the German, 'Er hat Bohnen im Öhren', which is a means for saying of someone (male) that he has beans in his ears. *Begriffschrift*, if a language, is meant to be a thoroughly formal one. What its sentences would speak of, if anything, would thus be (no more than) structures within the conceptual, or ways bits of it relate, identified independent of identifying to what any particular bit of the conceptual reaches. The sorts of facts it would be concerned to state would be, at first approximation, like what one might know in knowing (if it is so) that, whatever else, being red excludes being green, whatever either of these bits of the conceptual reach in the nonconceptual, and hence whatever being red and being green may be. But I have already made the point that no relations between bits of the conceptual, identifiable as holding independent of identifying what reach, in particular, any of these bits have, can impose any reach on any of them. (So has Hilary Putnam. See (Putnam: 1977).)

So nothing *purely* formal, could manage to speak of such things as being red. Thus the above 'at first approximation'. The most one could state in *Begriffschrift* would be generalizations about ways for things to be, ones which required identifying no such way in particular—or none which required more for their instancing than that some purely formal generalizations hold. I suppose that it is some such qualification which encouraged Frege to think that *Begriffschrift* could contain sentences which said things about arithmetic. Might Frege be right? Perhaps arithmetical propositions can be conceived as no more than generalizations over domains of the conceptual, without reference to specific bits of it, or committing to there being any bit with some given reach within the nonconceptual (ones, e.g. concerning equinumerosity). Or perhaps some suitable notion of formality allows *Begriffschrift* to count as formal while committing to the reach of some of what it speaks of.

But perhaps again all that is more than Frege really needs. To say that *Begriffschrift* is not a language is not to disparage it. There is a more general category to which it might belong, *means for representing facts* (about something or other). Without being a language, it *might* be a very useful such means—perhaps just what Frege needed for his envisaged refutation of Kant. One salient species within this genre—another thing *Begriffschrift* might be—is a *calculus*. A logical calculus consists of some stock of representations of logical forms (forms *for* a thought, or, more generally, a bit of the conceptual), to take (on a decomposition), and some rules for calculating on these forms—for moving from given such forms to given others. If it earns the title *logical* calculus, then these rules capture (represent) some of what some laws of logic say. For a usual calculus, the moves from form to form pass along truth-preserving paths from form to form; some or all of the truth-preserving paths there are, given the relevant laws. Such is the technique of representing by which a calculus may represent logical facts.

Wittgenstein called logical calculi 'objects of comparison' (e.g. *Investigations* §§130-131.) He had the following in mind. Take some given discourse, or set of thoughts, or propositions—thoughts expressed in some way that interests us. One may use a calculus—say, some standard first-order one—to represent, say, entailment relations between these items. But first there is a step to take. I believe that the familiar term for this step is 'propaedeutic'. Since calculi deal in forms *for* a thought, thus for thought, to take, for each item in the set to be represented, one needs to assign it some relevant form. It needs to be a form the item may count as having, and as having in the context of all the assignments made to all the other items in the set to be represented. The calculus supplies the forms. But, notoriously, neither it, nor logic, tells us when a given such assignment is correct (for given purposes). *That* is not a logical matter. It is, so to speak, a question borne on from both sides of the conceptual-nonconceptual distinction. Anyway, if (but only if) we carry out the propaedeutic properly, the calculus will then represent some of the relations which in fact hold (or at least count as holding on the occasion of so using the calculus) between the items in our set.

We can now compare two conceptions of what laws of logic say, and, correspondingly, of what it would be for a law of logic to be correct. On the one, such a law is a reflection of a structure within the domain of all thoughts—that domain to which any thought belongs. Most notably, it reflects the presence in that domain of certain truth-preserving paths, whose nodes are *particular* thoughts. It is itself an element in that domain. Those paths connect other elements in that domain. The law thus tells us that *those* elements are so connected. (Perhaps the law does not require there to *be* just those elements. There would have been no such thing as the thought that Frege was bearded had his parents, as it were, missed the boat. I set such complications aside.) On the other, at least part—perhaps not all—of what it would be for things to be as per some law of logic—say, the law that a conjunction entails each of its conjuncts—would be for calculi which represent that law (as per above), and are otherwise correct, to have all (and no more than) the correct applications that they do—to represent just those bits of discourse which count as so related as so related. It then remains to say just what these applications are—a task liable to be occasion-sensitive. (Essay 1 expands and argues the second approach.)

Conceiving things in the first way, there is an answer (whether, as Frege would put it, we mere humans can see it or not) to the question which paths *from thought to thought* a given law reflects, and, thus, to the question what lies on these. So the law speaks in just that way to just those thoughts. It is at best not clear that there is any answer (available to us mere humans or not), provided just by things being as they are, to the question what correct applications a given calculus admits of (or to the further question just which calculi might capture some of what a given law says). Or at least an answer to questions of this second form has more room for appeal to our shared sensibilities. It is, correspondingly, not logic alone which tells us *which* thoughts are connected to each other in which ways. On the first approach, it is logic alone which fixes (at the most general level) just which thoughts are connected by truth-preserving inference. On the second, there is a new space in which, just *perhaps*, the parochial may operate (on which see essay 7). All of which, again, is to raise, not to settle, issues.

12. Coda

By now I have assembled a particular view of a more or less familiar landscape. Each of the essays collected here explores some of it so viewed. I hope the view is not so alien as to discourage, and that these explorations cast at least a little light. The essays appear here, so near as I can recall, in the order of their composition. I have tried to keep modifications to a minimum. About halfway through this series I ceased to use footnotes. Initially, that was provoked by a new word-processor. But it became a point of principle: if it isn't worth including in the text, save it for elsewhere. I am not sure just what the status of this principle is. But I think it has had a salutary influence on my style. So I converted earlier essays into that style. Twice, I think, but no more, that involved adding to the text. Somehow, a crucial point was lost from essay 1 on the way to its initial appearance. Its last section is now modified to include it.

Three of the essays here (1, 5, 9) were originally written as homages to Hilary Putnam, who, from the beginning, inspired all I have done. Four essays (6, 7, 10, 11) are on Wittgenstein. I mean them to offer an interpretation. But they also offer views to which I subscribe. Be warned. One essay (8) compares Austin and Frege. One (3) is on Quine (and why Quine and Putnam are two, not one). One essay (2) finds, and defends, a common thread in Noam Chomsky and John McDowell. Most of the essays are on Frege in one way or another. Here, too, there is a shift from early to late in seeing Frege more and more as a guide to truth. For this I would like to give thanks to Cora Diamond, whose provocative essays on Frege and nonsense incited me to read him more carefully. The essays on Putnam (and Quine) focus more on questions of, so to speak, the hardness of conceptual structure, and the idea of conceptual truth. The essays on Wittgenstein and Austin focus more on questions of occasion-sensitivity (the role the parochial assigns occasions for representing). Essays 1 and 6 have the most to do with logic. Essays 2, 4, and 5 focus most on (allaying) fear of the parochial. In the end, though, all of the above themes run through all the essays, each of which approaches these in a different way.

My doctoral dissertation (1967) was on innate ideas. Though I never returned to it, that, and the issues it addressed—as raised, for the most part, by Noam Chomsky, and responses to him—first provoked my interest in the parochial. By the mid 1990s I had begun to see those parallels between Chomsky's attitude towards the parochial and John McDowell's which I take up in essay 2. I thereby also began to see just how pervasively attitudes towards the parochial have informed (or misinformed) philosophy as it has been practised recently, and is practised now. This makes the topic worth considering purely in its own right, as I have done here. I also saw, though, that I, in particular, had to come to proper terms with the parochial in order to make the right kind of sense out of the phenomenon I had studied almost exclusively up to then, and which I think is (usually) crucial to framing philosophy's problems properly (where that can be done at all), namely, that phenomenon which I have called 'occasion-sensitivity' (see Travis 2008). Enough by way of motivation.

I began the first of the essays selected here in 1999 (if memory serves). The last reached its present form at the end of February, 2010. I hope to have made some progress on the way in framing issues clearly. A few friends have been a major influence throughout. I have already mentioned Hilary Putnam. I must now mention Peter Sullivan, Mike Martin, and Mark Kalderon. Larry Sklar helped with the first essay. Later pieces have benefited from my contact with Jocelyn Benoist. In the later stages of the series I was inspired, with new perspectives on the history of philosophy, but also, more importantly, with a state of mind more suited to philosophy, by Sofia Miguens. Though it may not show, when I write about Frege, or Wittgenstein, or Martians, I try to keep Jim Conant and Tom Ricketts in mind, mostly as exemplifying a clarity I can only aim for. The earliest work here was supported in part by an Arts and Humanities Research Council (UK) sabbatical leave extension fellowship. The latest was supported, in part, by a research leave fellowship from the Mind Association.

28 February 2010

1

What Laws of Logic Say

Suppose I said, 'Is blue has mange'. Suppose none of my words did anything other than what, in English, they are for doing. In English, 'is blue' is for speaking of some indicated object as coloured blue. It can do that only where something indicates what has been said to be that way. In English, 'has mange' is not for that. Nor, in the present case, is there any other such device. So 'is blue' cannot have performed that function here. Nor, by hypothesis, did it perform any other. Similar remarks apply to 'has mange'. So I did not say anything as to how things are. The words I used performed no function at all; *a fortiori* they said nothing.

The point here transcends English. It is also about thoughts; more generally, representations. A representation may represent some object as coloured blue. But it can have that feature only if it has a further one: for some object, it must have the feature of representing that object as being coloured blue. If there is one thought according to which *some* given thing is coloured blue, there are many. One such thought is distinguished from others, inter alia, by *what* it represents as blue. There is such a thought only if there *is* something it is thus about. So while there may be such a thing as representing Pia's cat as blue, there is no such thing as 'representing is blue as having mange'. There may be a thought that Pia's cat is blue. But there is no such thing as 'the thought that is blue has mange'.

If we consider severally all those features that distinguish some thought from others, only certain combinations of these are jointly features of what might be a way of representing things: only some combinations could identify a thought. A given such feature can be a feature of a thought only in certain combinations. So, it seems, thoughts come in certain forms. Whatever is a thought has one or another form that there is for a thought to have. Only certain forms are ones a thought might have.

That idea combines naturally with two others. The first is this. A representation of things as thus and so answers to the way things are: it is correct or not, or, perhaps, neither, according to the way things are. It is so evaluable because it at least purports to represent things as a certain way. What does not so purport is no representation, so not thus answerable to how things are. By the initial idea, there are limits to ways of intelligibly so purporting, fixed independent of anything the world might teach. What is, and what is not, a *possible* representation is decided independent of experience.

The second idea is that logic is an artefact of the forms of thought: the forms there are decide what logic must be. Predication can be done only where an object is, or objects are, its subject; true predication only where *they* are as represented. Hence existential generalization. Combine this idea with the last, and laws of logic are distinguished from other generalities about the way things are, for they are in no way answerable to the way things are. In the same way that it makes no sense to suppose that, contrary to what we always thought, 'Is blue has mange' really does express a thought, it makes no sense to suppose that such and such a law of logic might prove false.

Such is a picture with a powerful appeal. But points we owe to Hilary Putnam also make it suspect. Putnam's core point, for present purposes, is that our concepts are, on the whole, at least, world-involving. The world plays its role, not just in supplying things that fit them and things that do not, but also, crucially, in determining, by being the way it is, what it would be for something to fit, or not to fit, any one of them—what would so count—sometimes even whether there is such a thing as fitting them. For the world to do that is for it to show something about the forms it is possible for a thought to take. If time travel is possible, for example, then thoughts about before and after cannot take the forms we thought. So, it seems, the forms of thought are not independent of experience. Perhaps there is a fixed point at which the world's effects run out. Perhaps that is the point where logic starts. But why should one believe that?

No one sees better than Putnam why the picture is suspect. Still, it is hard not to feel its pull. Resolving that tension is Putnam's project in 'Rethinking Mathematical Necessity'. There he finds a qualitative difference between laws of logic and other generalities. At the core of that difference is the fact that 'logical truths do not have negations we (presently) understand' (Putnam 1994: 256). On the other hand, we should resist thinking that laws of logic are guaranteed immunity from proving wrong. We should reject, as he puts it, 'the idea of a nature of thought (or judgement, or ideal language) which metaphysically guarantees the unrevisability of logic.' (Ibid.) That, in fact, he tells us, is another idea we cannot understand.

Putnam is right. But there is more to say. It is what logic *says* that leaves little, though not no, room for its laws to prove wrong. What follows develops that idea. It retains the idea of logic as an artefact of forms of thought, but examines how, and in what sense, a thought might have a form. I will take more seriously than Frege did his idea that a thought has a structure only relative to an analysis.

The idea will be that we see thoughts as with given structures, and, correspondingly, apply logic in given ways, for particular purposes. We are not free to go in for such things in just any way we please. On the other hand, a thought itself dictates no one particular way of assigning it structure, and logic no one way of applying it to thought. The picture of logic that will emerge is found in Wittgenstein's *Investigations* §§96–131. I will refer to those passages in developing it. It is a very different picture from the conventionalism of which Wittgenstein is sometimes accused.

1. Making Sense

If someone suggests that laws of logic have negations we cannot presently understand, or that a present denial of a law of logic would lack a definite sense, some might suppose that that talk of sense, and understanding, cannot be fully literal: 'lacks sense' here can only mean preposterous, or something of the sort. For such English sentences as 'Some contradictions are true', or 'Snow is white and snow is not white', are perfectly meaningful. So, one might think, there is a definite way things are according to them—some contradictions are true: snow is both white and not white, and so on. Is there such a thing as the way things would be if such a statement were true? Deadpan disquotation alone cannot answer that. Putnam's point here is serious.

Putnam contrasts negations of laws of logic with other propositions which, no matter how preposterous, he thinks we can understand. As an example, he suggests the (or a) proposition that the moon consists of Roquefort cheese. But it is none too easy to see what such a statement would assert. Suppose that tomorrow you unfold your morning paper and read the headline, 'Scientists discover that the moon consists of Roquefort cheese.' What could that mean? 'Roquefort' is an *appelation contrôlée* for a ewe's milk cheese aged in certain specific caves in south-eastern France. How might that have got to the moon? Is this a hitherto secret part of French agricultural policy—some desperate attempt to deal with the European cheese mountain? Or is the point, perhaps, that the moon is made of a substance which, while lacking the official seal of origin, is phenomenally indistinguishable from Roquefort cheese? Or is it merely in some sense chemically the same thing, though perhaps phenomenally easily distinguishable? (Compare a statement, of a diamond, that it is really just coal.) Or has it been discovered that our current theory of elements is really quite wrong: there are really five *Urstoffe*, including water, fire, etc., and, most surprisingly of all, a stuff which has been known, up to now, in its pure state, only in the form of Roquefort cheese?

The above conjectures do not merely represent different ways in which the moon might consist of Roquefort cheese, or different reasons scientists might have for saying so. They also represent different understandings one might have of what it would be for the moon to be made of Roquefort. A statement describing the moon as made of Roquefort might bear any of these, among others, as the proper understanding of how things are according to it. According as it bore one or another of them, it would be true under one or another set of conditions. For example, on some of these understandings, but not others, such a statement might be true, even though the composition of the moon made no contribution to French agricultural policy. So if someone describes the moon as made of Roquefort, and we do not know more about why he would be saying that about the moon, so about what would make the moon the way he said, then we really do not know what it would be for things to be the way he said, so when the way things were would count as things being as he said. And we do not know that despite the fact that the English he produced is perfectly meaningful English, and we, being English speakers, know what the words he used mean. We have no adequate grasp on when his statement ought to count as true. Such a grasp must derive from further facts as to what he was doing in so describing the moon.

Now suppose someone said, 'Sometimes both a statement and its negation are true', or 'Snow is white and snow is not white'. As with statements about the moon and Roquefort, we would not, as things stand, know what was meant. Here not knowing that means not knowing when what was said would be true. If there is no knowing that, then there is no such thing as 'the conditions under which what was said would be true'. So no definite statement would have been made at all. In a case such as this, we would not know what was meant without some further story, parallel to the story that might have appeared under the headline about the moon and Roquefort. And now Putnam's point can be seen this way. While, with a bit of imagination, we can see what an adequate further story about the moon and Roquefort might be like, we presently have no idea of what a further story might be like for a statement negating some law of logic, so nor of what such statements might be used to describe as so. It is not that a claim that some statement and its negation are both true is preposterous. Such a claim does not get so far as being preposterous. For as things stand, there is no answer to the question just what way it is preposterous to suppose things are. To see Putnam's point in this way is to see that it needs to be taken seriously.

A problem about what sense the denial of a law of logic makes is in part a problem about what sense the law makes. One solves *that* problem by saying what laws of logic do—just how they connect with what we think. That is the present project.

2. Frames and Games

What, if anything, it would be for logic to prove wrong depends on the commitments, if any, that logic makes. If logic is committed to the world being thus and so, then one thing it would be for it to be wrong would be for the world not to be that way. But, on a widely held view of logic, it has *no* such commitments. What logic is committed to depends on what it is about. In some way or other it is about many things. In *some* way, it is about language and thought, and, specifically, about certain sorts of relations between statements, or thoughts—ones in terms of which *some* correct inference can be defined. What matters, though, is in just *what* way it is about those things. (If logic is to be an artefact of forms of thought, it matters just how, or in what sense, a thought may have a form.) This section begins to develop Wittgenstein's answers to these questions.

In *Investigations* §94, Wittgenstein speaks of 'the subliming of all of representation' through

[t]he tendency to assume a pure intermediary between the propositional *signs* and the facts. Or even to try to purify, to sublime, the signs themselves.

The remark looks back on the main work of the *Investigations* up to that point. The idea, in brief, is this. Suppose I call a certain tomato 'red'. When I would speak truly depends on what one should understand by a tomato's being red. The mere fact that I called it 'red' does not by itself decide what it would be for things to be as I represented them. By contrast, if my words had specifiable representational features which added up to the expression of a 'pure intermediary' (what Wittgenstein elsewhere called a 'shadow'), then those features in themselves, independent of further considerations, decide all that is decided as to when things would be as I represented them. The *Investigations* up to §88 has been an extended argument against the idea of such pure intermediaries. Whatever it is that makes *our* representations right or wrong, Wittgenstein has argued, it is not their having some representational identity which, on its own, decides when the world agrees with them, and when not.

The point so far can be seen as the atomistic form of an idea which also has holistic implications. On the atomistic side, the rejected idea is that a representation has a structural identity which determines all that is so as to when it would have represented truly. The counter idea is that any structure—any spelled-out constraint on representing truly—admits of understandings. The holistic idea concerns a range of representations. The idea is that that range is organized in *one* particular way into a system of connections, such as entailments, between its elements; and that each element has a structure which fully determines its place in the system, so that it is just these structures, collectively, that determine all that is determined as to where such connections hold. The counter idea is that there is no one way such ranges are so organized—no one system of connections—and no one structure in the elements on which, alone, their import depends.

In *Investigations* §97 Wittgenstein states the holistic idea of a pure intermediary as follows:

Thought is surrounded by an aura.—Its essence, logic, presents an order; in fact the *a priori* order of the world, that is, the order of *possibilities*, which must be in common to thought and the world. But this order, it seems, must be *utterly simple*. It is *prior* to all experience, must run through all experience; there must be no empirical cloudiness or uncertainty about it.

Thoughts (or statements), and so the facts they represent, stand in one particular order—notably, in one particular set of inferential relations. The task of logic thus becomes to locate thoughts, or statements, within this order. Describing ways one thought may relate inferentially to others becomes describing *the* ways thoughts and statements relate. Logic could do such a thing only by being sensitive to specifiable features that thoughts and statements have intrinsically. A thought must thus have, intrinsically, features adequate for logic to be sensitive to, a particular form or structure which decides its logical properties, so far as they are decided. Logic says what such a structure must be. That idea of forms of thought began this essay. Wittgenstein flags it as an illusion.

In §93, Wittgenstein warns that 'the forms that we use in expressing ourselves about propositions and thought' may engender 'a misunderstanding of the logic of language', one that makes us think 'something extraordinary must be achieved by propositions'. I have just described the misunderstanding. On engendering he says this:

The ideal is unshakable. You can never get outside it . . . There is no outside; no air to breathe out there.—Where does this idea come from? It is like a pair of glasses on our nose through which we see whatever we look at. It never occurs to us to take them off.

(1953: §103)

We predicate of the thing what lies in the method of representing it. Impressed by the possibility of a comparison, we think we are perceiving a state of affairs of the highest generality.

(1953: §104)

(*Tractatus Logico-Philosophicus* 4.5): 'The general form of a proposition is: This is how things are.'—That is the kind of proposition that one repeats to oneself countless times.

One thinks that one is tracing the outline of the thing's nature over and over again, and one is merely tracing round the frame through which we look at it.

(1953: 114)

In representing (rightly) we may structure what we represent. The structure in our way of representing may be mistaken for structure intrinsic to what we represent. That would be so if there were other equally right ways of representing as so the very thing that we did that did not structure it in that way—even if each, perhaps, structured it in some way or other. It might also be that what we represent as structured in a certain way may be rightly so represented only given the conditions of our representing it; if the world were otherwise, in ways we can imagine, then, though we would still be representing the same thing as so, it would not be representable as structured in that way. (Something, perhaps, may be seen, for certain purposes, but not for others, as structurable, in some given way.)

Different maps of a given city may divide it into different neighbourhoods, or draw the boundaries between neighbourhoods differently; some may divide it, not into neighbourhoods, but merely into quadrants. Some may divide it into a north and a south side, and different such maps may draw that division differently. It may well be of some such set of maps that no one map is, for such reasons, right (wrong) where the others are wrong (right). None of the maps, perhaps, misrepresents the city, though for each, some of the way it represents the city as structured lies in its method of representation, rather than in the city itself. Some methods of representation would, of course, cease to be ways of representing how the city is if circumstances were very different than they are. If the city rotated twice a day around some axis, we might be unable to represent it rightly as with a north side and a south side. If its bits continually rearranged themselves like a kaleidoscope, we might be unable to think of it (correctly) as dividing into neighbourhoods, or even into quadrants.

The idea here was broached by Frege, who suggested that, though any expression of a thought (an *Aussage*) structured it in some one way, the thought itself was structured only relative to an analysis (Frege 1892: 199–200). The same thought, he suggested, may predicate such and such of such and such on one way of structuring it, but predicate different things of different things on another. It might even be singular on one way of structuring it, general on another. (Frege does not seem to have suggested that whether a particular way of structuring a thought is available at all may depend on how the world is.)

In representing something we may structure it in *one* way it is structurable. The point applies only where we *represent* the world. That is not the only way we view it. Sometimes we just look or listen. In doing that we see, or hear, some of how things are. To do that is not to *represent* things as some way (controversial as that *may* be in some quarters). Nor is it to see things as structured in any one particular way. If Pia saw the petals falling from the rose, that report of what she did may have, or be seen as having, a certain structure—one naturally also seen in the sentence 'The petals fell from the rose'. But that encounter with the world is also describable (equally well modulo the point of the description) in a multitude of other ways. She saw the incidence of petals in the vicinity of the rose's centre on the decrease. She saw the centre of mass of a collection of rose petals shifting groundwards. And so on. No one such description exhibits *the* structure of what Pia saw in a way in which the others do not. In that sense, the world is structured in no one way; no one order is *its*.

One might think that representing the world to oneself as thus and so just *is* structuring it in some one particular way; if one has done the former then, *ipso facto*, for some particular structure, one has structured things in *that* way. But that is not correct. Suppose Pia *thinks* that the rose has lost its petals. So she represents the world to herself as one in which things are that way. One might say: she represents the rose to herself as (newly) petal-less. As with seeing, that account of what she thinks structures it in a particular way—or is naturally seen as doing so. But the question that needs asking is: How else might one (on occasion) say her to think just that? Might we (at least sometimes) equally well say her, for example, to think that gravity has robbed the rose of its petals, or that the petals, moved by gravity, are now elsewhere? Might there not be indefinitely many ways of saying what she thinks, each of which structures it differently? If so (as, on reflection, seems so), then taking things to be thus and so is not structuring them in any one particular way.

In describing, we structure. That point is of particular concern to Wittgenstein where what we represent are our representations, or representings, themselves. For, he says, 'the forms that we use in expressing ourselves about propositions and thought' may lead us to misunderstand 'the logic of language' (§93). Our ways of saying what it is that was said, by so and so, in such and such words, or what so and so thinks, may lead us to attribute structure to such things that is really only in our ways of representing them. What might that point come to in the case of representing language, or particular uses of it to say things? The words in which a statement is made seem really to have a particular structure, which is not just in some way of representing them. The sentence, 'The petals fell from the rose', is rightly understood as structured in a particular way. So what structure is it that we might wrongly see as in what is said itself, rather than just in a particular way of representing it? We can get a idea of (some of) what this might be if we follow up another, earlier, idea of Wittgenstein's.

In January 1930, Wittgenstein said to Schlick and Waismann that it only makes sense to think of a proposition as structured if we think of it as part of a system of propositions within which that structure plays some definite role. To think of a proposition as structured, we must think of it as part of some system (Waismann 1979: 90). In the *Investigations* that point takes on new significance. For we now drop the idea that there is some one system which is *the* one a proposition belongs to. Consider describing the colours of objects. Suppose I describe some tomato as red. Then what I say about it—the content of my claim—depends on what I have excluded—on the fact, if it is one, that I excluded its being green, or blue, or purple, or orange. For example, I may or may not be distinguishing between being red and being orange (or maroon, or burgundy). I may or may not have been making that distinction. I will have said one thing about the tomato if I was invoking that distinction, another if I was not. That point could be put this way: the content of my description depends on the place it has, or should be understood as having, within some system of descriptions of the colour of a thing. One might even see a content for it as fixed by a place for it in some such system.

With that rough idea in mind, let us set out a simple system for describing the colours of objects. Let the system provide this set of possible descriptions: 'It's red', 'It's blue', 'It's yellow', 'It's green'. Let the constituent words, 'red', 'yellow', etc., name the obvious colours. We need not elaborate on what it is for them to do that. What needs to be fixed is what way, within this system, one describes an object as being in describing it as coloured a given one of these colours. To fix that, we will say how the system is to be used. In using it one is to make certain suppositions. (If these cannot be made, then the system cannot be used.) First, suppose that, for a large range of objects, each is correctly described, within the system, by one of the descriptions it provides. Not all objects need be describable within the system. For example, none of its descriptions may fit a sufficiently variegated object. Second, suppose that no object is correctly describable within the system by more than one of its descriptions. Third, suppose that how an object is describable within the system is something one can see just by looking, without otherwise interfering with anything. The standard for correct description is as follows: an object is correctly describable by some one of these descriptions just in case, on the above suppositions, and on the supposition that it is correctly describable in some one of these ways, it is more reasonably counted as describable by that description than by any of the others within the system. So, for example, a tomato that is a uniform deep red on the surface is more reasonably describable with 'It's red' than with 'It's blue', or 'It's green'. If the tomato were mottled so that equal amounts of its surface were red and green, then it would be as reasonable, but no more so, to call it red as to call it green. So such a tomato would have no correct description within the system.

Where this system is committed to the world being, or not being, certain ways rather than others, it is liable to be mistaken. But finding such commitments is no simple matter. It might be, for example, that nothing is correctly describable within it: all objects the world could produce are so variegated that none is ever more reasonably describable as some one colour rather than various others. That would make the system useless. But being useless is not quite being mistaken. We do not yet have commitment.

The system has other notable non-commitments. Nothing within, or about, the system tells us that it is the only system for describing the colours of things. Nor is there anything about it that tells us what any other system would have to be like in order to be a system for describing colours. It is not even so that whatever is correctly describable as green, or red, or etc., in this system would be correctly so describable in any system for describing the colours of things. No plausible system could make such claims. To begin with the simplest case, imagine a system just like our original one, but with an enlarged set of possible descriptions, including 'It's brown'. Now consider a rennet apple, mostly encrusted with brown but which is, say, green wherever there is no brown crust. In the original system, this apple is correctly describable as green. For if one had to choose some one thing to call it from among the options the system provides, then green would be the most reasonable option. In the enlarged system, though, there is a more reasonable description: the apple may be described as brown. In the enlarged system, as in the original, that description is correct only if no other, including 'It's green' is. So what was a correct description in the original is incorrect in this one.

The sort of apple just described is sometimes correctly describable as green, or as red, and sometimes not as that, but rather as brown. So each system captures a sometimes-possible way of talking about the colours of things. Other things sometimes describable as green, or red, are not correctly so describable in either system. Nor is either system committed to there being no such cases. We sometimes distinguish between red and yellow melons by their interiors, so not by a feature to be seen *just* by looking (at an intact one). A rotten apple, no longer correctly describable as red within either system may nevertheless be, for some purposes, a rotten red apple. Watching the sun set over Dagenham one might remark, 'Look how red the sun is!' There are systems for describing colours (ways of doing that) in which that is a correct description, though viewed from Quimper, or Bath, the sun may not look red at all. Such systems are not our sample one, but nor are they ruled out by it.

Consequent on the above non-commitments there is another. Within the original system (enlarged by suitable devices for conjunction) there is no such thing as a correct description, 'It's both red and green (all over).' Necessarily, any such description of an object, *given within this sort of system*, is false. But the system is not committed to being the only one for describing the colours of things. Nor does it tell us what other such systems might be like. No system could do that. So, while the principle 'Nothing is red and green all over' necessarily holds within the system, the system does not tell us that it holds of *all* systems for describing colour—of all sometimes right ways of thinking of objects as coloured. The structure of a particular system does not confer necessity of that sort.

Our simple system provides a way of understanding some actual descriptions of the colours of objects. These can be understood as saying what such a description would. Which descriptions are correctly understood in that way? English cannot be our guide here. It provides the means for saying what colour something is. But the very fact that there are many systems for describing *colours*, each differing from others in its standards of correctness, shows that *English* makes no one of these *the* one in which descriptions of colour are given in English. Any way of thinking of an object's being coloured would be a right way of thinking of what some description in English said. Nor need *anything* about a description make some one system *the* one to which it belongs.

To view a description as within the system is to see it as subject to certain standards of correctness. That may be illuminating. Whether it is depends on how that description is rightly understood. It may be an illuminating way of viewing my description if, in whatever cases matter, I will have represented rightly just in case I represented rightly by the standards of that system: things will be as I ought to be understood to have said them to be just in case that description of them within the system is correct. That, in turn, is decided by the perceptions of those competent to understand it—those sufficiently au fait with the circumstances of its giving (so, inter alia, with English) and with normal human sensibilities.

Whether a description can be seen as within a given system also depends on how the world is—on what cases need deciding to settle whether things are as thus described. Max called an apple red, answering Pia's question about what sort he put in her lunch box. The apples there were for him to call that, fall unproblematically into two sorts, only one of which is reasonably called red on any way of viewing being coloured. Then it may be illuminating to see Max as operating with our original system. If relevant apples are more peculiar—some reaching bitter brown maturity only within a box, others more stably redskinned—that may give reason to see Max's words as part of a different system.

Our original system, for example, purports to be a system for describing the colours of objects. Now imagine the system modified as follows. In the system an object is correctly describable as such and such colour just in case your Aunt Ida would call it that. Being red and being what your Aunt Ida would call red are not the same thing. So this is not a system for describing the colours of things. It wrongly purports to be that. The system would also prove mistaken if the world conspired to make it so that the colour of an object is never something one can see just by looking. Perhaps, for example, there proves to be no such thing as how an object, in relevant respects, looks—it all depends on where you are standing, or on the day of the week, or on what you ate for lunch, or, perhaps, how an object will look on the next observation is always entirely unpredictable from how it looked on past ones. There may still be ways of thinking of objects as coloured on which some are. Our sample system would not then provide one such way. (We are particularly indebted to Putnam for making us aware of cases where notions that seemed to have coherent applications to the world in fact fail to do so.)

Perhaps we can only see how thoughts relate to the world in seeing them as structured, or formed, in some way or other. One reaction to that fact is to see thoughts as all part of some one system of forms of thought. Wittgenstein suggests that we are encouraged to that reaction by our ways of describing what is said and thought. He advises against it in pointing out that structure, or form, may lie in our ways of representing thoughts rather than in the thoughts themselves. Our brief look at systems for representing things, and at what such systems may accomplish, shows something which that idea may come to. First, a given system for describing such and such—colours, for example, does not exclude there being other systems, whose standards of correctness conflict with it, that are also systems for describing that. Nor does it show what such other systems must be like. A given system for describing colours makes no claims about what the possible form of any colour description must be. Second, if a given system provides a correct way of viewing given actual descriptions, that does not exclude there being other substantially different systems that also provide correct views. Two such systems may be mutually incompatible. So if some element of a given system is structured in a certain way by its place in that system, and if some *actual* description, given by someone on an occasion, is viewable as an instance of that element—as functioning as that element does—it does not follow that that actual description is per se (uniquely) so structured. Third, a system that provides a correct view of given descriptions, or thoughts, does so only given suitable occasions and circumstances for viewing them. In imaginably different surroundings it might have failed to do so.

3. Objects of Comparison

Wittgenstein treats language games and calculi as of a piece. In §81, for example, he says,

in philosophy we often *compare* the use of words with games and calculi which have fixed rules, but cannot say that someone who is using language *must* be playing such a game.

We can use language games, or calcluli, to model some of what we say and think. But,

we can avoid inaccuracy or emptiness in our assertions only by presenting the model as what it is, an object of comparison—as, so to speak, a measuring rod; not as a preconceived idea to which reality must correspond.

(§131)

That is Wittgenstein's response to the idea of logic as exhibiting 'the one essential order in common to thought and reality' (vide §97). The system of the last section shows what it is to think of a language game as an object of comparison. A language game is defined in terms of definite rules. We have seen in what sense those may be the rules governing actual things we say. If language games and calculi are relevantly of a piece, then those same features of an object of comparison should show up in logic's application to what we say and think. This section is about how they do, and how that matters to the question how a logic might be wrong.

Suppose we see logic as about language and/or thought. Then how is it about that? Logical calculi are one way of expressing logic and its laws. So one way to pursue our question is to ask what such a calculus says. A given calculus trades in given forms. One might see it as about specific items—thoughts or statements, say—which are of those forms. But if we think that structure is read into these items from the frame through which we view them—that such an item has one or another specific structure only on a way of viewing it—then it would be better to see the calculus as simply about the forms themselves. A calculus so seen provides a view of specific collections of thoughts or statements—one view, perhaps, among many—as a map provides a view of a city by structuring it, say, into neighbourhoods.

A calculus, so viewed, defines a system for thinking about the world. Thoughts or statements may be seen as within that system, just as a colour statement may be seen as exploiting some given system for colour description. Just as the latter system confers a particular sort of content on a colour description so seen, the calculus, viewed as a system, confers a particular sort of content on thoughts seen as placed within it. A thought, when properly so seen, counts as having the content thus conferred. That does not rule out other ways of seeing it.

No system within which given thoughts might fit can, as a part of what it is, exclude there being other systems within which those same thoughts fit, and which relate them differently. Nor can any system tell us what such other systems *must* be like. It is thus no part of logic's content, on this idea of it, that such and such thoughts are of such and such forms, thus related in such and such way. Rather, a logical system only provides *forms*, related in such and such ways. For those forms to be so related is just for the system to be the one it is. To deny that any such forms were so related would be to deny that there is any such system, any such forms for thought to take. There is thus an absolute hardness to the 'must' by which these forms *must* be so related, a hardness internal to the system. Some thoughts, perhaps, may be seen as of those forms—usefully, not inaccurately, *for certain purposes*. That means neither that they *could* not be viewed otherwise, nor that they could be viewed in that way no matter what. It is not for logic to pronounce on that. The hardness of the logical 'must' does not extend so far.

Consider the simplest case: a classical propositional calculus. Such a calculus deals in truth-functional forms. It tells us how any of these forms relates inferentially to any others. Roughly, a truth-functional form is a form a statement would have if its truth value were a function of the truth values of other things which, in some suitable sense, occurred in it. Depending on how we think of things, these other things might be truth-evaluable words used in the making of the statement, or things some of the statement's words said or expressed. All that matters for the moment is that they are things that can recur—not just occur in some one statement whose truth value they determine, but also, ad lib, alone, or in combination with any other such things, in further statements. For the moment we will suppose they have a truth value independent of any particular occurrence of them. Let us call these things statements. Then the calculus is about all the forms a statement might have, or be seen as having, definable by ways its truth value might be determined by the truth values of the statements that occur in it.

The present idea is that the calculus is simply about those forms. That is an idea about what it does not say, on its own at least, about actual statements.

What it does not say, it cannot be wrong about. First, it says nothing about English. It does not claim, for example, that such and such bit of English—'or', say—is a truth functional connective, nor of any English that it is of such and such truth-functional form. That is good, since it is not a logical truth that, for example, 'or' is truth functional. Second, it does not say of any statements made in English that they have a truth-functional form, or are truth-functionally related to such and such others. Suppose there is some statement, in perfectly proper English, in words 'P or Q', which is not true even though what that 'P' says is true. That does not show classical logic mistaken.

One might still think that the calculus relates to language in this way: for any actual statement, or even for any English sentence, and for any form within the ambit of the calculus, either that statement (or sentence) is of that form, or it is not, *tout court*. If it is, then the statement must have whatever properties the calculus assigns to that form. So, for example, one might think that any statements in words 'If ... then ...', if those words meant what they do mean, is of a certain truth-functional form ('material implication', as it is usually called), or that none is, or that such and such ones are, and such and such ones are not. It only remains to discover which of these possibilities are facts of English. On the present idea, though, we need not, and often should not, think in such ways. Instead, we might say this of a conditional: viewing it as subject to the calculus in the obvious way sometimes provides a correct view of some of the inferential relations it may sometimes count as bearing to some other statements. Perhaps that is the right view of most conditionals. It allows us to acknowledge what anyway seems right: there are clear insights to be gained, on occasion, into what a conditional says through the sort of exercise in symbolizing that we learn in elementary logic, but few, if any, conditionals have all the properties of something of that obvious truth-functional form.

Suppose we view each of some arbitrary collection of conditional statements as of the obvious truth-functional form, which we might write '... mc ...'. Relying on our intuitions as to which antecedents and consequents say the same as which others, we replace each by some letter of the alphabet, using precisely one letter for each thing that some antecedent or consequent says. So we might see one statement as of a form, A mc B, and another as of the form relative to it, B mc C. The calculus tells us that material implication is transitive. So, when so viewed, a statement of the form A mc C will follow from the first two. There are two general points about this scheme for viewing collections of conditionals.

First, to see a particular collection in this way is to assign each conditional in the collection a particular understanding, where, normally, that is only one of many understandings such a conditional might bear—so where that understanding may or may not be correct. Suppose, for example, that one conditional is some statement, 'If Pia leaves early, she will catch her train', a second is some statement, 'If Pia catches her train, it will be late', and a third, some statement, 'If Pia leaves early, her train will be late.' Does the third follow from the first two? It does if the calculus applies to the collection in the way just envisaged. But whether it in fact follows depends on the right way of understanding each of the first two conditionals. The second, for example, might have been offered as a remark on Pia's tardy ways. If so, there is a way of understanding it on which it might be true even though if (unthinkably) Pia did leave early, then she would catch her train, even if it were on time. Similarly, the first may bear an understanding on which its truth requires that she would catch her train even if it is on time. In that case the conclusion does not follow. The two conditionals do not, so to speak, mesh with each other so that transitivity applies (even though their antecedents and consequents match in the right way). There are other possible ways of understanding such conditionals on which they do so mesh. (Understanding them as meshing may just *be* one such way.) Where those other ways are, or count as, right, the calculus applies. Crucially, though, there are various ways of understanding conditionalization, for given antecedent and consequent. A classical calculus does not, and no calculus could, capture all of them in any one set of inferential rules.

A second point now emerges: whether a given set of conditionals counts as meshing may depend on how the world is. It may also depend on the point in counting those conditionals as meshing or not. It may even sometimes be a matter of choice. Here is an illustration. Wine affects Max badly, so Max seldom drinks it. But he occasionally succumbs. A dinner is in the offing, about which Pia remarks, 'If Max drinks wine, he will have a hangover.' Suppose there were an effective hangover-blocking drug. Suppose Max discovered it and took it before the dinner. Then he might drink wine without a hangover. That mere possibility does not show Pia's remark false. In speaking of this drug, we are talking fantasy, not describing what might happen.

We may know that Max is resolved not to drink wine at this dinner. He has already had, he reckons, one hangover too many. So we may tell the host to count Max out when it comes to calculating how many bottles will be needed. A fanciful observer might speculate on what would happen if Max came upon a hangover-blocking drug. Exasperated, we may allow, truly, that if Max discovers such a drug, then he will drink wine. As things stand, understanding Pia's conditional in the above way is understanding it so as to fail to mesh with what we would thus say. For if it did mesh, we would get the result that if Max discovers such a drug, then he will get a hangover, the falsity of which would show Pia's conditional false. But Pia's conditional is not thus shown false.

Suppose that, counter to our belief, there really is a hangover-blocking drug, Max does find it, takes it, drinks wine at the dinner, and does not get a hangover. Then, at least for many purposes, it would be a fair understanding of Pia's remark on which we could correctly point out that she proved mistaken. Let us try a weaker supposition. There is such a drug. Max might well have discovered it, but by chance did not, and did not drink wine. If we take the possibility of his discovering it seriously enough, then we have good grounds for counting Pia's remark false. The view that we thus take of her conditional is one on which we may well be able to count it, correctly, as meshing with our further conditional above. Change the facts as to how the world is, and we may also change what Pia's remark might count as meshing with.

When is the possibility of Max's discovering the drug serious enough for us to be able to view Pia's remark correctly in this last way? An answer need not follow simply from the circumstances of her speaking. The point in taking the possibility seriously, or not, may make the difference for what it is right for us to say. Or perhaps we can simply choose how seriously to take it. We might, accordingly, view Pia's conditional as meshing with our own, or as not. Either view may be sometimes correct, or at least permissible.

We apply a calculus to trace inferential relations between sets of statements (or thoughts). But which inferential relations in fact hold, or count as holding, between a given statement and others may depend on how the world is. It may also depend on the circumstances in which we would count given relations as holding or not. This is to say that the applicability of a given calculus to a given discourse also depends on these factors. Particles such as 'if/then' exhibit here a feature Putnam has always insisted on for any sort of language *we* could use. The content of given conditional statements, like the content of statements about water, or colours, or weights, depends not just on some understanding of them that we might have had no matter how the world was, but rather on what understandings the world makes intelligible. The world plays a substantive role, not just in questions of truth, but in questions of content. It decides what contents are possible.

No point made so far begins to show that a classical propositional calculus is mistaken. Such a calculus does not claim of any particular conditional that it has such and such form of which the calculus speaks, nor even that a conditional must either have such a form *tout court*, or lack it *tout court*. Nor does it claim of any set of conditionals that they must mesh, or even that they must either mesh or fail to mesh *tout court*. So far we have only been discussing ways a calculus may be applicable or not. The point has been that this calculus may provide a correct way of seeing some discourse, or may fail to, in just the ways our system for describing colours may be, or fail to be, applicable.

We have yet to speak of laws of logic. But we have reached a crucial point at which Wittgenstein and Putnam intersect. Suppose that the colour descriptions *we* can give are such that we could never describe anything truly as red and green all over. What kind of fact is that? For later Wittgenstein, the fundamental fact is that, within a given system for describing the colours of things, there is no such true description. We may regard that sort of fact as a hard, non-negotiable, necessity. Perhaps, too, as things stand, no colour description we gave would be correctly viewable as part of any system in which such a fact failed to hold. But neither of these facts entails that there could not be a system which both counted as a system of *colour* description, and in which there was such a thing as a true description of something as both red and green all over, nor that our actual descriptions could not *turn out* to count as part of such a system.

That is a way of formulating for colour descriptions a point Putnam emphasizes for logic in the essay now under discussion. Our present understanding of colour descriptions does not allow for true descriptions of a thing as both red and green. But the world can teach us understandings we cannot now imagine, so cannot now have. We cannot *now* entertain the possibilities that would allow for. But if two descriptions could be conjoined intelligibly into one possibly true one, it would not automatically follow that they were not of, respectively, things as being red, and things as being green. Here, then, Putnam and Wittgenstein are one (and not just lately). It remains to see how these ideas apply to logics, and to laws of logic.

4. How Logics May Be Wrong

In this Wittgensteinian idea of a logic as a frame through which we may look there is a familiar Putnamian theme: it is not as if the meaning of a particle selects some logic as *the* one that applies to it, nor as if, conversely, there is some logic, or specific set of inference rules, such that for that logic, or those rules, to apply just is for the particle to mean what it does. Meaning is just not that sort of thing. It is not as if *whenever* we viewed words as governed by other inference rules we would *ipso facto* be viewing them as meaning something other than what 'if-then' does. That fails to capture what we are prepared to recognize as to words meaning what they do. The point is the basis of his opposition to Dummett's ideas on capturing the *meanings* of connectives in terms of introduction and elimination rules, and of his opposition to Christopher Peacocke's related ideas about 'individuating' such concepts as conjunction or conditionalization in terms of 'possession conditions'. (See Peacocke 1992.)

One way of viewing this core point is: meaning leaves room for circum-stance—inter alia, the way the world is—to show what logics are usable, or best, for viewing given discourse. One thing that might mean—an idea that has at times appealed to Putnam—is that the world might show that one or another logic—classical predicate logic, say—or, again, some law of logic—excluded middle, say—is wrong. But within the present framework we need to ask what it could mean to call a logic, or a logical law, wrong. If laws of logic are features internal to particular logics, then they are not open to counter-example, just as a principle that nothing is both red and green all over, viewed as a constitutive feature of some particular system for describing colours, is not open to counter-example. Constitutive features of the frames through which we view things do not have *that* sort of content. On the other hand, it might be that a particular logic, seen as such a frame, is not one in terms of which given discourse is even possibly viewable. That logic would be wrong for that discourse, at least in the way that an architectural design may be wrong for the neighbourhood, or pliers the wrong tool for extracting teeth.

A purely hypothetical situation brings us closer to a way a logic can be wrong. Putnam's current view, as I understand it, is that quantum mechanics *could* have confronted us with such a situation, but does not. In the hypothetical case there are triples of propositions, A, B, C, with this feature: it is true that A and either B or C, but it does not follow—in fact is not true—that either A and B or A and C. For such triples, classical logic would not apply. Not only need they not be viewed through that frame; they cannot be: it provides no correct view of them. It is thus wrong *for* them. That does not make them a counter-example to classical logic. One might suppose such triples merely to show that the English 'and' and 'or' do not always behave truth-functionally (and similarly for other natural languages). Who would ever have thought otherwise? And, of course, no proposition of *logic* asserts anything about what English connectives mean. But the difficulty runs deeper. Suppose we tried to introduce two new connectives, 'et' and 'vel' into English. By stipulation these are to behave truth-functionally (in the obvious way). Then, in the imagined situation, our stipulations will have failed. For, though 'A et (B vel C)' may very well express a truth, '(A et B) vel (A et C)' cannot. So 'et' and 'vel' cannot always behave truth-functionally (if that is what truth-functional behaviour requires). Classical logic cannot be forced to apply to propositions such as A, B, and C by introducing new connectives into the language. Why, then, are they *not* counter-examples to it?

The answer is that nothing *in* logic itself asserts that it is applicable to absolutely any thought whatever. Distributive laws, since they are (partly) constitutive of classical logic, hold wherever it does apply. But the logic does not itself say where it applies. That answer is correct on the present Wittgensteinian view of what logics say. There is more to say about the case in hand. Triples such as A, B, and C, if we were forced to recognize them, would show something about our intuitive notion of a proposition. As conceived in the hypothetical case, each, singly, is a coherent description of the world. 'B vel C' is also a coherent description. So is 'A et (B vel C)'. But 'A et B' and 'A et C' are not. If we discovered such triples, it would certainly be a surprise. We intuitively suppose that coherent descriptions can always be built up, ad lib, truth-functionally into new, more complex, *coherent* descriptions. The discovery is that sometimes they cannot. So, importantly, *propositions* are not always quite what we supposed.

But, earth-shaking as that news may be, as soon as things are put this way, we see why we have, so far, no counter-example to classical logic. A logic, viewed as about thoughts, is a system for viewing, describing, or representing some inference relations between thoughts (which ones depending on the logic). It is *not* a system for describing relations between thoughts and non-thoughts, since none of these *are* inference relations. What has turned out, in the hypothetical case, is that there are no such thoughts as 'the thought that A et B', or etc. So with such monsters we leave the realm of logic—at an unexpected place to be sure. Nor is there any good reason to see classical logic as claiming that wherever there *is* a thought 'X et (Y vel Z)', there is also a thought 'X et Y', and one 'X et Z'. There is no reason to see laws of logic as saying such things.

5. Mistaken Logic

Systems for colour description *are* liable to be mistaken. A given such system does not claim to be the only one for describing colours, nor to be universally applicable, nor that some principle that holds, with the hardest possible necessity, within it, must hold in any other system for describing colours. But a given system does invoke certain notions. And it does claim at least to be coherent. Even if, perchance, no colour description we have occasion to give fits within the system, at least we can see how there could be descriptions that did fit. A given system's pretensions to be coherent *may* turn out to be bogus—for example, in ways such as those sketched for colours above. If, as I have suggested, such systems model the situation for a logic, then it should be conceivable that a logic—classical logic, say—should be mistaken in this sense too: that it should have pretensions to coherence that turn out to be bogus. That would parallel the sort of possible failure Putnam has detailed for systems for describing space or time. (See Putnam: 1962a).

The last section's discussion of the compositionality of coherent description provides a hint of what such failure might be like. Classical logic appeals to a certain notion of a proposition, or truth-evaluable item, where it is an imaginable discovery that there is no such thing. The truth-evaluable items this logic trades in have two features. First, each is free to occur in combination with any others as constituents of some more complex truth-evaluable thing. If A, B, and C are three such things, then for any (truth-functional) way of expressing a thought that involves the expression of three others, there is such a way of expressing a *thought*—a way that actually succeeds in expressing one—that involves the expression of all of A, B, and C. Second, for any such proposition, there is just one truth value which it has on any occurrence, whether in isolation, or as part of a complex. When we evaluate the truth value of a truth functional whole, on this conception, we may ask after the truth values of the constituents full stop. We need not ask after their truth values *as they occur in that whole*.

Though we may not otherwise have noticed, notions such as *thought*, or *proposition*, turn out to be cluster concepts in the sense Putnam has made familiar. (See, e.g. Putnam: 1962a.) As Putnam has emphasized, when a concept is presumably subject to a number of independent constraints—when we take all those constraints to fix the concept we use—the world may show that those constraints de facto form an incoherent whole; they cannot jointly govern any concept. In the present case, it is the strands of the cluster that, on inspection, formed our intuitive conception of a proposition, or a thought, that, in this hypothetical situation, unravel. *If* all of this is what it takes to be a proposition, and if '_ et _' is a context in which propositions must be free to occur, then neither A, B, nor C are propositions, for they cannot have both of the above two features. There is a perfectly good sense in which A, say, says the same, or represents things as the same way, on all of its occurrences. In a perfectly good sense, it speaks of, or is about, the same objects and properties throughout. But if it represents one element in all the above combinations, then it cannot be taken to have a truth-value independent of the combination in which it occurs. Conversely, if we assume that it has the same truth value wherever it occurs, then we ought not to assume that it occurs in all the mentioned combinations. If a thought must have a truth value occurrence-independently, then there is such a thought in the one combination, but no such thought in the other. (If 'A et B' does not describe a genuine, coherent, way for things to be, then neither, in that combination, does either 'A' or 'B'. It is no longer a disproof of that that 'A' would describe such a way if it occurred on its own.)

On the other hand, when the strands in a cluster concept come apart, what we may discover is that not all are needed, or always needed, to identify that of which that concept *is* a concept—in this case, what might count as a thought, or as a proposition. What we might discover—a point Putnam has always stressed—is something new as to what we *really* had in mind when we spoke, or thought, of thoughts (things there are to think) or propositions. What we may discover, as Putnam has argued so convincingly in other cases, is that the only *reasonable* course is to recognize some *thoughts*, or *propositions*, which do not have truth-values occurrence-independently, or which cannot occur in all combinations. Or even that the things we had in mind by *things to think* are regularly like that.

A logic tells us that there are certain forms for thoughts to take (whether or not such and such given thoughts take those forms). Classical logic speaks of forms whose ingredients are propositions, on that cluster-concept which we have just imagined unravelling. It would not falsify that claim if there were, here and there, thoughts that could not be ingredients in such forms. But suppose that, systematically, there could be no thoughts to be ingredients in such forms: our cluster concept has unravelled on a grand scale. (All thoughts, perhaps, turn out to be like the triples imagined above.) Then there are no such forms for a thought to take. In that case, classical logic will have been committed to something that is not so.

At a grand enough level of abstraction, we have now imagined what it would be like for classical logic to be mistaken. That does not yet take us very far. It is not as if we have yet been able to make sense of these presuppositions of logic failing in such a wholesale way. So far, we had better remain with Putnam: it would be rash to say that there is no such thing as logic proving mistaken, but we have no adequate understanding of how that might happen.

There is a further parallel with Putnam's view. It may be a feature of a given system for describing colours that within it there is no such thing as something's being red and green all over. That feature may be essential to the system. What the system cannot tell us is what other systems for describing colours must be like. Whether all of these must contain that principle depends on what would be recognizable as a system for describing *colour*. Similarly, it may be an essential feature of a given logical system that such and such a principle holds within it: without that feature, we simply would not have that system. There is all the hardness to that necessity that one might wish. But the system cannot speak to other systems. It cannot rule out ones in which the principle does not hold. Nor can *it* rule, or even claim, that no such system could count as one for representing *thoughts*, if by that we mean: things there are for one to think. In using the system we accept the principle as necessary in any application we thus make. That is not to say that it is a principle that could never rationally be given up, or even that there could never be a compelling case for doing so. With Putnam, though, we may say that there are limits to the systems we can presently conceive of, and with that may go principles we cannot presently conceive of being false. If there are such, there is nothing intelligible for us now to say in denying them.

This essay has presented a particular view of how logic is about language and thought. It is a view in step with Putnam in that it grants what logic says a special status. On it, truths of logic, insofar as there are such, do not confront experience in just the same way as, say, truths of physics, or even truths of geometry. The view carves out a restricted space in which it is not guaranteed that logic should not prove mistaken. But, by making logic's commitments minimal, it makes that space minimal as well. More argument would be needed to establish that this view is right. It was, anyway, Wittgenstein's (last) view. It provides one way of seeing just how deeply Putnam is right.

2

Frege's Target

'Hostility to psychologism', John McDowell writes, 'is not hostility to the psychological.'(1977: 181) 'Psychologism' is an accusation. But it may be one of several.

The psychologism McDowell is master of detecting is, as he sometimes puts it, a form of scientism. It is *a priori* psychology where, at best, only substantive empirical psychology would do. It often represents itself as describing the way any thinker (or any empirical, or language-using one) *must* be, as describing requirements on being a thinker at all. But it misses viable alternatives. It is just speculation as to how we are.

McDowell sees Frege as his anti-psychologistic ally. Frege attacked mis-guided applications of psychology. What he attacked might certainly be called psychologism. But his target was rather different from McDowell's, which is better seen as the mis-derivation of substantive psychological results. Frege objected to mistaking the psychological for the logical. That would involve appealing to perhaps quite genuine psychological facts as deciding questions on which they did not (thus) bear. It would be to suppose our design as thinkers of a special sort to shape, not just our particular ways of thinking of things, or our capacities to see in the world what we can, but also that which we thus think about—to make some realm of non-psychological fact what it is. That worry about reading the wrong significance into a special psychological design runs in roughly the opposite direction to McDowell's worry: failing to see where something *is* a question of special design, trying to derive from some supposed way any thinker *must* be what can only be a matter of how certain thinkers in fact are.

McDowell himself makes frequent appeal to ways in which we, or relevant thinkers, are thinkers of a special sort. Our special design opens our eyes, as he puts it, to particular tracts of reality. That our eyes may be thus opened shows where, and how, there may be facts that it takes special capacities, not enjoyed by just any thinker, to see. It also has metaphysical significance, for it identifies places where there are domains of facts which are not, or need not be, derivable from facts of other sorts—facts available to any thinker equipped only with somehow more basic, or more widely shared, cognitive capacities. It shows how facts, and domains of them, may have more varied and intricate shapes than such a reductionist demand would permit. As that idea plays out, our special capacities inform—decide in part—the shapes of the facts to which they open our eyes. We hope to read that: they decide, in part, to what shape of fact our eyes are open. But there is a risk that we will have to read it: they decide, in part, the shapes of those facts to which, anyway, our eyes are open. Or there may seem to be that risk. That idea would be the psychologism which is Frege's target. I do not think McDowell guilty of that. But to banish vertigo, one must see just where there is at least apparent risk, and how it may be disarmed. That is the main task of the present essay.

In some sense laws of logic are laws all thinkers must conform to—in whatever sense that is, they describe conditions on being a thinker at all. Depending on the sense, that may leave room for the idea that we have special capacities—features of our design as thinkers of a special sort—which allow us to appreciate the particular logical laws we do. A secondary aim here is to sketch what that room is. Failure to see it may lead one to slide (as Frege may have) from a legitimate view of laws of logic as holding for, and binding, any thinker at all, to a view of what any thinker must be like that would be psychologism in McDowell's sense.

1. Logic

For the most part Frege's anti-psychologism is highly domain-specific. It is psychologism about *logic*, specifically its laws, that is, for him, the devil. On occasion he takes a somewhat broad view of the logical, so that what is at stake is not just laws of logic. On at least one occasion he broadens his target beyond the logical to include what he calls the source of logic's brand of unconditioned necessity. Frege's views on laws of logic are encapsulated in the following:

The question why and with what right we acknowledge a law of logic to be true, logic can answer only by reducing it to another law of logic. Where that is not possible, logic can give no answer. If we step away from logic, we may say: we are compelled to make judgements by our own nature and by external circumstances; and if we do so, we cannot reject this law ... I shall merely remark that ... what is given is not a reason for something's being true, but for our taking it to be true.... Anyone who has once acknowledged a law of truth has by the same token acknowledged a law that prescribes the way in which one ought to judge, no matter where or when, or by whom the judgement is made.

(1893: 15)

Here Frege assigns two properties to laws of logic. The first might be called *absoluteness*. The truth of a law of logic depends on nothing, or nothing extra-logical. This means that a law of logic would be true (or would be a fact) no matter how things stood extra-logically, so no matter what experience might have to teach us. If we wanted to explain the truth of a law of logic by appealing to *our* nature—say to what, or how, we cannot help thinking—our attempt would misfire. And, though this may be reading things into Frege, if we tried to explain the truth of a law of logic by appealing to facts of geology, say, or chemistry, we would, presumably, equally be barking up the wrong tree (if not just plain barking). One possible source of this idea of absoluteness is the idea that laws of logic are among the most *general* facts of truth (so of thoughts). But there is another source for the idea which will emerge presently. The second feature Frege ascribes to laws of logic might be called *universality*. Whatever it is a law of logic says, it is something true of, or binding on, all thought whatsoever. It thus describes a feature of all possible thinkers, not just thinkers who share our special (human) design. (One might usefully take this mark of the logical as helping to identify what it is that a law of logic could possibly say.) That laws of logic are the most general truths, or most general facts of meaning, is an idea often identified in Frege. So, it seems, laws of logic have, on Frege's view, at least three identifying features: absoluteness, universality, and (maximum) generality.

Frege sometimes takes a broad view of the logical. Thus, in the introduction to *Grundlagen* he announces his determination 'always to separate sharply the psychological from the logical, the subjective from the objective' and 'never to ask for the meaning of a word in isolation, but only in the context of a sentence' (1884: p. x). If one violates the second rule, Frege thinks, one will inevitably try to find the meaning by staring at the word and seeing what comes to mind. What comes to mind will be one or another association one makes with the word—Frege supposes it will be what he calls an 'idea'—where the association in question is a psychological phenomenon. That will be to mistake the psychological for the logical. Whereas if one asks for the meaning of the word in context, one will be apt to answer the question by specifying the (or a) role the word plays in that context. If the context one chooses is a sentence, the role one finds is apt to be the contribution of the word to the conditions for truth of (or for being as represented by) the whole of which the word is a part. To answer in terms of role, or, at any rate, in terms of that role, is to answer by speaking of the logical, and to mistake nothing else for that. Roughly, the logical, on this conception, seems to be whatever it is (including relations to other representations) that fixes, or is fixed by, when a representation would be true.

Laws of logic, Frege insists, depend for their holding on nothing (extra-logical). There is a way in which this autonomy is shared by all logical facts, on the above broad conception of the logical. Suppose one asks why the 'Frege' in a given 'Frege was bearded', is such that if that whole is true, then that 'Frege' referred to someone. The answer might be, 'Because, in that context, that "Frege" functioned as a name.' Suppose one asked why that 'Frege' then functioned as a name. That might elicit an answer in psychological terms, perhaps on roughly these lines: 'Because that is how a competent speaker would understand it.' And indeed, that the 'Frege' in a given 'Frege was bearded' is a name does seem to depend on psychology in some way. But suppose one asked why a name is such that when it so functions in a true statement it refers to something. The question would seem to reflect some sort of misunderstanding. All one could say by way of answer is, 'That is just (part of) what being a name (or what referring) is.' That *names* have that property depends on no extra-logical fact (on our broad conception of the logical). If all competent speakers understood a given utterance, 'Frege', differently, then perhaps it would not be a name. But a *name* would have the mentioned feature no matter what. Just as with a law of logic, that *names* are thus depends on nothing.

The point extends throughout the logical in the present sense. So, for example, one might consider the English predicate, 'is a chair'. One might ask what makes that predicate such that it is true of (precisely) chairs. An answer might be that it is that by virtue of its meaning what it does. And there is presumably some psychological, or historical, story as to why it means what it does (perhaps the history of Indo-European languages). A way of capturing the fact of 'is a chair' meaning what it does is to say that it expresses the concept of being a chair. Now suppose we ask why the concept of being a chair is true of (or fits, or is satisfied by) precisely chairs. That question, too, seems to reflect a misunderstanding. For the answer that suggests itself is, roughly, 'For a concept to be the concept of a chair is just for that to be so of it.' Again, nothing extra-logical—in this case, nothing external to its being the concept of a chair that is in question—has any role in determining whether or not that concept has that feature.

At least in the cases at hand, the kind of autonomy which, in the case of laws of logic, is their absoluteness—independence of facts of any other sort—reflects the intrinsic nature of relevant features of relevant items. It is intrinsic to a name that (where there is truth or falsity at all) it identifies that item on whose being thus and so the truth of its whole depends. Nothing that lacks that feature would be a name. It is intrinsic to a certain concept that it fits whatever is thus and so. That feature is (part of) what makes a given concept *that* one. Without it, a concept simply would not be that one. So there is no way of picking out something there might be anyway—something determinately what it is independent of its having the relevant feature—and then asking why *it* should be a concept with that feature. If it *is* so identifiable, then, trivially, it is not that concept. Generalizing, facts hold absolutely in Frege's sense where their holding is intrinsic to the things they involve.

Absolute logical facts thus reflect intrinsic features of things they concern—conjunction and negation, say (and truth). A fact about those things depends on nothing just where that is just part of what conjunction and negation are (what it did not hold of *ipso facto* would not be those things). Such absoluteness is possible only for what is austerely enough conceived—what is sparse enough in intrinsic features. If there are too many things conjunction is per se—too many ways it is identifiable as the thing it is (say, both by a truth table and by some design which, per se, expresses it)—then it becomes possible to ask intelligibly how it is that what, per se, has some of these features also has the others. If, for example, conjunction has a certain distribution in our thought, then how is it that what has that distribution also has such-and-such truth table. A substantive answer to such questions, where there is room for one, is liable to make crucial (putatively) intrinsic features depend on something. (There may be absolute facts about the concept *chair* which could not hold *absolutely* of the English 'is a chair' precisely because there is something that English looks like (and the point holds even if we think of words as partly individuated by their content). That laws of logic are to be absolute in Frege's sense puts, I think, severe constraints on what such a law could say—constraints ignored in much discussion of laws of logic. (See essay 1.) It is easily forgotten that austerity is part of what absoluteness is.

On at least one occasion, Frege broadens the target of his anti-psychologism to include challenges to what he tells us is the source of logic's absoluteness: the objectivity of truth. He says,

If it is true that I am writing this in my chamber on the 13th of July, 1893, while the wind howls outside, then it remains true even if all men should subsequently take it to be false. If being true is thus independent of being acknowledged by somebody or other, then the laws of truth are not psychological laws . . . They do not bear the relation to thought that the laws of grammar bear to language; they do not make explicit the nature of our human thinking and change as it changes.

(1893: 13)

For whatever the notion of truth actually fits—whatever is, world willing, true, or, at worst, false—there is a substantive distinction between being true and being thought true (by whatever thinkers). If we think truly that such-and-such, then what we thus think so is so, and would be so no matter what, how, or whether, we, or any thinkers, thought. Whether what we think so is so, is thus not a matter of psychology. So, Frege tells us, neither are laws of truth (or of logic). To deny the objectivity of truth in this sense would just be to hold that what the facts are in those areas of reality we think about (or some of them) depends on what, or how, we, or certain thinkers, think. That doubtfully coherent conception of areas in which, as it has it, facts hold is just idealism. It is just that that McDowell (and with him Wittgenstein) must, but may seem unable to, avoid.

2. Grammar

As has emerged, Frege views grammar as, in some sense, a psychological phenomenon. He says, for example,

Grammar, which has a significance for language analogous to that which logic has for judgement, is a mixture of the logical and the psychological.

(1897:129)

If we think of the laws of logic as psychological, we shall be inclined to raise the question whether they are somehow subject to change. Are they like the grammar of a language which may, of course, change with the passage of time? This is a possibility we really have to face up to if we hold that the laws of logic derive their authority from a source similar to that of the laws of grammar

(1897: 147)

What the laws of, say, English grammar are really does depend, in some way, on psychological fact. Frege emphasizes this in part with didactic purpose. He contrasts grammar with logic in order to separate off a range of notions, such as those of subject and predicate, which, he insists, have no role to play in logic. Whenever we detect that a notion has psychological content in the way grammatical notions do, we thereby detect, in his view, that it is no part of logic. In any event, whatever objection there is to making logic out as dependent on psychology, there is no objection to making grammar out as so dependent.

Grammar, Frege tells us, is a *mixture* of the psychological and the logical. If so, in what sense is it a psychological phenomenon, and in what sense is it a logical one? For the answer to that we should look to Noam Chomsky (though not all philosophers, nor linguists, agree that grammar is psychological in the way Chomsky has pointed to). I will set out his view in terms suggested by his earliest exposition of it. But, though the terminology has changed with time, I think that, modulo one small detail, the view has remained much the same.

We might use the term 'grammar' either to refer to an explicit theory of some natural language, or to refer to the organization, or properties, that such a theory might truly ascribe to it. Thinking in the first way, we might think of a grammar as a theory which, with finite means, generates a set of sentence-descriptions, or, equivalently, a set of assignments of properties, to (what according to it) are sentences of its target language. What goals might such a theory aim to meet?

One reasonable goal would be to identify the sentences of the target language—to distinguish correctly between sentences of that language and strings of words or pseudo-words that were not sentences. To do that, a grammar should at least make some assignment of properties to each sentence of the language, and, for every assignment of properties it generates, there should be some sentence of the language that has those properties. In other terms, for every sentence of the language, the theory should generate some description that fits it, and for every description it generates, that description should fit some sentence of the language. Further, for certain designated descriptions the theory generates (think of them as full, or maximal, ones), those descriptions should fit no non-sentence of the language. One might further demand that, for descriptions of a designated sort, for every two such descriptions the theory generates, there should be two sentences of the language, each of which fits precisely one of these, and that, wherever there are two different sentences, no generated description of this sort fits both of them. (These desiderata leave it open precisely what a sentence is. For all said so far, it might just be a string of words.)

Meeting the above goal is less than one might reasonably hope for, for there seem to be clear grammatical facts a grammar need not capture in order to meet it. To take a hackneyed example, consider the sentences 'Zoë expected Des to spill his beer' and 'Zoë persuaded Des to spill his beer'. A grammar might meet the above goal without marking any structural difference between these sentences. Yet we (any reasonably fluent English speaker) can, on brief reflection, see that there is a difference. To tell the story quickly and sketchily, one expects events (or people, or objects, to arrive) whereas one persuades people (or other thinkers). If sentences may have such things as direct objects, and if direct objects are constituents, then the two sentences just mentioned must have significantly different structures. Any grammar that did not assign them such would miss a syntactic fact.

What goal could we impose on grammars that would require them to capture such facts? I have just pointed to a fact we competent English speakers are prepared to recognize, to a way we, the competent, see, or are prepared to see, such sentences as the above to be structured. One goal for a grammar might be that, in addition to meeting the above goal, it should assign sentences (just) those structures that the fluent are thus prepared to see in them. Or, more liberally, we might require a grammar to assign properties to the sentences of its target language in that way which best reflected what the fluent are thus prepared to recognize (at least so far as it is determinate which way this would be).

There are ways we see the sentences of our languages to be structured. A grammar which said which ways these were would, to that extent, at least, be saying what structure these sentences had, and, more generally, just how the language was organized syntactically. (A remark on the factivity of 'see'.) That there are such structures to describe has implications for the notion of a sentence, and thus for what it would be even to meet the lower goal set above. For it follows that a sentence is not just a string of words, but rather a string of words structured in a particular way. It follows that there might be two sentences made up of the same words in the same order, but differing in their syntactic structure. That idea corresponds to our ordinary way of thinking of a sentence. For we think of a sentence as having such things as a subject, a direct object and a main verb. Strings such as 'Flying planes can be dangerous' are, we can see, structurally ambiguous. What the subject of that string is depends on the structure it is read as having. This means, so thinking, that ordering of words is a common feature of two different sentences.

A grammar which met our higher goal would be capturing facts a grammar might miss in meeting the lower one. When we now shift to the other understanding of 'grammar' as those properties of a language which a grammar, in the first sense, might truly ascribe, we get a certain picture of what a language is. If a language is identified by its sentences, then a natural language is identified, not by some set of strings of words, but rather by some definite range of syntactic structures—those structures that its sentences might have. A language thus is, or incorporates, a particular system for forming such constructions.

This view of syntax brings out in just what way grammar is a psychological phenomenon: the syntactic facts of a given natural language are, or include, what its fluent speakers are prepared to see in it. One might view that as a form of idealism: if English speakers thought differently about their language, there might not be the syntactic facts of English that there are. But that is innocent idealism. It only makes what is plausibly the psychological, and not some domain of non-psychological fact, depend on given psychologies.

In what way, then, is grammar a logical phenomenon? 'Des', as it occurs in 'Zoë persuaded Des to spill his beer', plays a particular syntactic role. It has a particular place in a particular syntactic structure. There are two things one can say about that. In one sense (on the present view), for 'Des' to have the syntax it there does is for fluent speakers to see that syntax in it. It has that syntax because of what it is to fluent speakers, and would not have it were it something else to them. In another sense, for 'Des' to have that syntax is for it to have a certain syntactic role in that sentence—a role that a correct grammar of English (by our higher standard of correctness) would spell out. That is what it is to have the syntax 'Des' there has. That role, and not speakers of the language, is what a grammar would speak of. To speak of it is to speak of the logical in the sense of *Grundlagen*. On the view set out here, the psychologies of fluent speakers decide, at least in part, what the grammatical facts are. But to say that need not be to mistake the psychological for the logical. Nor is there any other reason to refuse to say it. So to refuse would be, it seems, to deny manifest facts.

Chomsky's work on syntax began in a climate in which a certain sort of empiricism was taken very seriously. It would not be genuine work if that empiricism were correct. His view of syntax as a psychological phenomenon is essential to his rejection of that empiricism. Next I will describe that empiricism, and then how that rejection works.

3. Empiricism:

What follows is meant, not as stipulation, but as, recognizably, a description of a family of actual positions. Empiricism is, first of all, a position arrived at a priori. Its guiding notion, put one way, is that we are universal thinkers: we enjoy no cognitive capacities, so see nothing of the world that would not be shared by any thinker with our sensory sensitivity to the stimuli that impinge on us (such things as light, sound, pressure). That idea is doubtfully coherent, presupposing as it does that there are enough capacities one *must* have (when equipped with sight, hearing, and so on) to qualify one as a thinker at all. But it is a useful way of thinking of what would move an empiricist to allow, or disallow, us the particular avenues of knowledge that he does.

The principal a priori rationale for the empiricist's view of our capacities, and our access to the world, is, I will suggest, epistemological. The epistemology at work there is sceptical. It is this epistemology that can make the empiricist's contentions that we lack cognitive capacities which would be features merely of a special psychological design seem, at least at first blush, something other than blatant psychologism. For it will be stressed that cognitive capacities are, by definition, *knowledge* yielding, and the doubt is whether any features of special design could merit that status. Since Hume, empiricists have typically allowed that we may have all sorts of special tendencies to think or feel things, or otherwise to react to sensory impingements. To that extent there are few a priori limits to the ways human beings may be creatures of a special sort. The question is whether such tendencies could ever, strictly speaking, amount to an ability to see, or to discover, how things are. The worry is that only in certain circumstances would such tendencies get things right; the design which confers them is not one for telling whether we are in such circumstances, so the design that confers them on us could never (thereby) confer on us a special route to knowledge.

That qualm is in view, for example, in empiricist attitudes towards 'ordinary language'. There are, the empiricist admits, things a fluent speaker is inclined to say. Part of being fluent may be having such inclinations. In certain cases we just would say that Pia had seen the pig loose in the turnips, or that Zoë had hurt Sid's feelings. Being so inclined is, in some sense, part of the way an unreflective fluent speaker ought to be. What the empiricist does not grant, though, is that what the fluent speaker thus exhibits is an ability to see when things are those ways the relevant bits of his language speak of being—when someone saw a pig, or caused anguish. What is in question is whether the special design that makes for relevant fluent speaking is the sort of thing that could confer the ability to gain such *knowledge*, to enjoy positions in which such questions are really settled.

When empiricism comes to a particular domain of fact, it is marked by three, or, often, four, features flowing out of the general train of thought just sketched. First, it will hold that, relative to that domain, there is a particular, specified domain of privileged fact. Privileged facts are, typically, what, for relevant purposes, is, strictly speaking, *observable*—that is, observable by any thinker with our sensitivity to the relevant sensory media. One might also think of them as what would *always* count as observable by us, no matter what doubts there may be as to how things really are. Empiricism, cast in this form, thus invokes a proprietary notion of the observable. Where there might be a thinker with adequate sensory equipment, but unable to see how things stood in the relevant domain (e.g. because he lacked relevant concepts), the privileged facts will be ones he could, in principle, be aware of, or ascertain, anyway. In such a case, the privileged facts would be distinct from those (supposedly) holding in the relevant domain.

Second, for a given domain, the empiricist will claim to identify those procedures, or abilities, which are the knowledge-yielding ones with respect to that domain. What these are is, from the empiricist perspective, something to be arrived at a priori. They will be just those capacities enjoyed by any thinker at all with relevant sensory sensitivities. Again, the guiding idea may be that for any purported capacity conferred by special design, there would be a substantial question as to the right one had to be confident in its deliverances. If we just happen to be designed to take things to be thus and so, perhaps, for all that, they are not that way—perhaps our design happens not to be a design so as to get things right. If we could, in principle, have proof that our design does not thus let us down, that proof would, the thought is, be by exercise of some capacity *not* conferred by special design. But then it will do to suppose that we have natural *tendencies*, plus universal knowledge-yielding capacities.

Third, the empiricist will hold that we can know a fact in the relevant domain only where that fact is provable, or ascertainable (with sufficient certainty) from privileged facts by application of the specified knowledge-yielding procedures. Fourth, an empiricist *may* claim that there are facts in the relevant domain only insofar as these are derivable from privileged facts according to the principles defining the correct operation of those knowledge-yielding procedures. Typically, such an empiricist will hold that the facts in the chosen domain are far fewer, and less interesting, than we would have supposed.

The relevant domain for present purposes is grammar—that is, the grammars of particular natural languages. Here the empiricist par excellence is Quine. For Quine the privileged facts are what he calls 'behaviour' (of relevant language users). Of course, Quine uses 'behaviour' in a proprietary sense. Sid tells all the women he meets he loves them. That is his wayward behaviour. But it is not behaviour in Quine's sense. The behaviour of English speakers, for Quine, is that (supposed thing) which is observable equally by an English speaker and a monolingual speaker of Tagalog. Or, better, what is observable both by a Tagalog speaker and a Martian. Quine's knowledge-yielding procedures are what might be called unconstrained hypothesis formation and confirmation. By those procedures, a given hypothesis about the grammar of the target language is confirmed just where, or insofar as, every conceivable rival hypothesis is (shown) incompatible with the privileged facts.

In the case of grammar, Quine holds not just the third, but also the fourth, tenet on the above list. So, for Quine, the facts of grammar are, in principle, much less rich than Chomsky supposes them to be. Specifically, Quine argues that for any two grammars, both of which meet the lower goal of the last section—that is, both of which distinguish correctly between sentences and non-sentences of the target language—neither is incompatible with any set of privileged facts. So at any point at which two such grammars disagree, it is not the case that one states a *fact* of grammar which the other misses. As we have seen, there is much that that excludes from the domain of grammar. The syntactic difference between 'expect' and 'persuade' is one small example.

There is a level at which Chomsky agrees with Quine's result. So long as the only standard of correctness we have for a grammar is the lower one of the last section—the one that does not require syntax to be a psychological phenomenon—there is no sense in which it can be a fact that 'persuade' behaves differently from 'expect' in the way described above. If privileged facts and knowledge-yielding procedures were as Quine claims, we would have only that lower standard of adequacy. Since Chomsky thinks that such things clearly are facts, it is necessary for him to contrapose. He must deny that we are confined to the lower standard of correctness. To do that, he must deny Quine's empiricism. The next section describes how that is done.

4. Anti-empiricism (I)

If empiricism about syntax is mistaken, it is either because it is mistaken about what the relevant privileged facts are, or because it is mistaken about knowledge-yielding techniques. Chomsky holds it mistaken on both counts. The more important count for his programme, hence, perhaps, the most prominent, is the second. The first, though, plays a crucial role in Chomsky's initial case against Quine.

Chomsky's case against Quine begins with a Moorean technique. If we abstract from Moore's execution of it, he had a core idea that went like this. Suppose we wanted to know what we were speaking of in speaking of chairs (or of something's being a chair). We would have, to begin with, two sources of information. There are, first, facts as to what we are prepared to say about particular cases: *this*, anyway, is a chair, or, more subtly, here is a case where something was correctly called a chair. Then, second, there are, or may be, facts as to what we would suppose something must do to count as a chair—be an artefact, say. Given the way human beings are, it would be reasonable to suppose there to be a defeasible presumption in favour of the first sort of data against the second, should the two come into conflict (and provided people were not mistaken about the natures of the things they were calling, or refusing to call, chairs). Moore's idea was then simply that, if we want to see what we are speaking of when we speak of someone knowing something, and hence, what would be cases of someone doing that, we should suppose the same rules of the game to be in force. To see what it is we speak of when we speak of knowledge, we must, accordingly, give a due role to what we would say as to when someone knew such-and-such.

Chomsky uses essentially that Moorean idea to turn empiricism upside down. As noted above, empiricist principles are arrived at a priori. That goes for Quine's ideas about knowledge-yielding procedures. The empiricist would be in a far different position if we could make his principles empirically testable. Relying on the Moorean idea, that is what Chomsky does. For, he observes, if we are to give particular cases and intuitions about principles their due, it should be non-controversial, by any reasonable standard, that we (tolerably competent English speakers) do know about 'expect' and 'persuade' roughly what has been said about them above. It is not as if there is any serious risk of our being mistaken about such things. What we know are facts. So it is a fact that 'persuade' behaves differently from 'expect' in roughly the indicated way. Such could not be *knowable* fact if Quine were right about knowledge-yielding procedures. It could not be a fact at all given Quine's plausible view about the knowability of syntactic facts. Thus is it empirically demonstrable that Quine is not right.

This case against Quine highlights Chomsky's rejection of Quine's conception of privileged, or (strictly speaking) observable facts. To begin with, if we reflect on what we know about our own language(s), we can see that it is a good bit more than we could know if Quine were right. We thus see ourselves to see our own language as a complex system of syntactic structures. But what we thus see are not *just* facts about ourselves. Solipsism can get no beachhead here, for we see that we can see what others patently can see as well. The above view of 'expect' and 'persuade' is no idiosyncratic one. It is just what any English speaker can readily see. Nor is there any serious question that other speakers do see it, or that we can, if necessary, confirm that they do. Second, 'expect' and 'persuade' are the first small step along a route to seeing the kind of syntactic complexity that English has. But that general sort of complexity is manifestly no idiosyncrasy of English. We can appreciate it as something distinctly human. We thus reasonably come to see (if we did not already) the languages of others as things of similar complexity. If we approach other languages in that way, there is no reason in principle why their speakers' views as to their syntactic structure, and ways of forming such structures, should not be open to view.

If Quine is wrong about the class of privileged facts—facts from which syntactic facts must be derivable—he is also wrong, on Chomsky's view, in his ideas about knowledge-yielding procedures. His fundamental mistake, given our present change of focus, is to suppose it to be discoverable a priori what these procedures are. If the procedures are to be ones for arriving at what we in fact know about our languages, then it must be an empirical matter just what avenues are, in fact, at our disposal. That will depend on our special psychological design. To say that empiricism is demonstrably mistaken, as argued above, is, inter alia, to say, against Quine, that our special psychological design—the ways we are *contingently* the sorts of thinkers that we are—may confer special knowledge-yielding capacities on us. I will say more presently in defence of that idea. Here, though, is a very abstract sketch of how it is possible for Quine to be wrong.

I will speak of H-languages, without defining that notion precisely. An H-language is, by definition, a language whose grammar satisfies a number of severe constraints—which has a highly specific, determinate, form. Precision here would be specifying exactly what these constraints are. Now we may compare two problems: first, working out from given data what the grammar of a certain encountered language is, supposing that the language may be any conceivable one; second, working out from given data which H-language a certain encountered language is, given that the language in question is an H-language. In both cases we will suppose the data confined to facts as to what speakers of the language do, and do not, produce in speaking it (and perhaps some facts as to utterances they reject as incorrect). If the constraints on an H-language are tight enough, the second problem may be considerably more tractable than the first (if the first is even soluble at all).

Suppose, now, that we (humans) are so designed as to see ourselves in certain situations as confronting H-languages, approaching the languages we thus confront accordingly. Such insight would consist in being liable to form certain hypotheses as to what speaking correctly from a grammatical point of view would be, but simply failing ever to entertain other hypotheses. What we had seen of the language might lead us to go on to novel uses in certain ways, but not in others. If such special design conferred a knowledge-yielding capacity, then we could describe things as follows. In certain situations, we see ourselves to confront human beings (using language). Part of what it is for us to see it to be human language users we confront is to see in them a certain frame of mind, that of an H-language user. We see them to be engaged in H-language speaking, just as we may see one of them to be expressing pique, or joy. Of course, if what the design conferred was not a *capacity* to discover how things are, then we should describe things differently: we are inclined to treat these people in certain ways; it is another matter whether that is treating them, and their language, as what they are.

Operating in the sort of environment we are designed for, and de facto are always in, a human being doing what we are thus designed to do would, peripheral deficiencies aside, arrive at correct views of the syntax of the encountered language. For the design is one for interacting with other humans. And, de facto, when we encounter language users, that is what we have to deal with. Someone doing what we are thus designed to do would thus arrive at just those syntactic perceptions of the target language which a human being, functioning as humans do, would have, so at perceptions his fellow speakers, if human, by and large share. Given the sense in which grammar is a psychological phenomenon, such perceptions are, in the nature of the case, correct, provided only that the target language is indeed the natural language of some community of human beings.

In normal situations, then, we are, to say the least, non-accidentally right in treating the languages we confront as H-languages. One might still resist the idea that what special design thus confers is a *knowledge*-yielding capacity. One thought would be that if the special design does, in fact, lead us to grammatical fact, then there should be a proof we could have, without relying on it, that the grammatical facts are, indeed, what, by the design, we would take them to be. But then the design is dispensable: the grammatical facts are just what they could be shown to be without it. We thus revert to our original empiricism. Another thought is that the design in question is fallible. In environments hospitable to it, perhaps, it leads us to take to be so what is so—it is a sort of access to *fact*. But in inhospitable environments it might lead us to take to be so what is not so. That might happen, for example, if we came upon a community of very human-seeming Martians. Fallibility, the thought is, makes vivid what would be so anyway: we can *know* to be so what, by the design, we would take to be so only where we had a proof that the design was not leading us astray. In that case, the design cannot be, in itself, a design of a knowledge-yielding capacity. By this line of thought, special design could confer no such special capacities, available only to thinkers of a special sort.

The first of these lines of thought is simply a mistake. The proof, in a given case, that the grammatical facts are what the design would lead us to take them to be is just that the language of which they are facts is a natural human language, so that what the special design would lead one to see in it is just what a human being (being so designed) would see in it. We may then appeal to the sense in which grammar is a psychological phenomenon. None of that suggests that the grammatical facts are only what they could be seen to be without appeal to the design, or that someone, neither so designed, nor with adequate access to the facts of what those so designed would see would be able to see what the grammar of the relevant language was.

The second line, though I think it is a significant part of what moves empiricists, is just bad epistemology. It is typical of the abilities we rely on to gain knowledge that they would *be* abilities only in hospitable environments. I can learn whether there is a cat on the mat by looking. In doing so, I rely on my ability to tell a cat when I see one. But that ability, like most, is an ability at all only where the world cooperates. If, unbeknownst to me, I am surrounded by extremely feline Martians, or marsupials, then, perhaps, I cannot tell a cat when I see one, and have not found out whether there is a *cat* on the mat just by looking. If I know there is a cat on the mat, then I have (even if I cannot give) proof that there is. Such proof as I may get, relying on my ability to tell a cat when I see one, contains no proper sub-proof that there are not Martians or marsupials about. But it is a mistake to suppose that only what contained such sub-proof could ever count as proving there is a cat on the mat, and a mistake about knowledge to suppose that without such sub-proof I cannot really know whether there is a cat on the mat. Similarly, one might suppose that to *learn* what an expression's syntax is, I must have proof that that *is* the syntax. If reliance on my special design supplies proof, that proof will have no proper sub-proof that it is human beings, and not Martians, who surround me. But it is equally a mistake to think that I could have such proof only in having such a sub-proof. Whether such proof is called for depends on how things are. (Where circumstances mandate relying on more than my design, or my ability to tell a cat on sight—where there *might* be Martians—nothing in that design, or that ability, prohibits my doing so.)

The case of grammar shows the form an anti-empiricism takes. The core idea is rejection of the empiricist's conception of our relation to the universal thinker. The anti-empiricist insists that what we can see about the world is not limited (certainly not a priori) to what universally shared capacities would allow. We have, or may have, knowledge-yielding capacities of special designs, with special shape and scope, part of our design as thinkers of a special sort— capacities each of which it is quite conceivable that a thinker should lack. These extend the range of facts that we might know. That leaves it at best unclear whether those capacities, if any, a thinker *must* have would be enough by themselves to qualify anything as a thinker at all.

If special psychological design may bestow such capacities, it is, contrary to empiricism, an empirical issue as to just what our cognitive capacities are. Empiricism, against that background, is at best the sort of psychologism McDowell targets: the supposed a priori deduction of how things must be in an area where it can only be a question of how things are.

On Chomsky's view we are so designed as to see certain sorts of phenomena in what we experience, or particular compartments of it. Specifically, we are so designed as, in confronting a human language, to think of it in a given way. There is, by that design, a way we (that is, a human) would come to think of the language in mastering it (given adequate exposure to all about it to which we might, by that design, be sensitive). To think in that way is to see certain syntactic structures in the language and its expressions. That they are so structured is, on that way of viewing things, what one is to think. The anti-empiricist point in the case of syntax is that, where such is so, the language *is* so to be thought of. In so seeing things, we are seeing how things are. The relevant design, operating in normal circumstances, is no less than a design for seeing that. So operating, it is thus the design of a genuine cognitive capacity.

Language being the psychological phenomenon it is, that we think of our languages as we do—so that we are designed so to think of them—is part of what makes the facts about them what they are. Such helps to make anti-empiricism about syntax seem innocuous, and, to Frege, not psychologism. The question to be raised now is how far anti-empiricism can be extended beyond the realm of grammar while remaining innocuous, and, specifically, immune to Frege's anti-psychologism.

5. Anti-empiricism (II)

Anti-empiricism, as exemplified by Chomsky, begins with the idea that special knowledge-yielding capacities, not shared by every possible thinker, may be part of, or conferred by, our design, or certain thinkers' design, as thinkers of a particular sort. Such capacities may gain us access to some range of facts refractory to one equipped only with the capacities an empiricist allows us. The facts to which we thus gain access may fail to connect with any empiricist's 'privileged' facts in the way the empiricist demands. Anti-empiricism so construed represents a clear area of common cause between Chomsky and McDowell. It is evident in McDowell's consistent and wide-ranging anti-reductionism, every instance of which turns essentially on crediting us with knowledge-yielding capacities of domain-specific and design-specific sorts, capacities which come in view when we take at face value the facts as to what we are prepared to recognize. The most conspicuous difference between McDowell and Chomsky is that, while Chomsky is mainly interested in species-specific design, McDowell tends to suggest that he is thinking of the designs of people with certain upbringings, or initiations into certain perhaps non-obligatory human practices. But that difference, so far as it exists, is over what ought to be a purely empirical question.

Another difference between Chomsky and McDowell is the domains at which anti-empiricism is directed. Chomsky, of course, directs it at the domain of grammar which is, as indicated by Frege's attitude towards it, a somewhat special case, one in which a certain degree of idealism may be harmless, and exempt from any Fregean accusation of psychologism. McDowell directs it at a wide variety of domains where its application may be somewhat more contentious. For example, he directs it at facts about the good, and Aristotle's conception of that; and he directs it at facts about human attitudes such as thinking that such-and-such, or intending to do such-and-such. To show what

McDowellian anti-empiricism is like I will consider those examples in turn. Then in the next section I will consider the scope and what I take to be the source of the general position these examples instance.

There is an idea of the good, or of what is good for us, on which the good is fixed by how a human being ought to live, or aim to, by what a worthwhile or desirable life is. On that conception, something is good just insofar as it is, or may be, part of, or may contribute to, such a life. One might also think that there are facts of human nature. On one conception, at least, of human nature, we may think of such facts as simply a matter of what human beings are, independent of what is desirable for them—facts purely within the domain of ethology, or psychology. As a matter of fact, people tend to—perhaps invariably—seek certain things. Certain things promote, others frustrate, the projects people in fact set themselves. It is natural for human beings to behave in certain ways. One might ask how, and how on Aristotle's view, these two sets of facts relate. For example, should the facts about the good so conceived, if any, be derivable from, or reducible to, facts about human nature so conceived? Here is McDowell's answer:

It is because a certain life . . . is a life of doing what it is the business of a human being to do, that that life is in the relevant sense the most satisfying life possible for its subject . . . How one might argue that this or that is what it is the business of a human being to do is left open. It does not have to be by showing that a life of such doings maximizes the satisfaction of some set of 'normal' or 'natural' desires, whose role in the argument would need to be justified by a prior theory of human nature.

We may still find an intelligible place, in the different position I am considering, for some such idea as this: the life of excellence is the life that most fully actualizes the potentialities that constitute human nature. But the point will be that the thesis . . . that this or that is what it is the business of a human being to do can be reformulated, with an intelligibly 'value-loaded' use of human nature; not that the justification of the thesis about the business of a human being is to be found in an independent, 'value-free' investigation of human nature.

(1980: 18–19)

This irreducibility of facts about 'the business of a human being' in no way impugns, on McDowell's view, the idea that there are such facts, or that we can know them. Such knowledge requires special knowledge-yielding capacities, part of a special, not inevitable, way of thinking of the world. But, on his view, at least if properly brought up, we may have such capacities.

Special knowledge-yielding capacities may be insusceptible to cognitive prosthetics. That is, what, with them, one is equipped to see need not be what would be derivable from some statable set of principles by a thinker lacking those capacities. Thinking otherwise, McDowell suggests, reflects a misconception of the deductive paradigm that leads us to suppose that the operations of any specific conception of rationality in a particular area—any specific conception of what counts as doing the same thing—must be deductively explicable; that is, that there must be a formulable universal principle suited to serve as major premise in syllogistic explanations of the sort I considered above.

(1979: 62)

To see what our special capacities allow us to see, one may need nothing short of human sensibility, or the sensibility of human beings properly initiated into a given way of thinking of the world. No principle graspable by a thinker devoid of the right sensibility need entail all that is open to the view of a thinker with that sensibility. That is to say that the facts such a capacity makes accessible to us need not be equivalent to any construction out of facts of some other sort, notably not out of facts which, by some empiricist's lights, might have privileged status.

The position, then, is this. Human beings, or humans of a certain sort, have a special knowledge-yielding capacity, conferred by a special psychological de-sign, not necessarily shared by just any thinker whatever. That capacity enables such humans to see facts of a certain sort—facts about the proper business of a human being, or the good for a human being. Such a capacity involves an irreducible sensitivity to facts of the relevant sort. It is not constructible out of other capacities a rational being just would have anyway, together with facts such capacities might anyway make accessible. Correspondingly, the facts this capacity makes accessible are, in general, ones it takes this particular sort of sensitivity to see. They are not derivable from facts of some other sort which might be accessible anyway to one who knew nothing of the good. They are not privileged facts in the empiricist's sense, since they are not accessible to one without a knowledge-yielding capacity of a special sort. Nor do they relate to any range of privileged facts in the way an empiricist demands. The irreducibil-ity of the facts of this sort is shown (in one way) by the ineliminable role of a special knowledge-yielding capacity in seeing them.

I turn to the second example: McDowell's attitude towards attitudes such as thinking something to be so. That attitude emerges, among other places, in a debate between McDowell and Michael Dummett over the shape a theory of meaning might take. Here, acknowledging a point of Dummett's, McDowell says,

If communication is to be possible, that in which our understanding of the language we speak consists must 'lie open to view'.

(1987: 94)

From an empiricist standpoint, the idea that our understanding expressions of the language, or particular uses of them, as we do, is open to view is likely to suggest, for example, that for someone to understand some utterance as he does is for such-and-such other fact to hold, where that other fact is observable in some sense in which that fact about understanding is not. For example, depending on his conception of privilege, an empiricist might suppose that the requirement McDowell endorses means that facts about how people understand utterances are reducible to facts about behaviour, again in some proprietary sense of that term.

But, McDowell suggests, we need not think that way. We may, instead, see relevant facts of understanding as themselves open to view, at least for someone with a suitable special knowledge-yielding capacity. With a proper appreciation of the capacities of fluent speakers, we can allow that

to be a speaker of a language is to be capable of putting one's thoughts into one's words, where others can hear or see them.

(1987: 99)

The others who can thus see or hear them are, of course, others competent in the relevant language. Someone so equipped can see, often enough, both that such-and-such is the expression of such-and-such thought, and that such-and-such is someone expressing what he thinks. That is a way of just seeing, or hearing, the speaker to think such-and-such. On McDowell's view the capacity that allows us to see such things is a particular kind of sensitivity to a particular range of facts, acquired in that exposure to the language and its use through which one becomes fluent. That is not a sort of sensitivity that could, in principle, be acquired otherwise, through learning such facts as that for someone to say such-and-such is for such-and-such other facts to hold, to which one might have access without such sensitivity—facts, say, as to how that person would 'behave'.

So there are both facts about what people think, and facts about what given utterances said, which are accessible to one with the right kind of knowledge-yielding capacity. That idea brings facts about the attitudes of others into the realm of the observable. But the relevant capacities here do not admit of prosthetics. They are not constructible out of capacities which any thinker, or even any language user, must share. Correspondingly, the facts to which they gain us access remain resistant to empiricist strictures. Again we have an instance of anti-empiricism of just the form that Chomsky deploys against Quine, though deployed in a different domain. We must still face the question whether difference in domain makes a difference in the acceptability of such anti-empiricism. First, though, I will consider just how this anti-empiricism might generalize.

6. Generalized Anti-empiricism

Generalized anti-empiricism can be developed from a simple idea. Suppose that some indefinitely expandable group of thinkers take themselves to discern some way for things to be, 'F', and agree, or would do, non-collusively, and productively (that is, in an indefinitely expandable range of cases) as to what is, and what is not, 'F'. Then they are marking a genuine distinction. There is at least a genuine distinction between that which is such that they would classify it the one way (as 'F'), and that such that they would classify it as not 'F'. Those, at least, are two genuine ways for things, or a thing, to be. So there is, at least, some genuine way, G, which some things are, and/or some things are not, such that these thinkers, in thinking as they thus do, are distinguishing between things which are that way, and things which are not. That idea is not an explanatory hypothesis, not a piece of psychology. It is rather an idea about what it is for there to be a distinction in nature. Given such productive agreement (as I will term it) in how to treat things, what more could one want for a genuine distinction (at least of some sort)?

The point so far, though not quite what we want, does gain at least some purchase against empiricist strictures. For the point is that there is a sort of productive agreement among thinkers which guarantees that there is a genuine way for things to be—really such a thing as things being that way—without thereby guaranteeing that any particular set of empiricist strictures is satisfied. If people agree in this way as to what they would, and would not, call a novel, or a teaspoon, or elation, then, for at least some way things, in fact, are or are not, their treatment of the world distinguishes between what is, and what is not, that way. It remains, for all that, an open question whether what they are thus distinguishing is capturable so as to satisfy empiricist strictures. Perhaps it is. But we are not entitled to the idea that it must be. To insist that these people could only do what they do in responding to what does satisfy such strictures would be that psychologism which is McDowell's target.

On this core idea, there is a sort of agreement among us, or among whatever creatures, that guarantees that there is something—a genuine way for things to be—to which they are responsive. That core point does not quite yet bear on *thinking* things to be such-and-such way. The anti-empiricist's concern is, not with mere responsiveness to some way for things to be or not, but a responsiveness that consists, in part, in thinking in terms of things being that way or not, and in part in an ability to recognize the, or at least some, facts as to things being that way or not. So we must elaborate the core idea so as to accommodate some features we know the phenomenon of thinking in terms of being such-and-such to have.

First, thinking in terms of such-and-such is, as a rule, an imperfect way of responding to (things being) that. Relevant thinkers (those for whom productive agreement is in question) sometimes disagree, sometimes, in practice, irresolvably. They are sometimes deceived as to how things are, or just ignorant, sometimes irremediably so. Some relevant thinkers are recognized, and recognizable, as better at telling how things are in relevant respects. (Think of telling fine shades of colour, for example.) Such shows where agreement is wanted: not in what people in fact say or judge, all their limitations operating, but in what they would be prepared to recognize as to what is to be judged (what judgements are correct) as to how things are in relevant respects. That is an idealization. By it we may ignore an actual performance if reasonably ascribed to some disturbance in the responsiveness for which these thinkers are equipped. And, as with the simple core point, there need only be enough productive agreement here to show that there is something to which they are thus equipped to respond.

Second, we typically think in occasion-sensitive ways. Where we think in terms of such-and-such way for things to be, we recognize room for different understandings of what something's being that way might be; on different ones there would be different truths to tell as to what was, and what was not, that way. We further recognize the possibility of speaking, or judging, of things being that way on such different understandings. So we recognize that there may be different truths to tell as to how things are in that respect on different occasions for saying how things thus are. Productive agreement that allowed for that would be, not simply agreement in responses to given situations in the world—to given items being as they then are—but in responses under particular conditions for producing them. Since it is thinking that is in question, that would be (sufficient) productive agreement in what it is, or would be true to say *when* as to how things are in the relevant respect, agreements as to the truths there are to tell (or judge) in speaking (or judging) of how things thus are.

Finally, in thinking of such-and-such we (must) operate with a conception of that of which we think. We are thinking of some given way to be only where our conception is near enough to a right one. We are thinking of a feature of things to which we are thus responsive only where our conception is near enough to a right one of that. Where we think of things as being F or not, there is something we take being F to be, and a way we take questions as to what is F to be treatable. We are thinking in terms of being F only where the conception thus embodied in our way of treating things is near enough to a right way of thinking of what being F is.

It is thus possible to be responsive to some feature of things while thinking, neither of it, nor of any way for things to be. Given thinkers may take themselves to think in terms of women being, or not, witches. They might agree productively as to who is, and who is not, a witch. Perhaps they are responding to a certain hormonal condition present in a minority of women. As they conceive things, witches are malevolent women with supernatural powers. But they are not responding to anything of which that is true. One might still say that there is such a thing as being a witch, and it is that that they are responding to—they are just radically wrong about what is involved in being that. But, for most purposes, it is manifestly fairer to the facts to say that there is no such thing as being a witch (or what they thus purport to think of), so that, though responding to a genuine enough feature of the world, they are in fact thereby thinking of nothing at all. If this is right, whether a conception is good enough for thinkers to be thinking of something to which they are responsive is a question of what is reasonable. That is to say: we correctly count thinkers as thinking in terms of F only where their way of conceiving what they thus think of is reasonably seen as close enough to a right way of conceiving F.

A good enough conception may be significantly wrong. We take ourselves to think of paths in space as straight or not. Perhaps thinking of such things as we do, one could never, travelling in a straight path, return to where one started. Perhaps there are no paths in space of which such is true, or even of which such makes sense. There may still be something we are thus responsive to, whose nature we are most reasonably seen as in error about, so that it is true, for all that, that we think in terms of paths in space as straight. Our conception of such paths may be near enough to a right one for us so to count, without its actually being right.

Such features of *our* thinking show that where productive agreement is to be the mark of thinking in terms of a feature of things to which one thus responds, it must be productive agreement of a certain quality. Thinking of things as a certain way involves thinking in a certain way of what one does in reaching verdicts as to how things are in that respect—of what one thus judges so, and of how questions of that being so are treatable. Thinking of things as a certain way means thinking *in* a certain way of the sort of thing being that way is. Agreement among a given range of thinkers has the right quality when the way they thus think of what it is they think of meshes (well enough) with the verdicts in which their productive agreement consists. Those thinkers will see their verdicts as mandated by the sort of thing the way in question is, or at least by their way of thinking of that. Meshing means that doing so is consistent with the verdicts: their conception must not, per se, dictate different ones. And the conception, together with the verdicts, make sense as a rational way of treating the world. Other thinkers (ourselves, perhaps) need not be able to join in this way of thinking. The relevant thinkers' eyes may be open to features of the world to which ours are shut. One must grant this much in allowing special psychological design the role that anti-empiricism does. But there must be enough coherence in that way of dealing with the world for it to be sufficiently determinate (or reasonable to suppose so) what, on that way of thinking, it would be correct to think and judge. We correctly count thought as with this quality where such coherence is visible to us. The anti-empiricist idea is that agreement has the right quality if there is close enough to mesh. In that case, these thinkers, in thinking in the way they do, think in terms of the way for things to be they take themselves to think of, and to which they are thus responsive. There is, the idea is, no further room for failure on their part to do that.

Productive agreement, with or without near enough mesh, is responsiveness to a feature things may have or may lack. That was the simple core point. Now the idea is: if a way of thinking of what that agreement is about, suitably engaged in, would lead (nearly enough) to that agreement, then it is a way of thinking of something to which, in so agreeing, relevant thinkers are responsive—thus, a way of thinking of a genuine feature things may have or may lack. Thinkers whose thinking is close enough to such a way thus think of something to which, in their agreement, they are responsive.

Insisting that productive agreement has this quality does not lose the anti-empiricist force of the core idea. We agree productively as to the colours of things. We think in certain ways about objects being coloured: colour is a visible property of objects, so, in certain standard ways, one can tell the colour of a thing by looking. For most purposes, we suppose the colour of an object to be stable—something it takes chemical processes to change. Supposing that to be the sort of thing an object's being coloured is, and thinking of things as we thus would, one would, intelligibly, reach roughly the verdicts we do. Thinking as we do, we thus think of ways for things to be—being coloured blue, and so on—to which we are thus responsive, and which are correctly thought of as we thus do. That is so, independent of any relation an object's being coloured thus and so may bear to facts of some other sort (privileged ones, perhaps, by some empiricist's lights).

Suppose, then, that given thinkers take themselves to think in terms of things being some given (putative) way, F. They agree productively in verdicts as to how things stand with respect to things being F—the truths there are to tell, on occasion, as to, or involving, things so being. They think in a certain way of what it is they thus agree about. Suppose we assume that they are doing what they thus take themselves to do: there is such a thing as being F, to (things being) which they are responsive, which they think of in a way near enough to a way in which it is correctly thought of. Suppose that, on that assumption, it is determinate enough what truths (and falsehoods) there would be to tell as to how things are with respect to things being F—clear enough what such truths would be if these thinkers really were thus thinking of a genuine way things may or may not be. Then, the current point is, these thinkers *are* nearly enough right. There is such a thing as being F, and a way things stand with respect to things being that. And these thinkers, at least in what they are prepared to recognize, are roughly right as to what way that is. There is no further room for them to fail of that. In being designed, or equipped, to react as they do, they enjoy a knowledge-yielding capacity. Where that equipment is special psychological design, it is a special such capacity, enjoyed by some thinkers, but one that need not be enjoyed by all.

Such is the main burden of generalized anti-empiricism. Where thinkers take themselves to be thinking in terms of a genuine way things may or may not be, they can be wrong about that only if they are behaving stupidly, randomly, inconsistently, or something of the sort—if they fail to produce genuine productive agreement, or their way of thinking of what they agree about is too far from a coherent way of viewing that. That is the point of Wittgenstein's remark that to say that given discourse did not fit the concept truth would be like saying that pawns did not fit the concept check. But

to say that check did not *fit* our concept of the pawns, would mean that a game in which pawns were checked, in which, say, the players who lost their pawns lost, would be uninteresting or stupid or too complicated or something of the kind.

(1953: §136)

It is also the idea, I think, that Wittgenstein worried, 'seems to abolish logic' (1953: §242), but insisted does not. We will next consider how anti-empiricism may give the impression that it does.

7. Idealism

Chomsky's anti-empiricism contains the idea that how things are in the domain that concerns him depends on how relevant thinkers think: grammatical facts just are what we are designed to think them. It is harmless for our mental equipment thus to shape *grammatical* facts. As Frege noted, grammar *is* a psychological phenomenon. But generalized anti-empiricism, as evidenced in McDowell, for example, does not restrict itself to domains of any particular sort—certainly not to the psychological in the sense that grammar is psychological. The idea the anti-empiricist wants is that one's mind's special design may, in McDowell's terms, 'open one's eyes to some tract of reality'—facts there anyway, with or without our capacity to see them. In that case, though special design may select which tract we see, and *perhaps* select in such a way that we are thus designed to think so just what is so, it had better not be that what we are designed to think shapes the facts in that tract—that how *it* is shaped depends on how we think. On the core idea, suitable agreement is engagement with the world: to agree (suitably) is, per se, to respond to *something*. But is that idea sustainable? Can mind-design *select* which tract of reality we deal with, on the anti-empiricist plan, without also deciding, of the selected tract, how things there are—without shaping the *world* along with our responsiveness to it?

Suppose given thinkers take themselves, in thinking in a certain way, to be thinking in terms of things being, or not, some given way, and thereby to be thinking, and judging, what is so or not. Suppose it is determinate enough what, on that way of viewing how things are, it would be true to say or judge. Then, the anti-empiricist insists, in thinking as they thus do, these thinkers are responsive to a genuine feature of things, of which they thus think. In that respect, at least, they in fact do what they take themselves to do. What it would be true to think and judge given that so thinking (with the verdicts that involves) is genuine responsiveness, is what it would be true to think and judge *tout court*. Thus it is that special design may confer special knowledge-yielding capacities.

The main point of this idea is to defuse empiricist critiques, on which genuine matters of what is so or not are not what we intuitively think—Quine's critique of meaning, for example. But there is an immediate worry, easily expressible, at least crudely. Coherence may take many forms. We share a rough conception of being a chair, and, nearly enough, a sense for when something is the right sort of thing to count as one. That makes it clear enough when one would be speaking truly, and when not, thinking of such matters as we in fact do. But if our sense for what a chair is is a feature of special psychological design, then, it seems, we might have had a different one— even while retaining much of our general conception of what is involved in *something's* being a chair. That might have made for differences in what, on our way of thinking of such things, it would be true to say as to things being chairs, the presence and absence of chairs, and so on. Or so it seems. Our thinking would still cohere enough to be genuine responsiveness. But what it would be true to say so thinking, so true to say *tout court* of that of which we thus thought, would be different. So it seems that had we been differently designed, that would have mattered to what could have been said truly about chairs: some of what it would now be true to say would not have been; similarly for some of what would now be false. In speaking truth we do nothing less than saying what is so; and in speaking falsehood, nothing less than saying what is not so. So, it seems, had we been differently designed, in ways we might have been, different things would have been so about chairs. If anti-empiricism means that, then it is precisely Frege's target. That, I think, would make McDowell Frege's target rather than his ally.

This worry, we hope, rests on a mistaken view of things. But before trying to say how it does, let us make it slightly less crude. For the anti-empiricist, a way of thinking is identified, in part, by the thinkers who engage in it. It is their responsiveness to things that fixes what it is that is being responded to (and responded to in thinking of it). Nor is that responsiveness eliminable in favour of some set of principles, available to those without it, which would generate precisely those same results—an algorithm, as it were, for determining how things are thus to be responded to. That is the point of speaking of sensibilities—a sense of what responses are called for, on novel occasions, by novel things, or situations, which one confronts. Two points about such sensibilities bear emphasis.

First, where it matters in confronting some empiricism, such a sensibility is a feature of a special psychological design. It is a feature a competent empirical thinker need not have had. The knowledge-yielding capacity it confers is one a competent thinker might have lacked. (Vide Chomsky.) There is such a sensibility only where there are alternative ones. We have our sense of when something is to be called a chair. Other thinkers might have had a different one, or at least a different sense of how to respond to the things we thus respond to.

Second, where it matters to empiricism, such a sensibility is, in an important sense, irreducible. What someone equipped with it could see (where it constitutes a genuine knowledge-yielding capacity) is not identical to the deductive consequences of any statable set of principles, or at least any such set graspable by thinkers without the relevant sensibility. (This does not rule out our sometimes having statable reasons for classifying as we do.) If sensibilities could not be like that, empiricist demands for accountings in terms of privileged facts would be in order. (And we would have to be able to make sense of the idea of facts available to any empirical thinker, the availability of which depends on no special psychological design.) This says something about the relation between sensibilities and conceptions. Insofar as a conception of being a chair is identifiable in terms of the sort of thing *something's* being a chair is, and is fixed independent of what it would be right to say, on novel occasions, of novel cases, our sensibility regarding the truths about chairs is not derivable merely from that conception. This means we could have had an alternative sensibility while still retaining that conception of what, in general terms, a chair is. Or, again, other thinkers might have had a different sensibility while sharing that conception with us. We think of chairs as certain sorts of seats for one. With such a different sensibility, we would still so think of them. Our sense for the right *sort* of seat, though, would yield different results as to when some novel item was correctly counted as of the right sort. By the general anti-empiricist idea, a different sensibility might have changed when one would, or at least when we would, be speaking truly in speaking in terms of things being what we thus thought of—being chairs or not—if a general conception may identify it as that which we (or other thinkers) thus think of. If that could mean that something it is in fact true to say might not have been, thus that something so (what would thus be stated) might not have been, then it is enough to make anti-empiricism Frege's target.

We can now broach a ready response to this worry: any sensibility as different as what is now envisioned would, *ipso facto*, change the subject. Had we had a different sensibility, we might still have used such words as 'chair', and we might still have conceived of what we thus spoke of as a certain sort of seat for one. But we would no longer have been speaking (or thinking) of being a *chair*. That, at least, must be so wherever a sensibility is different enough to make for differences in when one with it would be speaking truly in speaking of that in terms of which they thus thought. For, the thought is, a way for things to be is identified precisely by the truths there are to tell about it. And that, correctly understood, rules out as mere fantasy any instance of the above worry.

But this ready response is suspect. It is so because, for the ways for things to be we name, we are prepared to recognize different ways of thinking of things as being *those* ways or not, where, on these different ways of thinking there are different truths to tell, and where these different truths are all *truths*. Sid buys a DIY chair kit. On bringing it home he discovers that it is much more difficult to assemble than he had imagined. It remains a neatly stacked pile of chair parts in his spare room. One day, someone, pointing at the pile, asks, 'What's that?' 'It's a chair,' Sid replies, 'I just haven't got around to assembling it yet.' On a later occasion, Sid and Pia, with guests, find themselves a chair short for dinner. 'There's a chair in the spare room,' Sid says helpfully. But there is still only the pile. Recognizably, Sid spoke truly the first time, falsely the second. It just takes a different way of thinking of being a chair to see the truth of that first thing from the way it takes to see the falsehood of the second. Such contrasting ways of thinking are a common everyday part of our way of dealing with the world.

Different ways of thinking of things can even be systematic without changing the fact of thinkers thinking of things as being such-and-such way. Suppose some people—Northumbrians, perhaps—regularly call slippers shoes, while others—Mancunians, perhaps—regularly refuse to do so. Northumbrians think of slippers as house shoes, and count them as shoes when saying, for example, how many pairs of shoes they own. Mancunians regard that as comical. It would be natural, in such a case, to count both the Northumbrians and the Mancunians as thinking of the world in terms of things being shoes. It is just that they think of shoes in slightly different ways. A Northumbrian would often speak of shoes on the Northumbrian way of thinking of such things. There would thus be truths for Northumbrians to tell, among themselves, at least, the truth of which requires counting slippers as shoes. There would, similarly, be truths for Mancunians to tell, the truth of which requires refusing to count slippers as shoes. Perhaps there are different truths for Northumbrians and Mancunians to tell about shoes. Perhaps thinkers of the one persuasion could never get themselves into a position for telling some of the truths tellable by those of the other. The truth of those distinctively Mancunian truths does not mean that what Northumbrians say to be so in telling distinctively Northumbrian truths is not so. There is no such threat. This is a clue to a better way to avoid Fregean psychologism than what the ready answer offers.

Suppose, now, that Mancunians and Northumbrians and all the rest of us agreed on the right way to talk about slippers. That would exhibit an alternative sensibility, and an alternative way of thinking in terms of things being shoes. There might then not be some of the truths for us to tell about shoes that, on the original supposition, there would be for at least some of us to tell. That simple example shows one thing it might be like for alternative sensibilities to be alternative ways of thinking in terms of things being such-and-such—some given way for things to be. There should be no psychologistic threat in such possibilities. The next section will attempt to spell out precisely why there is not.

8. Platonism

The ready response is unconvincing. It is implausible that thinkers would never count as thinking of the same thing—of being such-and-such—where, on their different ways of thinking of *that*, different things would count as something's being that way. In fact, the ways for things to be that we have names for, or could name, admit of understandings. We speak truth as to things being those ways in speaking of them on some such understanding. There is thus, or so it seems, the possibility that different understandings of being such-and-such might be available to differently designed thinkers, or different ones the ones on which they would speak, or judge, in given circumstances, of things being that way. What we need is, not to rule that possibility out, but rather to see how, while that might make for different truths for such thinkers to tell (than there are for us to tell), nothing we truly state, or take, to be so might thus be thought, truly, not to be so: whatever we think so that is so, would be so no matter how any thinker thought.

To see how psychological design might work that way, we need to dispel the very idea that suggests the ready answer. Trivially, a statement is true just when things are the way they are according to it. That suggests, innocently enough, that a statement's truth depends on precisely two factors: first, how things are according to it, and, second, how things are. Innocence ends if one supposes that one can specify how things are according to a statement—which way it speaks of things as being—in such a way that the truth of any statement which speaks of things as that way can depend only on whether that is, in fact, a way things are. Let P be a way a statement might thus represent things. Then, accepting that idea, we may still innocently allow that the way given thinkers think decides whether some one of their statements stated that P, or, say, that Q, where that is another such way for a statement to represent things.

But one cannot, accepting this idea, allow that, where a statement spoke of things as being P, whether it thus stated truth depends on how a particular (sort of) thinker thinks. For what thinkers could thus decide, in thinking as they do could only be, within this framework, how things were: whether that which is so according to any statement which states P *is* so. That would be mind-dependence of the worst sort. Yet, with the end of innocence in place, anti-empiricism is under pressure to say just that. For, given the role it assigns to sensibilities, it seems, where thinkers think in terms of, say, things being chairs or not, still, for all that, whether things are as they say (on some occasion) in saying such-and-such to be a chair depends in further ways on how they are designed, or equipped, to think. If that dependence must be a dependence of how things *are* on how they think, then, except, perhaps, in special domains such as grammar, anti-empiricism becomes precisely Frege's target.

We must, then, reverse this end of innocence. But we *have* reversed it with rejection of the ready answer. Sid spoke of an object in the next room as a chair. Rejection in that case means allowing that differently designed thinkers, each thinking of objects as being chairs or not, might think so differently as to make for differences in when what each thought, in thinking a given object to be a chair, would be true. Generalized rejection is insistence that the point holds for any specifiable way Sid may have said the object to be. It would still hold, for example, if he spoke of chairs, where we are to understand such-and-such by being a chair. The generalized point is just Wittgenstein's insistence that there is no such thing as a 'pure intermediary' between a statement and the world—something which still represents the world as thus and so, but which, unlike 'mere' words, is immune in principle to different possible ways of under-standing what being as thus represented might be. So for any way of specifying the 'thus and so', there remains room for a way of thinking to contribute to fixing *what* was thus thought (judged) so, by fixing the understanding of things being *that* way on which that was what was thought. The influence of thinkers on what it would be true for *them* to think or judge thus never need be—as at some specifiable point it would have to be if the platonist end of innocence were right—an influence on how the world judged about was shaped. Nor need it change what it would be true for *us* (or other thinkers) to say or judge in thinking of things as being, or not, that very same specified way.

In the special case, for some ways an item may be, whether that item is what Sid spoke of in speaking of being a chair may all depend on what one understands (or means) by being a chair. Where such different understandings are open, one may speak, or think, in terms of something's being a chair in thinking of it as being one on any of these. Our differently designed thinkers are equipped with different senses for when something is the right sort of thing—the sort of thing in question when one speaks of chairs. By hypothesis, each sense is compatible with thus thinking in terms of things being *chairs* or not. These different senses, or sensibilities, form, in part, the understandings on which these thinkers think, or speak, of things as chairs or not. Those different understandings make for differences in when what they thus think, or say, would be true. The generalized point is that differently designed thinkers might stand differently, in this way, towards any way we can specify that things may or may not be, so any way we can represent them as being or not. For differently designed thinkers, different understandings would be available of being such-and-such way (for any way that is thus specifiable), and different understandings may be right for given situations in which to speak or judge. Those different understandings would matter to the ways they represented things as being—the ways things were according to their statements—but not the ways the things they thus represented as one way or another were. The anti-empiricist needs this point at least to whatever extent the ready answer is not available. The point is available when we reject the above end of innocence.

Sid said, 'The grass is wet.' I tell Pia, 'Sid said that the grass is wet.' If the world is nearly enough what he and I suppose, then the way it is will leave no doubt as to whether he thus said what is so. I said him to have said certain grass to be a given way—wet, on the relevant understanding of grass being so—and so to have said the world to be a certain way—the way it is when certain grass, on a relevant understanding of what that is, is, on the relevant understanding, wet. If all went well, then whether things are as he said they were, will not depend on further issues as to what one understands by being those ways of which I said him to speak. But it is not as if things *must* go well. Whether a strange enough world was the way I said Sid to speak of, would have depended on what one understood by its being so. That might make room for different understandings as to what it was Sid said so, and would make room for different understandings on which to speak of that which Sid spoke of as so. That such things are possible is no hindrance to seeing whether, in fact, Sid was right, given that he said what I said he did. Nor do we aim to speak, or to say what others said, so as to eliminate such possibilities. Yet, where they exist, there are different things to be said in speaking of the ways for things to be we speak of, or specify in saying what others said. The idea that ended innocence thus supposes, as we now do not, that there are ways for things to be, and ways for us to say, or think, them to be, for which no such possibility exists.

Pia said that Sid had red hair; Zoë said that he had not. Each spoke of Sid's having red hair. But dye would make what Pia thus said true, while it would make what Zoë thus said false. For each spoke of having red hair on a different understanding of what it would be to have it. What the one said thus does not contradict what the other did. If Zoë spoke truth, that does not mean that what Pia said is not so. For thinkers with a different sense of the sort of thing one might call a chair, who, for all that, still thought in terms of things being chairs or not, there might be different truths to tell about chairs than there are for us to tell. Where we spoke truth in calling such-and-such a chair, they might speak truth in denying that it was that. They would do so in speaking of being a chair on an understanding of being one which their sensibilities made available, and right in given circumstances. Perhaps we could not have that understanding, or speak on it, as, perhaps, they could not have some of ours. Such thinkers, insofar as possible, would stand to us as Zoë does to Pia. In speaking of things being chairs or not, they would, to the extent that they so differed from us, say, and deny, different things to be so than what we state in so speaking. The truth of what they thus stated would do nothing to show that what *we* think, and say, truly, in thinking in those terms, was not so.

To see our mind's involvement in shaping what we think, we must, so to speak, catch ourselves thinking. In the first instance that is a perfectly mundane thing to do. From the perspective of one occasion on which we find ourselves, we examine how we would stand towards the world on another. It would be correct, in certain circumstances, but not in others, to describe Sid as having red hair. That is how, in those circumstances, one would naturally think of things. So we see how ways of thinking, interests, purposes, and so forth, may work to shape truth. It is not as if to do that we need to look at thought without actually doing any, or being governed by the specific ways of thinking we are thus involved in. Mind dependence is visible from the inside. Where knowledge-yielding faculties depend on *special* psychological design, different psychological designs must be conceivable. Anti-empiricists, such as Chomsky or McDowell, need the idea of special design. So they must allow the legitimacy of thinking of ourselves as having been otherwise in relevant respects. Where an anti-empiricist needs the idea of special sensibilities—as, I think, McDowell often does—he also needs to make sense of them in terms of the above role for understandings in fixing what is said in speaking of a given way for things to be. But if we are to think of what we might have been, we must do it, just as in the mundane case, by *thinking*, from our actual perspective on the world, with full involvement of our actual sensibilities. That may limit what we *can* think—what we can sensibly suppose. It also means that how things *might* thus be is what they might be by those ideas of what is sensible, rational, and right which govern, and are fixed by, the way *we*, in fact, thus think.

9. Domains

We have now seen how anti-empiricism steers clear of idealism where it needs to. Where we think so what would be so no matter how one thought, thinkers who thought otherwise would either be thinking of different ways for things to be, or would be thinking of the ways we thus think of, but on different understandings of things being those ways. The coherence of a form of responsiveness to the world, in ensuring something independent of us to which we are thus responsive, ensures no less than that. At this point, though, a question arises. For, for all their common ground, there seemed to be a distinction between Chomsky and McDowell. That distinction turns on Frege's idea that there is something special about grammar. It is (he thought) harmless to suppose that English grammar would have been different from what it is, had English speakers thought differently enough about their language—or, in a still more Fregean vein, may some day be different from what it now is, if English speakers change—in a way that it is not harmless to suppose that the ink in Frege's inkwell might not have been black, or the wind not blowing at gale force, if only people thought differently enough. (For all of which, the facts about what English grammar *is* would be what they are no matter how one thought: differently designed linguists would not change the nature of the object of their study.) What is the difference between these two sorts of cases?

   The answer is simple. It is part of our way of thinking of the colours of things, or the forces of winds, that such things are what they are no matter how one thinks; whereas it is (if Frege is right) part of our way of thinking about grammar that grammar is but a reflection of how fluent speakers are prepared to think of what they do in speaking. In each case, that is just part of how we conceive things. In each case, that conception meshes, in the way the anti-empiricist demands, with the rest of relevant practice, as a coherent form of responsiveness to how things are. So in each case, what is thus so on that way of thinking of things is so. There is, on Frege's plausible idea, a significant way in which grammatical facts are a matter of what relevant speakers are *prepared* to recognize—Dutch 'erkennen' (acknowledge), whereas facts about colours or wind velocity are what suitable thinkers are *equipped* to recognize—Dutch 'herkennen' (tell, identify). In each case, that that is so is internal to a particular form of coherent responsiveness to the world.

Objectivity was, for Frege, the root source of (what he called) the laws of truth. Genuine objectivity may be internal to a special-design, non-universal, way of thinking, so as to reign provided that way coheres as described above. That suggests a certain possibility for logic. Perhaps we, for example, enjoy a logical competence conferred by a special psychological design, not necessarily shared by any thinker whatsoever. We are designed, say, to see ourselves (and, perhaps, others) as thinking in terms of certain particular notions of conjunction and disjunction, and to see our thought as organized accordingly. That we think in those specific terms would be part of a special design. For all that, it might be part of the way we thus conceive things that there are facts about those special notions that hold absolutely, that is, depend on nothing, neither on how anyone thinks, nor on how things stand extra-logically. That might be a coherent way of thinking, provided it is directed at sufficiently sparse, austere, notions of conjunction, disjunction, or whatever it is of which such facts are to hold absolutely. For, as seen in section 1, absoluteness and austerity must go hand in hand. (And we, at least, do not know how to specify so austerely as to exclude, in principle, any say from the world as to what coherent responsiveness to it might be.) But, if such a way of thinking is responsiveness, then what is so, so conceiving things, is no less than what is so. So there are absolute facts about those notions of conjunction and disjunction.

That possibility separates several ideas in Frege's thought. One thing Frege wanted for logic was absoluteness. Absoluteness is compatible with special psychological design—though Frege might have regarded it as a cheapened form of absoluteness (given that there is always room for a word from the world as to whether a way of thinking coheres). Another thing Frege wanted was universality: in some sense, the laws of logic should hold for all thinkers. There are several things universality might come to. It might be a matter of how all thinkers must be viewable by us. Or it might be a matter of what all thinkers must be prepared to recognize. In this second case, one might have absoluteness without universality. Frege also had the idea that the laws of truth are the most general laws of thought. The idea of special logical competences threatens to rob that idea of sense. All this, though, just gestures at issues needing much more detailed examination. That task is a separate project.

3

The Twilight of Empiricism

1. Answerability

The most striking feature of traditional empiricism, from Hume to Quine, is what it tells us there is not. Hume tells us that nothing causes anything, *if* causation is what we naturally take it for. Quine tells us that there is no linguistic meaning, or at least no facts of the sort we naturally suppose as to what expressions do mean: it is neither a fact that 'renarde' means *vixen*, nor that 'vixen' means *female fox*. As Austin noted, often in such cases 'there is the bit where you say it, and the bit where you take it back' (Austin 1962: 2). First a surprising thesis, then some intricate backpedalling, in which it is suggested that not *much* is lost—that there are good enough *ersätze* for the things we naturally supposed there were. I want to concentrate on the moves which get us to a point where backpedalling seems called for. The *Ersätze* will emerge as false coin.

Such empiricist claims concern what I will call 'answerability'. A central case of that is taking something to be so, where I mean thus to refer to a stance or attitude properly expressed in flat (bald) assertion. I begin with background.

The world thrusts attitudes, or stances on us; as a rule, we do not choose them. That is a feature equally of disgust at Sid's table manners and of taking his face to be smeared with food. Both stances are, where held, not optional. I may respond with disgust to Sid's manners; I do not decide whether to. If I needed to, I would not be disgusted. Equally, to need to decide whether Sid's face is smeared with food is not yet to take it to be. But there is a difference. Disgust is not optional *for me*. I am saddled with it by the way *I* am. Someone who did not feel it might be just as alive to things being as they are. By contrast, if my taking Sid's face to be smeared is what it aims to be, then it is the *world* that does the forcing: my attitude would be forced on *anyone* suitably exposed to, and discerning of, things being as they are.

To take Sid's face to be smeared with food is to see oneself as purely registering how things are; as doing what proper sensitivity, and suitable exposure, to the world makes compulsory. It is, further, to see one's stance as so elicited by precisely that way which the stance consists in finding things. As a rule, such an attitude may be, in this respect, illusory. There may be nothing to do the envisioned sort of imposing. It is only the lighting that makes Sid's face look that way. The attitude is correct or not, in one way, as it is thus illusory or not. There is the noted difference between such a stance and disgust at Sid's manners: if the stance is thus correct, then it is the world that would have to have been different for it not to be, and vice versa.

To say this is to say that a stance's correctness in this sense is independent of any taking of it: there is the stance there is to take; if it is correct, then it is correct whenever, and however, taken, and similarly if it is incorrect. In general, stances, or attitudes, may be exclusive. Insofar as I am disgusted by Sid's manners, thus far I am, *ipso facto*, not indifferent to them. Insofar as I take Sid's face to be smeared with food, thus far I do not take it to be foodless. In the first case, two thinkers may take mutually exclusive attitudes while equally responsive to the way things are—equally faultless in their responding to it. Not so in the second case. If any case of taking Sid's face to be smeared with food is thinking correctly, for the present sort of correctness, then any taking of an attitude that one excludes is *ipso facto* incorrect. So contingent accompaniments of particular takings of a stance have no bearing on its correctness in the present sense. The way things are holds *sole* sway over that.

I will call a stance admitting of correctness of this sort *answerable*. To be truth-evaluable is to be answerable, though answerability can be seen as having wider scope.

The empiricist claim, in a given case, is that the relevant stances are not answerable: by empiricist lights they fail some requirement on being that. If they are not, there is no such thing as what they pretend to answer to. Causal facts, if any, are what causal stances pretend to answer to. If those stances are not answerable, there are no causal facts. Similarly for linguistic meaning. What requirement do such stances fail? Why require it?

2. Empiricist Tools

The present notion of answerability is minimalist. An answerable stance, if correct (true), is so on any taking of it. Its correctness (truth) excludes that of any stance it excludes. So one can construct stances logically related to it—for example, one correct just in case it is incorrect, and vice-versa. Suppose someone thought our causal stances to satisfy that condition. We all thought so until Hume arrived. They seem to. Hume says not. Who is right? If anything decides in Hume's favour, it is more than merely what answerability, or truth-evaluability, is as such.

So the empiricist demands more of answerability than our present notion itself does. What? Empiricists strikingly insist on three things. First, answerability (at least to the sublunary) is ultimately to the observable. Second, the argument from illusion is a means of locating the observable. Third, answerability is to what could not but be, given something there might be to be observed, and (so) to what any thinker is equipped to learn from that.

The argument from illusion begins with a premise which must be supplied case by case for each candidate for the observable. If there are genuine candidates for which it cannot be supplied, then there we have arrived at the observable; the argument stops at that point. If the argument *locates* the observable, there is somewhere it does stop. If the claim is to have observed X to be present, or so, or that someone once did that, or might do that, then the premise is that there is, or is such a thing as, a ringer for N's situation regarding X (where N is the one claimed to have observed X). The conclusion of the argument is that N did not observe X, or, if N is just dummy for anyone, then X is not thus observable. If the result is indifferent to N's situation, then X is not observable full stop.

'Ringer' is a technical term. Let us say that a ringer for N's situation regarding X is a situation such that were N in it, he could not tell that he was in it rather than his actual situation (from the way things looked or seemed, or from anything experience might inform him of), but in which X is not so, or present. So if N claims to see a pig to be before him, then a ringer might be a situation in which there is a stuffed mechanical pig—so cleverly done as to look *just* like the real thing. All that is needed is that there is such a thing as that, not that anyone has ever actually made such a 'pig'.

How are we meant to get from premise to conclusion? The step has struck most empiricists as too obvious for words. But suppose our intuitions need jogging. Patter might then take any of various forms. For example, if N were in a ringer situation *in re* that pig, nothing he could be aware of (experiencing) would reveal that. So if it needed proof that he is not in such a situation, he could appeal to nothing he *is* aware of experiencing to show this. So he is really taking it on faith that his situation is not a ringer. He has no proof. Or, if something he knew already proves that it is not, then he is concluding this from that fact. In neither case could he simply see (observe) a pig to be before him. For if that is what he observed, no faith is called for, and he need not *conclude* this from something else. Whatever the patter, the crucial idea is this: if there is a ringer for N's situation *in re* a pig before him, then N's situation might be a ringer, or might be for all he has actually seen, or is aware of experiencing. For if it were a ringer, it would be for all he had actually seen or experienced.

Empiricism's third demand is that answerability be to what some observable would (for any thinker) recognizably necessitate. What was not thus necessitated would incorrigibly admit of ringers. By the argument from illusion, its obtaining (if there were such a thing) would then be in principle unrecognizable (unknowable). For an empiricist, answerability cannot be in principle unrecognizable: our stances could not float that free from what we could see to matter. So there could be no such thing to answer to. Nor could it take a parochial capacity to see what relevant observables thus meant. For there are ringers for a capacity only some thinkers have—masqueraders which are mere designs for prejudice. On pain of regress, only universally available capacities (if anything) could distinguish such ringers from the real thing. But then, the thought is, the parochial drops out as in principle superfluous.

Empiricism is not replete with arguments for these three demands. I have tried to make them plausible pro tem. But we can see the ideas at work, for example, in Quine's attack on the 'traditional' notion of meaning. Here is Quine's crucial starting point:

In psychology, one may or may not be a behaviorist, but in linguistics one has no choice. Each of us learns his language by observing other people's verbal behavior and having his own faltering verbal behavior observed and reinforced or corrected by others. We depend strictly on overt behavior in observable situations.

(Quine 1987: 5)

Facts about a language must be recognizable by its speakers, so, plausibly, learnable by them by observation. Quine assumes from the start severe limitations on what one might observe. They are contained in his proprietary use of 'behaviour'—roughly as bodily movements and emissions. Not that *behaviour* admits no ringers. But why is it, here, *the most* one might observe? Observing speakers of an unlearned language, why could one not observe, say, that someone is complaining over spilled beer, or asking someone to leave? Quine does not say. No more speaks for *that* limitation on observation than this: complaining, for example, can be faked; it has its ringers. So, the thought is, where I take someone to be doing that, I do so on faith, or in concluding it from something else, which means that it is not observable. That idea just instances the argument from illusion. Following long empiricist tradition, Quine implicitly relies here on familiar doctrine. From the result thus reached he argues, plausibly, that no data we could have would eliminate all ringers for, say, 'renarde' meaning vixen (if it could do that). No non-parochial capacities could bring any such consequence in view. Data could necessitate no such fact in the way empiricism demands. So, by his empiricist lights, there can be no such fact.

For Quine, it is not a fact that 'renarde' means vixen. There is then some backpedalling to the effect that we humans prefer some 'translation manuals' over others—such is the way of our people. But those are mere facts about human predilections and prejudices. Our preference for a manual cannot make its contents *answerable* stances: where prejudice is thus called for, correctness is precisely not what the world alone decides.

3. Privacy

Frege presents a powerful anti-empiricist line of thought. He states the theme in Frege 1884, where the targeted idea is that meanings are 'ideas'. He elaborates it in Frege 1918, where the targeted idea is that thoughts are ideas. These two ideas merge.

In 1884 (p. x) Frege warns of a pitfall: taking meanings (*Bedeutungen*) for ideas. (Russell was driven to this in (Russell 1918)). What would it be to do that? That depends, for one thing, on what one understands by meaning. In 1884 Frege had not fully worked that out. Meanings *might* be what words speak of, in which case if meanings were ideas, ideas would be all we could ever speak of. Ideas in Frege's sense are, whatever else, private property. So I would have only my ideas to speak of, you only yours. But there is a more interesting understanding of the idea that meanings are ideas.

One might approach the question of what meanings are by asking what meanings do. That thoroughly modern idea began with Frege. A natural answer would be: the meaning of a sentence fixes when it would be true, that of a sub-sentential part makes a systematic contribution to fixing that for each sentence in which the part occurs. To say that meanings are ideas would now be to say that such truth-conditions refer essentially to an idea: for a given sentence to be true is for it to relate in such-and-such way to some idea(s). Ideas being private, the meanings I could assign to sentences would thus be available only to me; and similarly for you. A sentence, with a meaning I could assign it, would be true on a condition only I could grasp. That is the most general understanding of the idea that meanings are ideas; for meanings to be what words speak of would be a special case, *one* way for it to be only me who can grasp the truth conditions imposed by the meanings I assign.

The question in Frege 1918 is whether thoughts are ideas. Here Frege aims at a comparison. He sets out certain central properties of what he means to call ideas, then he asks whether thoughts could have those properties. These properties are: an idea is part of the content of someone's consciousness; an idea needs an owner (for it to be is for it to be a particular part of someone's consciousness); no idea can be part of two different thinkers' consciousnesses (Frege 1918: 67–68). *If* we are aware of our ideas, then I am aware only of mine, each of which is contemporaneous with my awareness of it. That is one half of the comparison; now we are to try to suppose that thoughts are like that. If so, then only I (if anyone) can encounter my thoughts; only I can have them, so entertain them; only I can grasp them. To grasp a thought is to grasp when it would be true (how things being as they are matters to its having answered). So if only I can grasp my thoughts, then they have private truth conditions in the same way that sentences would if meanings were ideas.

If you cannot grasp a thought of mine (or what matters to its truth), then you can neither assent to it, nor negate it, nor entertain any thought of which it is a constituent (Frege 1918: 69). One thing Frege tells us about that situation is that in that case science must be private: there can be no common inquiry into anything. I can have, at best, my geometry, you yours (Frege 1918: 68). But could there be so much as private science? Frege gives good reason to think not.

To make his case against private science, Frege continues his comparison between ideas and thoughts. Here is the first term of the extended comparison:

When the word 'red' is meant not to state a property of things but to characterize sense-impressions belonging to my consciousness, it is only applicable within the realm of my consciousness.

(Frege 1918: 67)

Suppose that in thinking of things being coloured red we are thinking of a property of objects *to be met with* in our environment—apples, drapery, and so on. Then we are thinking of a property with systematic import for indefinitely many aspects of the behaviour of the object with it. It is very intimately connected with how the object looks—not just with how it looks to some observer on some occasion, but how it looks, full stop: something open to observation on indefinitely many occasions, and to an indefinitely wide range of observers. It also has roles in other aspects of the behaviour of the object; both known and unknown ones. The property's being what it is poses no definite limits on just what these roles may be. (An object's being red may *mean* things (factively); what these are is a matter for discovery.) Whether a given object has this property is thus open to proof, where it is not fixed in advance just what proof might be. So, too, any substantive reasons for taking it to be red—say, that it looks red to me now—are open to being outweighed by others, where it is not fixed in advance just what these may be.

Properties of ideas cannot have the sort of systematic, or extensive, import for their behaviour that properties of environmental objects do for theirs, for ideas exist only as a content of a consciousness, a given idea only as long as it is part of someone's consciousness. A property of an idea thus cannot have that factive meaning which is open to discovery: investigation is just not on the cards. Further considerations about the idea cannot bear on its having such a property in the same potentially open-ended way as in the case of objects to be met with. There is not, as with those objects, always room for further observation, or investigation, yielding further proof, perhaps outweighing what is already in hand. What sense is to be made of the idea that properties that are different are really one—that it is *one* thing, being coloured red, that is a way both an object to be met with and an idea may be? Frege suggests that there is none. *If* ideas have properties, one of these might be *called* 'being red', but that would be one *only* an idea could have.

Someone might compare one of his ideas with a tomato, *say* them to look the same way, then rule that to be red in his sense just is to look this way. What is to count here as an idea and a tomato looking the same way? Objects have looks. A tomato may, as such, look thus and so (red, orange in this light). We are not yet entitled to suppose ideas, as such, to have looks in any such sense. For we have not yet distinguished an idea's *looking* red, say, and its merely so impressing, or so looking to, its owner. So an idea and a tomato cannot yet look the same in that sense of looks. Nor will it do merely for the idea to impress its owner as looking like the tomato. For that it *does* so look was to be the object of an answerable stance, so that an idea's having the right property—one an object to be met with might also have—could be the object of an answerable stance. That is not achieved unless there is something on which the correctness of such impressions turns—as, so far, there is not. So we remain at a loss as to in what sense it could be that the tomato and the idea look alike, so in that way share *one* property.

So much for the first term of our comparison. The second term is private thoughts: ones with private truth conditions. Here Frege says this:

I said that the word 'red' was applicable only in the sphere of my consciousness if it was not meant to state a property of things but to characterize some of my own sense-impressions. Therefore the words 'true' and 'false', as I understand them, might also be applicable only in the realm of my consciousness, if they were not meant to apply to something of which I was not the owner, but to characterize in some way the content of my consciousness. Truth would then be confined to this content and it would remain doubtful whether anything at all similar occurred in the consciousness of others.

(Frege 1918: 68–69)

What is it like for a *public* thought to be true? There are parallels with an object's being red. First, like the drapery, such a thought may be encountered—grasped, entertained—by many. Many may thus see what it would be to grasp, or to think it, and thus *may* see who does grasp it, and who thinks it. Many can see when the thought would be true; no one is thus the sole arbiter of its truth. Such insights are within reach of anyone suitably equipped and positioned.

Second, just as something's being red has an indefinitely extensive role in its behaviour, so a public thought's being true has an indefinitely extending role in the way things are: for it to be true is for something to be so with such a role. One may think that the ball is red. There is no end to the experience that may show, or matter to showing, whether that is so. There is no fixed limit on what other aspects of the world may bear on its being so. What is involved in a ball's being red is open to discoveries. Similarly for what it means (factively) for this ball to be red. Perhaps it is observably red. Then it is observably so full stop: not just in some fixed battery of encounters. So there are, in principle, an indefinite range of ways in which the truth of the stance may be investigated, or discovered, in which it might be shown, or proven, true.

The 'truth' of a private thought would be nothing like this. It would not engage with phenomena there are to be encountered as that of a public stance does. It would not be open to investigation, discovery, or proof in any of the ways just sketched. It would not be at all what *truth* is—the truth, that is, of stances there are to take. It would be senseless to suppose oneself, in using 'true' of one's private thoughts, to be attributing to them the same status as a public thought would have in being true. 'True' so used could not mean what 'true' does. Someone might be inclined to call a private thought true, but there is nothing it would be for this inclination to be right.

So private thoughts would be neither true nor false, not truth-evaluable. They would not be answerable: there would be no genuine *demands* on their having answered. With investigation and discovery excluded in principle, there could be nothing for a private thought to live up to, not even something visible only to its owner. To be thus bound to no standard for correctness is to be bound *by* no logic (no spelling out of *truth*). For Frege that line reverses. Logic, as he conceives it, could not bind private thought, *therefore* such thought could be bound to no standards for having answered. This condenses a second case against privacy.

Laws of logic, for Frege, spell out what truth is: what it is, in general, for something to be true (Frege 1918: 59). They contain 'prescriptions about asserting, thinking, judging, inferring'; ones which hold for any case of this (Frege 1918: 58). In these respects logic is *universal* in import. Frege also stresses logic's indifference to particular subject matter. For that, its laws must be maximally general, abstracting from mention of anything. Now here is the second line of thought in brief. If there were private thoughts, then there could be no logic so conceived. That can also be put by saying that private thoughts would not be governed by logic. To say that is to say that they could be governed by no standards of correctness at all. But then there is nothing it would be for them to be answerable. To be a thought *is* to be answerable. So there are no private thoughts.

Here is a quick way to the point. Suppose that Sid and Pia can each entertain some private thoughts. If we consider the thoughts available to Pia, we can abstract away from their particular topics, quantifying where something is mentioned, thus arriving at the most general thoughts available to her. We may do likewise for Sid. What we would thus arrive at are the most general thoughts *available to Pia*, and the most general ones *available to Sid*. But there would be no sense to the idea that these are the same thoughts. So there would be no sense to the idea that there are most general thoughts *tout court*. If there are not, then, on Frege's conception of logic, no thought whatever could have the content of a law of logic. No thought would say with complete generality how *one* must think to think truly. So to suppose there to be private thoughts is to suppose there to be thoughts not governed by logic. But that cannot be.

Here is another way to see the same point. If a law of logic mentions nothing, how can it, in any sense, speak to anything? How can any prescriptions on thinking, or judging, follow from it? A most general truth has nothing but its structure to make it true. So it must speak via the import of the truth of something with that structure. There may be such import insofar as the law's structure reflects that of some inferential network to which both it and more particular thoughts belong. The truth of the law may reflect the truth-preserving nature of certain paths through some such structure. But Sid's private thoughts and Pia's are logically incomparable: Pia's bear *no* inferential relations to Sid's. So they do not jointly belong to any network whose structure a law might reflect. Some generality might reflect the structure of some network to which Pia's thoughts belong, but then it would not do that for any network to which Sid's belonged. For it cannot belong to both. And for it to be structured thus and so just is for it to belong to a system in which its parts have systematic roles. So, again, no generality can have the scope (all thoughts) that a law of logic must.

A law of logic, on Frege's conception, governs thoughts in relating inferentially to them. Nothing could so relate to all thoughts if some were private. So if there are private thoughts, there is no logic. By the same token, private thoughts are governed by no laws of logic. So there can be no private thoughts (no privately answerable stances). A private stance could be governed by no genuine standard of correctness. Let the stance be what it might, and let the world be as it may be. Now, has the stance answered? One may as well say yes as no. Neither answer can conflict with anything else that is so. For without logic there are no consequences of saying either, or, equally, one might just as well take anything as anything else to be a consequence, or not to be. With such freedom, there is nothing it could be for one's stance to have answered, or to have failed to.

To be answerable is to be bound to how things are in some particular respect, so that things being as they are matters to one's (or to the stance's) status in some definite way. The idea is that one cannot be bound to anything in particular unless one is already bound by logic. Could not one be bound by private logic? But that would just be to be bound by further private stances; ones which one took, where a thinker might have taken others, in being the special sort of thinker one happened to be. If the problem was how any private stance could bind, the solution cannot be that some can if others do. Being bound by logic, as Frege conceives it, is being bound merely by what thinking is as such; merely by there being no such thing as illogical thought. A *thinker* need be committed in no special way to manage that.

On this second line of thought, the *soi-disant* private thinker could have only the impression of being subject to a certain condition of correctness; there is no such thing as that impression being right. That is a point of intersection between this second line and the first. On each, no *answerable* stance can have a private truth condition. The second, but not the first, turns on Frege's conception of logic.

4. Anti-empiricism

I spoke of Frege's anti-empiricist line(s) of thought. Frege billed his case, not wrongly, as anti-idealist. Are these the same? They are if the argument from illusion stops nowhere short of ideas. Empiricism then becomes idealism. Here, too, Frege had the right idea. It begins with the first feature he assigns ideas:

Ideas cannot be seen, or touched, or smelled, or tasted, or heard. . . . . . I see a green field, I thus have a visual impression of the green. I have it, but I do not see it.

(Frege 1918: 67)

Ideas, in short, are not objects of perception. Not all we can think about is. But perception has some crucial features lacking in our contact with ideas. Perception is a form of contact with (things in) our surroundings. It is contact with things to be met with, with what is there, and the way things are, independent of that contact with it—with how things would have been had we not seen, etc. That permits a certain battery of notions to fit—*capacity, investigation, discovery* crucially among them. For what may be an object of perception, one may have, and exercise, capacities to tell how things stand with respect to it—whether, say, there are pigs in the environs. A capacity is, in the nature of the case, to get something *right*. There must then be something to get right: a way things are anyway, independent of the capacity's exercise. Similarly, if, but only if, there is something to get right—a way things are anyway—the notions of investigating, and discovering, how things are apply. The notion of capacity applies just where there are, or may be, ways of finding out how things are. So what we experience may bear on whether things are thus and so, or may just *be* their being that. Experience may thus show, or prove, various things as to how things are. These notions—*capacity, investigation, discovery*—must fit whatever we can *think* so.

With that framework in place, one may take answerable stances towards what one experiences, thus to the sublunary. Since perception keeps that framework in place, one may *think* things about the objects of perception. There is a way such things are independent of one's contact with them. One may thus bind oneself, or be bound, to that being one way rather than another. One *could* be discoverably right. Frege's point is that no such framework is in place for our contact with ideas. An idea, in Frege's sense, must be a particular content of consciousness. It is nothing without an owner. So there is no way it is anyway, independent of our contact with it. So the framework cannot fit. So we cannot take answerable stances towards our ideas. The idea of answerability does not fit there. So if ideas are what we experience, we cannot take answerable stances towards the objects of our experiences. We cannot *think* things about them. So we cannot think about the sublunary world. Such is the fate of this form of idealism. It mirrors, in experience, the point that a *thought* cannot have a private truth condition.

What does it take, then, for the framework to be in place? Frege tells us,

> If man could not think and could not take as the object of his thought something of which he was not the owner, he would have an inner world, but no environment. . . . By the step with which I win an environment for myself I expose myself to the risk of error.

(Frege 1918: 73)

To experience, and think about, an environment is to relate to what is there anyway, independent of one's contact with it; to that which, by exercise of one's capacities (such as they are) one may get right or wrong. That allows, at one stroke, both for answerable stances and for error. I may get so far as taking there to be a pig before me: I may be answerable. But then, for all that I take one to be there, there may be no pig: the risk of error. This 'risk' in a given case may come to no more than that there is such a thing as a ringer for my situation *in re* pigs. Risk may be that attenuated, but it must be that much. *Perception* requires ringers. So, too, does answerability, at least to the sublunary.

Austin saw the point here:

> To stipulate that a sense-datum just is whatever the speaker takes it to be . . . is to make non-mendacious sense-datum statements true by *fiat*; and if so, how could sense-data be, as they are also meant to be, non-linguistic entities, *of* which we are aware, *to* which we refer, that against which the factual truth of all empirical statements is to be tested?
>
> (Austin 1962: 130, footnote)

Ayer, an exemplary empiricist, missed it:

> The possibility of my being mistaken, in what is not merely a verbal sense, depends on the fact that my judgement goes beyond the evidence. . . . It is held to be characteristic of an incorrigible proposition that it is completely verified by the existence of the sense-datum which it describes. . . . If one uses a sentence such as 'this is green' merely to designate a present sense-datum, then no proposition is being asserted to the truth of which any further evidence would be relevant.
>
> (Ayer 1940: 82–83)

For Ayer, thus, there can be, indeed regularly are, *propositions*, either true or false, but answerable to nothing beyond one's present idea being as it is. Just this is what Frege and Austin see to be nonsense.

Frege's point can be put as follows. There must always be ringers for whatever (sublunary) affairs there are to answer to. So the argument from illusion, if valid, can stop nowhere short of ideas. By empiricist tenets it is thus ideas to which our stances (towards sublunary affairs) must ultimately answer. But there are no answerable stances towards ideas. So empricism becomes idealism, thus abolishing answerability *überhaupt*.

Frege's prognosis for empiricism is realized by Quine. In the last section of 'Two Dogmas' (Quine 1950) he tells us:

> The totality of our so-called knowledge or beliefs . . . is a man-made fabric which impinges on experience only along the edges. Or . . . like a field of force whose boundary conditions are experience. . . . A conflict with experience at the periphery occasions readjustments in the interior of the field. Truth values have to be redistributed over some of our statements.
>
> (Quine 1950: 42)

Our beliefs, Quine tells us, face experience as a corporate body. And they face it thus:

> Any statement can be held true come what may, if we make drastic enough adjustments elsewhere in the system. Even a statement very close to the periphery can be held true in

the face of recalcitrant experience by pleading hallucination or by amending certain statements of the kind called logical laws.

(Quine 1950: 43)

So no experience, as such, means, or shows, that any belief in particular is false. For any belief one might have, no experience is, as such, inconsistent with it. So far as any experience goes, *any* belief might be true, depending on what one supposes of others. What, then, could our experience be of? How could it bear at all on belief, or on the truth of *anything*? How could it be recalcitrant? (In the space of a page Quine has shifted from talk of beliefs, to talk of 'statements'. Perhaps he means to duck a problem here in conceiving a statement as what leaves entirely open what is so according to it, and then avoiding talk of anything which raises a *question* of truth in there *being* what is so according to it. But, since *nothing* is so according to a statement so conceived, it could hardly be *correctly* held true, or false, no matter how things were. Nor would it help to insist that nothing ever makes anything either true or false. Ducking *this* problem would just be ducking the issue entirely—a point on which I plan to harp.)

We sometimes identify experiences by what, in fact, was experienced: a stuffed mechanical pig, which I took for the real thing. If that is what I experienced, then there is one belief in particular, if I have it, which must be false: that there is a pig before me. For such experience, revision of belief cannot come just anywhere. I could, of course, have the experience and retain my belief that I face a pig, but if I do, then I retain a mistaken belief, one inconsistent with my having had *that* experience—one thus incorrect in precisely answerability's characteristic way. We sometimes identify an experience by what one in fact perceived, or made out, in having it: a pig rounding the corner, say. The same point applies. I *could*, perhaps, see a pig before me and plead hallucination, or etc. But if I did see a pig before me, I would then be wrong. So Quinean experience cannot be like that. One cannot experience a stuffed pig, or have the experience of seeing a pig to round the corner. Just what *can* one experience?

Quine helps himself to the idea that experience can *conflict* with a body of belief. As he puts it, an experience can be *recalcitrant*. But just what entitles Quine to any such notion? Perhaps there is a clue in this:

As an empiricist I continue to think of the conceptual scheme of science as a tool, ultimately, for predicting future experience in the light of past experience. Physical objects are conceptually imported into the situation as convenient intermediaries—not by definition in terms of experience, but simply as irreducible posits comparable, epistemologically, to the gods of Homer.

(Quine 1950: 44)

So we are meant to be able to predict future experience. Such predictions would not be about such things as porcine encounters: for Quine we experience no such things. Pigs are posits. Still, though, a *prediction* is, by nature, what may come true or not. It is an answerable stance. Depending on future experience, it might not come true. In that case, experience will not be compatible with revision anywhere—with holding on to just *any* belief by making revisions elsewhere. There is one belief—the prediction—which it refutes. Hold onto that, and you hold onto something definitely false. In Quine's paradise, such things cannot happen. But that is just to say that in that paradise there are no predictions to be made. Posits, such as pigs and sofas, are thus not convenient intermediaries. There is nothing for them to mediate.

The point can be put another way. Let us make a Quinean prediction. Now let experience continue its course, however it may. Has the prediction turned out false? There is no answer to that. Or rather, by Quinean lights, you are free to say whatever you like, without thereby lapsing into error. But a prediction compatible with any future course of things is no prediction at all. A 'prediction' that fits into Quine's paradise could not be an answerable stance. Then the rest of a Quinean body of beliefs—the posits and such—has no function. So nor can some totality of belief be answerable corporately. Experience, no matter how it goes, cannot be recalcitrant. For, in Quine's paradise, there cannot be anything we do experience. Experience cannot be of anything, or at least of anything towards which one might take answerable stances. In which case, one can just as well hold onto any *body* of 'belief' no matter what. There is, in Quine's paradise, nothing to investigate, nothing on which one might exercise capacities. There is nothing encounterable to which one might be answerable—just what Frege saw empiricism's fate to be.

That Quine has given up on answerability, corporate or not, is clear in this:

> Certain statements, though about physical objects *and not sense experience*, seem peculiarly germane to sense experience—and in a selective way: some statements to some experiences, others to others. . . . But in this relation of "germaneness" I envisage nothing more than a loose association reflecting the relative likelihood, in practice, of our choosing one statement rather than another for revision in the event of recalcitrant experience.

(Quine 1950: 43 (my italics))

We do not, in fact, change belief in just any way. A given experience may change our belief as to whether a pig is in the tulips, or the sty has been left open, but not as to whether there are over five million Parisians, or one can see St Paul's from Primrose Hill. We *take* the experience to bear on the former, not on the latter. Such is *our* perception of germaneness. Such, for Quine, is the way of our people—what we (humans) are inclined to do—nothing more. So if a given belief is what *we* would recognize as true, that is substantially a matter of the sentiments we are inclined, or designed, to have. For Quine there is nothing else it might be for the belief to be true full stop. If truth values are to be distributed in some given way over a body of belief, once again, such is the way of our people. An answerable stance was meant to be one whose correctness was decided *only* by the world's being as it is, precisely not by any idiosyncracies of thought with which its taking might be accompanied in given cases. That is just what is not so, given Quine's notion of germaneness; neither for individual stances there are to take, nor for corporate bodies, whose status as a body depends on the way of our people in distributing values within them. Quine speaks of distributing truth values over such bodies. But he has no right to the idea that what is being distributed is in fact *truth* values—values only answerable stances may take.

One might rightly sympathize with the idea that no belief is absolutely immune to proving false. But it is not that idea that sows debacle. That emerges in the contrast between Quine and Hilary Putnam. (See, e.g. Putnam 1962.) Like Quine, Putnam rejects the idea of beliefs which *essentially* stand fast (are true) no matter what. But, as for the import of experience, he quantifies differently. Quine insists that for any experience, any belief might be revised or not. Just that bars us from experiencing *anything*. Putnam's idea is: for (almost) any belief, there is such a thing (or at least not no such thing) as a course of experience that would show it to be false. That does not challenge our ordinary notion of experience. It is not that there are no experiences of pigs or vixens—experiences which may (flatly) prove particular beliefs false (say, that there is no pig in the garden). For all that, our most cherished beliefs about pigs and vixens are not immune to proving false. But if they do, they *prove* false; it is not all a matter of how we choose to distribute truth values, or the way of our people in such matters. Such would be a lesson about that which our experience, in point of fact, was of. Putnam's worries about analyticity thus do not, as Quine's do, bring meaning itself into question.

I have pictured Quine's debacle as empiricism's. One sees the equivalence in this: one cannot get so far as thinking that a belief might be held onto no matter what, unless one has already stripped experience of any substance. One must first, with Quine, remove pigs and sofas from the realm of sense experience. One must, more generally, remove as any object of experience (all the more as anything visibly, recognizably, that) anything towards which an answerable stance might be taken. Only when experience is *thoroughly* impoverished—well after perception has left the picture—could it be that any belief—say, my belief that that pig is munching tulips—can be retained *correctly*, no matter what the experience. We can, without error, preserve our belief that there are no pigs—plead hallucination, etc.—only if pigs are never simply what we see, or actually experience. There is no better reason for thinking that than that such things admits of ringers. The argument from illusion is what is then needed for stripping experience of that import which it must not have if we are to be able to retain any belief no matter what.

It would be false advertising to pretend that it is a scientific view of things that thus impoverishes experience. Explaining how the retinal patterns we receive allow us the contact with our environment we in fact have may be a project for psychology. That it is those patterns which permit us contact does not yet decide with what that contact might be, given that endowment which a solution to the psychologist's problem would, in part, spell out. Not without additional empiricist assumptions. Quine has the merit of executing empiricism thoroughly. Thereby he becomes empiricism's twilight.

5. The Parochial

Suppose that one sort of thinker (humans, say) can grasp, or entertain, thoughts that another sort (Martians, say) cannot. The one sort can perceive ways of answering to the world that the other cannot catch on to. This would not be a case of privacy. Humans being what they are, there can be, in principle, as many of them as you like. Similarly for Martians. The thoughts envisioned here are ones it would take a parochial capacity to grasp: its absence need not disqualify one as a thinker. Call such thoughts 'exclusive'. Might answerability take exclusive forms, though it cannot take private ones? Frege's second line of thought, but not his first, works equally well against both.

Suppose there were exclusively human, and, perhaps, exclusively Martian, thoughts. Then thoughts available to humans would form one system in which, by abstraction, one would reach one set of most general truths. Thoughts available to Martians would form another. But human thought and Martian would be, in part, at least, incomparable. Just as with private thought, there would be no reason to suppose that the most general human thoughts and the most general Martian ones are the same, so that there are any most general thoughts *tout court*. In fact, that suggestion makes no sense. Some human thoughts are logically incomparable with all Martian ones: they stand in no inferential relations with them; and vice-versa. Just as in the case of privacy, this rules out any thought's having the import that a law of logic must. No thought can speak as a law of logic does to *all* thoughts. So neither we nor the Martians could be bound by *logic* as Frege conceives it. Neither we nor the Martians could then bind ourselves to any specific forms of answerability at all. That rules out exclusive thought.

On Frege's conception of logic, exclusive thought, just as much as private, blocks any thought from having the content that a law of logic must. So, equally with private thought, it abolishes logic. The line then continues just as well in the two cases. That locates, in one way, a worry not obviously misplaced. Suppose that other thinkers, lacking our parochial sensibilities, would be unable to see how it was that the *world* decided the correctness of some of our purportedly answerable stances—unable to see on what in things being as they are correctness turned. Then what right would we have to our certainty that those stances were genuinely answerable, rather than merely giving us that impression? What right would we have to so much as that distinction? As Frege conceives logic, such worries are serious. For, we now see, a law of logic will be what Frege insists it must be, only given what I call the Martian Principle:

Martian Principle: For any answerable stance, any thinker must be able, in principle, to grasp when it will have answered; to see something in the way things are or might be, on which its having answered or not turns—thus to see it to be answerable.

Frege's conception of logic requires this principle, which bars, impartially, both privacy and exclusivity. Whether it is correct is not obvious, but to be discovered.

Why might one resist the principle? Austin points to one way. Logic alone does not provide determinate standards for having answered. What answers or not is a stance, a particular representation of the way things are. What it is answerable to is things being as they are. On the one hand, the stance is that the ball is red; on the other there is the ball. When would it be as *that* stance has it? Logic does not say. So far this is nothing Frege would deny. Austin, though, presents a particular take on this aspect of answerability; part of a thoroughly un-Fregean conception of truth:

The statements fit the facts always more or less loosely, in different ways on different occasions for different intents and purposes. What may score full marks in a general knowledge test may in other circumstances get a gamma. And even the most adroit of languages may fail to 'work' in an abnormal situation.

(Austin 1950: 130)

Austin's idea is this. Suppose someone gives a given description of the way things are, applying given concepts to given things, in a certain structured way. As it may be, he describes the drapes as red. When will that description have answered to the way things are? There are various standards one *might* apply to settle that; one might hold *that* description to any of various conditions on its truth. Which of these standards *is* to be applied is not decided merely by the description given, by the concepts there deployed. All are compatible with that much. So there is a definite result as to truth only if the circumstances of the describing, or those of its evaluation as to truth, somehow make one standard or another the right one for the purposes in hand. In effect, Austin here gives one take on the idea of occasion-sensitivity: there are various things that might be said in describing drapes as red; various things that might count, or again, not count, as their being red. The mere notion of something's being red does not, as such, choose any of these as what one would say, or what would so count.

Austin's idea so read is, as noted, thoroughly un-Fregean. For Frege, a concept is a function from objects to truth-values. So when it is fixed which concepts are applied to what, in what structure, the truth value of the whole stance must also be fixed. There cannot be various ways of answering the question whether a stance so identified has answered, where those ways might yield different results. (The *word* 'red' might, for all that, express different concepts on different occasions. Austin's point is not merely that. It is about given descriptions, and the concepts they deploy.) A thinker could not grasp a thought that the drapes are red if he lacked the concept red. But if he had it, there would be, on Frege's view, no further barrier to his seeing what it would be for that thought to have answered. The Martian Principle tells us that he could at least come to see (in principle) when it would be that something satisfied the concept red.

Austin thus departs from Frege. Does he also depart from the Martian Principle? I think so. For Austin's idea can be put this way: one can be all a thinker must be, and all that logic captures of that, and, further, one may grasp all that one must grasp to count as having the relevant concepts—one may know all there is to know as to what being coloured red would be as such—and for all that, one may not yet be in a position to see whether a given judging, or stating, say, that the drapes are red is to count as having answered to the way things are. So now suppose a given candidate thinker simply could not grasp certain standards for a given stance's having answered—certain things it might be, say, for drapes to count as red. Suppose he was intractably blind to what those standards demanded for truth. He could not, say, catch on to the way stains would matter to the truth of the particular judgement in question. Would that disqualify him as a thinker, or even as a grasper of the concept red, etc.? Austin's point entails that it need not. In fact, whatever it is that allows us to see how to evaluate (as to truth) a given deployment of concepts of things—a given describing of drapes as red, say—*is* something a being could miss out on without simply failing to be a thinker, or a possessor of the relevant concepts. It is thus something parochial.

If truth is what Austin portrays it as, then our capacities to see when our (each other's) judgements and representings would be true rely essentially on the parochial. That violates the Martian Principle. Conversely, if the above is right, then the Martian Principle rules out occasion-sensitivity.

The argument from illusion generates loss of (sublunary) answerability: for the answerable, its premise can always be supplied. That, in other words, was Frege's point. The empiricist hope was that the argument should prove unsound within the realm of the observable. That hope has been dashed—witness Quine. Answerability requires the argument to be invalid in this strong sense: there must be cases of its application where the premise is true, the conclusion false. Empiricism would then be wrong. How could there be such cases?

For the argument to be invalid, there must be facts of a form illustrated thus: there are ringers for Pia's situation *in re* a pig before her; nonetheless she sees a pig to be there. In such a case it would not be so that her situation might be a ringer—for all she actually experienced, or can tell, or is aware of. For it is not a ringer if there is a pig before her.

What sorts of facts would the required ones—as to what was seen; as to what might be—be? Would they be accessible in principle to one unaided by parochial sensibilities? There is a ringer for Pia's situation; one involving a stuffed mechanical pig, say. It cannot be that such eventualities are never to be counted possible—that it is never so of an experience: one could not tell from Pia's that it might be such a ringer. So whether that is so of Pia's situation all depends. Or it does if there are the facts needed to defeat the argument from illusion. (On this issue see Clarke 1972.)

On what might it depend? On *her* circumstances, for one thing—on such things as the incidence of such stuffed pigs in her environs. But that is not all. Even if there never was such a 'pig', Pia may have no right to rely on that. She may even have (good) reason to watch out for them in her environs.

Another factor now comes into play. Suppose *we* have occasion to count Pia as having seen a pig (to be) before her, or to refuse to do so. What are we to say (in saying what is so)? Suppose *we* have no right to suppose her environs to be 'pig' free. Perhaps we have no right to suppose it is not such a 'pig' she actually confronted (or none not deriving from our right to take her to have seen a pig). So, we must then admit, it *might* have been a stuffed pig. And, we ought further to allow, it might have been for all Pia could have seen. *We* cannot count Pia as having seen whether it was; we would be wrong to accept her word (her report of her experience) as proof. So *we* would be mistaken in counting her as having seen a pig to be before her.

What it is true for us to say as to what might have been for Pia thus depends on *our* circumstances as well as hers. That is to say this: if there are facts such as to make the argument from illusion invalid, they must be occasion-sensitive ones. What counts as what *might* have been in Pia's situation must depend on the occasion for saying, or judging, what might have been. 'Might have been' must admit of varying understandings, where it takes an occasion to fix how, on it, the notion *is* to be understood.

This is to say that there is room for facts of the required sort only with Austin's conception of truth in play. But we have seen that that conception is inconsistent with the Martian Principle. Contraposing, with that principle in play, there can be no facts such as to defeat the argument. The argument from illusion would thus be valid. (On this point see Bernard Williams 1978: 64–67)

So the Martian Principle yields the argument, and thereby empiricism. It is neither logically, nor historically, fanciful to see it as empiricism's deeper source. It also yields empiricism's downfall: given it, empiricism abolishes answerability. So *it* abolishes answerability—just what it was directed at preserving. What this shows is that the principle is incorrect, despite the many (understandable) current temptations to appeal to it. Losing the principle loses us Frege's second case against private answerability. But we retain the first. We also lose his conception of logic, thus gaining impetus to seek a better view of how logic speaks to thought.

In any case of answerability there is, on the one hand, that which is answerable, and when it *would* answer, and, on the other, its answering or not. It is on the second side of this divide that the world must hold sole sway. This it cannot do where, as empiricists are wont to propose, human responses choose between stances which are optional, for all of the world's being as it is, and whatever our exposure to it. (Germaneness, for Quine, is a classic case of this.) Here the human does what, for answerability, would have to be the world's work. Without the Martian Principle, the parochial may work, innocuously, on the first side of the divide. Parochial human responsiveness may now, not just choose between stances visible to all, but *make* visible particular things to answer to in taking things to be some given way (Austin's point). More generally, it may enable *seeing* some of what, anyway, is there to answer to, though visible only to thinkers so enabled.

4

Psychologism

'Psychologism' is a term of abuse. It has been used recently of several different flaws. The main ones run in roughly opposite directions. One flaw does away with a phenomenon absolutely central to thought. The other inflates the demands of that phenomenon, thus deciding too much in advance as to what thought must be. I will call the phenomenon *answerability*. I begin with a simple, intuitive, idea of it. Elaboration will be needed. But in due time.

Thinking something so is a special sort of stance, or attitude, towards things being as they are. Where one thinks something so, there is, first, that which one thinks so. Whether what one thus thinks so *is* so—whether things are as one thus thinks them—can be determined only by things being as they are, what one's stance is towards. A stance of this sort is eligible for a particular kind of correctness. In terms of it, there are, for any such stance, two ways for things to be in being as they are. If things are the one way, then in taking that stance one thinks correctly in this sense. If they are the other, one thus thinks incorrectly. Where the world works this way, a stance it makes correct on any taking of it, it makes correct on all. *Perhaps* one who finds chocolate banal is no more correct or incorrect than one wholly in thrall to it. That would thus be a stance without the features just mentioned. So it would not be the special sort of stance that thinking something so is.

Thus is such correctness decided (if at all) solely by how things are. Factors peculiar to a taking of the stance can play no role. Properly spelled out, the correctness involved here is truth. The sort of eligibility for truth I have just described is what I mean by answerability—being answerable to things being as they are.

Now for two opposing thoughts, each of which has driven a very great deal of philosophy, each of which is difficult to give up. Again these are intuitive ideas. Again elaboration will come. The first begins with the idea that we—let that be we humans—are thinkers of a special, *parochial*, sort. Not all thinkers need think as we do. It continues: the parochial sort of thinker one is, shapes how it is open to one to be answerable to the way things are. In particular, it helps to determine what it is in things being as they are to which one *can* be answerable, the sorts of aspects of things being as they are with which it is possible for one to have that sort of rapport. So if, so to speak, a Martian is as different from us as any thinker could be, then there will be things we can think so, that the Martian cannot, and, perhaps, vice versa. There will be cases where the Martian cannot see what it is we are answerable to, and vice versa. For all of which, the thought goes, we are, in those cases, thinking things *so*—being answerable.

Where the parochial is assigned the wrong work in making us answerable to what we are, it instead abolishes the answerability it was meant to make for. For it will then intrude on, or compromise, what was to be the sole province of things being as they are. The resulting stances (if any) will not fit the required notion of correctness. The world will lose the *sole* authority such correctness calls for. Making the parochial thus intrude is one thing that has been called psychologism.

The second thought is that there can be no answerable stances except those available, in principle, to any thinker. So (minimally) we cannot think it *so* that P, if a Martian, could not grasp when things would be as we thus thought. That is why these are opposing thoughts. A *very* great deal of philosophy has been a working-out of this second thought. As we shall see, this second thought places heavy demands on answerability. The stronger the demands, the more the range of (genuinely) answerable stances shrinks. If, developing this second thought, some supposed area of answerability seems to disappear—we are apparently left, say, without stances that it is *so* that such-and-such caused such-and-such—there are two possible reactions. One is to accept the loss. The other is to save that region of presumed answerability by enlarging the powers and workings of *The Mind*, that is, the common property of all who qualify as thinkers—so that the Martian turns out after all to be able to take those stances that seemed, for a moment, lost.

If there are risks in seeing the parochial as working to make aspects of the way things are available for us to be answerable to, there are risks in the enlargement of The Mind as well. Enlargement may become inflation. It may banish some of the plasticity our thought requires. Building too much into The Mind narrows the ambit of empirical psychology. That sin in the opposite direction might also be called psychologism. Such psychologism would be specialized scientism—a mistaken insistence as to how empirical investigation *must* turn out.

Just how might the parochial threaten answerability? What constraints on answerability might it violate? I will pursue that question by developing Frege's conception of answerability, and his correlative views on psychologism of the first sort. Compared to prior philosophers, such as British empiricists, Frege is a minimalist in the demands he sets on answerability. If he is ever less than minimalist, that is something that flows out of his particular conception of logic. I will then turn to Wittgenstein's (last) conception of answerability, by which Frege is not quite minimalist enough. That will allow us to see how the pursuit of answerability might lead to psychologism of the second kind.

I. *Grundlagen*

For Frege, psychologism is confusing the psychological with the logical. That would be psychologism of our first form: involving (our) psychology in (pre-sumed) standards of correctness in a way such as to frustrate any suitable form of answerability to *how things are*. Frege's first attempt at spelling out the transgres-sion that yields such loss was in *Grundlagen der Arithmetik* (Frege 1884). There the crucial transgression is a form of privacy: making the way in which a (supposed) judgement is answerable graspable, in principle, by no more than *one* thinker. The idea of this particular transgression continued to play a role in Frege's thought; for it matters to his conception of what logic is, in a way soon to be spelled out. As an account of pyschologism, though, this idea lacks the right generality. It leaves many untouched whom Frege meant to target. Moreover, it flows less obviously, or directly, from the idea of answerability itself than later Fregean elaborations. By the time of *Grundgesetze der Arithmetik* (Frege 1893), Frege's attention was thus focussed elsewhere. Nonetheless, this first idea merits some expansion.

Frege introduces the idea in the preface to *Grundlagen*, where he vows

always to separate sharply the psychological from the logical, the subjective from the objective . . .

never to ask for the meaning of a word in isolation, but only in the context of a proposition.

(1884: x)

and comments:

In compliance with the first principle, I have used the word 'idea' always in the psychological sense, and have distinguished ideas from concepts and from objects. If the second principle is not observed, one is almost forced to take as the meanings of words mental pictures or acts of the individual mind, and so to offend against the first principle as well.

(Ibid.)

The cogency or import of the context principle is not the issue here. What matters is the sin into which one might be tempted: taking the meanings of words to be 'ideas', by which he means 'contents of an inner world', such as sense impressions, creations of imagination, experiences, feelings, moods, inclinations, and wishes (1918: 66). Here is the crucial feature of ideas which makes the sin here a sin:

The sense impression of green which I have exists only through me; I am its bearer. It strikes us as nonsense that a pain, a mood, a wish should occur on their own, without a bearer. An experience is not possible without an experiencer.

(1918: 67)

Thus

Ideas must have a bearer.

(Ibid.)

Every idea has only one bearer; no two people have the same idea.

(1918: 68)

So if meanings were ideas, then no two people could take words to have the same meaning; no two people could attach the same understanding to given words.

What happens if meanings are ideas? The simplest thought would be that then all we ever talk about are ideas (our own, if we can grasp what we say). There is a second, more encompassing, idea. Meaning (as Frege sees things) fixes when words would say what is so—just how they are answerable, how the way things are matters to them. Where meanings are ideas, it takes ideas to identify the conditions on such correctness. So for any given words, if they *are* answerable, then at most one person, in principle, can grasp how. At most one person can mean words to answer in that way. So at most one can *think* what is so answerable. Two people can thus neither contradict nor endorse each other's views. Wherever meaning works like that, Frege tells us, there can be neither genuine disputes nor genuine shared knowledge:

There could be no science which was in common to many . . . but I would have perhaps my science, namely the totality of thoughts whose bearer I am, another would have his science. Each of us would concern himself with the contents of his own consciousness. A contradiction between both sciences is then impossible; and it is really silly to dispute over truth, almost as ridiculous as if two people disputed whether a hundred mark note was real, when each meant the one in his pocket, and each understood the word 'real' in a different sense.

(1918: 68)

One thing this stresses is that if there were answerability under these conditions, each thinker would be answerable to what was, essentially, his own private tract of reality—some expanse of the way things are that was in principle inaccessible to anyone else. So for no thinker would there be another whose views (or information) as to what was right could matter to whether this first thinker was right or not.

That is a terrible situation. If we were all in it, would that abolish answerability, so logic, *tout court*? If someone were in it, would it abolish answerability for him? Might there be private answerability? Or is that very idea incompatible with what logic must be? Frege certainly thought this last thing. To see why, we need to spell out how the mere supposition of private conditions of correctness is destructive of answerability itself.

Frege remarks that if everything were an idea (so if meanings were) then 'psychology would also rule logic and mathematics' (1918: 74). That, he takes it, would make logic, at most, a collection of psychological truths. But, he remarks, 'neither logic nor mathematics has the task of investigating . . . contents of consciousness belonging to individuals' (Ibid). So it is an error to see logic as psychology. That might be called psychologism. Just where does this error lie? Genuine psychology is answerable. That is not the trouble. But, for Frege, logic has a special content. Its task is to set out precisely what truth, so what answerability, as such is. To do that it must say what it would be for a *thought* to be true. It will not do merely to say what it would be for such-and-such thoughts to be true (or, more properly, to be in some particular condition). Nor can it be that whether thoughts in general, or some given thinker's thoughts, do answer (are true), given the world's being as it is—or whether they are in that condition of which logic speaks—depends on some thinkers' psychologies. That would be precisely not to have the matter decided solely by the world, so it would not be answerability at all. So logic would not have explicated the notion that is its proper subject. And, Frege tells us, things do thus go wrong when meanings are ideas. He expresses the key idea as follows:

> The words 'true' and 'false', as I understand them, would apply only in the area of my consciousness . . . Then truth would be limited to the content of my consciousness, and it would be doubtful whether anything at all similar occurred in the consciousness of others.

> (1918: 68–69)

If 'true' and 'false' have a sense in which I might take my private stances to be true or false, then that is not a sense in which any other stances might be true. So there can be no saying what it is for a *thought* to be true. So there can be no proper logic. At most *a* logic might try to say what it is for, say, *my* thoughts to be what *I* understand by true. But *a* logic—one among others—would not unfold the laws of truth (the task Frege assigns logic). For *they* apply, intrinsically, to *any* thought.

They say precisely what answerability as such demands. To be a thought just *is* to be answerable. What *a* logic explicated could not be answerability as such, so nor truth. That is a sketch of a story of how loss of publicity loses answerability, and of how, conversely, if there could be genuinely answerable private stances, then that would abolish logic. It remains to spell out details.

For Frege, laws of logic are *the* most general truths; arrived at by abstraction from less general ones. They mention *nothing*, insofar as it is possible to abstract away from such mention, to generalize instead. Such truths have nothing but their structure to make them true. So they can speak to thought, or thoughts, only in this way: their structure reflects (is an image of) the structure of a system to which both they, and the thoughts to which they speak, belong, a system structured by inferential relations, and by commonalities in ways of representing (or in what would thus be represented). This idea yields an alternative route to the above point.

So conceiving logic, let us try to suppose answerability a private matter. So the thoughts each thinker thinks are available only to him. One thinker's thoughts, if they were that, might form a system. By abstraction, one could reach most general thoughts within it. But these thoughts would be most general only relative to it. For each thinker, there would be a different such system. So to be most general within some one such system would not yet be to be most general *tout court*. Further, no one such system contains a negation, or any other logical compound, of anything in any other. This is to say that there are no inferential relations between the elements of one such system and those of another. Thus no principles of logic span two such systems. Rather, the most general truths of one system reflect nothing of the structure of another, nor of its inferential properties. Nor are there any truths save those belonging to one such system or another. So no truth speaks, in the way a most general truth would speak, to *all* thought. (There *is* no maximal generality *tout court*.) But a law of logic was to be a partial characterization of what *truth* is: that is, of what it is for a *thought* (full stop) to be true. If answerability is a private matter, no thought does that. So no thought says what a law of logic would. There *is* no logic. The idea now runs: thoughts not subject to logic are subject to *no* genuine standard for having answered. No matter how things are, one might just as well say that they did answer as that they did not—or, once logic is abandoned, say both. Such 'thoughts' would not be answerable, so not thoughts at all. Nothing could say of them what a law of logic is meant to say. That is a *reductio* on the idea that answerability is a private matter.

There is a more minimalist case against private answerability. In explaining what answerability is we needed, crucially, the idea that what is answerable is a *stance there is to take*, where what the stance is is identifiable independent of any particular taking of it, identifiable by that to which the stance is answerable. Where a stance must be identified in terms of ideas, it is, essentially, a stance only one person could take. That erodes distance between the *stance* and a particular thinker's taking it, and, again, a particular taking of it. That, one might argue, deprives us altogether here of the idea of a stance there is to take. This would make it impossible to say what, in this case, answerability comes to. There are thus several different cases that might be developed—but still need to be.

2. *Grundgesetze*

The idea was: things are *judged* to be some way only where whether things are that way depends exclusively on how things are. This dependence on the way things are, most straightforwardly elaborated, would mean: if things were otherwise, they might not be as judged. That idea, though, does not quite serve Frege's purpose. Instead, we might try to identify answerability in terms of what must *not* share the role to be played by the way things are. That is Frege's strategy in *Grundgesetze*. The rough idea is: thinking cannot make it so. An answerable stance is answerable to something in particular: to whether things are thus and so. Such a connection between stance and world is answerability only where whether things are in fact that way could not be changed by different reactions towards, or senses for, their being so. Historically, most worries about psychologism have been about transgressing that requirement.

Frege expresses this particular condition as follows:

> There is no contradiction in something's being true which everybody takes to be false.... If it is true that I am writing this in my chamber on the 13th of July, 1893, while the wind howls outside, then it remains true even if all men should subsequently take it to be false. If being true is thus independent of being acknowledged by somebody or other, then the laws of truth are not psychological laws.

(1893: xvi)

He later elaborated this theme as follows:

> If anyone tried to contradict the statement that what is true is true independently of our acknowledging it as such, he would, just by his statement, contradict what he stated.
>
> If, namely, something were true only for him who held it to be true, there would be no contradiction between the opinions of different people. Someone who held this view should not, in point of consistency, contradict the opposing view; he would have

to pay homage to the principle, *non disputandum est*. He could not state anything at all in the usual sense, and if he gave something this form, it would still only have the value of an interjection; that is, the expression of a mental condition or process, which could not stand in contradiction to mental conditions or processes of other people. And his statement that something was true only for us, and through our acknowledgement of this, would also have this value. If this opinion were true ... there would be no science, there would be no error, no correction of error, there would really be nothing true in the usual sense of the word. The independence of *this* from our acknowledgement of it is so tightly bound up with it, that it cannot be separated out from it.

(1897: 144)

Transgressing *Grundlagen*'s demands on answerability would eliminate the science that we know. Does it leave room for private science—for each person, his own physics? If *Grundlagen*'s demands are genuine demands on answerability, then no. What is at stake in *Grundgesetze* is very clearly answerability as such. What would be lost with it can be no less than science full stop. What Frege demands is, as he sees it, essential for anything's being either true or false. So it is a minimal condition for logic. In fact, he suggests, logic is no more than an elaboration of what comes into play when the demand is met.

For something to be true is one thing; for everyone to think so is another. So, perhaps *ceteris paribus*, either thing might occur without the other. More generally, where a stance undertakes to answer to things being thus and so, its truth should be compatible with any views or perceptions by anyone as to whether things *are* that way. This idea comes into play only after it has been fixed to what the stance in question *is* answerable. What different views of things would not change is whether things, as they are, are *that* way. The views that cannot change things are, crucially, views as to how things are. They might also be views about how to think about how things are. Or they might simply consist in a particular (non-obligatory) way of thinking of how things are; a way of viewing things. What such views cannot change is whether that which is so according to any answerable stance is so.

Frege's example, that the wind howled on a certain day, is particularly compelling in part because of its subject matter. Suppose the judgement were that everyone now thinks the wind howled. That would be answerable to what all present earthlings *think* (as to the wind's howling). That actual thinkers in fact have certain attitudes is as much part of how things are as anything, so part of what there is to be answerable to. Trivially, where a stance is answerable to *such* a feature of reality, whether it in fact *answers* to how things are depends in some way on the attitudes certain thinkers in fact take. If it is correct, then, had those thinkers not had those attitudes, it would have been incorrect. That is what it is like for such a stance to depend on how things are. What answerability demands here, the idea is, is that whether such a stance is correct cannot depend on how, or what, or whether, *one* thinks about the way things in fact are—one's views, or preferences, in taking, or evaluating, these stances towards so-and-so's attitudes, as if thinkers with different ways of viewing things might equally correctly take either the stance in question, or the opposing one. What must not be is that one may correctly take the stance if one thinks in one way, but also correctly reject it if one thinks in another.

Suppose Sid takes *andouilletes* to be disgusting. Is that an answerable stance? That may well depend on its ambitions. The stance may undertake no more than disgust at *andouilletes*. In that case, not. For otherwise either all those disgusted by them, or all those not, would be getting something wrong as to how things are. But in matters of taste for *andouilletes*, if anywhere, *non disputandem est*. Suppose, though, that Sid's attitude is part and parcel of a view that denies what I just said—a view on which there *is* something observer-independent to get right as to what is disgusting and what is not. So it is part of his stance that *amateurs* of *andouilletes* are getting something wrong. Then his stance may be both answerable and false. *Andouilletes* are not disgusting in the way he means. A stance may *undertake* to be answerable: to take it is to take oneself to be answerable, and in a certain way—to mean to bind oneself to how things are. Whether a stance *is* answerable is sometimes decided by whether it undertakes to be. How could a stance which undertakes to be answerable, for all that, fail to be? By failing some requirement on answerability, of course. Section 4 will present an idea by which such failure is none too easily suffered.

One can see both the core idea of *Grundlagen* and that of *Grundgesetze* as different attempts to work out the intuition that answerability requires a distinction between—in fact, logical independence of—thinking something so, and thereby being right. That distinction goes missing, the *Grundlagen* idea is, when what being right would be is something private. In *Grundgesetze* it shows up in the stability of what is thought so under certain variations in attitudes towards that being so: an answerable stance-to-be-taken, correct on any taking of it, is, *ipso facto*, correct on all. That is the mark of the answerable. *Grundgesetze*'s demand on answerability more directly, and fully, touches the target of concern to Frege. His concern was that there should be something for logic to be about—genuine *thoughts* that such-and-such is so; and, most particularly, that logic itself should be answerable, but not to any fact about (particular) psychologies. Logic presents a special case of answerability. Here are some preliminary remarks on how.

For Frege, a law of logic is, to begin with, true. So it is answerable: for each such law, to a specifiable aspect of how things are. Second, Frege insists that there is no *explaining* why a law of logic is true (except in terms of other laws of logic). He tells us,

The question why and with what right we acknowledge a law of logic to be true, logic can answer only by reducing it to another law of logic. Where that is not possible, logic can give no answer. If we step away from logic, we may say: we are compelled to make judgments by our own nature and by external circumstances: and if we do so we cannot reject this law . . . I shall neither dispute nor support this view; I shall merely remark that what we have here is not a logical consequence. What is given is not a reason for something's being true, but for our taking it to be true.

(1893: xvii)

A law of logic depends on, is hostage to, *nothing*. It does not hold by virtue of things being one way rather than another. That is how there is no explaining it. It is only a very special case of that to say that it in no way depends on facts of human psychology. It equally cannot depend on facts about meteorology. But in any event it will be a form of psychologism (the second sort just mentioned) to make a logical truth depend for its truth on anyone's attitudes. These two points mean that answerability does not always mean a liability to vary in correctness according to how things are. Thus the *via negativa* of *Grundgesetze*: identifying it in terms of what must *not* matter.

For a law of logic (or anything) to be hostage to nothing is for there to be no such thing as things being other than it has them. If there is no such thing as, say, being F without being G—for example, being a conjunction but not subject to conjunction elimination—that means that being G is just part of what being F is (what it is to be F). A model might be: there is no such thing as a married bachelor: being unmarried is part of what it is to be a bachelor. Or: there is no such thing as a conjunction that might be true without both its conjuncts so being: nothing would so count; that is part of what it is for something to be a conjunction. (This supposes these claims true.)

So the truth of laws of logic is part of what it is to be something or other. What? A superficial answer would be: logical laws involve certain logical constants—conjunction, disjunction and so on; their truth is part of what it is for something to be what those constants form—a conjunction, for example. There are problems with that view. What makes something a logical constant, to begin with? If disjunction *is* one, how can we be so sure that there is really no such thing as *disjunction* behaving differently than it would if the laws Frege takes for laws of logic are true? It is, in any case, not Frege's view.

Frege tells us,

The meaning of the word 'true' is unfolded in the laws of being true.

(1918: 59)

Logical laws (the laws of truth) are thus part of what it is for something to be true; that is, part of what it is to be answerable. It is clear how this is meant to work in the case of propositional logic. Where there is answerability, a certain notion of correctness applies: one on which (on Frege's view) what is answerable has, outright, precisely one of two values: correct, incorrect. One can define the usual trivial functions of these values (the usual truth functions). One can then define compound thoughts (compound answerable stances), and the connectives that form them, in terms of these functions. If we regard the laws of (propositional) logic as holding of (so, for Frege, as being) such compounds, then that they hold is a trivial consequence of the nature of that particular sort of correctness such that to be answerable is to admit of it.

This view of the matter sets up some small distance between laws of logic and the thoughts they concern. There is a natural truth-functional correspondent of conjunction. That the laws of logic hold of conjunction *defined as that truth-functional connective* is, perhaps, just part of what answerability is. So, perhaps, there is no such thing as things being otherwise in *that* respect. But *is* conjunction nothing other than what is so defined? Must anything that would ever count as conjunction be that? One *might* think: we have an intuitive idea of conjunction which *may* be adequately captured in that way, at least for some purposes, but then again, *could* turn out (sometimes) not to be. Such might depend on what the world is like. Perhaps, at least, it is not quite right that there is simply no such thing as *conjunction* behaving other than in this truth-functional way—nothing that would *ever* so count. If not, and if, for logic, conjunction is truth-functional by *fiat*, then logic treats conjunction at one remove. *Its* conjunction is at best a proxy for *conjunction*. Our conjunctive thoughts are subject to the relevant laws only where, and insofar as, they are correctly viewed as so definable. Plausibly, Frege failed to note the distance here because it seemed inevitable to him that conjunction was so definable. The point, though, begins to suggest a view of logic very different from Frege's. We will return to that in the last section.

There is one more strand in Frege's view. For Frege, logical laws are the most general truths. If they are *most* general, then they make no mention of such things as functions, or connectives, or thoughts, or anything else. So there is nothing but their structure to make them true. If the law is no more than an unfolding of what being true is, thus of answerability, then the relevant unfolding is in that structure. To be *that* law is to be so structured; to be so structured is to be true just where that law is, which is to be true *simpliciter*. That what is *so* structured is true *where* it is, so true full stop, is simply part of what being answerable, or being true, is. Where truth depends on structure in the way the truth of a law of logic does, there is thus no such thing as things being otherwise with respect to it.

If, by virtue of their generality, logical laws do not mention anything, how can they be *about* thoughts, or thought? How can there be, in fact, anything to which they answer? Here is one response. Logical laws are true in virtue of their structure. But a thought *has* a structure only insofar as it belongs to a system of thoughts. The elements of which it is structured are nothing but reflections of particular samenesses in ranges of thoughts—what is in common, for example, to the thoughts Fa, Fb, Fc, ... A thought's structure is thus a reflection of the structure of the system to which it belongs. And so it is for a law of logic. Its structure reflects the most general structure of *the* system to which it belongs: the most general, so the hardest, most non-negotiable, network of truth-preserving paths within and through that structure. By its structure it identifies those paths. It is thus answerable to the structure of that system. (If there is the distance between logical laws and actual thoughts that we began to notice above, Frege is not entitled to this view. But that is an issue for later.)

To what system does a law of logic belong? A thought belongs to the same system as a given thought if it is logically related to it—if there might be an argument leading from the one to the other, or involving both, or a thought compounded of both. For Frege, a law of logic is (must be) related to *every* thought: it bears on each thought in unfolding in part what it is for that thought to be answerable. What it did not relate to logically simply would not be a thought. So every thought belongs to the system it does. So there is but one system to which all thoughts belong.

3. The Martian Principle

How can demands on answerability limit the role of special design in shaping it? Here is one line of thought. Suppose that a special design—ours, say—is essential for being able to detect a certain thing to which to be answerable—things being, or not being, F, say. So without that design, no such thing to answer to could come in view. Without it we would have detected nothing to be answerable to at that place where we in fact do. The Martian can, in principle, see no *such* thing to which thought might answer. There are, then, two sorts of special design (ours and the Martian's). With the one, one would detect a certain way things might or might not be—or so it would seem to one so designed. With the other, one would detect no such thing. Is there, then, in fact such a thing to which to be answerable? Each design offers a standard by which that question might be answered. By that standard, there are just those ways for things to be which one so designed might recognize. By the standard of the first design, there is such a thing to which to answer. By that of the second, there is not. By that standard, those of the first design are condemned to suffer an illusion. They suppose themselves to be taking answerable stances which, in fact, are answerable to nothing.

Which design, if either, yields the right answer to the question? Is there really, in the way things are, something to be answerable to, which the first design then allows one to detect? Or is there not? We will get nowhere on this question (the idea is) while relying on the one, or on the other, design. It is already clear what answer such reliance would yield. Each design gives us only a thoroughly parochial view of the matter. So if the question has an answer, it will have to be what is the right answer by the standards of some third design. That will have to be a third *special* design. For if the question were settled merely by the answerability conferred by *The* Mind—what any thinker must be like— then it would be settled already by what we and the Martian share in common, as it is not. But a third special design, if it yields a result at all, only makes our problem arise anew. It gets us no further. *It* cannot supply an answer to our question when we did not have one already. So there is no answer to that question. Put otherwise, there is no answerable stance that could be such an answer. For nothing could make that stance correct outright, aside from some parochial way of thinking of things. So it is not a fact that those with the first design are thereby enabled to be answerable to something; that their apparent answerable stances are in fact that.

This line of thought suggests what I will call the **Martian Principle**: No thinker, or stance, could be answerable to anything to which any other thinker in principle could not be. For any answerable stance, any thinker whatever could, in principle, grasp what it was to be answerable to what that stance is, and could thus take a stance answerable to that. (This idea gets sympathetic treatment in Williams 1978, especially chapter 2.) How might one transgress this principle?

Consider, for example, Noam Chomsky's relation to the principle. Chomsky, he tells us, deals in the empirical. Empirical psychology or linguistics is, by definition, concerned with the parochial. As Frege reminds us, experiment is otiose if the question is what any thinker (or language user) *must* be. But psychology's involvement with the parochial may seem non-threatening to one persuaded of the Martian Principle. For it aims for *explicit* accounts of parochial capacities and sensibilities. And one might think an explicit account would make the parochial eliminable: in its explicitness, it would not require a parochial sensibility for grasping it; its issue would be just those perceptions, or intuitions, which it originally took the relevant parochial sense to see (or feel). The *eliminably* parochial—what one could, in principle, do without—is no threat to the Principle.

Chomsky certainly aims for explicitness. But is it an explicitness that makes the parochial eliminable? His interest is in a specifically human (thus parochial) language faculty. But there are various ways to be interested in it. Chomsky's interest is, for one thing, in explicit grammars of specific languages (and in constraints on the form of any such). Such a grammar would eliminate reliance on one sort of intuition, peculiar to speakers of its language: intuitions about the syntactic shapes occurring in that language. It would do so in this way: by a finite set of principles (graspable not just by those speakers) it would generate individuating descriptions of each such shape. Those descriptions would be available to one not sharing the native speaker's intuitions *as to how his sentences are shaped*. The speaker has a feel for when well-formed strings are syntactically different. Given an ability to match such surface strings to the structures the grammar provides for them, one could rely on the grammar for identifying, by those structures, just where there are such differences, and how each such difference relates systematically to others. One need no longer consult the native speaker's feelings. For argument's sake, suppose the Martian, too, is thus served. Chomsky is also (perhaps more) concerned with universal grammar: an account of the general form of the syntactic shapes of *any* human language. We can think of a universal grammar as a schema which became the grammar of a particular human language when values were assigned parameters in it. Let us suppose the Martian equally well served by that theory.

The Martian might be *that* much better off. There remain at least two problems. First, individuating descriptions of syntactic structures need not enlighten us as to the representational roles of those structures, insofar as they are dedicated to specific ones. So the Martian may well remain unenlightened on that score, thus unable to speak or understand a human language. One might wonder whether a theory of those roles which met the psychologist's normal standards of explicitness, thus relieving human beings (in principle) from reliance on a feel for what happens when a given such role is played, would, necessarily, also enlighten the Martian.

The second problem is one on which Chomsky has been explicit. It is that of making out which shapes occur in some language one encounters—what it is that given humans are up to syntactically. To eliminate the parochial in this domain, one would need (at the least) a discovery procedure for grammars— some set of principles which, for given non-syntactic (in fact, non-linguistic) facts about what the speakers were up to, would predict the syntactic shapes of the sentences they produce. What a universal grammar would say about such procedures is just this: 'Assign values to *these* parameters as, here, a normal human would.' To which a Martian could only reply, 'Thanks, pal.'

On this problem there is one point of agreement between Chomsky and Quine. It is highly unlikely, at best, that any Martianly-accessible discovery procedure would predict the presence, in any language, of syntactic shapes of the complexity and subtlety which, Chomsky has argued, humans are prepared to *recognize* in the grammars of human languages. The moral Quine draws is that there are no such shapes in human languages. Or, more cautiously, that there can be no fact of the matter as to whether any given such shape is *the* shape of some sentence or not. That reflects Quine's adherence to the Principle. The moral Chomsky draws is that there are (most likely) no discovery procedures for human grammars. That is to say, in this special case, our ways of telling what our fellows are up to do not reduce to Martianly-accessible principles. They rely ineliminably on the parochial. It was in arguing precisely this that Chomsky effected his initial radical re-orientation of focus in linguistics. This aligns Chomsky with such philosophers as John McDowell, and against such others as Quine, Michael Dummett and Bernard Williams. It manifests his firm rejection (and resolute transgression) of the Martian Principle.

Where some area of purported answerability is unquestionably the real thing, adherence to the Principle might lead one to the conclusion that The Mind—the common possession of all thinkers—is a richer and more elaborate affair than one would have thought. Where the purported area can be made to seem open to doubt, the Principle might be used to show that there is no genuine answerability there at all. There might be less of that than one would have thought.

Empiricists, such as Hume, or Quine, are notorious for theses of the second sort. Hume, for example, entertains such a thought about our stances as to one thing's having caused another. He does aim to describe that parochial endowment which yields our *perceptions* as to what causes what. But he makes it difficult to think of this endowment as a *capacity* to *detect* things in the world to which to answer. Quine takes such a view of stances as to what words mean. In each case the conclusion might flow directly from the Principle. In fact, though, typically for an empiricist, Hume and Quine each appeal to two different ideas. The first is that all answerability must ultimately be answerability to the observable; the second is that the argument from illusion is a tool for identifying what really is observable. By that argument, it is not observable that P, if anything that might count as such an observation, admits of ringers: a situation which, if one were in it, would be not detectably different from that of the supposed observation, but in which not P. For if there are ringers, then the situation putatively of observation might be one in which not P—which could not be so where one had *observed* that P. The upshot in the causal case is that no more than events and their concatenations are observable. In Quine's case, it is that no more is (relevantly) observable than behaviour in a highly attenuated sense: bodily movements and emissions (notably of noises). Neither causation nor meaning is plausibly constructible from such materials.

The Principle so applied thus means that neither our attitudes towards causes, nor those towards what words mean, have anything suitable to which they could be answerable, so are not answerable. If there were causes, or things words mean, that is what these stances would answer to. Since they answer to nothing, there are neither causes, nor things words mean.

These specifically empiricist ideas may be an unnecessary detour. Adopting a suggestion by Bernard Williams, perhaps they both just follow from the Martian Principle. (See Williams 1978: 66–67.) Here is a sketch of the idea for the argument from illusion. That argument would be blocked just where, though there is a ringer for the observing situation with respect to P—say, with respect to observing a pig standing before one—there is no doubt that one's situation is *not* a ringer; nothing one need establish to establish that it is not. That is needed since if one did need to establish something, that would be in order to *conclude* that P (that there is, in fact, a pig before one), which is precisely what one does not need to do where this is something one can just observe. But, plausibly, facts of the required form—that such-and-such does, or does not need establishing—if there are such facts, would be visible only to a thinker of a certain special design (ours, say). We (humans, readers of this essay, or whatever) have, perhaps, our shared sense of what ought to be doubted. We cannot expect a Martian to share this. So, by the Martian Principle, there are no such facts. So the argument from illusion is valid.

The Martian Principle is thus perhaps prior to, and more general than, traditional empiricism. Empiricism, though, does highlight one feature of it. The empiricist idea is that where a stance purports to be answerable to the world in some particular way, we can step back from the stance and turn our gaze to the world to see whether there is, in it, anything to which to be answerable in that way. Our investigation will be philosophic, not scientific. Our tools are the argument from illusion, not physical measuring devices. Crucially, though, we can examine the world while the scrutinized stance itself remains *sub judice*, thus without deploying it. We look to the world as it is anyway, independent of how it would be if such stances, or their negations, really answered to it. The world, so viewed, must turn up something to which the stance might be answerable. Or, the idea is, there is no such thing. That, we may now note, is also the modus operandi of the line of thought that led us to the Martian Principle. On that line of thought, there is a special design which, if taken as conferring a cognitive *capacity*, permits detection of some features of the world to which one might be answerable. But, the idea is, there is a question as to whether the design can be taken in that way: as conferring a capacity rather than a mere illusion of one. That question, the line goes, must be settled by what there really is to answer to, as visible without aid (or interference) of that special design. Unsurprisingly, that idea, whether in its special empiricist form, or more generally, tends either to reduce the scope of our answerability, or to inflate the powers of The Mind (or both).

The Martian Principle lies on one side of two opposing intuitions. One is that, for any *answerable* stance, that to which it is answerable would be just the way it is no matter how anyone was designed to think about such things. No thinker's design could change which stances answered and which did not, among the answerable stances there are to take. (Everything would have been coloured just the way it is no matter how we were designed to think.) The other intuition is: where we are answerable, that to which we are answerable must be identified by what we are prepared, or equipped, to recognize. The phenomenon we thereby think about cannot be other than what we are equipped to acknowledge it to be. (Roughly, being coloured green cannot *diverge* from what we would understand by, or recognize as, being coloured green.) Correct intuitions cannot conflict. The next section explores how these two may be reconciled.

4. Investigations

There is an idea with which one might oppose the Martian Principle. Wittgenstein expresses it in *Investigations* §136:

What a proposition is is in one sense determined by the rules of sentence formation (of the German language, for example), and in another sense by the use of the sign in the language game. And the use of the words 'true' and 'false' may be among the constituent parts of this game; and if so it *belongs* to our concept 'proposition' but does not 'fit' it. As we might also say, check *belongs* to our concept of the king in chess (as so to speak a constituent part of it). To say that check did not *fit* our concept of the pawns, would mean that a game in which pawns were checked, in which, say, the players who lost their pawns lost, would be uninteresting or stupid or too complicated or something of the kind.

(Wittgenstein 1953)

Truth may *belong* to a stance: it may be part of the stance, not just that things are thus and so, but that *it* is answerable (to whether they are). Truth and falsity may, in that way, belong to its ambitions. Suppose that, taking these ambitions to be achieved—holding the words, or stances, answerable as they would thus be understood to be—yields sufficiently orderly results: the stance belongs to a range of stances such that if one supposes them to be answerable to something, it is then not too stupid, complicated, or etc., to sort out those which then would be correct from those which would then not be. As it may be, the stance is that the lake is blue; there is another that it is not blue; if precisely one of these *must* be the correct one, it is not too stupid to suppose that, with information enough, one could say which. And so, more or less in general, through some impressive enough range of related stances. If this condition is met, the idea is, the stance *is* answerable; there is no further way for it to fail to be, so no further requirement to be met. In particular, satisfying the Martian Principle is no such requirement.

The core of the idea is that the only intelligible questions there are as to answerability are resolvable by what is visible to those taking, or able to take, the relevant stances. Answerability, or lack of it, does not turn on what would be visible of the world, or of the stance's relation to it, only, or *even*, to a thinker differently designed, or from some viewpoint independent of what enables the taking of that stance itself. *Grundgesetze* proposed necessary conditions on answerability, ones whose satisfaction it takes no such foreign form of thought to see. The present idea is, roughly, that such conditions are also sufficient—all that answerability demands. (This is not to say that answerability, or its absence, is always settled by what takers of the stance in fact do say as to what is too stupid, what not. One can be wrong as to just how stupid a given way of treating stances really is.) To put things imagistically, a special design may, in a special way, articulate the way things are into particular ways things are; different special designs might do that differently; the articulations in things that one special design makes visible need not be visible to a thinker embodying another.

Despite this reference to *different* special designs, the main use for this idea is in resisting challenges to our answerability posed by philosophers of our own design, such as Hume and Quine. If the idea is right, then it is an adequate response to such challenges to point to the manifest discipline and coherence of the stances within the challenged area: its being not too stupid, or complicated, etc., to treat them as what they represent themselves as being—answerable stances, it being clear enough just how they would thus be treated. If causal stances are answerable, for example, it is clear enough when to say the man on the next stool spilled Sid's beer, when to say it was rather Sid himself, and that where the barmaid pushed the man who bumped the beer, there are two things to say as to who it was who spilled the beer. The idea just is that no more than that is needed to show that Hume was wrong. Similarly, if, by our ordinary standards in such matters, 'livid' means pale, and not purple, with rage, then there is no way for Quine to be right about meaning. Martians, of course, have a right to this idea as well. That matters to us precisely so far as we can see enough about their taking stances to raise specific questions as to whether such-and-such among these are answerable. That need not be very far.

This idea is not answerability by fiat. A stance can take itself to be answerable, but fail to be. The world may be not what it was supposed. We assign weight to cheeses, taking ourselves to be dealing in a stable feature of them. If measurements of their weights turn out to vary wildly and unpredictably, it will perhaps turn out that there is no stable feature of a cheese that its weight might be (given what weight was supposed to be); so nothing to which these particular stances might be answerable, so no facts as to what cheeses weigh. That would be, conspicuously, a *mundane* discovery, something the world might teach us in teaching us how it was—a physical, and not a philosophical, discovery.

The idea does, though, exclude the Martian Principle. It allows special design to make thinkers so designed *aware* of something there is in fact to which to be answerable—simply by making us so designed as to satisfy the above requirements in some particular way. By design, we take, or may take, stances which hold themselves answerable in some sufficiently determinate way; it is not too stupid, or etc., to regard them as doing what they thus purport to. Within these bounds, special design may operate ad lib. Nothing invisible to us, nor anything on the order of the Martian Principle, would show that expressions of such stances 'really' fall short of saying how things are.

Since Wittgenstein, that idea has been most prominent in the work of John McDowell. He insists, for example, that special design may locate for us a phenomenon of memory which may yield non-inferential knowledge of the past, a phenomenon of kindness, facts about which are intrinsically motivating (in a certain way), or a phenomenon of knowledge, including, sometimes, ways of standing towards, say, the pig's being in the sty, which are proof against the argument from illusion. That memory sometimes yields non-inferential knowledge of the past is part of the concept—not in the strong sense that the concept as such somehow makes that *true*, but simply in that, as things stand, it is part of what memory is to be presumed to be. We take stances aimed at answerability to what fits that conception. Is it too stupid to take those stances to be answerable in the way they aim to be—too disorderly to suppose there to be such a phenomenon for them to be about? Patently not. So those stances are answerable to what they purport to be: there is, in fact, *that* phenomenon of memory.

Where special design shapes answerability, *what* those so designed are answerable to is fixed by what they are thus equipped to recognize as to how the relevant form of answerability would work. That captures the second

of our pair of opposing intuitions; and thus may seem to threaten the first—
that where a stance is answerable, what it answers to, if correct, is what would
be so no matter how, or what, or whether, anyone thought. But the threat is
only apparent. For insofar as the second idea captures what answerability is, it is
part of the way a stance undertakes to work in undertaking to be answerable.
So if the stance does work as it aims to, then any role for what we are prepared
to recognize, for our responses, for agreement among us, or for any other
feature of our (perhaps special) design, is confined to fixing *what it is* to which
we are thus answerable, and not, of any such thing, whether that is so. And
now the Wittgensteinian idea applies. Is it too stupid to regard these stances as
achieving that aim? Is their behaviour too disorderly for that? If not, then they
do achieve it.

An issue, so far suppressed, must now surface. Frege's idea about howling
wind was: for each answerable stance, there is the way things are according to it;
whether things are *that* way cannot depend on what, or how, one thinks as to
their being so. But there are several notions of a way things are. Sid said that the
wind is howling. To say that *is* to say what way he said things were: such that
the wind was howling. It is that, that is, on one understanding of *the way spoken
of*. Now, *is* the wind howling? When would it be? When, for example,
howling, and not merely whistling? The answer might be: it depends on
what you understand (mean) by howling wind. There is (suppose) a way of
thinking of wind howling on which the wind Sid spoke of qualifies as doing
that, but also another way of thinking on which it does not. Whether that is
right depends on that wind. But suppose it is. Then a further question arises.
Should Sid be taken to have spoken of howling wind on the first understanding? On the second? Perhaps on neither in particular? More generally, should
the way *that* wind was be counted as the way Sid said it was, in saying it to be
howling? Or should it not?

If special design makes wind howling something we can think about, then it
cannot ever work to determine whether wind is howling. That would undermine answerability in just the way Frege suggests. But, without doing that, it
can work to point us to answers to the above questions. By its lights, for
example, taking Sid to have spoken on the first understanding may be the
only reasonable thing to do. It is free to shape our answerability so long as all
that it shapes is what we are committed to in thinking, say, that wind is
howling—how, for purposes of that commitment, wind howling must be
thought of. When, one might ask, should it count as shaping answerability
rather than that to which some stance stands in a mere pretence of answerability?
Wittgenstein's answer is: it shapes *answerability* (and nothing less) for what represents, or takes, itself as answerable, provided it is not too unreasonable, or foolish,

to hold so. That is, *count* it as working towards answerability when it is not too stupid to.

For all *that* latitude, Wittgenstein's idea still collides with the Martian Principle. It was meant to. It is opposed accordingly by Michael Dummett (1993). Dummett's opposition helps exhibit what is at stake. It shows up in his insistence on the possibility of what he calls a 'theory of meaning'. Such a theory, for a given language, targets this phenomenon: fluent speakers of the language can recognize, of indefinitely many novel cases, when it has been used correctly—notably, when given words would have described correctly what they were used of. He insists on two conditions of success for such a theory. First, it must consist of a set of stated principles which generate, from specified inputs, everything competence would allow one to recognize of novel cases—all there is to be recognized, given the language as it is. (The theory must specify what inputs it requires; these will presumably consist in facts about the novel cases, other than facts about what words of the language mean.) Second, the principles must be adequate to serve, in principle, as a cognitive prosthetic for the Martian: perhaps the Martian cannot, unaided, get the hang of what we are on to in recognizing what we do as to what is describable as what; but (considerations of time, attention, and so on, aside) he could operate the principles so as to derive all that we can see intuitively.

Accepting Wittgenstein's idea, one would want to ask why we should think that our sense for what is describable as what can be captured in such a theory. The phenomenon is that there is a range of facts we are prepared to recognize. With Wittgenstein's idea in place, it is not required, for there to be such facts, that they follow from any such set of principles—that there be, even in principle, a prosthetic for the Martian. To insist on that would be to demand more for answerability than answerability itself demands. So to a philosopher like McDowell, Dummett's insistence will look like no more than armchair psychology, thus psychologism of our second sort. Dummett in fact supports his view with a sweeping claim (1993: 36): any ability to recognize some range of facts is representable as theoretical knowledge, that is, captured by some set of principles. He does not appeal to any special facts about our *linguistic* competence. That heightens the impression of psychologism of this second sort.

Things look otherwise with the Martian Principle in place. Then, where a (supposed) capacity to *recognize* failed Dummett's demands, there would be no such capacity at all. In the case of meaning, we were meant to be able to recognize a certain range of *facts*—such-and-such was correctly described as mauve, say. But if a Martian cannot grasp what it would be for such a fact to obtain, or when it would, then there *are* no such facts. Our stances were meant to be *answerable*, but, failing what Dummett insists on, there would be nothing for them to answer to. The fact was meant to be that you *cannot* call that mauve, that it is not true to say so. But, by the Principle, without a cognitive prosthetic for the Martian, there *are* no facts as to what is, and is not, correctly called mauve. If the principle moves Dummett, he understandably insists on what he does.

Is Dummett guilty of psychologism (not Frege's target, but that other form)? That depends on whether the Martian Principle is correct. We have seen one intuitive case for it. How might a case be built against it? The general form of a case would look like this: the Principle's rationale rests on envisioning a certain alleged way of failing of answerability, but when we try to do the indicated envisioning, we find that there is really nothing there to be envisioned. Conversely, whatever we *can* envision we can accommodate without being pushed towards the Principle. What the Principle tries to envision is some state of affairs—some way things 'really are'—visible only from (what turns out to be) an imaginary vantage point, one outside of, and neutral between, all special designs. But there is no such vantage point, a fortiori, nothing visible from it. What we *can* envision are mundane ways of being under an illusion of answerability—of failing at what we in fact aim at in aiming at that. The Principle rests on the idea of an ultramundane way of suffering illusion; a way that would not frustrate anything we can recognize to be our aims or interests. But, the idea is, there is no such way.

We sometimes, for one purpose or another, classify some things as mauve, others as taupe, others as heliotrope, and so on. We take ourselves thus to be saying how some things *are*. The Principle tries to raise a certain spectre of illusion: in a certain special way we may not be doing what we suppose ourselves to be doing in so classifying things. Our stances here rest on certain expectations of the world, but some of these may, in fact, be disappointed. We may be let down in unnoticed ways—moreover, in ways in principle beyond our ken. We certainly *can* be let down by the world. There *is* such a thing as having one's expectations dashed. But, the thought is, to be let down as to what *we* expect of the world is to be let down in a way representable by *us* as obtaining, from the parochial perspectives available to us in the positions we, in fact, occupy. Perhaps if we looked harder at the things we are classifying, we would notice that what looked mauve one moment looked taupe the next, change being so disorderly here that there is really no point in insisting, in the way we had, that the things in question really *are* mauve, taupe, or etc.

Such intelligible, here discoverable, disappointment does nothing to move us towards the Martian Principle. There is no need yet for the source of our disappointment to be visible to a Martian. Such disappointments happen. But it is enough for disappointment that *we* are capable of grasping them. The disappointment that yields the principle need be no disappointment to us at all. It *would* be nothing we could recognize as such. It is meant to be what *ought* to disappoint us if we could but see the world from some unattainable vantage point—if we could but be the purely neutral observer. But why call that disappointment? Just *what* expectations of ours are dashed here? Precisely what did we suppose ourselves to be doing, in taking the supposedly answerable stances we do, that we in fact are not doing? Just *what* are the relevant stances meant to be, which they are not? Plausibly, nothing they undertook in undertaking to be answerable. If that is so, then there is no reason to accept the Martian Principle.

This, though, must be read as a scheme for a case, and not the case itself. Such a case would need to be detailed beyond our present limits. What matters here most is how the Martian Principle matters to issues of psychologism, and just what makes it seductive.

5. *Nouveaux Essais*

The Martian Principle seems, all too often, to present us with a choice: either we are much less answerable than we supposed, or we share much more in common with the Martian than one would have thought. To put this second option in other terms: there is much more to what any thinker would have to be (to be a thinker at all) than seemed at first; much more structure to The Mind, as opposed to merely minds of particular designs. Our current sense of philosophy's task makes us rightly chary of the first option. So the principle militates towards more detailed and elaborate specifications of what any thinker must be. (The problem is not just about moral facts, or facts about so-called 'secondary qualities'. As McDowell has noted, it extends to the correct expansion of such-and-such arithmetical series—a purely arithmetical problem when, but only when, it has been fixed which series is in question. In fact, it arises for any descriptions of sublunary affairs.)

Dummett, moved by the Martian Principle, is led to a priori conclusions about how empirical psychology must turn out. If one shares Wittgenstein's more relaxed view of answerability, one will, with McDowell, find this a particular kind of psychologism—not Frege's target, but what we can now see as lying at an opposing pole: *a priorism*, or scientism. One lands at that pole when, to avoid being Frege's target, one ascribes more to The Mind than it rightfully possesses. From a Wittgensteinian perspective, one cannot insist a priori that, say, our appreciation of when something is properly called a chair— a specifically human sensibility—must be reducible to principles which say when something *is* to be called a chair, and which could be applied to decide this without reliance on those very human sensibilities. Dummett insists otherwise; a second form of psychologism just in case the Martian Principle itself is.

On Frege's view, logic concerns what any thinker must be. There are two elements in that idea. First, there is the idea that the laws of logic apply to any thought whatever—whether Martian, or ours. Second, there is the idea that the laws of logic capture something one must be prepared to recognize in order to be a thinker at all. Each of these ideas bears various understandings. Might the second form of psychologism lie hidden in either?

The first idea may be innocuous. It can be a valuable insight that the sort of thing a statement of a law of logic undertakes to say is different in kind from, say, the sort of thing a definition in physics undertakes. The latter aims to say what something—perhaps a certain physical quantity—*is to be supposed to be* (in given circumstances, for given purposes). It is consistent with its ambitions that subsequent events should show that, while those suppositions are not right of anything, the quantity it aimed to define is definable in some other way. Definitions in physics represent themselves as such as to be replaceable by others, should the facts so dictate. That feature identifies, in part, what it is they do say. (The point is Hilary Putnam's.) By contrast, a statement of a law of logic aims to say—represents itself as saying—what is hostage to nothing; so what is never to be retracted, what nothing would ever count as making, or showing, false. Such a statement *may* succeed in what it aims at. If so, it is correctly treatable as answerable as it purports to be. So to treat it is to treat *what* it states as what depends on nothing. That treatment is correct *if* the statement can be taken at face value. For it thus to be correct is just what it is for a way things are to depend on nothing. What *can* be so treated need not be a world-independent matter.

As with definitions in physics, this feature of the ambitions of a statement of logic helps fix just what its content is. To state what is hostage to nothing, it must state, so undertake to state, nothing that could be falsified by any way patterns of entailment in the world turn out to be. A logical law must thus not be about conjunction, for example, insofar as conjunction is something open to *proving* to be truth-functional or not. So if the fact to which a statement of logic answers is that conjunction elimination holds, that fact may come to little more than what it is for that rule to hold within a given calculus. In the one case, it simply is not that calculus without that rule. As for logic itself, it is simply not the conjunction *logic* is concerned with unless that rule applies to it (for all of which, some, or all, conjunctive thoughts we think might not involve *that* conjunction). Such restriction of the import of the law may prove the price that must be paid for depending on nothing.

It can also be part of the content of a law that it is, whatever else it may be, something universally valid (something holding, say, of *all* thought). That is a demand that *might* be satisfied vacuously. Suppose the law is, or means, that a disjunction follows from either of its disjuncts. Then it might be true of any thought, whether Martian or human, that wherever a disjunction occurs in such thought, it is so related to other thoughts, which are its disjuncts. That is compatible with no disjunct ever occurring in Martian thought at all. Perhaps disjunction is not a form in which Martian thought can be answerable. The idea here is not that Martians might think disjunctive thoughts, but not ones for which the law holds. Precisely not: that *would* conflict with the universal scope of the law. Rather: the law holds universally by virtue of this: what it would not hold for cannot count as instancing what it applies to.

This, though, is not how Frege sees things. For him, logic limns features that any thought whatever must have; features that follow from the mere idea of answerability. So whatever a principle about disjunction tells us, Martian thought encompasses disjunction. That might consist in an insistence that Martian thought, whatever it is, and whether Martians think disjunctive thoughts or not, can be formed into disjunctions: one can take any two Martian thoughts and disjoin them, the result being something thinkable. (But by whom?) The principle then applies. This commits Frege to a view of what disjunction really is. What for him follows from the mere idea of answerability is that the calculus of truth functions applies to anything that could possibly count as thought. The extra premise is that disjunction could not but be a certain truth-functional connective.

There is now the second idea: one could not be a thinker at all without grasping the laws of logic, that is, without being prepared to recognize that to which a statement of them answers. So here are particular cases of answerability which must not be beyond the grasp of the Martian, even if the Martian Principle is not true in general. What the Martian must be prepared to recognize in the case of propositional logic would be that any thought (available to him) can be put in truth-functional combination with any other, and that the results are *thoughts* with the indicated truth-values. Notably, he can recognize, of any thought he can think, that such-and-such is a negation of it. For Frege (by the move discussed) this just amounts to recognizing conjunctions, disjunctions, etc., and recognizing them as truth-evaluable in the way they in fact are. There will be parallel things to recognize in the case of predicate logic, though it is more difficult to say just how they follow from the idea of answerability. All of this would be just part of recognizing a thought as a *thought*—that is, as answerable.

Frege tells us that one cannot recognize anything to be any way without thereby, or therein, finding a certain thought true (1918: 61). So one cannot judge at all without judging as to truth, thus without grasping what truth is. He also tells us that truth, though indefinable, is unfolded in the laws of logic (that is, of truth). So one must grasp them to know what truth is, so to judge, or think things, at all. We have just had an idea of what such grasp would come to. It would align Frege with Leibniz, who, in the *Nouveaux Essais*, argues, contra Locke, that knowledge of logical laws cannot be acquired, since one cannot begin on the project of learning anything—one cannot so much as think— unless one already recognizes certain basic laws. (See Leibniz 1753, book I, also 1696.) Leibniz thought that we can do that because we have certain innate ideas, which, he insists, are equivalent to innate knowledge of certain princi- ples. (This is a particular notion of *part of the concept*, shared by Kant and Frege.) Leibniz thus ascribes to us a specific logical competence—part of our human design, without which we would not be thinkers at all.

The ideas are thus, first, that certain forms of thought must be available to any thinker. (Whatever thoughts he thinks, these are combinable truth-functionally into *thoughts*.) And, second, any thinker must be able to recognize the truth- functional structure of the range of thoughts he can think, and the truth-values and truth-functional dependencies that this imposes on certain elements in that range. (There will be a parallel point for predicate logic.) Is there in this, perhaps, a subtle form of the psychologism of which Dummett's ideas about meaning stand accused?

I close with a speculation. In taking an answerable stance, one employs a conception of just *how* it is answerable. The stance is, in part, that it is answerable in a certain way. Part of any such particular conception is a conception of what answerability itself would be. Again, such a conception must be at work whenever we consider whether a stance has, or should count as having, answered. Frege spells out considerable specifics of what the operative notion must involve. Logic—the laws of truth—*is*, for him, that spelling out. We do recognize our notions of being true and being false in Frege's unfolding of them—though one might haggle over where, on our conception, those laws apply. (One might well resist, e.g., the idea that any answerable stance *must* be either true or false, and any reading of the laws that forces that idea on us.)

But is there, in these respects, only *one* way of conceiving answerability? Is it really so that nothing could *ever* count as answerability, but in a different form— that there is flatly no such thing as that? Since Frege, we have come not to expect our concepts to work like that. Even in the case of vixens, it is not quite right to say that there is simply no such thing as something counting as a vixen but not a female fox. (Perhaps 'female' turns out to be not quite *le mot juste* for that one side of a familiar recognizable distinction.) Answerability is, perhaps, the most central concept in our thinking, and thus an exception to the rule that concepts alone do not make things true. (For there to be such a thing as being F, and for such-and-such propositions to be true is, except in particular circumstances, not just two sides of a single coin.) One need not doubt answerability's centrality. One might doubt that the normal plasticity of thought ossifies in the face of that centrality when it comes to thinking about answerability. To the extent that it does not, Frege's picture of logic is a very subtle form of psychologism.

5

Morally Alien Thought

What is Hilary Putnam to morality, or morality to him? I mean: How do Putnam's central insights on the form of our thought and its involvement with the world play out in the case of moral thought? And what does that playing out show about those insights themselves? Putnam has spoken eloquently to the first question, notably in two recent books (2002, 2004). Here I will but add a perspective on that. The thrust is against two Humean ideas, or, more broadly, the influence of traditional empiricism—one which continues to be pervasive today (perhaps because, despite the work of Frege, its sources have not yet been defused adequately). As to the second question, the case of morality brings out in sharp relief an *apparent* tension between two ideas in Putnam. I stress the 'apparent'. Exposing an appearance can be the first step in dissolving it. The first of these ideas has two mutually informing parts. The first of these, for which Putnam is well known, is that the content of our thoughts, or at least our worldly ones, is world-involving. The second is that our thought about the world is pervaded by the parochial. By 'parochial' I mean to refer to features of our thought which are not features of thought as such, marks of the human, not required merely for qualifying as a thinker *überhaupt*. The point will be: there is no access to the way our concepts in fact apply to things without a view informed by the parochial. Our form of thought is, so to speak, a reference point in terms of which the application of our concepts is fixed. That may smell of idealism—an apparent odour which generates traditional empiricism by reaction to it. So it will be important to be clear on why there is no idealism in it.

Putnam's second idea can be put as a rejection of a view of Tractarian Wittgenstein. It can be put this way: one way of applying concepts, or, again, the applicability of one set of concepts, may exclude another. That works against this Tractarian idea:

Newtonian mechanics, for example, brings the description of the universe to a uniform form. Let us imagine a white surface with irregular black spots. We now say: Whatever kind of picture these make I can always get as near as I like to its description, if I cover the surface with a sufficiently fine square network and now say of every square that it is white or black. In this way I shall have brought the description of the surface to a unified form. This form is arbitrary, because I could have applied . . . a net with a triangular or hexagonal mesh. . . . to the different networks correspond different systems of describing the world. Mechanics determines a form of description by saying: All propositions in the description of the world must be obtained in a given way from a number of given propositions—the mechanical axioms.

(Wittgenstein 1922, 6.341)

And now we see the relative position of logic and mechanics. . . . That a picture like that instanced above can be described by a network of a given form asserts *nothing* about the picture . . . But *this* does characterize the picture, the fact, namely, that it can be *completely* described by a definite net of *definite* descriptions.

So too the fact that it can be described by Newtonian mechanics asserts nothing about the world.

(Wittgenstein 1922, 6.342)

If this is right, then Newtonian mechanics is not involved with the world in such a way that it may prove false (or senseless). That is, of course, not so. Though Putnam is not (and never was) alone in thinking that, he does have, as we shall see, the best account of why it is not so. Again, as he has argued convincingly, if Riemannian geometry is part of the correct description of space (assuming that *space* itself is an applicable notion), this excludes room for the application of Euclidean geometry: there are no Euclidean straight paths.

One system for classifying colours may treat blue and green as just *one* colour; another may treat them as importantly different ones. Either system may be a perfectly good way of classifying colours. The possibility of treating colours in the one way does nothing to rule out the possibility of treating them in the other. In matters of the geometry of space, for one example, things are not like that. One true description of the shapes of paths in space—one way of classifying these—*may* rule out another. In that respect, Tractarian Wittgenstein did not yet see what was coming. What matters here, though, will not be the point as such, which, by now, should be uncontroversial, but rather how it interacts with the first idea, and, particularly, with the role assigned the parochial.

1. Worldly Content

Frege's view of truth contained the following two elements. First, to judge something (think something so) is to be beholden, for a particular sort of success or failure, to things being as they are: one's fate in this respect depends *solely* on how things are. This particular sort of success or failure is truth or falsehood. Second, *how* one is thus beholden, in a particular case of judging, is fixed by (and fixes) what it is one judges. For one to have judged that things are such–and–such way is for it to be fixed *what* it is one judged. So for that much to be fixed is for it to be fixed *just* how one is beholden to the way things are. So whatever fixes that what was judged is that such-and-such also fixes how the judger is thus beholden. To know that someone judged that such-and-such is thus to know how he is thus beholden. That what was judged was such-and-such fixes all there could be to be fixed as to *how* things being as they are makes that whole enterprise of judging the sort of success or failure that truth, or falsehood, is.

Later Wittgenstein, J. L. Austin, and Putnam, each in his own way, departed from this last bit of Frege's view. The general common point would be this: it can be fixed what someone judged, namely, that things are such-and-such way, and, for all that, substantive issues may remain to be settled as to whether what he judged is true, and when it would be. Such issues, of course, must be settled by *something* other than what he was to be understood to have judged. My concern here is with Putnam's departure. That will give us the world-involving part of his first idea. I will approach Putnam's departure through some somewhat artificial examples. Insofar as these involve science fiction (as they will), one might, understandably, baulk at the idea that what they depict as possibilities are really possible. I will not pause to discuss such worries. My concern is to expose a certain form in our thought. The examples illustrate this form.

My first example departs from what Putnam himself has said. What is a vixen? A female fox, or so one would suppose. I am also going to suppose that one would suppose it is a certain familiar sort of animal. If we have not all seen foxes, at least people have—a not uncommon event; the vixens, I will suppose, are, or seem to be, identifiable at sight. So it would make perfectly good sense for a moderately experienced bucolic type to say, 'Look! There goes a vixen.' Now a discovery is made. Somehow, to its embarrassment, the relevant branch of zoology had made a mistake. Foxes do not quite come in genders. Let us say they are hermaphroditic. (In another version, their 'gender' at a moment may depend on a subtle interplay of environmental factors, including stages of the moon.) They do type in another way, though. Through physiognomy cum personality, they type themselves for either male or female roles. They are, so to speak, either 'butch' or 'femme'. It is the femmes who bear the young. So if there are any vixens, then what one would have supposed was true of them, and distinguished being a vixen from something else, in fact is not true of them. If there are vixens, then, whatever else, they are not female foxes. If there are not vixens, then, inter alia, vixens are not that common kind of animal which bucolic types are so good at identifying (and which you could easily have learned to identify too, if it but existed). In the circumstances, the right thing to suppose, I claim, is, or well might be, that we were wrong as to what vixens are. They are not female foxes. They are vulpine femmes.

My second example concerns gold. I take this example from Leibniz (see 1753: 269 (book 3, chapter 6)). The aims of alchemy are realizable to this extent: scientists succeed in fabricating something with all the supposed phenomenal qualities of gold. It is heavy, yellow, and malleable. It even dissolves only in aqua regia. At about the same time, though, scientists develop a test which infallibly distinguishes between the gold there would have been anyway, before the fabrication, and the fabricated stuff. Leibniz leaves it unspecified what this new test might be. But we might suppose it to be a test for atomic number. (Accepting this as a test for gold would also mean giving up our idea that (pure) gold is yellow.) Leibniz suggests that, on account of the importance for commerce of the rarity of gold, we would not count the fabricated stuff as gold. A more Putnamian idea would be: as the new test shows, the fabricated stuff is not the same *stuff* as the gold we knew and loved. That gold is a kind of stuff is central to what we always would have supposed it was for something to be gold. On either line, the fabricated stuff is not gold. This means that what it is to be gold is not (just) to be heavy, yellow, and malleable. In fact, it is not even to be all of that.

What is the common form here? There is something one would suppose it is for a creature to be a vixen, similarly for being gold. There are explanations to be given as to what being these things is, explanations which would be the right ones for introducing the concept of being a vixen, or of being gold. If these explanations are understood aright, they actually do explain what it would be to fit these concepts. But all of these statements are tensed. Given the cognitive positions we are now in, there is something one would rightly suppose as to what it is for something to be a vixen. In fact, there may be something we know about this. (Though in my hypothetical example we turned out not to know what we thought we did.) As things stand, there are now explanations to be given, which would be the right explanations (now) to give of what property being a vixen is. One would understand the explanations aright if one under-stood them as stating what it is that is to be supposed about this, and enough of what is to be supposed to fix what the concept of being a vixen is. To grasp the explanations would be to know how things were said to be in saying that there is a vixen in the tall grass there. It is enough, as things stand, to fix what it is that would be judged in judging there to be a vixen over there. But all these statuses for these explanations are compatible, so far as they go, with the falsity of these explanations, so with its being possible that they are false. Their falsity would be their falsity of *vixens*. So it is compatible with there being something it is to be a vixen, such a thing as something's being one, but with its being false that vixens are female.

The explanations which fix, correctly, what it is to be a vixen do this thanks to the circumstances in which they are given. They fix what it is to be a vixen in stating (enough of) *what is to be supposed* about what it is to be this. They *may* do more than this, insofar as there is more that we in fact know about vixens. But it is in capturing what is to be supposed that they earn their status as identifying that particular way for a thing to be: being a vixen. And their enjoying that status is compatible with their falsity, in fact, with their discoverable falsity of *vixens*. Thus do the cases of vixen and gold fix the general form of our relation, in thought, to those particular ways for things to be of which we think. This captures the way in which such thought is so shaped as to be world-involving. It captures Putnam's departure from Frege. It may be fixed that someone judges that things are such-and-such way; and still, when what was thus judged would be true depends on how the world (things being as they are), in fact, makes *that* judgement depend on how things are for being true or false.

Our understandings as to what it is to be a vixen, or gold, are open to evaluation in light of what we learn about the world. Similarly for any other way for things we grasp to be. Why might evaluation be called for? Frege holds, correctly, that there is nothing wrong with the concept *iron wood*. It has its uses. It merely has a null extension. If it is part of our understanding of being a vixen that vixens are a certain familiar sort of beast (we could show you them), and that they are female foxes, then, perhaps, it is our understanding that they are the conjunction of those things. Since (in the imagined case) no familiar beast is a female fox, the concept of a vixen would turn out to be like that of iron wood. But it is not like that. For the concept of a vixen to be like that of iron wood would be for it *not* to be of a certain familiar sort of beast. That would be inconsistent with our present understanding as to what it is to be a vixen. So if we are driven to the conclusion that being a vixen is like being iron wood, then our present understanding cannot stand. The world can make it impossible to hold onto our present understanding of being a vixen. That is when evaluation is called for of the sort that interests Putnam. The point then is: the correct upshot of such evaluation may be that there are such things as vixens (so such a thing as being one), and we have misunderstood what being a vixen is.

It remains to spell out how the parochial is involved in this world-involvingness of thought. From (Putnam 1962a) on, Putnam has been absolutely clear about its essential role. Perhaps the best way to see the point is to compare Putnam with a contemporary, Paul Feyerabend (1962), who also saw, around the same time, that that Tractarian idea, above, would not do. Feyerabend saw that there are identifiable things to be supposed as to when a given concept (or putative concept) would apply, and that these, whatever they are, for all that they *are* to be supposed, *might* prove false. (As Feyerabend saw this point, it was required by a consistent and thorough empiricism, on which *every* proposition must be answerable to experience.) His further view was that where such a proposition did prove false, the associated 'concept' was only a bogus concept. In the present example, if the proposition that vixens are female is not true, then there is no such thing as being a vixen. (This idea is crucial to such sometimes-heard views as that there is no such thing as believing something.) Feyerabend thus does not depart from Frege. If that there is a vixen in the grass is a *judgement*—something that might be true or false— then, in identifying what is so according to it—that there is a vixen in the grass— one identifies precisely how, in fact, its fate depends on how things are.

Putnam expressly rejects this part of Feyerabend's view. Of course it may turn out that we reject some bogus 'concepts'. Sometimes—*perhaps* with such ideas as being a witch, or being phlogiston—what one would have supposed these things to be is *so* far from anything that is actually so that we need to conclude that there are really no such things. But when is what would have been supposed *too far* from the truth? When is a divergence too wide? An answer can be: in a broad enough range of cases, we have the capacity to see such things. It is a matter of what is reasonable, and we are able to see, well enough, what is reasonable. If, as was once suggested by a biochemist, 'witches' were in fact women with a certain hormonal imbalance—if it is the visible effects of such a hormonal state which would lead the surrounding populace to identify someone as a witch—then, for all that, it is just not very reasonable to say that there *are* witches, and to be a witch is to be a woman in such a hormonal state. Our use of 'witch' just cannot shake those (supposed) associations with devils, evil, and so on. Similarly, one *might* say that phlogiston is valence electrons. Valence electrons do much of what phlogiston was meant to. But this would not fit well enough with our full prior conception of what phlogiston was meant to be. It would not be reasonable to suppose that valence electrons are phlogiston. So *phlogiston* is not valence electrons: they are not what we were thus speaking of all along. Conversely, if you just cannot define momentum as mass times velocity (because, as we learn, there can be no physical quantity of that shape), it would be plain unreasonable to react to that by supposing that there is no such thing as momentum. There is such an obvious alternative candidate for momentum to be. Similarly for gold. If gold is an element, then it is a white one. If it is an element, then it could be one we often spoke of, dealt with, recognized lumps of, and so on. We would just have been a bit wrong as to what made the samples we encountered yellow. Might it be, in virtue of that, that we simply have never encountered any gold, because there is no such thing? That would be an absurd thing to say.

So if there really is such a thing as gold (though pure gold is white), if there is no such thing as a witch, all of that is in part because of what it would be reasonable, or, again, absurd to say, given the way the world in fact proved to be. And if there is, that is because the concept *gold*, and any other, in fact works in such a way that what is reasonable, what absurd, and so on, *matters* to whether there is—to what, in fact, fits, and what does not fit, *that* concept. But what *is*, in fact, reasonable, what in fact absurd? Often enough, we know these things when we see them. We have a sense for the reasonable and the absurd. It is something we can detect. Suppose a (putative) thinker had a different sense for such things, in some respect or other. Such a thinker could not see what was unreasonable about saying that there is no such thing as gold (though the thinker I am imagining is not Feyerabend—his different sense of what was reasonable would play the role in his thought that *our* sense of the reasonable plays in ours). Would this putative thinker thereby simply fail to qualify as a thinker at all? There is no more reason to suppose this than there is to suppose that our sense of the reasonable could be grasped by, or communicated to, a being without this sense—that it is a sense for what is reasonable, itself reducible to something else. Given the shape Putnam sees in thought, this could not be. For that something else would only be what being reasonable *was to be supposed* to be.

There is, in any case, no reason to expect such reduction. In any event, such a different sense of what is reasonable *need* not disqualify someone as a thinker. That was (part of) Wittgenstein's point in his example (1953, §185) of the pupil who continued series of integers in a different way than we do. Different things come naturally to such a thinker, for all of which, he is a thinker. We deploy concepts which apply to things as we do because, or only given, our sense of what is reasonable—a presumably parochial sense for this. That is so of all our concepts. That is the way in which the parochial pervades our thought.

2. Is Reason Cool?

'Or what?', asked the neophyte. But I do not mean it thus. My question is whether reason's deliverances may be enough in themselves to motivate, or whether, for motivation, one must add to such deliverances some further passion. That is one question Hume made bear on the issue of whether there are moral facts. One present concern is how Putnam's ideas bear on that question. So it is time to say something about the area of our thought on which those ideas are thus to apply. I will consider what may well be only one portion of morality: questions, as they arise in particular cases, of the thing (for so-and-so) to do. Not all such questions, of course, are moral ones. But some are. If I wonder what it would be like to eviscerate a living person, then, we may hope (at the moment we can only hope) it is so that eviscerating the next passing stranger is not the thing to do. Similarly, watching the old woman leave the bank, having just cashed her monthly pension cheque, I know that if I snatch her purse, I can buy a new video-enabled iPod. Still (we may only hope) this is not the thing (for me) to do. If it is so that these are not the thing (for me) to do, then (*mirabile dictu*) there are moral facts.

Hume, however, thought that there were not. His starting point was the following correct idea:

Reason is the discovery of truth or falsehood. Truth or falsehood consists in an agreement or disagreement either to the *real* relation of ideas, or to *real* existence and matter of fact. Whatever, therefore, is not susceptible of this agreement or disagreement. is incapable of being true or false, and can never be an object of our reason. Now 'tis evident our passions, volitions and actions, are not susceptible of any such agreement or disagreement . . . 'Tis impossible, therefore, they can be pronounced either true or false, and be either contrary or conformable to reason.

(1739: 458)

Truth is a form of correctness of attitudes whose correctness is settled entirely by things being as they are—by matters of fact. In Frege's terminology, it is a property of judgements. Hume's idea is that there are no such moral states of affairs for a *judgement* to be beholden to, that it is not part of things being as they are that, morally speaking, they are such-and-such ways. If I take you to be eating *ortalans*, I am right or wrong according to what it is that you are eating. Here there is judgement. If I am revolted at the thought of eating *ortalans*, there is no such question of being right or wrong. I am simply revolted. If I think it (morally) reprehensible of you to be eating *ortalans*, that, for Hume, gets classed with my revulsion, and not with my judgement that you are eating *ortalans*. That is, the view I express is not liable to be true or false, correct or incorrect in that special way. He has two reasons for holding this. One is an idea that moral verdicts are intrinsically motivating, whereas reason, as per above, is essentially cool. Whatever I *judge* to be so, some 'passion' or 'volition' must be added before I am motivated to act (or refrain from it).

Hume's second reason is this:

A speculative reasoner concerning triangles or circles considers the several known and given relations of the parts of these figures, and thence infers some unknown relation . . . But in moral deliberations we must be acquainted beforehand with all the objects, and all their relations to each other; and from a comparison of the whole, fix our choice or approbation. No new fact to be ascertained; no new relation to be discovered. . . . In moral decisions, all the circumstances and relations must be previously known; and the mind, from the contemplation of the whole, feels some new impression of affection or disgust, esteem or contempt, approbation or blame.

(1739: 289–290)

When we reach a moral verdict, we do not arrive at any new fact: all the *facts* were already in before our deliberation began. So moral verdicts do not express facts. Both these ideas are misunderstandings. I will now try to say how.

As the credits start to roll across the screen, I get up to leave, hoping (just) to catch the last train home. There is an exit to my right, and one to my left. Looking, I see that the aisle to the right is blocked with elderly gentlefolk engaged in avid conversation, with no inclination to engage in (submaxillary) movement. Short of mayhem, exit right is just not in the cards. The aisle to the left is clear. The thing for me to do is to take the aisle to the left. I so conclude. Is this verdict motivating? I *might*, for all of reaching it, turn right and try to fight my way out. I *might*, for that matter, simply sit still until the underground stop is closed. To do these things I may not need to fight some compulsion to do otherwise. To reach my verdict is not per se to acquire any such compulsion. The most we can say if I do such things having reached my verdict is that I have behaved irrationally. But *should* verdicts as to the thing to do saddle us with compulsions? Should they energize us to overcome the obstacles in the way of carrying them out? Some such verdicts *may* energize. But that is not what it is for their content to be that such-and-such is the thing to do.

The thought that exiting left is the thing to do has a special role in my deliberations (if I do deliberate). It marks their end. It states their upshot. Other bits of deliberation may state a consideration for or against exiting left. But that exiting left is the thing to do is not itself a consideration either for or against doing so. It would be solecistic to say, 'Exiting left is the thing to do; that counts in favour of doing it; but, on the other hand, turning left is a more difficult manoeuvre for me to execute than turning right, so, on balance, what ought I to do?' If the difficulty of the manoeuvre counts against exiting left, then that belongs in the deliberations at an earlier stage. If it counts at all in favour of one course or another, then it is already counted in the verdict that exiting left is the thing for me to do. Such a verdict is the *end* of deliberation (though, of course, if, having reached it, I suddenly realize that there are considerations I have overlooked, I may start all over again). For deliberation to be at an end (or obviated by the patency of the facts) is for my course to be set—for me to be committed (in thought, at least) to exiting left. In that sense, a verdict that such-and-such is the thing to do *is* motivating. Being motivating need not be being energizing, or putting one under psychological compulsion.

Do we have a right to expect any more of a moral verdict than that much by way of motivation? Must *moral* verdicts energize, while verdicts as to how to leave the theatre need not? I suggest that such would not be a reasonable expectation of morality. It would be a misunderstanding of 'motivating' to think otherwise.

So if reason is cool, it is not simply too cool, at least when it comes to motivating exit left. What of Hume's second point? Again, there is something obviously right about it. But what is right here does not dictate the conclusion Hume wants. We reach a verdict as to the thing to do, or, anyway, a correct verdict, only after all the facts are in *which are relevant to that verdict*. That is just another way of saying: a verdict that such-and-such is the thing to do marks the *end* of deliberation, in the sense set out above. It marks deliberation's issue: a setting of course. So far, this is not to say that it is *not* a fact that exiting left is the thing to do. If Hume means more than this—if he means that moral questions arise only after *all* the facts are in, *sans phrase*, then he is simply begging the question which needs to be decided. He is begging it not just in the moral case, but for upshots of deliberations in general, for deliberations as to how to leave the theatre. This (I think) he does not mean to do. For he tells us,

One principle of moral praise being supposed to lie in the usefulness of any quality or action, it is evident that *reason* must enter for a considerable share in all decisions of this kind; since nothing but that faculty can instruct us in the tendency of qualities and actions and point out their beneficial consequences to society and to their possessor.

(1739: 285)

Where it is a question of the utility of a course of action, reason may instruct us. If, in some particular case, reason dictates a unique answer to the question what is the most useful, or fruitful, or prudential, course of action—if *reason* dictates this—then that which it dictates is, by Hume's lights, as by ours, a matter of fact. Reason *dictates* the answer; that answer is the only thing rationally to think (given that things are as they are).

That exiting left is the thing for me to do is motivating in the only sense that matters—the only sense in which a moral verdict *must* be motivating. Though one can arrive at it only after all the facts relevant to how to exit are in, it might, for all that, itself be a fact. It would be if one may think it *so* that exiting left is the thing to do, and do so truly or falsely. There is reason to think this as to exiting left being the thing to do, and no good reason (even by Hume's lights) to think otherwise. If, exiting left, I encounter a hitherto unnoticed obstacle and miss my train, whereas, while struggling against the obstacle, I notice the knot of elderly gentlefolk suddenly melt away, then it was wrong that exiting left was the thing to do. Whereas, in the contrary case (smooth exit, made train,

persisting knot of the unmovable) the verdict was right. Its rightness or wrong-
ness is decided, so far as we can see, by things being as they are. This does not
mean that any such verdict must always be decided unequivocally as right or
wrong by the way things are, any more than that any judgement that a ball is red
must be so decided. It might just be a very peculiar ball. (I elaborate this general
point in Travis 2008, essays 5 and 7.)

Both the Humean ideas with which we began are thus wrong. Judgements
(as to the thing to do) may be motivating in the only sense that matters (even if
they are *moral* judgements), while, for all that, *judgements*—either true or false.
They may be judgements (pleonastically as to matters of fact) even though they
are correct or not only in light of *all* the facts that are relevant to them, so
reachable correctly only after all *such* facts are in. But Hume's concern, and that
of his present day successors, is really with morality in particular. Perhaps when
a verdict that such-and-such is the thing to do has *moral* content, then there is
something in that which prevents it being a judgement. I have not pretended
yet to consider *moral* verdicts. There is so far no reason to think I would be
morally censurable if I tried to exit right. (Not, at least, before the mayhem.)
Perhaps there is some special bar in the moral case to eligibility to count as
judgement. Hume indicates one thing this might be: a moral verdict would
have to be (he suggests) an expression of 'passion' or 'volition'. This could not
be because it must be that to motivate, though perhaps Hume thought otherwise. Perhaps there is some other reason. If so, then while reason may instruct
us as to utility, or prudence, it stops short of full instruction when it comes to
the moral. There we cannot reach conclusions as to the thing to do unless
informed by sentiment. We must now explore the reason for thinking such a
thing. This will bring us back to Putnam.

3. The Marquis

That exit left is the thing for me to do is just part of how things are, whether it
is is thus something there is for a *judgement* to be right or wrong about,
something on which its truth or falsity might turn. (Nor need the fact that
exiting left is the thing for me to do be constitutionally iffy. True, I need to exit
left if I am to get home expeditiously. But getting home expeditiously might
also be, for countless reasons, the thing for me to do. Nor does the presence of
reasons per se make *that* fact constitutionally iffy.) Humeans *need* not deny this.
Matters apparently change where that something is the thing to do is (in part) a
moral matter. For, the idea is, any moral verdict expresses sentiment in some
way that prevents it being right or wrong (that is, true or false) according to

how things are. So that the thing for me to do is not to snatch the woman's purse is *not* part of how things are, not something for a judgement to be right or wrong about.

So there is something special about the moral case. The first question, then, is: What *is* the moral case? I do not need a general answer here. But in the area of morality I have marked off already, one mark of the moral, it seems to me, is obligation. If in point of morality the thing for me to do is not to snatch the purse, I have thereby incurred an obligation, whereas there is no such obligation in the case of my exiting left. I may say, 'I was obliged by the sudden unruliness of the crowd to leave unobtrusively by a side door.' Circumstances obliged me: I was (in some suitable sense) forced; I had no choice. By contrast, the sort of obligation I incur if morality does, in fact, dictate that I not snatch the purse is one which stands even (and especially) where I have the choice. Moreover, its presence is indifferent to variation in my interests, or what I want, insofar as there is room for such (rational) variation. It stands even if I very much want the iPod. If I snatch the purse, even in the complete absence of impediments to doing so, I have failed to live up to my obligations. Whereas if I try to exit right, then, given only what has been said so far, I have merely been foolish. Or, if I suddenly develop a consuming interest in befriending gentlefolk, then perhaps even sage.

It is easy to see how incurring obligations can make one uneasy. Perhaps here is the source of resistance to the idea of moral facts. The general form of the resistance, I think, is as follows. Not snatching the purse is, indeed, the thing for me to do *if* we allow that question to be decided by what we (relevant humans) are prepared to recognize—that is, by the verdicts we are prepared to accept as correct or reject as incorrect, given that some notion of correctness fits here, or given whatever such notion does. But what we are prepared to accept as correct is informed by our parochial traits of mind—a particular parochial sense for such things. Parochial traits are precisely ones some being might lack while not failing to be a thinker *überhaupt*. So some other sort of thinker might not be prepared to recognize that snatching the purse is not the thing to do. But now, it seems, we have the option of siding with the one sort of thinker or the other (while remaining rational). We are no more out of tune with the facts if we go by what this other form of thinker is prepared to recognize. So I am free to take it that not snatching the purse is not the thing to do, that snatching it is among the things I might do. But then I cannot be under an obligation not to snatch it, or none of the sort which is morality's hallmark.

The thought might be spelled out this way. Things being as they are is not enough to dictate the correctness of the verdict that snatching the purse is not the thing to do. For such a verdict is correct, insofar as it is, only by virtue of certain sorts of responses, by certain sorts of thinkers, to things being as they are. That is shown by the possibility of two different sorts of thinkers, as per above. But the thing about a judgement was to be that its correctness is decided *solely* by things being as they are, and independent of how anyone reacts to their so being. So the verdict here cannot be a judgement. I think we had better see how to respond to this line of thought *given* its premise that there is room for such different forms of thinkers. For that I will turn to Putnam. But first I will explore, briefly, the idea that there is really no such room.

Frege suggested that the laws of logic (or of truth) captured the most general structure of thoughts—a structure in which *any* thought must find a particular place. He also held that they, thereby, spelled out something about 'The Mind', that is, something about what it is to be a thinker at all. (See Frege 1918: 74.) *Any* thought has a place in the structure thus identified: any attitude without a place in this structure is simply not a thought (judgement). It is not that such-and-such is so, not what might be either true or false. To be a thinker is (inter alia) to think things (so). Any being whose attitudes did not include ones with places in this structure would not think things, so would not be a thinker at all. To this one might add a stronger thesis: to be a thinker, a being must be (sufficiently) sensitive to the places of his relevant attitudes in this structure— where the attitude is a thought, for example, that it forms a pair of mutually exclusive things to think (or is of a pair of mutually exclusive things that might be so); where there is a thought, there is its negation.

The stronger thesis, at least, removes some work for the parochial to do. It seems to exclude the possibility of two different sorts of thinkers, one suitably sensitive to the structure Frege has in mind, the other constitutionally blind to it. So we cannot get so far as supposing that this structure *is*, in fact, the most general structure of thought, not merely in virtue of things being as they are, but also only by grace of the responses of a particular sort of thinker to things being as they are. So, one might plausibly think, it takes no parochial sensibility to recognize that the laws of logic hold, or at least not in this way. So we can see their holding as something there is for *judgement* to answer to. Whether or not Frege held this stronger thesis, I think there is *something* right in this general line of thought, though it remains to spell out just what this is, and though I do not think it rules out all roles for the parochial in logic. The present point, though, is not to evaluate the line. It is to set out a term of a comparison, the other term of which is to be morality.

By way of a parallel, one might try to see morality as spelling out (some, perhaps not all, of) the most general structure of agency. For some doing to be an action at all, the idea would be, is for it to have some definite place in the structure thus spelled out. A being whose doings had no place in this structure would simply not be an agent at all. (Since being an agent is, arguably, essential to being a thinker, such a being would not be a thinker either.) There would then be the parallel stronger thesis: a being who was not sufficiently sensitive to the places of (some of) his doings in the structure thus spelled out would simply not be an agent. So, in this sense, the content of morality is part of being an agent *überhaupt*.

In one sense, it is not implausible to see morality as pretending to the kind of universality spelled out here. That not snatching the purse is the thing to do, the idea would be, is part of a structure into which any *action* fits. The strictures which dictate it are in force (even if, sometimes, beside the point) for any action by any agent. Perhaps so. On the other hand, suppose, as seems imaginable, there is a being, as clever as us in most practical affairs, but constitutionally unable to see anything the matter with purse snatching. Think of this being, if you like, as locally morally challenged. (Let us not dwell (yet) on just how local this might be.) Would this being thus fail to qualify as an agent? That seems implausible. Of course, he need not do so even on the above story. For he might see *some* of his doings as having their place in the structure that story posits. But then, do his purse snatchings fail to be actions? That, again, seems implausible. Yet if we do not say these things, then we have made that room for the parochial in moral matters which our initial argument supposes. Or at least we have not ruled it out in a way that parallels the story in the case of logic.

Some see hope for a weaker position here. Perhaps our morally challenged being falls short of being a *fully rational* agent. So the content of morality would spell out (part of) the most general structure of *full rational agency*. To put the point another, not quite equivalent way, seeing one's actions as occupying the place they do in the structure morality captures—as subject to morality's constraints—would be part of being fully rational. One can (some do) hear that idea with a particular spin: the content of morality follows from general principles of rationality which any being must be prepared to recognize as holding in order to qualify as a thinker at all. That is a very strong thesis, *not* equivalent to the idea that (assuming that my contemplated purse snatching is, morally speaking, not the thing to do) snatching the purse would be irrational. The content of morality may be an *irreducible* part of rationality. But then, presumably, not a part which any thinker must be prepared to recognize merely to qualify as a thinker. There would be room for the idea of a morally challenged thinker. Which would leave room for the parochial to work.

In any event, the parallel between logic and morality breaks down when it comes to the obligations that go with the things for one to do morally speaking. On Frege's idea, no one is under any obligation to conform to the laws of logic. Either there is no such thing as doing otherwise (no such thing as illogical thought), or, insofar as there is (one may make mistakes in reasoning), it is not that one thereby fails to live up to obligations; it is merely that one will fail to think in the way one must to attain the goal *truth*. This is entirely parallel to my failing to exit left, thereby failing to attain the goal *making the last train*. One cannot be obliged not to do X when there is no such thing as doing X. And when there is such a thing, logic is indifferent to what you in fact do. Conduct yourself as you like. Whereas morality is, presumably, not like that. X can be the thing for you to do, and you can thereby be under an obligation to do it, only where there is some kind of choice about it. There is a choice for an agent just where he *might* act in one of several ways. (I may or may not exit left, even if not to do so would be irrational.) And here the crucial part of the parallel—the part that would exclude the parochial from moral matters as, on Frege's picture, it is excluded from logical matters—breaks down.

I sympathize with the view that, as one might put it, evil eats the soul, so is best shunned. But, first, I doubt that either the goal of an uneaten soul, or that of avoiding evil, dictates (recognizably) what we are to do in particular cases independent of a parochial sense for what an uneaten soul would be, or what, by the maxim, would eat one. And, second, I doubt that the force of a moral thing-for-you-to-do is that it is your best bet. Given the maxim, morality *may* unfold limits to variations in the interests and goals one, or at least we, might rationally have. This is not to say that its dictates, or what follows from them, must be, in principle, recognizable to any thinker, or agent, at all (on pain of not so much as being one).

So we need to face the argument for the non-factuality of the moral head on. That argument, I think, is the natural expression of the unease one feels when finding oneself saddled with obligations, willing or not. I will grant it its initial premise. What follows from that? In *Philosophical Investigations* §185, Wittgenstein presents a case of someone with idiosyncratic understandings of *the same*, applied in particular cases. The understandings that come naturally to us when we are told to go on in the same way in continuing a series of numbers do not come naturally to him. Let us imagine the same sort of phenomenon in the case of colours. I can point to, say, a ball, a scarf, some wine in a glass, the sun at sunset, the exposed bricks in the restaurant wall, and say of all of them that they are red. What I say is something you, too, are prepared to recognize. Can we imagine a being who just cannot see how to go on to novel cases of what counts as red and what does not in the way we do? We show this being, red samples (as in a paint store, say), and then various items which are (count as) coloured red. The being gets the hang of when something's being coloured as it is would be its being coloured red, by and large, but with exceptions. He simply cannot see how you could call a scarf red, no matter how coloured. Or, more plausibly, he cannot see why in the world, if a certain ball is a central case of red, one would want to call *wine* red, or how you could say that of the sun at sunset, knowing what we now do about astronomy.

If such a being is imaginable, as I suggest it is, then the parochial is at work in the application conditions for the concept *being coloured red*. There is what *we*, with our parochial sensibilities, are prepared to recognize as something's being coloured red; to see when something would, indeed, count as coloured red— when it would be correctly so characterized, insofar as the notion of correctness fits here—one would need to see what *we* do in recognizing what we are prepared to recognize. Does this show that whether something is coloured red is not the object of a judgement? Certainly not. I respond to the tomato you show me with this attitude: it's red. The argument against this attitude being a judgement, if it parallels the initial argument above, would run: whether the attitude I thus hold is correct must depend, not just on the tomato's being as it is, but also on the responses to that on the parts of particular sorts of thinkers, namely us.

But *what* depends on this? The attitude I took in response to being shown the tomato. But what attitude is that? *How* is the tomato according to me? If our parochial sensibilities fix the relevant notion of the same in the compound notion *same in respect of being coloured red*, then the answer to that question depends on what work those sensibilities thus do. Without them there is no answer to the question what it is that is to be correct or not by virtue of how things are, just *how* my attitude is to depend for correctness on how things are. When they have done their work in fixing that much, we so far have no reason to suppose that whether things are as they are according to the attitude thus fixed is not determined simply by things being as they are. It may take a parochial sensibility to see how a given attitude is to depend for its correctness on things being as they are. It may take such a sensibility to discern in things being as they are that particular way for the truth or falsity of something to be decided, that particular way for things to be. It does not follow that whether things are the way someone with a suitable parochial sensibility might thus think them to be is not decided simply by things being as they are—just as truth or falsity requires. So the argument which I portrayed as an expression of unease at the idea of moral obligation is simply a bad argument. In the next section I will try to improve it. For the moment, though, I want to paint a Putnamian picture of just how the parochial is involved in moral thought—as Putnam tells us, in just the same way as it is involved in any thought, notably, in scientific thought.

For this purpose I will introduce the Marquis de Sade. Here is someone who feels more than unease at the idea of moral obligation. In fact, he might feel a bit resentful. For, for him, cruelty to others is what makes life worth living, or is at least its greatest joy. So he would like to renounce any obligation not to practise it. In fact, for the actual Marquis, he would *like* to do this rationally. So he would like his being under such an obligation not to be simply part of things being as they are, and any idea that he is under such merely the expression of (distastefully sentimental) sentiment. What are his prospects?

It seems apt here to consider the concept *cruel*. Now, on Putnam's model, what it is to be cruel (as what it is to be gold, or a vixen, or a straight path in space) is fixed, in our current circumstances, by some (or perhaps all) of what is to be supposed about this. If *cruel* is like any other concept, then it is fixed by enough independent such suppositions to form a motley, a totality which, given the way the world in fact is, *may* fail to be capable of joint truth of *any* way there is for things to be. (There is an imaginable condition in which there is *nothing* being which is both being a familiar sort of animal, being vulpine and being female. To say, in this condition that there are no vixen would be to reject a central supposition as to what vixens are.) We may suppose that *cruel* is at least eligible for this sort of discord. We can get a handle on the relevant motley, for the Marquis's purpose, if we invoke a conceit of Michael Dummett. Let us think (imagistically) of *cruel* as governed by an introduction rule and an elimination rule.

The introduction rule decides of certain specific treatments of others (some moral agents, some not) that such are cruel, and of others that such are not cruel. To invoke another conceit, and to speak very loosely, it assigns an extension to the concept. The elimination rule dictates (some of) what follows from something fitting the concept. What follows, I think, is that *ceteris paribus* (that is, perhaps with small exceptions, and perhaps excepting cases where cruelty is an unavoidable by-product of satisfying more pressing moral demands), cruelty is not the thing to do. By the rule as stated, this consequence does not depend on any particularities of the perpetrator. These enter the picture, if at all, only on the introduction side. Whether a given treatment is cruel *may* depend, for all said so far, on who is doing it. And we may think of this consequence as carrying the force of moral obligation: if you violate the rule, you have not lived up to your obligations.

There is one more feature of the motley here. It is a way in which logic and morality are alike. Perhaps it underlies the desire to find, in morality, some most general structure of agency. Consider the concept *is a conjunction*, applied to things we think and say. We may apply the Dummettian conceit. Here the introduction and elimination rules will not be those rules for conjunction which one finds in a standard calculus. Rather, the introduction rule will assign the concept an extension. It will decide, of some of the things we say, or might say, that they are conjunctions. For example, if I say, 'Touch my glass and I'll break your nose', that is presumably not a conjunction in the meaning of the act. The elimination rule will tell us that if something is a conjunction, then that introduction and that elimination rule which one finds in standard calculi apply. Now, suppose the motley just described turns out to be a mess. Some of the things we would have supposed to be conjunctions are not such that those logical rules can apply, as per the elimination rule for this concept. Then there is a further regulative principle which is characteristic of the logical. Revision of our suppositions should come, if at all possible, on the introduction side. We do not (or at least try not to) conclude that, after all, a conjunction does not entail each of its conjuncts. Rather, we conclude, if at all possible, that some of the things we thought conjunctions are not really that.

A similar regulative principle governs moral notions such as *cruel*. We are prepared to learn that some things we thought cruel are not really, or vice versa. But the idea that if something is cruel it is (*ceteris paribus*) not the thing to do is one we would not give up if at all possible. It is, at least, a good thing to have concepts like *cruel*, which can play the sort of role this concept does in deliberations as to what the thing to do is. One might think of *cruel* as occupying a penultimate place in deliberations. Arriving at the conclusion that something would be cruel may be hard and complex work. But when we get that far we are almost home. We apply the elimination rule, and we have arrived at the end of deliberation, at something which is *not* merely a consideration against doing something, but which is the simple fact that something is not the thing to do. It is a good enough thing that as long as we can hold onto what gives the concept that role, holding on to that would be the thing to do when our suppositions— what is to be supposed about cruelty—get into trouble.

In describing the concept *cruel* I hope so far to have been describing, nearly enough, what we are all prepared to recognize (or all of us who grasp what cruelty is)—what we are prepared to recognize, that is, as to what being cruel is to be supposed to be. That is the Putnamian model. If what is to be supposed here is, in fact, the case, then the Marquis's ambitions are doomed. For the things he would like to do no doubt are cruel by the supposed introduction rule, and then, by the elimination rule, he is under an obligation not to do them. He cannot rationally duck out of it. So the Marquis had better be able to show the above suppositions to be in a mess—not jointly true of any way for things to be. What are his prospects here? To begin with, he does not really want to challenge the introduction rule, or at least not relevantly for his case. He wants there to be things that are cruel, or where's the fun? He is satisfied if these are roughly what we suppose they are. If greater sensitivity to suffering would show that even more things are cruel, so much the better for him. The problem is all with the elimination rule. So what needs to be shown is that that rule really does not fit with the introduction rule, and that, further, contrary to what we suppose in the above parallel between logic and morality, the elimination rule must go.

To say that the elimination rule must go is to say two things. First, our reigning suppositions are in a mess. Second, the correct (rational, or most reasonable) resolution of the mess is rejection of the elimination rule—counter to what is to be supposed of moral notions such as *cruel*. How might the Marquis argue this? For one thing, if he were *au courant* enough, he *might* complain that *cruel* is not a conservative notion. With it one can prove things not involving it which, without it, one cannot. But it is hard to understand this complaint in any way on which it is impressive. If someone were blind to cruelty (as the Marquis, a connoisseur, is not), he would not be able to see what it is that is wrong in a certain range of instances of treating someone in a given way. Perhaps he would thus be unable to see anything wrong with the treatment in question. Where we *are* blind to cruelty we are so handicapped (as in Putnam's example of the father who browbeats his son, thinking to make a man of him). Similarly, someone blind to the chemical composition of water would be unable to see how it is that you can generate hydrogen from water in such-and-such ways, or why it is that flushing a lump of potassium down the toilet will cause an explosion. That is no mark against the concepts of hydrogen and oxygen, or of chemical composition. The concept *cruel* identifies something the *same* in certain range of cases where something has (clearly enough) gone wrong. It does that in capturing a particular notion of the same. It is hard to see how that could be objectionable.

To illustrate what is objectionable in the non-conservative, Dummett produces the concept *boche*, governed by an introduction rule on which it applies to anyone born German, and an elimination rule on which to be a boche is to be despicable. That is surely an objectionable concept. It is morally objectionable. The problem is not that with it we can prove things we could not prove without it: it is *what* we can thus prove. The Marquis's complaint against the concept *cruel* is that what one can prove with it is similarly objectionable. The suppositions about being a boche do not cohere here in just the way the suppositions about being a vixen did not cohere in my imagined case. There is no way for someone to be which is both per se despicable and assured by being German, just as in the imagined case there is nothing for a creature to be which is both a way a familiar sort of thing is and involves being a female vulpine. Similarly, according to the Marquis, for being cruel. It is mere sloppy sentimentality, he claims, to suppose that those cases admitted by the introduction rule are cases of not the thing to do.

If this charge is right, then most of us suffer an illusion. We need to change our view as to what is to be supposed as to what being cruel is. (Moreover, we need to change this view in the most radical way. The concept, as we now conceive it, is in the worst shape it could be in for applying to the facts. For, counter to what, by our present lights, is to be supposed, what needs changing is our view of its elimination rule, and not, as was to be supposed, our view of the introduction side.) Perhaps there is a claim here to adjudicate. Adjudication would bring the parochial into play. But the parochial that comes into play is just that which comes into play when there is a claim of this form to adjudicate for any concept. And it comes into play in just the same way. It is our parochial sense of what, if anything, it is most reasonable to take us to have had in mind all along in thinking of cruelty, what sort of revision of our view, if any, it would be most reasonable to make. We certainly may suffer illusions as to how some supposed concept works (as with the concept *gold*), or, indeed, whether there is any way it works (as with the concept *witch*). Then there are other cases where we suffer no such illusion, as is in fact the case with the concept *vixen*. Given that there are cases of both kinds, in which class is it most reasonable to locate *cruel*? The question, as posed here, is not specifically a moral one. The classes of illusions and non-illusions at issue here transcend any such category. An answer to the question so posed will settle the Marquis's claim.

So the question is: by the light of what we are prepared to recognize as reasonable in such matters, what is the reasonable classification of this case? The parochial is invoked here, but, as Putnam stresses, only in the way it is invoked for settling the correct application of any concept, including scientific ones. We have already developed reason, in rejecting the initial argument, above, against the parochial, for thinking that such invocation does not impeach the claims of the products of its exercise to be *judgements*, correct or incorrect purely by virtue of things being as they are. And we can now invoke a familiar idiom. Nothing along the lines of the case the Marquis has to make outweighs the intuitive considerations in favour of the view that cruel things are, *ceteris paribus*, not the thing to do. The reasonable view, given what we now know, is that this is not among those cases where revision is called for.

There is a word for the Marquis. He is perverse. He is, indeed, perverse in Freud's sense: his sexual instinct has taken a non-species-serving turn. That does not matter much. More importantly, he is perverse in refusing to be reasonable. He refuses to recognize what is reasonable by our parochial lights. But our lights are his lights. But for his local perversity, our sense of what is reasonable is the sense he depends on—to take one small example, in his grasp of the dictates of the introduction rule for *cruel*. So far, then, here is our position. There is no less reason to think it a *fact* that, say, not eviscerating that passing stranger, or not snatching that purse, is the thing to do than there is to think that, in point of fact, exiting left is the thing to do. And there is plenty of reason to think this last thing. But we are not done. I began with two ideas in Putnam. A more radical challenge to the credentials of the parochial will also bring these ideas into apparent tension. There is thus one more challenge to defuse before we can call it a day.

4. The Martian

We are considering judgements of a certain form: that such-and-such is the thing (for me/for so-and-so) to do. I have defended the claim that some of these *are* judgements, including some where being, as judged, the thing to do carries moral obligation (where, in present terminology, such-and-such is *morally speaking* the thing to do). To say that these are judgements is to say that there is something identifiable in the way things are—things being such-and-such way—on which their correctness (truth) turns, namely, whether such-and-such is the thing to do. For such-and-such to be the thing to do—for it to be the *correct* answer to the question what I, or what he, is to do, what all the considerations there in fact are dictate—may *be*, in favourable cases, a particular way things are.

Facts as to the thing to do (morally speaking) come into view, on the present story, only for a thinker in whom a suitable parochial sense for such things is operative. But, following Putnam, this is no more, or differently, so in the moral case than it is for facts about the thing to do *überhaupt* (e.g. that it is to exit left), or, again, than it is for facts about the behaviour of bodies in space and time (or spacetime). Nor does it decide against such things being genuine objects of judgement.

There are two ideas here. One is that it takes the parochial to bring facts as to the thing to do (morally speaking) into view—not just for one to see what the facts are, but to so much as see what there is in this domain to be deliberated about, investigated, at all; to see what it would be for things to be one way rather than another in such respects. The second is that, to that extent, the operation of the parochial is pervasive. It infects *all* judgement. So merely that much dependence on the parochial does not impugn the claim of an attitude to be a judgement.

But there is another idea in Putnam that may seem to threaten these. It is this: if one thinks correctly of the way things are in thinking in a certain way— deploying concepts which would function in a certain way—that may mean that one could not think of things correctly in thinking in a certain other way—deploying concepts which would function thus and so. If one thinks of space correctly in conceiving *straight path* as per Riemann, then space cannot be correctly thought of by conceiving *straight path* Euclideanly. Now here is a *seeming* application of that idea in the case of things to do.

If a parochial sense is needed for seeing what there is to judge of, morally speaking, then there may be a thinker, a rational agent, who at least lacks our sense for such things, who, in fact, may have some other, for us alien, sense of them. Let us name this alien sort of thinker The Martian. We will make his alternative sense what, for argumentative purposes, it needs to be. Thus, let us suppose that Martians do deliberate, sometimes, as to the thing to do, and do, in many cases, share our perceptions as to things which are just not on—which one is obliged not to do. But now here is Alf, a harmless chap, out for a Sunday stroll. If a Martian were to think in accord with what he is equipped to recognize, he could find no reason why eviscerating Alf (for sport, say) was not the thing to do. Perhaps to the Martian, Alf, or his life, simply does not count in any way that would rule this out. Or perhaps the Martian thinks of this as a (mild) good deed: unsaddling Alf from a life not worth living. But if Martian thinking is scrutable to some such extent, it is useless to argue with Martians about this: their reasons for such views are inscrutable to us, and vice versa.

We and the Martians cannot both be thinking correctly about the thing to do (assuming there are ways things in fact are in such respects). It cannot be both on and not on to eviscerate Alf. Nor is it part of our idea of the thing to do that it might be all right for Martians to eviscerate Alf, but not for us. If Alf were eviscerated, it would be horrible, full stop. So of ourselves and the Martians, at most one of us could be right. If concepts are applicable as we apply ours— notably such concepts as *cruel*—then no concepts are applicable as the Martians apply theirs. If, by design, we are equipped, or prepared, to recognize what we are equipped to as to how (our) concepts would properly apply, and similarly for the Martians, then one of us, by design, must be condemned to error. Competing ways of conceptualizing things need not be mutually exclusive. If you conceive *purple* so that violet is a shade of purple, then purple is not always a mixture (of red and blue). If you conceive it so that it is always such a mixture, then violet is not purple. But *purple* may admit of being conceived of in either way: there are just different understandings as to what it might be. If, on one understanding, you say, 'Purple is a mixture', and on another you say, 'Not always', you will not have produced a contradiction. You will merely speak on different understandings. It is not like that in the present case. If, so far as we are *equipped* to see, eviscerating Alf is not the thing to do, then either we or the Martians are equipped for error.

Now it seems that it can *be* that our way of thinking of the thing to do gets us to the *facts*—opens our eyes to some region of reality (of the way things are)—only if there is something *in rerum natura* which adjudicates in favour of us and against the Martians. And it may seem that this would need to be something accessible—visible—to a thinker relying neither on our parochial equipment, nor on the Martians', nor on any other. For if it took our parochial equipment to grasp the adjudication—to see the proof in our favour as *proof*—all that would have been shown is what to think if you think as we do. Similarly if it took Martian equipment to see what was right. And similarly if the adjudicator relied on Neptunian equipment. But, by Putnam's second point, this would mean that there could be no adjudication. For, by it, there can be no *thinking* about anything without aid of the parochial. But, the idea is, if there is no such adjudication, then there is no fact as to whether we, or the Martians, are right, for example in our thinking about evisceration. So there is no fact that we are right. So there is no fact that eviscerating Alf is not the thing to do. And so in general for facts as to the thing to do, or at least in moral matters.

This line of thought misunderstands Putnam's point about the incompatibility of ways of conceiving things. For the incompatibilities he presents us with are ones which we can see, incompatibilities by our sense for what is incompatible. If one cannot think Euclideanly of straight paths in space, that is because doing so would be wrong in a way that recognizably matters to us. For it to be mistaken would be for there to be a mistake about it which we are equipped to recognize as a *mistake*, a mistake on our way of deploying the concept of a mistake. It is not as if we might be mistaken in some way unrecognizable to us as a mistake, some way in which being mistaken would not matter to us as a mistake should. If the above line of thought were right, then an adjudicator would be called for whose notion of a mistake was uninformed by any parochial sense. But that would be no notion of mistake at all. In fact, such an adjudicator would not be a thinker at all, which shows already that this line of thought could not be right.

We are asked, by the line, to suppose that we might be thinking incorrectly, the Martians correctly, where what was incorrect about our way of thinking was something we could not (were not equipped to) recognize as *being incorrect*. The response is that that idea (so far, at least) has no sense. It is easy to imagine Martians who, thinking as they are equipped to, see nothing amiss with eviscerating Alf. We already have such things as wolves as models. What we need to conceive of, though, is their so thinking and thus thinking *correctly*, where what makes that *correct* thinking is something we cannot grasp. *That* is none too easy a thing to do. (Not that we might not learn from actual Martians, if there were any, some valuable lessons as to how to lead our lives. But that is not to the present point.)

Putnam puts the point the right way in (Putnam: 1994). There he tells us, thinking of the cases of logic and mathematics,

In my view, if we cannot *describe* circumstances under which a belief would be falsified, circumstances under which we would be prepared to say that B had been confirmed, then we are not presently able to attach a clear *sense* to 'B can be revised'.

(1994: 253)

Logical truths do not have negations that we (presently) understand. It is not that we can say . . . that the theorems of classical logic are 'unrevisable'; it is that the question 'Are they revisable?' is one which we have not yet succeeded in giving a sense.

(1994: 256)

'We might be (are) mistaken as to such-and-such' (say, as to how introduction and elimination fit together in the case of *cruel*) requires, to be true (or so much as false), a sense not conferred on it by 'might' alone, nor, in all cases, by the sense that would attach, as things stand, to the given filling out of 'such-and-such'. 'Sense', in this sense, is not meaning. In a remark, 'The scarf is purple', what 'purple' speaks of may be fixed by what it means in English: (*the colour*) *purple*. What is *said* in the remark is liable to depend on some further sense attaching to that word on that speaking of it—for example on whether 'purple' is *here*, for this purpose, to be understood as including, or excluding, violet. Whether *anything* true, or false, is thereby said is liable to depend on just what such further sense attaches—for example in the case where the scarf is, in fact, violet. (On this see essay 1.) So Putnam's point is, if someone were to say, '(Perhaps) (I put it to you that) sometimes, though P, and though, further, Q, it is not so that P and Q', though all his words mean what they usually mean, and we know that much about them, no sense that we are presently able to attach to his words, or that the circumstances of his speaking might confer on them, yields something either true or false. As we are presently able to understand him, he has not said anything liable to be either.

The point here should be seen as corollary to Putnam's core point about the world-involvingness of concepts (the same point which calls for the pervasive invocation of the parochial). So far as we are equipped to tell, *cruel*, as it *is* to be introduced, works such that eviscerating Alf, for example, would be cruel, while, at the same time, also eliminating such that, since eviscerating Alf would be cruel, it is not the thing to do. On Putnam's view, though, *any* such perception as to *any* concept—that purple is a mixture, the vixens are female foxes, that *this*, for example, is purple, or is a chair—has (at best) the status *what is to be supposed* (given *our* occasions for supposing things). The point of which is: we cannot say that, if a concept worked differently in such a respect, then, *ipso facto*, no matter what the circumstances, merely by virtue of what a concept (or *same concept*) is, it would be a different concept. To say that would be to blind oneself in advance to lessons the world may sometimes have to teach. Sometimes it has such lessons. That is not to say that for any such thing to be supposed, perhaps the world *does*, in fact, have a lesson as to that. (A comparison. It *could* be that, sometimes, when one looks at something visually indistinguishable from a vixen, it is not a vixen, but, say, a dummy. If no one has ever actually rigged such a cunning ringer, at least it could, in principle, be done. It does not follow that what you are now looking at—manifestly a vixen—might be a dummy.) If, given the general world-involvingness of concepts, notions such as *might*, and, correlatively, suggestions, hypotheses, etc., are to retain *any* sense—if they are to be intelligible parts of truth-bearing discourse—then their sense, where they fit into such discourse, must derive in part from the particular circumstances in which there are particular determinate ways for them to be right or wrong. As Austin said, we *could* decide to make 'I might be wrong' appendable to *everything* we say, just as we could decide so to talk that 'D. V.' fits after every expression of intention. So far, that would merely be to license empty gestures.

If eviscerating Alf is *not* something not to do, then, depending on one's tastes, one may be missing out on something, saddled, as we are, with our perceptions as to when there is proof as to the thing to do. Whether it is or is not the thing to do certainly makes a difference to *us*. But it is not (just) that about which we might be wrong on the line of thought which calls for the (impossible) adjudicating standpoint. What we are to be (possibly) wrong about is how *cruel* introduces and eliminates, or some other similar workings of the notion *thing to do*. And the point is that we are to be (possibly) wrong in a way we are congenitally unequipped to see. So the mistake here would be, no matter how much input from the world, not something we would be able to recognize as a *mistake*. It would not be the sort of thing that could matter to us as (recognizable) mistakes might. It would not make that sort of difference to how we organized our lives. It is that (supposed) inability on our parts to see the mistake *as* a mistake which seems to call for the neutrality of the imagined adjudicator. This, if we think with Putnam, threatens the idea that anything has been introduced here which would be a mistake at all—that what the line of thought is trying to imagine is something which would *be* a mistake.

It may help here to think of Pyrrhonian therapeutic manuals. The point of the manuals was to dissuade people from believing things. The method was to exhibit, in a raft of particular cases, *isostheneia*—an equal balance of reasons for and against believing the thing in question. One such exhibition concerns the proposition that grass is green. The argument runs: grant that it looks green to us, but who knows how it looks to a cow. Unless we were in a position to see this, and to adjudicate any disagreements between cows and us, we would not be in a position to see the truth here. So far as it is open to us to see how things are, there is *isostheneia* for the question whether grass is green. A natural response to this is: whether grass is green is not a matter of how it looks to cows. *If* being green *were* a matter of looking green to suitable observers, cows just would not get a vote. Or, better, insofar as bovine reactions do matter to whether grass is green—for example, perhaps cows give more milk in green environments—that is something we are equipped to recognize. Now the point can be put this way. As to whether (not) eviscerating Alf is the thing to do, or, more properly, whether our concepts *cruel* and *thing to do* introduce and eliminate as we take them to, the imagined Martians do not get a vote. Or, rather, they matter to these questions only insofar as we are equipped to see the way they stand towards them as *mattering*. Again, it is easy enough to imagine Martians who sometimes eviscerate for sport. What we need to do, though, is to conceive of their deliberations in such matters as right. Our ability to do that is bounded by what we are equipped to conceive as *right*. Correlatively, so is our ability to speak sense in saying that the Martians *might* be right. So far, then, neutral, absolutely non-parochial, adjudication is not called for. So there is, so far, no threat to the idea that whether something is the thing to do is, or may be, even in the moral case, something to be judged of.

Putnam locates the work of the parochial at just the right place. For him, its work is in informing—forming, itself informed by the world as it may be—those things there are *for* us to judge (or not); that to which we might assent or not. We commit ourselves—chance our hands—as to things being one way or another in ways that are intelligible to us. So we are liable to be right or wrong—to have mis-committed ourselves, to be mistaken—only in ways that are intelligible to us. Our mistakes concern that to which we might be sensitive. To be mistaken now just *is* to be intelligibly so. (Intelligibly, not necessarily knowably.) Is being *really* right being right to the eye of an absolutely unparochial (purely cosmopolitan) observer, by a standard uninformed by the parochial? But such a cosmopolitan observer, uninformed as he would be, could not grasp what it was we were to be right or wrong about. For, now, that itself is informed by our parochial sense for how our concepts would reasonably apply. So our being correct or mistaken could not be a matter of what such an observer would find: that suggestion is unintelligible. What we need to avoid to be correct is not (could not be) being unintelligibly mistaken, any more than we need to achieve being unintelligibly correct to be correct. The idea of the cosmopolitan vantage point, so expanded, has little power to attract. Cosmopolitans among us may have perspectives provincials lack but would be well served by. (And if provincials have perspectives cosmopolitans could use, being cosmopolitan does not in principle debar one from sharing them.) Such are contrasts one can draw within the realm of thinkers of our sort, parochially equipped as we are. It is mere fantasy to think of these sorts of comparisons as transcending that limit.

A truth-bearer (an attitude there is to take) is a (potential) common element in the postures of thinkers towards things being as they are, a way for different thinkers, or one at different times, to go wrong, or right, in their dealings with things as they are, a way for their expectations to be frustrated or vindicated. If we put the parochial to work on truth-bearers available anyway, without it, and without any parochial equipment, it would then show up as yielding merely the result that P is what one would think if, as to whether P, one thought in a certain way—a result indeed beside the point where the question is whether it is *so* that P. Which merely shows that if there is no thought but thought informed by the parochial, its work had better not be placed there. There is a parallel misplacement of the parochial in Quine. He begins with given things to which one might subscribe or not—things thus in the role of truth-bearers. For him, those objects of commitment, together with things being as they are, or at least with what one might experience of things being as they are, do not jointly dictate anything (on their own) as to what one must think to think correctly. If, in the light of experience, we hold onto commitments to some of these things, reject commitments to others, that can reflect no more than the way of our people—what thinkers of our parochial sort are inclined to do, which has the immediate result that our experience cannot be of things being thus and so, nor, in fact, can it be of anything. So much for experience. The very notion of judgement—a stance whose correctness is decided precisely, and exclusively, by what the stance is, and things being as they are—soon perishes with it. Putnam does not share Quine's starting point. For him we do not begin with commitments to be made anyway, and then put the parochial to work on them. That difference, as we now see, makes all the difference.

Putnam shows us how the parochial's role is equally as essential as the world's in forming how our concepts in fact apply—how the two must work together if we are to have intelligible, rational, engagement with the world. In expanding that idea as he does, he guides us to defusing the apparent threat of the Martian, as set out above. We can see it as merely apparent by seeing it to expand as does that idea of the cosmopolitan observer just canvassed. *One* thing that becomes visible by this route is this: that such-and-such is morally the thing to do may just be part of things being as they are. Eviscerating Alf is *not* the thing to do, full stop.

6

To Represent As So

Agreement . . . in judgement is part of communication.

(*Investigations* §242)

Throughout Wittgenstein had Frege in mind. We should too, to understand him. This is as true for *Philosophical Investigations* as for the *Tractatus*. In fact, the later work is, in an important way, closer to Frege than the first—even though the *Investigations* makes a target of what *seems* a central Fregean idea. It directs Frege's own ideas at that target, using something deeply right in Frege to undo a misreading of what, rightly read, are mere truisms.

The *Tractatus* presents a view of what it is, essentially, to represent as so. The *Investigations,* I will suggest, presents a different view, but on the same topic. Wittgenstein, of course, rejects essences, on some conceptions, in some employments:

'You speak of language games . . . but never arrive at saying what the essence of a language game, and thus of language, is. What is in common to all these processes and which makes them all language, or parts of language. So you let yourself off that part of the investigation which used to give you the biggest headache, namely what to say concerning the *general form of a proposition* and of language.'

And that is true.—Instead of specifying what is in common to all that which we call language, I say that all these phenomena have nothing in common in virtue of which we use the same word for all.

(§65)

We see that what we call 'proposition', 'language', is not the formal unity I had imagined.

(§108)

But he also says,

It is part of what communication is, not only that there is agreement in definitions, but also (strange as this may sound) agreement in judgements.

(§242)

It is hard to do philosophy, even of a new sort, while espousing no commitment to what things—in this case, propositions, representing—are as such. As we shall see, what I have just quoted *is* a view of this. The *Investigations* opens with a fundamental point—a thesis—which paves the way for this.

1. The Opening Move

The *Investigations* makes its first point by deploying a notion, *language game*. The items it thus deploys to make its point are fictions, precisely what they are said to be, best thought of as identified by how they are to be played. It will help *here* to think of each as containing some specified set of moves, each move governed by specified rules, these jointly fixing how the game is to be played. A game is thus *just* what its rules make it. Those rules spell out a notion of correctness: a move is correct, on this notion, if it conforms to the rules which govern it. A language game *may* have a given point, something to be achieved in playing it. Such *can* sometimes give sense to the idea that there is something its rules *ought* to be.

For present purposes, language games are (as Wittgenstein repeatedly insists) objects of comparison. We speak of them to serve philosophic ends. (See §§81, 130, 131.) To think of them as fixed by their rules, apart from any playing of them is just to assign them a particular role in the comparisons to be made. One thing they may accomplish, thus conceived, is to make perspicuous ways for representing to connect to action. For this end, and for suitably chosen games, we may think of the rules governing a move as dividing into introduction and elimination rules. An introduction rule specifies under what circumstances a move would be made correctly. It may say, say, that a player may say 'Slab here' only if there is a slab at some specific place. The elimination rule specifies what must, or may, be done if the move in question was correctly made. The prescribed consequences of the move may just be more talking. But they may be actions of various non-linguistic kinds. A correct move 'Slab!' in some game might, for example, require bringing a slab to a certain point. In ways I will try to bring out, connections with action are central to a representation's content being what it is (or, indeed, to its being anything at all). So, that a language game may connect words with action in a given way is an important feature of it, given the purposes it will serve in the *Investigations*.

I begin now on the basic point. One half of it is stated in §10:

Now what do the words of this language *designate*?—What is supposed to show what they signify, if not the kind of use they have? And we have already described that. So we are asking for the expression "This word designates *this*" to be made a part of the description. In other words the description ought to take the form: 'The word . . . designates . . .'.

As said already, the fundamental point at the start of the *Investigations* departs from Frege. But we see already how the point is made by taking very seriously another on which Wittgenstein and Frege agree. Frege made the point this way:

What is distinctive about my conception of logic is that I begin by giving pride of place to the content of the word 'true', and then immediately go on to introduce a thought as that to which the question 'Is it true?' is in principle applicable. So I do not begin with concepts and put them together to form a thought or judgement; I come by the parts of a thought by analysing the thought.

(1919a: 273)

A thought, for Frege, is, in this sense, the fundamental unit of analysis. In just this sense, a whole move in a language game is the fundamental unit of analysis when it comes to content. What does this mean?

Suppose that, taking a thought (judgement, proposition) as fundamental, we ask the question whether such-and-such is an element of such-and-such thought—for example, whether Frege, or something naming him, is an element of a proposition that Frege smoked. If the proposition comes first, we can begin with when *it* would be correct, in that distinctive way in which a proposition, as such, is liable to be correct. For a given proposition, there is such a thing as things being as they are according to it. The distinctive sort of correctness, seen one way, just consists, for it, in things being as they are according to it. So thinking, we can say: for Frege, or something representing him, to be an element of a given proposition just is for him, or it, to make (or be correctly viewable as making) a particular identifiable contribution to when things *would* be as that proposition has them: whether things being as they are *is* their being that way turns on how Frege thus is. The proposition has an element naming Frege just where that element so works to make the condition on that proposition's correctness what it is.

As Frege notes, what the elements of a given proposition are is all relative to an analysis. There are two points here. First, there *might* be various alternative ways of carving up a whole proposition into parts. For to carve a proposition into parts is just to divide up *its* main task—being true (correct) just when it would be— into identifiable sub-tasks: the elements, on that carving, are just what perform, respectively, these sub-tasks. A thought that Sid grunts would be true just where Sid grunted. So it would be true just where *Sid* is a given way. A sub-task can thus be making its truth thus turn on Sid. It would be true just where someone was a grunter. So a sub-task can be to make its truth turn on whether someone or other grunts. These tasks, if performed jointly, make the whole true just where Sid grunts. To be an element of a proposition on this analysis just is to perform (or perhaps be) one of these sub-tasks. That a proposition's task *can* be parcelled out into sub-tasks in some given way does not preclude also parcelling it out differently. *Any* such parcelling out what the proposition does into sub-tasks would be a correct analysis of it, on which what performed some sub-task thus identified would be an element of the proposition.

If elements are what one thus carves out of a proposition, on some division of its job into sub-tasks, there is no intelligible question as to how the elements of a proposition (on an analysis) can form that unity which the proposition itself is. For there is nothing it could be for something to be an element other than to contribute to that unity. The element has no identity other than as that which performs such-and-such sub-task.

The second point here is Frege's context principle (cited by Wittgenstein in §49). An element of the thought that Sid grunts can make the truth of that whole turn on whether *Sid* is some way or other only in concert with some other element making the truth of that whole turn on whether *someone* is such-and-such way—say, a grunter. There is no such thing as making truth turn on how Sid is apart from any *way* it is so to turn. Words which made the truth of a whole turn on whether Sid was some way might be said to *name* Sid. Similarly, words making the truth of a whole turn on whether someone was a grunter might be said to name *being a grunter*. By analogy one might say the same for an element of a proposition, or of a thought. Where naming is of logical signifi-cance, to name X just is to perform some such role. Naming so conceived *could* be done only in the context of a whole in which elements, in naming what they did, jointly performed the task that the whole did—here being true just when that whole would be. In that sense, naming cannot be done in isolation. This is the context principle.

A move in a language game is the basic unit in the game in just the same way as a proposition (thought) is the basic unit in thinking. For something to be an element of a move is for it to contribute, in some definite way, to the conditions for the correctness of that whole move. All the above remarks apply to this. This is Wittgenstein's point in §49. For an element of a move to name something just is for it to play a particular logical role in that whole move—to have a particular place in a particular parcelling out of the task of the whole move into sub-tasks. If an element of a move *names* X, does that fact identify a unique role as the one it thus performs? That is the main question to be addressed. First, though, I will pause for a moment over a different conception of what it is to be an element.

2. Occam's Razor

This second conception is what Wittgenstein refers to in the *Tractatus* as 'Occam's Razor' (3.328, 5.47321). He stated it clearly in January 1930. (See Waismann 1979: 90.) It is there put thus. For something to be an element in a proposition is for that proposition itself to be an element in some specific system of propositions. For the proposition to contain that element is (inter alia) for there to be, within that system, a range of propositions which are *the same* in some determinate respect. The element thus shared is, or identifies, that respect. For there to be that element is for there to be that way for *those* propositions (the range) to be the same. For it to occur in that proposition is for that proposition to belong to that range, within this system.

To be an element of a proposition, on Frege's view, just is to contribute, in a way there is for *an* element *to* contribute, to the truth conditions of a whole. That way of contributing, Frege insists, is detachable from its occurrence in that whole. There *could* be a range of cases of an element contributing in that way. So far, this does not require there to be such a thing as *the* range (or set of them), or the system, which is that to which the whole thus analysed belongs. For one thing, for Frege, the same proposition may be analysed in many ways—and would fit in different ranges of propositions on each. Nor is it some Fregean quirk to allow for multiple analyses. If a proposition were, essentially, such-and-such construction out of such-and-such building blocks, it would not have the pride of place Frege sees for it. One could give no more than lip-service to that idea of pride of place.

Tractarian Wittgenstein cannot share this view. For, as he says in January 1930, 'It is the essential feature of a proposition that it is *a picture* and has compositeness.' (Ibid.) That is part of his conception, there, of what it is for a proposition to represent: it represents what its elements name as structured *just* as that proposition is by its elements. There is an *identity* of structure between that of what is *so* if the proposition is true and that proposition itself. Such a proposition *must* be built up in just one way, of just one set of parts. Different structurings of parts are *ipso facto* structurings of different propositions. Merely insisting that a proposition occupies a particular place in a particular system does not guarantee that this is so. A whole system of propositions might divide into sets of ranges, each of propositions the same in some respect, in different ways on different analyses of *it*. The whole system might admit of multiple analyses just as, for Frege, a proposition does. If it is the system that is to guarantee the uniqueness Tractarian Wittgenstein needs, something else must guarantee that the *system* decomposes uniquely into some one set of such ranges.

We are left with this in common to Frege and Tractarian Wittgenstein: an element of a proposition performs a role which is one for *an* element to perform in *a* proposition, a role thus admitting of further exemplars. A role is essentially detachable from an occurrence of it. Let us now put this idea to new use. I have spoken, so far, of two ideas of an element, each of which leaves it open that the *same* proposition might be structured in different ways, out of different elements. What, aside from a particular structuring of particular elements, identifies a given proposition as the one it is? We began with one feature of a proposition: when things would be as it has them. We might cite that as an answer. But there is another (non-rival) view available.

Frege remarks in 'Der Gedanke' that to judge something is to expose oneself to the risk of error (1918: 73). (This happens in two steps. To judge of an *environment* is to run the risk of error; an environment (as he has just argued before making that point) is all there is, or could be, to judge about. (See Travis 2005 and essay 3.) A proposition is the content of a judgement, detachable, Frege insists (1915: 271), from any particular judging of it. So a proposition is *a* way for *a* thinker to be exposed to risk of error.

The idea of an element as a respect in which some range of items are the same can now come into play. A proposition represents a particular, determinate, exposure there is to suffer to the risk of error. So *it* is a way in which a range of things would be the same. Which things? Each of us, at a time, occupies his own position of exposure to risk: each of us is *exposed* to risk of error, and exposed as he is. For each, there is his own distinctive way in which plans may go awry, actions may miss their mark, surprises may be in store. If today is Friday, I am in my own particular sort of trouble. (Proofs due by noon.) A proposition represents a determinate way for such distinctive individual exposures to be the same, so a range of cases of a thinker being exposed in the same way. The proposition identifies, and is identified by, that understanding of *the same*. (This is already to rule out the possibility of 'private language'.)

I think today is Thursday. I am not alone. Each of us who thinks so is thus exposed to a different specific form of trouble. Which of us, in risking what we in fact do, instances just this particular shape of stance towards things? What risk *would* one run in judging today Thursday? I leave that, momentarily, open.

Language games are apt for capturing specifics of exposure to risk of error. A move in one identifies common elements in different thinkers differently than a proposition does. If a proposition is that the flat is dark, what risk does one run in supposing it? When would one be running just that risk? Well, you risk your hand just wherever *your* answer to the question what the thing for you to do is depends on whether things are as that proposition has it. Where is that?

Consider the film-developing game. Two players go through a series of moves, at the end of which, if all is well, film has been developed. In the game there is a move, 'The room is dark'. By its elimination rule, player 2 may remove film from its canister and place it in developer. When one removes film from a canister (for this purpose), there is a way in which darkness matters to whether one's project will go awry. So, with this project in view, there is a way in which darkness matters to whether removing the film is the thing for one to do. If we were designing a game that was to have this envisioned end, then, that elimination rule settled, there is something the move's introduction rule ought to be. Let us now suppose we have made the introduction rule accordingly. You are playing the game. The room is dark enough for you to bump into things unintentionally. Objects loom as shadows. May you make the move, 'The room is dark', correctly? Not according to the rule we would thus have made. Those conditions would spoil film.

If, in the game, you make the move, 'The room is dark', you are in error just in case you breach the imagined introduction rule. But now that will be just where relying on the room's being dark where it bears on the thing for you to do would lead to doing the wrong thing—what missed its mark—where that thing was what the elimination rule licensed, and the mark was what showed here what the introduction rule ought to be. In the case at hand, this is just where opening the canister would spoil film.

What of our envisioned *proposition* that the room is dark? Again, in supposing it you are in error just where, in fact, things are not as they are according to it. But that introduction rule for it has not yet been linked to any elimination rules by the route just covered for the above move in the game. So would (supposing) that proposition be in error in the circumstances just envisioned—objects looming as shadows, barked shins, etc.? Nothing said so far about what proposition it is decides this.

3. Frege's Limitations

Consider the proposition that Sid grunts. How might this decompose? Perhaps into a part which makes it about Sid, and one which makes it about being a grunter. Making a proposition about Sid could count as naming him. Similarly for naming being a grunter (a way for someone to be).

To be an element of a proposition is to play a logical role. So to name Sid is to play some logical role. To be an element of a proposition is to make some determinate contribution to its condition for correctness (truth). It is to be part of a particular way of parcelling out that condition into sub-parts. Is to name such-and-such to make some one such contribution? If I say that an element names such-and-such, have I thereby said what its contribution to its whole is?

Here we come to an idea of Frege's which, from late Wittgenstein's point of view, is a bad one (on one straightforward reading). It damages the good idea of a proposition enjoying pride of place which Frege and Wittgenstein share. If we accept everything Frege says on this question, then what an element of a proposition names does determine what its contribution to its whole is. There is just one such contribution thus to make. For Frege, in the simple sort of case now on hand, logical roles fall into two categories: naming objects, and naming concepts. If, in the present case, there is an element which names Sid, then there must be another which names a concept. This would be the element proposed, above, as naming being a grunter. Naming Sid is identifying what it is that has to be some way or other (for the proposition to be true); naming that other element is identifying which way something or other must be.

So far, so good. Now the fatal step. For Frege, a concept is a *function*, namely, one from objects to truth values. (See Frege 1891.) If words 'Sid grunts' decompose into an element 'Sid', which names an object, and an element 'grunts', which names a function from objects to truth-values, then the whole, 'Sid grunts', names the value of that function for a certain argument, namely, Sid. This is to say that it names a truth-value: true if Sid grunts, false if he does not. This is to say that for parts jointly to play these roles is, *ipso facto*, for them to decide a unique and determinate truth condition for their whole. *Mutatis mutandis* for propositions, of which words 'Sid grunts' could be but one instance, or expression. This is why Frege's answer to the question must be yes.

Not that taking concepts for functions is at all quirky. It is a natural reading of a truism: to apply a concept to (predicate something of) an object is to say (or think) *the object* to be thus and so, which it is (if it is) or is not (if not) purely in being as *it* is. Only the object's being as it is makes that predication true or false. On the reading of this truism, a concept thus behaves as a function would: fix the object it applies to, and you fix the truth-value such application takes. To see this as misreading, one must first find another. To which task we now turn.

In matters of decomposition (on the view late Wittgenstein and Frege share), a proposition and a move in a language game raise exactly the same questions. So we may now ask this. Suppose there is a move in a language game—say, 'The room is dark'—which we have decomposed, somehow, into parts, and that, for each part we have identified something it in fact names (on that analysis). For example, on our analysis, 'the room' names a certain room, 'is dark' names (the property, or concept, or whatever, of) being dark. Have we fixed what the correctness (truth) condition for the move is? Do our parts, in jointly *so* functioning, uniquely, or univocally, fix some one such condition?

Clearly not. For we can imagine two games. In the first, if I have made the move, 'The room is dark', correctly, then I am excused from carrying out certain orders. For example, I need not bring you your copy of *Zettel*, on grounds that I cannot see to find it. In the second, if I have made the move correctly, then you may remove the film from its canister (and rely on doing so safely). Let us suppose that each game is well constructed: the move is made correctly in it just in case there would, in fact, be those consequences (or at least such consequences would be to be expected). Then the correctness conditions for the move must differ from the one game to the other. For I may be, reasonably, unable to find your copy of *Zettel* (knowing it is on the shelf) where it is quite unsafe for you to remove the film.

One might correctly say of either game that in it 'is dark' names (speaks of) being dark. But the role it plays in naming this differs from the one game to the other. In the one game, but not the other, it contributes to a condition on being as said which is not satisfied if, where whether to remove film turns on whether the room is dark, removing film is not the thing to do. So if a move consists (on an analysis) of parts, for each of which there is a such-and-such it names, those facts about the move are compatible with any of indefinitely many mutually exclusive conditions on correctness (answers to the question when things would be as thus said).

The point is general. That words name such-and-such determines no unique contribution which is that which such words make to conditions on the correctness of the whole they thus are part of. Such is just part of what *naming* is. It holds equally for naming in the context of a move in a language game, and naming in the context of a proposition. The fact of my speaking of being dark is compatible with my saying any of many things in, and by, doing so. There are many different things, each of which being dark may, sometimes correctly, be taken to be (or come to). Being dark admits of understandings. The same goes for being a grunter. On Wittgenstein's new view of representation, these are to be taken as illustrating something intrinsic to the idea of a way for a thing to be; if a concept is identified by what it is of, then something intrinsic to the notion *concept*. *Investigations* opens with this point. It is the first point the idea of a language game is used to make. It advances us far towards our emerging new picture of representing as so.

We needed a new reading of a truism to see how it could be a misreading to make concepts into functions. We now have it. It is on an *application* of a concept to an object, on an occasion, that one says the object to be thus and so. The rest of the truism then holds. The concept as such admits of many applications, each excluding others. So it alone cannot assign an object, in being as it is, a truth value.

4. Comparisons

Words may name in the context of a proposition (or its expression). May they also name in the context of a language (such as English or French)? Not in the same sense. For a language asserts nothing, thus neither correctly nor incorrectly. Our fundamental point about naming makes this no mere nicety. The words 'is dark', in the context of a move in a particular game, contribute to a particular condition of correctness. That is what it is for them to name, in the sense in which they may name in such a context. What the English words 'is dark' mean does not choose between different conditions of correctness such as the two just indicated. The English 'The room is dark' is governed no more by one such condition than by any other. So there cannot be 'the proposition they express'. They can be used to express *various* propositions, where the use in question fixes just how one may be in error in speaking of such-and-such as dark—some one such condition on correctness.

But there *is* truth to tell in saying the English 'is dark' to name (speak of) being dark. Here naming is not playing a role in some given thought. Aspects make the difference here. There is a switch in my kitchen which turns the dishwasher on and off. This does not make me apprehensive as to what the switch may be up to while I am away. If I did worry, I would be missing the aspect with which 'turns on' occurs in that expression of truth. The point thus made is: to turn the dishwasher on, or off, flip that switch. Turning the dishwasher on and off is what the switch is *for*. Similarly (at least at first approximation) for the English 'is dark'. English does not go around telling people things. I need not worry whether English can keep an Oxford secret. But if you want to tell someone something, and it is to your purpose to speak of something being dark, then, if you are speaking English, uttering the words 'is dark' will generally be a way of doing so. That is what they are for.

Crucially, there is no particular thing you have to be in course of saying in order to use 'is dark' to speak of being dark, just so long as speaking of being dark has a role in saying it. It does not matter whether you are speaking of a room being dark in a way that would license opening film canisters, or merely in a way that would excuse your failing to find *Zettel* on the shelf. English is indifferent to such things. It is, as one might say, plastic. This is why it is so useful. To put things (so far) picturesquely, we might say: the words 'is dark' would speak of what they do in English, in any move in any language game, provided only that, in that move, they speak of (name) being dark.

What language games *are* played in some speaking 'The room is dark' (in speaking English)? The notion *playing a language game in speaking English* is not yet defined. It is (normally) not as if, where I say, 'The room is dark', we have agreed to speak according to such-and-such rules. Nor does *English* provide the rules of some game for us then to play. But we can think of playing a game in another way. If, in given circumstances, I say of a given room, 'The room is dark', the rules of a game with that rule may be such that I would thus have spoken truly only if I would have moved correctly by those rules. Such rules identify some of what it would be for things to be as I said. We might speak of that move, so that game, as modelling my words.

In the game, if 'The room is dark' is said correctly, another player may remove film. A parallel condition can govern what someone said: things *are* as he said only if removing film (for developing) can be the thing to do, insofar as this turns on the present darkness of the room. (That there is no other way the film will be spoiled need not be in *this* bargain.) Such may be a condition on the correctness of what one says in calling the room dark. It contributes to *an* understanding of what it would be for the room to be as thus said. When I call the room dark, I may be said, in this sense, to be playing any game which thus captures some of what it would be for things to be as I thus say. By that measure, I might correctly be said to be playing indefinitely many different games.

Where I speak of the room being dark, I must do so on *some* understanding of it so being. The language games I thus play, on our current understanding of playing one, may make explicit some of what that understanding is. Their elimination rules show some of how things would be if as I said: what is licensed or demanded by them is what one can, or must, do so far as that turns on things being as said. Their introduction rules must then be what these elimination rules require. If I said things to be thus and so, things *would* be that way, on the understanding on which I said so just where *those* introduction rules permitted saying so.

Where I speak of a room as dark, there are things you may expect if I am right, among which ways you may, on the occasion, expect this to bear on the things for you to do. Licensing such expectations is a way of exposing oneself to risk of error. An identifiable such exposure may be a common element in a range of cases of thinkers taking things to be as they do. It may thus identify something to be thought or said—a proposition. For a given way *for* things to be—thus and so—there are many such exposures to risk one may incur in taking things to be that way, so many propositions. There are many ways of exposing oneself in taking a room to be dark.

Supposing this point to hold for *any* things words might name (in speaking of sublunary affairs), and a concept to be what one names in speaking of a determinate way for things to be, a concept cannot be a function from objects to truth values. The fact of having named one cannot by itself fix when what one thus said of something would be true of it. Logic is so built that, when it speaks to particular thoughts, it requires treating what plays the role of a concept (on an analysis of a thought) as such a function. This means that when we apply logic, that to which we do so must be, for our purpose, viewable in those terms. So far as matters to an application, it may be as if 'is red', as such, has some definite extension. Concepts are sometimes treatable as functions. That is another way an identification may be understood. This suggests, perhaps, another way of reading Frege.

There are as many games to play in calling a room dark as there are things one *might* understand by a room being dark. Who is 'one' here? When I speak, there are those my words are *for*, for whom they *should* be usable as they ought to be. I cannot speak to people on understandings of being dark they cannot grasp, or could not recognize as understandings of *being dark*. On the other hand, for anything those my words are for *would* sometimes understand being dark to be, I can sometimes speak of being dark on that understanding of it. This remark fits together with another. We sometimes recognize someone as having spoken of a room as dark, while also recognizing certain things as to when things would be as he said. We are constrained here by the limits of *our* ability to understand being dark in different ways. Those limits are also the limits of our ability to take an audience as having taken *being dark* to be what was spoken of. Our limits here, and those of those for whom I speak, are fixed by an entirely parochial sense for when it would be being dark that was in question. To call such a sense parochial is to say that sharing it is not part of being a thinker as such. A being would not fail to be a thinker merely in lacking it. The sense in question is part of *our* equipment for engaging with the world, for all of which, what it helps pull off is *engagement* with the *world*.

Where I did say 'The room is dark', what standard of correctness governed it? Only the parochial can answer this. I tell you the room is dark. You prise the lid from the canister. The light on the smoke detector blinks. No one will ever see that judge's peccadilloes. Did I speak on an understanding of being dark on which the room was that? *Is* there such an understanding? If I spoke understandably, there are those equipped to understand me. There are things such fellows would be prepared to recognize—say, that there is an understanding on which the room was dark, and another on which it was not, that, circumstances what they were, I ought to have been taken, or one had a right to take me, to be speaking in the second way. In which case, things were not as I said.

There need not always be such outcomes. Those for whom I speak need not always see such things in one way rather than another. But sometimes there are. I call the room dark. The canister is opened. The tabloids have their field day. *Is* there an understanding of being dark on which, for all that, the room was not dark? That may be hard to say. But should I be so understood that things being as they were is things being as I said? About that there may be no doubt.

We have arrived at the new picture of what representing is. What I said to be so in representing things as some given way is what it ought to be given how one ought to expect to be able (or need) to act on what I said, as the introduction rules of a *good* game with a *point* are what they ought to be given the elimination rules they mesh with. Questions as to what it is I said—where I spoke of things being thus and so, on what understanding of their so being I in fact spoke—are thus answered by our common parochial sense for what ought to be expected of my speaking as I did in the circumstances in which I did—in the artificial terms here used to make the point, by our parochial sense for the games I was, or would be, playing in speaking as I did, on our present notion of what it would be for me to be playing a language game in speaking, say, English.

5. Truth

A further contrast with Frege's view may help focus the new picture. Frege's conception of a truth bearer (1918) starts from this question:

Is a picture as bare visible, tangible, thing really true? And a stone, or leaf, not true?

(1918, p. 59)

The answer is, clearly, no. A picture, so conceived, might represent anything, or nothing, as so. So far, as Frege sees it, there is no intelligible question as to whether what it represented as so is so. There is no 'what it represented as so'. And (a critical assumption), one cannot ask whether words represented as so, what is so, except by asking of that which they represent as so (that such-and-such) whether *that* is so.

Suppose a painting does represent something as so—something, say, as to how the cathedral at Rouen looks. No question of truth arises, the idea is, until it is fixed just *how* the cathedral is thus supposed to look. Only with that fixed can we ask whether the cathedral is as represented. Suppose the painting is a Monet. In its image of a wall is a patch of blue paint. Does this represent it as so that the cathedral has a partly blue wall? Or that the wall was in shadow at the time it was painted? Monet's ways aside, there is no saying. If not, the idea is, no (determinate) question of truth has arisen.

A question of truth thus arises for Frege only where there is no unanswered one of this form: 'Is the representation to be taken as representing *this* as so, or rather *that*?' For what raises a question of truth, there is no such open question as to what is so according to it, when things would be as it represents them. Frege thinks that beginning with visible, tangible representations we can arrive at non-visible, non-tangible, representations which meet this condition—and that any representation which did so *would* be neither visible nor tangible.

This conviction is another version of the idea from which I have already signalled Wittgenstein as departing: the idea that a concept is a function from objects to truth-values. Suppose there is an identifiable way for things to be such that if things were represented as that way, there can be no further open question as to whether they were thus represented as *this* way, or rather *that*. Such a way for things to be would admit no understandings. The zero-place concept of it would thus map *things* being as they are into a truth value. Where naming a (non-zero place) concept is a contribution to representing things as this way, the concept named could only behave as a function from objects to truth values would. What raises such a question of truth is a representation on a different understanding of that term: something *to* represent as so. Such a thing (as Frege argues) is neither visible nor tangible.

That the parochial decides *which* way words represented things is, for Frege, an anodyne idea. Whether 'is dark' then named one concept or another may all depend on us. But, on this conception, there is *no* role for the parochial once a question of truth has been raised. From the question when someone should be counted as having spoken truth—as having said no more than what is so—we have separated out a question which does not refer to him, or his utterance, at all: for a given thing that might be said, when *that* thing would be true. On the Fregean idea, such a thing—something *to represent* as so—is not susceptible to understandings, as mere visible, tangible representers—words, pictures, etc.—are. It *is* an understanding for such things to bear. So there is no role for the parochial, or anything else, in choosing between understandings of *it*.

A language game provides a different story. We can now abandon the idea that there are ways for things to be which brook no competing understandings, and the idea that the only questions of truth are whether things are one or another of these ways. For any way for things to be, there may always be questions as to how one may expect to act on that, admitting of different, and competing answers on different occasions for considering a question how to act. On the other hand, on the new picture, words are true if one can do all they license, must do all they require if correct. How things are according to the words is then fixed by those standards for their introduction which such standards for their elimination impart.

If a painting represents part of a cathedral wall as blue, there is this question: might it be true to represent the wall like that? The question *may* have a clear answer. Or, again, not. There are all sorts of things it *could* be for a wall to be blue there; all sorts of understandings of it so being. Would a crude *graffito* count? For each such thing, there are the language games in which it is what would so count. That there are such further understandings of being blue *need* not matter to truth in the case at hand (given the way the wall in fact is), though it might. As to whether the painting is subject to any such further standards of correctness—whether it is the playing of any such further games—this is a matter for the parochial to rule on, just as it does where Frege concedes it room to operate.

My calling the room dark raises a question of truth: *is* it dark on the understanding on which I spoke of that? This question still leaves room for the parochial to work. There are things to be decided as to the understanding of that on which I did so speak. Now, the idea is, say what you like as to what that understanding is, and there is still the same sort of room for the parochial to work. There is always room for fresh questions of truth to arise. Find new circumstances of which my words might be true or not, and there are, correspondingly, new language games for me to have been playing or not, games which provide for such circumstances in any of many ways (or none). With that, there is more of the usual work for the parochial to do. The parochial, like rust, never sleeps. On this new picture, as opposed to Frege's, it never cancels out absolutely.

Invisible, intangible truth bearers thus lose the special status Frege accords them. The parochial takes on an ineliminable role in representing as so. Such a view must be seen as a picture of what representing is as such—though it is as yet unclear how it could be that. This sets an agenda for much of what follows this opening move in the *Investigations*. I now turn to that agenda, and one bit of its execution.

6. Thinking, Meaning, Understanding

So far I have discussed the work of the first 27 paragraphs of the *Investigations*. It sets an agenda for much, if not all, of the rest, notably for the rule following discussion (§§84–87, §§138–242). Two issues are on that agenda.

One agenda item is to apply the new idea of representation to a sort of representation not yet in the picture. I have spoken above of what belongs to representation as such. So far we have considered only linguistic representation: representation in, or by, vehicles. I utter some words, or make some signs by waving my hands, or use smoke signals, or whatever, to which one is to react in a certain way. The signs—the physical bearers of this way of being taken—make my representing perceivable, so that you can be aware of being represented to, and then, if things go well, take yourself to be represented to in a certain way. Where there is such a thing as how signs are to be taken, a parochial sensibility *may* decide that. Wittgenstein's point could then just be that there are no bounds on the room for such decision—what Frege suggests there *must* be for there to be questions of truth at all.

But representing with such a physical face to it—with bearers of content—is one case of two. There is representing to, or for, an audience—those who are to take the representing in one way or another. Then there is representing things to oneself as so. One *can* be the sole intended audience for representing of the first type: I leave myself a note (which, on finding, I *may* disbelieve). But there is a case where it is not that. Representing something as so may just be taking (holding) a certain view. I will call that *autorepresentation*. For me to think that my keys are in my pocket is, per se, for me to represent the world to myself as a certain way. For me to represent the world to myself as a certain way is for me to *stand* towards it in a certain way—in a certain posture. To write a note would not be so to stand. Representational vehicles have no clear role in my so standing (though some have postulated them by way of supposed empirical hypothesis). Nor, in any clear sense, is my representing something to myself as so something that is to be *taken* in one or another way, so that a parochial sensibility might decide how.

Where there is something which is to be taken in a certain way, there is a role for the parochial to have: determining *what* way. Autorepresentation seems to involve no such thing. So it is as yet unclear what role the parochial could have there, so how the new picture applies. The first agenda item is to see how it might.

The second is to see what calls for the new picture. This, I will argue, is the task of the rule following discussions (§§84–87 and §§138–242). This section treats the first item, the next section the second. As a preliminary, though, I now summarize that first discussion. §§84–87 discusses how the explanations we give one another can *explain*—can say no less than what to do, or how things are. I tell you, 'To find the post office turn right at the second street', or, if that does not suffice, 'That alleyway is not a street.' I may thus tell you no less than what route to follow. The instruction, 'Turn right at the second street' *admits of* competing understandings, as does every other. For all of which my giving of it need not. My explanations, the things I say, are *for* thinkers of the sort we are, or those I give (say) them to. Such thinkers *would* take them in a certain way. Such is part of being the sort they are. What explanations which are for such thinkers in fact say is what they would thus be taken to. Their content is formed by the sort of thinker they are for, thus by what is peculiar to thinkers of a certain sort—by what is *parochial*. 'The sign-post is in order—if it meets its aims in normal circumstances' (§87). It is aimed at a certain sort of thinker. Its content is what its aims and their fulfilment make it. I will apply this idea to the first agenda item.

How, then, does the new picture apply to autorepresentation? I will focus on one case of it: someone meaning his words in a certain way—so as to say such-and-such. Here meaning is what *someone* does, not what 'vrijgezel' does in meaning *bachelor*. It is non-factive, so unlike Pia's frown meaning Sid is driving. I *meant* to post the letter. I meant to say 'begleiten', not 'beleidigen'. It aims at something, with all the usual accompaniments of that. If I mean to say X to be so, and for X to be so just is for Y to be so, I need not have meant to say Y to be so. Which need not mean that I can mean to say something where there is no such thing to say. What can one mean the words one speaks to say? On one view, anything one can think. Thus, as Wittgenstein portrays the view (§205),

> 'But it is just the queer thing about *intention*, about the mental process, that the existence of a custom, of a technique, is not necessary to it.'

The counter idea here can be put: ignorance is strength. A small child can jump off a tall building and try to fly—if, as may be with a small child, he does not know that he cannot do this. But only if that. I can jump off a tall building and flap my arms. But I cannot thus be trying to fly. For I know I cannot. You cannot try to do what you are fully convinced you cannot do. So I cannot, in the bakery, try to ask for bread by saying, 'Would you like to go for a drink?' At least not in normal circumstances. For, as I know full well, I will *not* have asked for bread in doing that. English does not work that way. I am a competent speaker of English. So I know what I will say (if anything) in the bakery in uttering 'Would you like to go for a drink?' So, contraposing 'Ignorance is strength', I cannot try, in so speaking, to ask for bread. So I cannot mean my words to be asking for bread.

Insofar as I am competent—I know what would be said in speaking given words on a given occasion—I can only mean my words to say what they will, in fact, say. If I say 'The room is dark' in circumstances in which that would be taken to mean it is safe to remove film, and I know this is how it would be taken, I cannot, consistent with that, mean my words to say that the room is dark on some other understanding of it so being. The new picture of representation now applies. What would I say, on a given occasion, in saying, 'The room is dark'? Refer to the new picture. Now insofar as I am competent, *that* is what I meant my words to say.

My readers and I are all competent in speaking English, but none of us perfectly so. Even where competent enough, we do not always see what we will say in uttering given words on a given occasion. We may always fail to appreciate fully the circumstances in which we speak. I may, say, misuse the word 'careen' because I do not know, or properly grasp, its nautical origins. Or I may misuse it in a particular situation because though I do know those origins, my audience does not, so that I am aiming for a metaphor unrealizable under the circumstances. A boat tilting from side to side in high seas may be said to be careening (on what is now, anyway, one recognized use). I might think of a truck heaped high, creeping from the dust bowl towards California, as like such a ship. So I speak of it as careening down the road. The metaphor falls flat. I do not say what I mean to. Equally, I might threaten someone, 'I'll careen you', and not succeed in saying what I mean to say—that I will keelhaul him—because that meaning of 'careen' is currently unknown.

There is that much room for divergence between what I mean my words to say and what they do say. None of this spoils the core in the idea that ignorance is strength. I thought 'careen' meant *keelhaul*. In the context I used it, it did not. But we know what it would be (roughly) for a word to mean *keelhaul*. The word 'keelhaul' means that, for example. Suppose 'careen' had meant *keelhaul* (in that context). What would I then have said? In the above case, that is what I meant my words to say. Again, the new picture of representation stays in place. Suppose I drag you under my canoe. Would that be keelhauling on the understanding of this on which that is what I would have threatened my audience with?

My perceptions as to what I would say in given words may intelligibly deviate from what is so. They may be, understandably, that I would say such-and-such else there is to be said. Then, in choosing my words as I did, *that* is what I meant to say. I was able to suppose I would then speak, in those words, of things being such-and-such way. So I meant them to speak of that. I was able to suppose the circumstances to be thus and so. So I meant thus to say what one would in speaking of things as that way in such circumstances. When would things *be* as I thus meant to say they were? Well, what language games would I be playing were my suppositions so? Our new idea of what representation is now takes its grip. How I meant things were now falls within the scope of the parochial.

Here, then, one illustration of how the new picture can be a picture of autorepresentation. Details differ from case to case. There is a further point. In saying Sid to think the room is dark, one might say him to think any of various things, depending on what, for purposes of so saying, one is to understand by a room being dark. But not: what Sid thinks in thinking the room dark (where he so thinks) depends on what one understands by a room being dark. (Nor even, I think, on what *he* understands by this.) Rather, in thinking the room dark, Sid thinks something *so*. What can be *thought* so is what, *ceteris paribus*, either *is* so or not. Which it is can then only depend on how things are. Equally, then, for whether things are as he thus thinks. So equally again for what he thus thinks. There is (roughly) no room here for whether things are as Sid thinks to depend on what one understands by a room being dark; equally little for *what* he thus thinks to so depend.

So far *what* Sid thinks seems to follow the pattern of a Fregean truth-bearer. Such a truth-bearer represents things as such-and-such way, where there are just *no* competing understandings of something being that way; so whether something is that way *cannot* depend on what you understand by something so being. Similarly, what Sid thinks in thinking what he does here is that things are a certain way; whether things are as he thus thinks cannot, it seems, depend on what one understands by things being such-and-such way, for *any* substitution for that 'such-and-such'. The phenomenon of thinking so *seems* to take this shape. Such may be one important source of the idea of a Fregean truth-bearer. But how *can* there be objects of thinking so—thoughts, or propositions—which thus admit of no competing understandings? We need to understand the terms of the line of thought, above, which can seem to suggest so.

Wittgenstein explores this topic in §§429–465. The key idea here is:

'An order orders its own execution.' So it knows its execution before it is there?—But that was a grammatical proposition, and it says: If the order runs 'Do such-and-such' then carrying out the order is called 'doing such-and-such'.

(§458)

'If you said that Sid grunts, what you thus said would be true iff Sid grunts.' Whether this states truth depends on what one understands saying that Sid grunts to be. But if we understand this antecedent as speaking of your having said such-and-such to be so, where that *is* (presumably) something so or not— if, that is, we understand it as we did Sid's thinking something so, above—then the remark is a truism, unfolding part (though not all) of the concept of truth: a grammatical proposition in Wittgenstein's sense. But why? In the consequent, the words 'Sid grunts' speak of Sid being a way he (presumably) is or not. To do that, they must bear some particular understanding of being a grunter. If *I* made this remark, then I spoke, in that part of it, of Sid being a grunter, on some particular understanding of him so being. In the antecedent I speak of you speaking of Sid being a grunter. Again, if I thus speak of you saying things to be thus and so, then I *thus* speak of Sid being a grunter on some particular understanding of him so being. And now a grammatical point: it must be the same understanding both times, which guarantees the truth of the whole. Which is to say nothing as to just what understanding this might be. So far we have learned nothing as to just when you would be right.

Suppose now that I say 'If Sid thinks the room is dark, what he thinks is so just in case the room is dark.' If, in the antecedent, I speak of Sid thinking things to be thus and so, then all the above remarks apply. In the consequent I use the words 'the room is dark' to speak of a room as dark on some particular understanding of its so being. In the antecedent I do the same. In the consequent I do it to say how things must be for Sid to be right. In the antecedent I do it to say what it is he will be right or wrong about. Again, necessarily, one understanding of a room being dark is in force throughout. Again we so far know nothing as to what it is Sid thinks.

'In thinking the room dark, Sid thinks something so; which *is* so, or not, independent of what you understand by a room being dark, or by things being any other given way.' That is so in just the way it is so that if I *say* the room to be dark, I thus *say* something so, which *is* so, or not, independent of what you understand by a room being dark. So things are as I said, or not, independent of any such understanding, just as things are as Sid thus thought independent of this. Neither truism suggests Fregean truth-bearers. Rather, the parochial retains the role assigned it, on our new idea of representing, equally, in the one case, in making determinate *what* it is I said, and when things would *be* as thus said, and, in the other, what it is Sid thinks, and when things would be as thought. That role once played, there is no need for playing it anew in fixing those understandings which, as we saw above, are not there to be fixed. (But if Sid thinks the room dark, could it not turn out that whether he thus thinks *correctly* depends on what you understand by *being* correct in so thinking? Of course.)

7. Particular and General

For Frege there is something on which the parochial *must* be silent: *when* (in what particular cases) things would be thus and so. A way for things to be speaks for itself in all such matters. If such speaking is meant to silence the parochial, then for Wittgenstein the idea is incoherent. Here is the key point:

We say 'The order orders *this*—' and do it; but also 'The order orders this: I am to . . .' We translate it at one time into a proposition, at another into a demonstration, and at another into action.

(§459)

Such translation—from something to be done to a case of doing it, from things being such-and-such way to a case of their so being—is blocked where the parochial is so silenced—for reasons Frege himself identifies. The rule following discussion points this out. Wittgenstein is here most deeply Fregean.

There is, Frege notes, something intrinsically general about a thought:

A thought always contains something reaching out beyond the particular case so that this is presented to us as falling under something general.

(Frege 1882b: 189)

Reaching beyond the particular case: a thought true of things as they are might still have been true without things being *just* as they are (in every respect). Nor need things have been just as they are in order for there to have been such a thought at all. If it is true that my cup is empty, it might still have been had it just been drained of different tea. Were it undrained, there would still be the thought that it is empty.

The generality of thoughts is found in a notion of a way for things to be. Being empty is a way for a cup to be. Being fuller than is a way for an ordered pair of cups to be. My cup being empty is a way for *things* to be. My cup being as it is may *be* (or not), its being empty. As I will say, it may *instance* this (or not). Not everything about my cup matters to it, as it is, instancing being empty (whereas everything about it matters to its being as it is). What being empty is, fixes what does matter and how: what is demanded for qualifying as an instance. There is an indefinitely extensible range of cases of what would instance being empty, equally, a range of different ways of being (doing) what a thing thus must.

That my cup is now empty is not a way for things to be. It is the circumstance of things so being. In things being as they are, they are so. There is indefinite variety in the way things could be while so being (that my cup is empty). There is, again, a range of cases. So the generality of a way for things to be (as I will say, of the conceptual) is the generality of thoughts, equally, of that which is so according to them.

'A satisfies (falls under) the concept W' is here just a variant for 'A's being as it is is its being W.' A concept is, intrinsically, of being thus and so. A concept may be satisfied by single items, by ordered pairs, and so on. A zero-place concept is a thought, which is satisfied, or would be, by things being as they are, or were.

There is a class of concepts (the first-order ones) which are satisfied by what is not itself conceptual. The characteristic mark of the non-conceptual (the particular, as I will say) is that there is no *range* of cases of something's being as it is being *it* (much as there is no range of different items, each of which would be Frege on some satisfiable condition).

There is no satisfying the particular. It makes no demands on, so nothing could matter to, so doing. My cup is not a way for things to be. 'Things being as they are is it's my cup' does not so much as express a thought at all. There is, by contrast, such a thing as being my cup. This *is* a way for things to be. To be sure, the only thing that could be that way is my cup. But my cup may do that chipped, in Dublin, and so forth. There is a range of cases here.

What satisfies a concept? In mathematics, one can say, 'an object'. The number 2 satisfies the concept *smallest prime*. In sublunary affairs this will not do. My cup satisfies the concept *empty*. *Now* it does. It is about to cease. Tea is on the way. It is my cup's being as it is now that is its being empty. *This* is what satisfies concepts. Equally for 0–place concepts. It is things being as they are which is its being so that my cup is empty. There is no range of cases of my cup being as it now is. To be that, a thing would need to be *that cup*, as it *now is*. There is just one case of that. So my cup's being as it is, things being as they are, belong to the particular. My cup is the way it is. But that is not a way for *a* thing to be, only a way for my cup now to be. Terminology should not mislead us into misclassifying my cup's being as it is with the conceptual.

In defending his idea of the invisibility of truth-bearers, Frege points to a crucial difference between particular and conceptual. My cup—a particular—is visible. That my cup is empty is not visible on the same understanding of *visible*. For, for my cup to be empty is for things being as they are to belong to a certain range of cases. To see that it is empty, one must recognize the membership. Neither such membership, nor the range thus joined, are visible things. One cannot *see* that to which precisely what would be cases of a cup being empty belong, nor are those other cases themselves in sight. (See Frege (1897; 149), and (1918: 61).)

Frege tells us that the particular's relation to the general in belonging to ranges is the *fundamental* logical relation. In his words,

> The fundamental logical relation is that of an object's falling under a concept: all relations between concepts reduce to it.

(Frege 1892–1895: 128.)

For a way for things to be, or concept, to bear this relation to given particulars is for a generality to reach all the way to the particular case—Wittgenstein's translation from order to action: I am to do such-and-such; I am to do *this* (doing it). A cup's being empty is a cup being empty; *this* is a cup being empty.

The rule-following discussion concerns this fundamental relation. What is it for this to hold? When would it? What might answer these questions? The relation holds between my cup as it now is and its being empty, but not between my cup as it is about to be and its being empty. What is the difference?

The obvious answer: my cup is now empty, but is about not to be. But that is just to say: the relation holds where it holds, and does not where it does not. It does nothing to explain its holding: to say why it is, or how it can be, that the cases of its holding are just the ones they are. (Why, e.g. my cup's being as it is bears it to a cup being empty, while other things do not.) Suppose one answered *that* question by citing some condition *on* its holding: the relation would hold just where that condition was satisfied. Such a condition belongs to the conceptual. How does it translate to instances of *its* satisfaction? We might thus be told when the non-conceptual would relate to the conceptual if we already knew enough as to when it would. That there might be *such* an answer was never in doubt. But it is hard to see how *that* could answer the question posed.

What *is* to be said as to when the fundamental relation holds? We can explain a given instance of its holding in terms of other instances of its holding—my cup is empty if innocent of liquid. Or we may cite *examples* of its holding. But there seems nothing *else* to say. We understand relations within the conceptual in terms of the fundamental relation, falling under. We cannot understand *it* in the same way. But perhaps in no other way either. This fits with Frege's conception of the zero-place case. For things being as they are to fall under the zero-place concept of my cup's (now) being empty is just for it to be true that my cup is empty. Truth, Frege tells us, is indefinable (equivalently, truth is part of the content of *any* judgement). To know when it would be *true* that my cup is empty is just to know when my cup would be empty. But what we wanted to know in the first place is in just what instances this would be so. To know what would fall under *my cup being empty* is to know what the correct transitions are from the conceptual, *my cup being empty*, to the particular cases of what are, or not, its instances. But what is it for given transitions to be the right ones? How *can* there be something to be known here?

I can, it seems, only explain the instancing of the relation by my cup (as it is) and being empty by appeal to other instances of the relation. So perhaps asking for more than this is asking a bad question. Frege says something on these lines for questions as to why a law of logic holds. Such *may* admit of explanation within logic. But it admits of no extra-logical explanation. (See Frege 1893: xviii). In logical matters, there is no such thing as things being other than as logic has them. For, insofar as there were, there would be room for explanation as to why things were *not* otherwise, such explanation being, necessarily, extra-logical.

But if there is no such thing as saying why logic is not otherwise, one *can* say why this is so. Logic (on Frege's conception) unfolds the most general structure of judgement, or truth. What was not so structured would, *ipso facto*, not be judgement, nor truth. Being so structured *belongs* to the concept *judgement*, which we have just understood in terms of the fundamental relation. So there is no such thing as *thought* being otherwise than logic says; but all logic says is how thought must be. (I do not defend this story. What matters here is just its availability.)

Now the thought would be: perhaps there is no saying why the fundamental relation is instanced as it is and not otherwise, in the same way as there is no saying why logic is as it is and not otherwise. We need to work out what this means. But there is at the start a crucial disanalogy. Logic traces relations within the conceptual. It does not speak to, but rather presupposes, the fundamental relation. If, as Frege says, truth is part of every judgement, then knowing when it would be true that my cup is empty is just knowing when my cup would be empty. So when it would be is part of what truth is. But logic is not concerned with that part. What we want to see, then, is whether those same ideas as to there being no such thing as otherwise, which find some application for that part of thought, or truth, which logic does unfold, also apply for that part which it does not.

Logic, conceived so as to fit Frege's story, deals in a certain structure which is *intrinsic* to the conceptual, a certain way in which given bits of the conceptual relate to others. To repeat, relations between bits of the conceptual are understandable in terms of the fundamental relation. It is in terms of such understanding that we can understand what it is for such a relation to hold intrinsically. If Frege's story fits, then this understanding of *intrinsic* will make sense of the relevant idea of there being no such thing as things being otherwise. But we do not have the same means at our disposal for understanding the fundamental relation itself, so nor for understanding what it could be for *it* to have a certain structure *intrinsically*.

This idea has work to do. Take any instance of the fundamental relation holding, or of it not, between some particular and some concept—say, between my cup as it now is and the concept *empty*. If the relation holds, then it is part of what being empty is that my cup's being as it is is so to count. That is *the* correct translation from being empty being such-and-such to its being *this*. Any competing one is a mistake. But there is no saying what makes this so. So that this is correct must be intrinsic to the structure of *falling under*: whatever did not have that feature simply could not be that relation. Similarly for every instance. How to understand that?

The picture is now this. There is no saying why *falling under* has the instances it does (except why it has certain ones given that it has certain others). For it is intrinsic to it to have *precisely* those instances that it does. Since the ordered pair, ⟨*my cup as it now is, being empty*⟩, instances *falling under* just in case my cup as it now is instances *being empty*, the same goes for every concept. It is equally intrinsic to *being empty* to have just the instances it does. All of this is part of the *intrinsic* structure of the relation of the conceptual to the particular. But we do not yet understand what *intrinsic* could mean here. We understand its application within the conceptual because we understand the conceptual in terms of the fundamental relation. We cannot have *that* understanding of it applied to relations between the conceptual and something else. Which leaves us, so far, with no understanding at all.

If my cup's being as it is is its being empty, one *can* rightly say: it is part of what being empty is that *this* particular *is to count* as something being empty. What we want to understand is *what* truth we thus state. The wanted reading cannot plausibly be: anything which did not have just *this* instance would not be being empty. There are two reasons. The first is the point with which the *Investigations* opens. The concept *concept* does not work like that. My cup is at the bottom of the fish tank, along with others. The others are all filled with fish food. Mine is not. Is mine empty? We would still be speaking of *being empty* if we spoke so as to count it as that way, but also if we spoke so as to count it as not that way (water being what it is). It is *not* intrinsic to being empty to be instanced by precisely what may so count. This point points in several directions. Here it makes vivid an understanding on which the conceptual does not relate intrinsically to the particulars which instance it—to *this* being as it happens to be. Whatever we count as its instances, a bit of the conceptual—a way for things to be—does not require just *those* for being the way for things to be it is. That would be a misreading of the correct idea that *this* just is what it *is* for something to be empty.

The second point. My cup might have been full. Had it been, there would, and *could*, not have been that very particular, my cup's being as it is, which in fact bears the falling under relation to being empty. Being empty would still have been the very thing it is. Ten minutes from now my cup will be as it then happens to be. Its being as it then is may *be* its being empty, or, again, may not. What way for a thing to be being empty is will be the same no matter what the outcome. So, again, there being such a thing as being empty, and its being what it is, does not turn on just which instances this turns out to have. That, again, is an understanding on which it is not *intrinsic* to being empty (or to any bit of the conceptual) to have just the instances it does.

What is *intrinsic* to being empty is what would belong to it no matter what its instances happened to be, ways one could *think* it to be while thoughts about any given instance of it were unavailable (while the instance was not available to think of). So it cannot be intrinsic to it to bear the fundamental relation to what might not have been: my cup's being as it now is. *Mutatis mutandis* for the fundamental relation. Nor could it be intrinsic to my cup's being as it now is that things being precisely *that* way bears the fundamental relation to that bit of the conceptual, the cup's being empty, as if were this not so to count, my cup would not be as it now is.

Our aim is to understand (and not to impeach) the transition from what being empty is—being thus and so—to the particular case—my cup, as it will be in ten minutes, being that way, or, again, not. We have found no help in the idea that all instances of the fundamental relation are intrinsic to its structure, thus impervious to explanation. It is hard to see how 'intrinsic' could bear an understanding on which this was both true and an advance in understanding.

This is just to develop Frege's idea. We can understand relations between bits of the conceptual in terms of the fundamental relation—one between particulars and the conceptual. We can thus give sense to the idea (whatever its merits) of such relations holding intrinsically. But we cannot understand the fundamental relation itself in such a way. So nor can we so understand what it would be for *it* to hold intrinsically between such-and-such particular and such-and-such bit of the conceptual. Nor would it accord with our understanding of the conceptual—of *concept*, of *way for things to be*—to equate 'holds intrinsically' with 'just does'. In fact, it is simply obscure what 'intrinsically' could mean here.

One understands *falling under* in grasping, for example, when things would count as my cup being empty; just as one grasps what truth is in grasping such things as how the world decides the correctness of a judgement that a cup is empty. Here the first rule-following discussion (§§84–87) comes into play. I *can* explain (rightly or wrongly) where the post office is by pointing the way. *What* I thus explain—how I say to go—is fixed by how such explanation would be taken by thinkers of the sort we are. As we saw in the previous section, with the parochial thus in operation, I can say, 'The post office is closed' and *mean* it in a certain way, and my meaning can stop nowhere short of the particular case: instances of the fundamental relation. So if one can walk into the building, but the counters are all closed, things being *just* as they thus are can be their being as I meant, or, again, their not. The explanations we give, so the things we say, and mean, are, normally, *for* thinkers like us. This fact shapes how it is they represent things, and so what the correct translations are from 'he meant that/to do . . .' to 'he meant *this*'.

Thus does my meaning stop nowhere short of the facts. (Cf. §95.) But the point now is: *only* with the parochial thus in operation is this so. When would a cup count as being empty? Exactly which instances of a cup being as it was would be it being that? When, that is, would it be the way I just asked about? Which way did I ask about? Now the above point applies. Operating as per the first rule-following discussion, the parochial fixes which way it is I spoke of, or meant. In this it stops nowhere short of fixing that way's participation in the fundamental relation: which instances of things being *thus* are instances of their being that way. Here stopping nowhere *short* is *stopping—nowhere—short*. Whatever the parochial achieves by way of relations between the bit of the conceptual I spoke of and other bits of the *conceptual*, this will not achieve relations between the way I spoke of and bits of the *particular*—those things which instance it. Such is just what it is for the fundamental relation not to be reducible to relations between concepts as relations between concepts are (on Frege's view) reducible to it. Nor is there, operation of the parochial aside, any other way for there to be facts as to how being such-and-such way translates into being, for example, *thus*.

With the parochial at work, it can be correct to say that it is intrinsic to what being empty is that *this* is a cup being empty: things could not be any other way in that respect. For it to count as *true* that the cup is empty may well be for such instancing to count as thus mandated. Not that there is some other mandating than that which the parochial allows for. Nor does this exclude what is sometimes so: that it is intrinsic to what being empty is that *this* is being empty—*only* on a certain understanding of what being empty is.

The parochial reaches all the way from the conceptual to the particular. With that idea properly in place there is no problem as to how rational relations, such as falling under, can have given instances. Our parochial equipment grants us understandings of what it is for the fundamental relation to hold. No others are to be had.

The parochial is precisely that of which one cannot say, 'There is no such thing as things being otherwise.' It is part of *human* thought—thus of human life, of *our* ways of going right or wrong in our projects in, or for, the world. So, it is something psychological—part of how *we are*, not part of how any thinker must be. If the parochial forges transitions from the conceptual to the particular, as just sketched, then, with this in mind, it can seem that:

We are at most under a psychological, not a logical, compulsion. And now it looks quite as if we knew of two kinds of case.

(§140)

Logic does not treat relations between the conceptual and the particular. If logical compulsion is what *logic* must place us under, then there *is* no logical compulsion to count my cup's being as it is as its being empty. But, while one might turn my cup over to see whether it is empty, one would not do so to see whether its being as it is is its being empty. Nor would I pass out questionnaires on trams to see whether I am getting such transitions right. Except insofar as being empty admits of understandings, there are few or no open questions as to what would so count. If I say, truly, that my cup is empty, that is because it does so count. We are rationally compelled, in pursuing the goal truth, to recognize those instances of the fundamental relation which in fact obtain. This remains so even if, for those bits of the conceptual we think in terms of, those instances are what would so count for thinkers such as us. *Our* exposure to risk of error is shaped by what we would, or could, count as error; what might abash us. Still, *you* must count my cup's being as it is as its being empty (where that matters) if you are to reach the goal truth.

If it seems as though there must be some *other* sense in which our hand ought to be forced here—as if we knew of some other kind of compulsion than that just sketched—then we need to recall the fundamental point of this discussion. We understand how there can be compulsion in transitions from one bit of the conceptual to another, an understanding available to us by reference to the fundamental relation. In the case of the fundamental relation itself we cannot understand compulsion in the same way. We do not have the same means available. It is this that casts suspicion on the idea that we *do* know of two kinds of case.

If we were different sorts of thinkers we would speak to, and for, different sorts. That *might* change which ways for things to be we spoke of. We would at least speak on different understandings of things being as we said. What it would be for things to be the ways we thus spoke of, so when the world would bear the fundamental relation to the concepts we thus expressed (deployed as thus deployed), would change accordingly. This does not mean that if we thought differently, my cup might be as it is without being empty. The conceptual that figures in our thought—the ways we think of things as being or not—is *formed* by that thought. It is, for all that, the *conceptual*, relating to the particular, as is the conceptual's prerogative. There is no *other* way of enjoying those prerogatives.

Such is the moral of the rule-following discussion. In drawing out this line of thought in the *Investigations* I have had two morals of my own in mind. First, to understand Wittgenstein, it is always a good idea to think of Frege. Second, and correlatively, the *Investigations* treats the very same problems that concerned Frege. It speaks to his concerns. These morals are for those—both admirers and detractors—who share the view that at some point, probably around the summer of 1930, Wittgenstein had an experience like Saul's fall on the road, or Godard's, thus abandoning philosophy for some new form of self-help. The *Investigations* offers new approaches to problems very much philosophy's.

7

The Proposition's Progress

I will trace the progress of an idea, *proposition*, in Wittgenstein's thought. Caveat: insofar as I discern a finished view, I share it.

What is a proposition? There are three familiar questions here. First, a proposition is the content of a truth-evaluable attitude. It is a way of exposing oneself to risk of error which one escapes or succumbs to *solely* in things being as they are. Which things *are* truth-evaluable? What *can* have its fate decided just in things being as they are? Second, what identifies a given proposition as the one it is? What features identify precisely that form of hostage-giving which it is? Frege's case for *Sinn* (1892a) speaks in one way to this question. Third, how can something which relates to the world as a *proposition* does, be formed from what are a proposition's parts? These may not all be *good* questions. They all concern Wittgenstein.

I will explore his views by tracing a path, in steps, from the *Tractatus* to the *Investigations*. I will focus on one intermediate step, found in *Philosophical Grammar*. It is, importantly, *intermediate*, not yet the *Investigations'* view. It is beset with problems. But it may make clearer in what way the *Investigations* addresses the same problems as the *Tractatus*, and how its very different answers are just what that fixed problematic requires.

The path I will describe was not, in fact, smooth. Old ideas, which do not fit happily into the emerging new view, still exert their force. They disappear and come back, and only with difficulty are eventually abandoned or transformed. Any story of a *path*, such as the one here, must be selective as to what belongs on it and what does not. I oversimplify, as a *reading* of texts such as the *Grammar* must. Another caveat.

Wittgenstein *always* had Frege in mind. One can read the *Investigations* as a reaction *against* Frege. It does depart from his ideas at absolutely crucial points. But it is also important to see how the case for these departures rests on Frege's own ideas. Wittgenstein was deeply Fregean throughout. One can read the *Investigations*—as one might read the *Tractatus*—as simply working out what Frege should have said to be true to his best insights.

1. A Tractarian View

A path needs a starting point—here the *Tractatus*. My account of that point will be minimalist. It leaves *much* unsaid as to what the *Tractatus* view was.

1.1 The essence of representation

The *Tractatus* contains a view of what is essential to representing something as so. (See §§2.12–2.15) As late as January 1930, Wittgenstein expressed that view this way:

> It is the essential feature of a proposition that it is *a picture* and has compositeness.

> (Waismann 1979, p. 90)

A proposition is a particular structuring of particular elements. Each of these elements represents an element of reality (that is, that which the proposition represents as a certain way). The proposition as a whole represents precisely those elements as *so* structured, where 'so structured' means in the very same way as that proposition itself is. A true proposition shares structure with what it represents as so. (I bracket the question what an element might be.)

The structure of a representation is, trivially, representational structure: a structuring of its way of representing something as so. It is a structuring of logical roles: of sub-tasks in the proposition's being true when it would be. What a proposition represents as so—say, that a pig is in the sty—does not represent anything as so (unless we so contrive). So it cannot have representational structure. But, on the view in question, a representational structure is also a structure of a broader sort. To give the broader sort a name, I will call it *conceptual structure*. That a pig is in the sty is (on the *Tractatus* view) also structured in a way instancing conceptual structure. A representation which represents precisely that as so instances the very same conceptual structure as that the pig is in the sty does.

If it is of the essence of representation (as so) to work in this way, then to represent a particular thing—say, that the pig is in the sty—as so, one needs a representation structured in a particular way. Any representation structured otherwise, or out of other elements, necessarily represents something else as so.

1.2 Is the proposition fundamental?

The above story *could* be read as accounting for the unity of the proposition; that is, as answering the third question above. The idea would be: a proposition is composed out of elements, just as a list is. But it is composed by something else which is not an element: a structuring of those elements. This would not represent some further element of reality, but instead would function as described above. Such may or may not have been Wittgenstein's intent. The thought, though, invites comparison with Frege. Frege writes,

> What is distinctive about my conception of logic is that I begin by giving pride of place to the content of the word 'true', and then immediately go on to introduce a thought as that to which the question 'Is it true?' is in principle applicable. So I do not begin with concepts and put them together to form a thought or judgement; I come by the parts of a thought by analysing the thought.

> (Frege posthumous 1919a: 272)

It is because of this primacy of the thought that Frege insisted, repeatedly, that, strictly speaking, something can *be* an element of a thought only relative to an analysis. (See, e.g. (Frege 1892b: 199–200), (Frege 1906: 203).) It is not that to be such-and-such thought just *is* to be constructed of such-and-such elements. A thought has a role: to be true just when such-and-such is so. An analysis of a thought divides that role into different sub-tasks. For such sub-tasks to be *elements* of the thought is just for their joint performance to be performance of the thought's role. There need be no unique path to that goal. Thus the relativity of elementhood to an analysis. For a thought to be true just in case Sid grunts, a sub-task might be: being true or not according to how Sid is. An element would then be that in, or by, which the thought was that way: being about Sid. Such a sub-task could be performed only where another was: being true or not according to whether the right thing(s) was/were *thus and so*. There is no being true or not according to how Sid is without a way Sid thus needs to be. Such is Frege's context principle. On this view of what it is to be an element, there is no intelligible call for explanation as to how elements can form a *proposition*. The proposition is that in terms of which elements are to be identified.

If, by contrast, elements of a proposition call for *structuring* into one, then that structuring *is* an answer to an intelligible question how elements can form one. Here elements are conceived as *naming* bits of reality—what *might* also be named in other contexts, say, a list. Now there is a question by virtue of what some given context in which these elements name what they anyway do is a proposition rather than one of the other sorts of contexts in which they may do their work. The *Tractatus appears* to depart here from what Frege rightly regarded as his most important insight.

In the remark of January 1930, cited above, Wittgenstein also says what it is for a thought to have a structure:

If there were only the proposition 'Φa' but not 'Φb', it would be superfluous to mention 'a'. It would suffice to write just 'Φ'. The proposition would thus not be composite. . . . But does 'Φa' presuppose 'Ψa'? Decidedly yes. For the same considerations tell us: if there were only a single function 'Φ' for 'a' then it would be superfluous; you could leave it out.

(See also Tractatus 3.328.)

Superfluous symbols (or elements) are meaningless. That is the *Tractatus'* Occam's Razor. An element is *not* superfluous only if it marks the place of a proposition in some range of propositions within a given system, marks a respect in which all these different propositions are *the same*. This is what it is for it to *be* an element.

As the *whole* story of being an element, this, like Frege's story, would leave room for multiple analyses of a proposition. So being an element would still be relative to an analysis. For, for all said so far, a given system of propositions might be decomposable in various competing ways into sets of ranges of propositions, each the same in some respect. A given proposition would find itself at the intersection of different subsets of such ranges under different analyses of the system as a whole. So this cannot be the whole *Tractatus* story. On it, something about the system to which a proposition belongs imposes a unique decomposition of that system into those subsets whose members share in common a given element. For, in the *Tractatus*, the *same* proposition cannot be analysable both as composed of elements E and as composed of different elements E⋆. What was composed of E would *ipso facto* represent a different thing as so, than would what was composed of E⋆. If elements need *structuring* into a proposition, and that structure does what the *Tractatus* says it does, then such structure must already be at work in fixing where elements are to be found.

The *Tractatus* thus departs from Frege. In this respect the *Investigations* returns to him. What is most central in Wittgenstein's later philosophy will prove to turn crucially on that return.

2. A First Step Towards *Investigations*

In the *Tractatus*, Wittgenstein tells us that the general form of a proposition is a variable. (6.) This variable is also described as the most general form of truth-function. There is thus a domain over which it ranges: roughly, elementary propositions (whatever they are), and truth-functional combinations of them. The *Grammar* turns on rejecting this idea.

2.1 *The indeterminacy of the notion* proposition

What does the propositional variable range over? The obvious answer would be 'All propositions'. The *Grammar* holds that answer senseless. (See especially sections §79, 80, 82, 122.) For the notion *proposition* leaves it under-determined just which things would count as one. In this respect, one might compare the notion *proposition* with *similar*, or *just like*. Is Tony Blair just like Jacques Chirac? That question makes no sense except in circumstances which fix more as to what is to be understood by being just like. The question 'What propositions are there?' is now cast as in the same boat. Here is a first example of what is to become the rule in later Wittgenstein: a concept does not decide what satisfies it except on some particular way of applying, or deploying, it. There are many ways of thinking of satisfying a given concept, on each of which different things would count as doing so.

In (1929) Wittgenstein portrayed it as a *project*, yet unachieved, to discover what the elementary propositions, thereby what propositions *überhaupt*, there are. The project would be philosophical; on the *Tractatus* view it could not be empirical. He quickly abandoned that view. In the *Grammar*, the notion *proposition* does not tell us what to look for to see what propositions there are, so nor what elementary propositions there are—any more than the notion *alike* tells us what to look for to see whether Chirac and Blair are alike. The *Grammar* also suggests that, in the same way, the notion *elementary*, if coherent, does not on its own tell us what to look for to see which propositions are elementary. (Part I, appendix 4.) Wittgenstein was later (9 December 1931) to call the idea of *discovering* elementary propositions 'arrogant', and something 'much more dangerous':

> I used to believe . . . that it is the task of logical analysis to discover the elementary propositions. I wrote, 'We are unable to specify the form of elementary propositions' . . . Yet I did think that the elementary propositions could be specified at a later date. Only in recent years have I broken away from that mistake.

> (Waismann, 1979: 182)

More generally, to see which things count as propositions one needs more of an understanding of what it is to be to count as one—for purposes of the question raised—than the notion *proposition* itself provides.

If I say, 'Blair is just like Chirac', and have said something to be so, it will usually be circumstance that has added the needed content. This is not the *Grammar*'s story. Before telling it, a remark. To lack the content to determine an extension is not to lack content altogether. There is something being the same is, independent of particular understandings of it. There is plenty to say as to what a proposition is, short of saying anything that fixes an extension for that term. Propositions are the contents of truth-evaluable attitudes. This points to the kind of answer later Wittgenstein will give to the first of the three questions with which we began.

2.2 *It is a language that gives the notion* proposition *determinacy*

That is the *Grammar* story. Each language is a different unfolding of the notion *proposition*. A proposition is, by definition, a way of being hostage to the world; a particular way in which it can be for the world alone to decide whether a certain attitude (judging something) has achieved its aim (truth). In telling us which things in it are propositions, a language tells us that there are such-and-such ways for the world to exercise such authority. In the *Grammar* there is at most one constraint on what a language may thus say: if it is to tell us anything, it must speak coherently. Which *may* mean that it cannot, for example, give content to *proposition* on which a proposition and its negation can both be true. But if there is such a constraint, it remains to say just what sort of constraint this is.

The grammar of a language says what its propositions are, in saying how each proposition in it works—what rules govern it (though such rules need not be explicit). For a proposition to function as it thus does is for it to have the sense it does.

The role of a sentence in the calculus is its sense.... It is only in a language that something is a proposition.... A proposition is *one* combination of signs among a number of possible ones, and as opposed to other possible ones. As it were *one* position of an indicator as opposed to other possible ones.

(1974: §84)

The language might, for example, provide an item 'This is red', which occupies a certain position in a system also containing 'This is yellow', 'This is blue'. For it to occupy that position might be, in part, for its correct application to exclude correct applications of those other items. In the *Tractatus* a proposition was not a string of words, but something more abstract: the namings of given things, structured (logically, not spatially) in a given way. *Words* which did such naming, presented as so structured, might themselves be (spatially) ordered how-ever you like. If a language determines what *its* propositions are, then, naturally enough, propositions are much closer to linguistic items. On the other hand, and by the same token, a proposition is no longer under any obligation to be a *picture* of reality in the way a Tractarian proposition must be. Its sense is its role in the language. Being a picture is no longer of the essence of representing as so.

It takes a language to give *proposition* enough determinacy to have an extension. So there are many different specific forms such determinacy might take. There are as many forms as there are possible languages: indefinitely many. As Wittgenstein puts it

'Language' is only languages, plus things I invent by analogy with existing languages. Languages *are* systems.

(1974: §122)

As he later put it, it does not take a logician to tell us what a 'real' proposition looks like. A proposition is just whatever something *we* would call a language makes a proposition. Bracketing coherence, there is nothing beyond this which could decide whether a language is telling us *correctly* what things are propositions. Nor are there any constraints on what the 'logical form' of a proposition might be, beyond the constraints on what the grammar of what we recognized as language might be. Perhaps this is commentary on Frege's idea of 'separating a thought from its trappings' (Frege: 1897). There is also here the germ of a need for a step beyond the *Grammar*—the final step to the *Investigations*.

2.3 Unfolding Truth

The notions *truth* and *proposition* form a package. One grasps either only in grasping both. Truth is a certain kind of success which it is the world's prerogative to grant or withhold from us. A proposition identifies a specific way for the world to grant or withhold it. One set of core properties of truth is unfolded, Frege tells us, in the laws of truth (logical truths). These fix the most general structure of the commitment one makes in allegiance to a proposition. For example, for each proposition there is another, true just when it is false. Allegiance to the first commits one to rejection of the second.

   If *truth* and *proposition* form this sort of packet, and there are indefinitely many unfoldings of the concept *proposition*, then, one would expect, there are also indefinitely many unfoldings of the concept *truth*. The *Grammar* is explicit on that point:

One can't of course say that a proposition is whatever one can predicate 'true' or 'false' of, as if one could put symbols together with the words 'true' and 'false' by way of experiment to see whether the result makes sense. For something could only be decided by this experiment if 'true' and 'false' already have definite meanings, and they can only have that if the contexts in which they can occur are already settled.

(1974: §79)

Frege tells us that the concept truth is unfolded in the laws of truth (or of logic). Wittgenstein is not here supposing that a language could be an exception to those laws—as if one could think, or operate, correctly according to the grammar of some language, but in violation of them. So he is not envisioning alternative unfoldings to those the laws of logic give. What alternatives *are* envisioned here?

The answer: the laws of logic are no more than half an unfolding of the notion *truth*. The other half emerges if we consider a notion of a way things might be or not—red, say. A *proposition* to the effect that Pia's dress is red would be something over whose success or failure (as a judgement) things being as they are may exercise its unique authority: things being as they are may *be* things being as they are according to that proposition; her dress being as it is, may instance a dress being red. Now consider what I might say, viewing the setting sun from my Hackney balcony, in saying the sun to be red. Do I express a proposition? If so, then, again, things being as they are may exercise its authority over that proposition's success or failure. But for purposes of that proposition (if such it be), the colour of the sun could not be independent of the conditions of its viewing—certainly not as the colour of Pia's dress is. The sun's being as I said in calling it red (if there is such a thing) would not suggest, as Pia's dress being red might, that it looks red independent of from where viewed. If Pia's dress is red, you need not be in Hackney to see it so looking. You would be equally placed to do that in Gravelines, if the dress were on view there. Not so the sun. So *could* things being as they are—inter alia, the sun's looking all the ways it does on all the ways in which it is on view—add up to things being as they are according to a proposition, such as I would have expressed on my Hackney balcony, to the effect that the sun is red? Would such a proposition really be a way for the world to exercise the authority it must over any proposition? Such is a question about truth—about what may *be* true or false—but not one which logic speaks to. It is an instance of that other half of truth's content. In the *Grammar*, it is a question for a language to speak to. Nothing not part of the language can dictate which way a language *must* decide it.

Frege tells us that the fundamental logical relation is that of an object falling under a concept. All others, he says, reduce to that (1892–1895: 128). We can generalize thus: the fundamental relation is between the non-conceptual and the conceptual—between things being as they are (or a thing as it is) and their (or it) being such-and-such way. Logic is silent as to which *are* the instances of being such-and-such way. It says little as to when there *is* a way to instance. It says no more than this: there is such a way only when there is another, such that the first is instanced precisely when the second is not. Things being as they are makes for success (truth) in representing things as the first way, precisely when it makes for failure (falsehood) in representing them as the second (and vice versa). For there to be something to instance, there must be such a thing as things (being as they are) instancing it, and (or) their not. *Perhaps* things must often enough do the one thing or the other (though *logic* does not so dictate). But as to how, and when, these conditions may be met—what a way might be of sorting instances from non—logic is silent. The *Grammar* point is: this is a matter for a language to decide for itself: where logic does not dictate to it, nothing else does.

It is a *fact* that the sun setting over Hackney is red; but not a fact that white chocolate tastes best. *De gustibus* and all that. So one might be inclined to say. But, the *Grammar* tells us, one *can* say such things only with reference to some given language. A *language* makes the one thing but not the other a proposition—*in it*. The notion *proposition*, so the notion *true*, do not, on their own, decide such things. Thus it is for nothing outside language to settle what engages with truth. As Wittgenstein recognizes, this can be an unsettling idea. The examples Wittgenstein has in mind are not quite like the contrast between taking the sun to be red and holding white chocolate to taste better than dark. They lead more directly to the most fundamental issues.

2.4 *The arbitrariness of grammar*

As things now stand, a language unfolds the notions *proposition* and *truth*. In one way among indefinitely many it adds enough content to these notions for there to be an extension for 'is a proposition' and for 'is either true or false'. Its grammar provides this content. Still bracketing conflict between grammar and logic, there is no perspective from outside a language from which its grammar is criticizable. With the proviso, grammars are not liable to be *wrong*—in conflict with the notion *proposition*. For, again on the proviso, that notion as such does not have enough content to support any such criticism. Grammars are, in this sense, arbitrary.

Wittgenstein worries about the arbitrariness of grammar. For grammar, so construed, connects with possibility. Bracketing the necessary, a proposition divides ways things might be into two disjoint, non-empty, classes: cases where things are as they are according to the proposition, and cases where things are otherwise. So if the proposition is that P, then there is the possibility that P, and the possibility that not. For the necessarily true (or false), there is at least one of these possibilities. But a grammar may tell us all sorts of things. If it thus tells us that such-and-such is *possible*—that there is such a thing as things being thus and so—is there really no position from outside it from which it can be decided whether it is right or wrong in this? Is such a grammar really not committed to anything determinately right or wrong independent of what it says? Is there really no such thing as a *proposition*, not referring to a language, that such-and-such is possible?

As Wittgenstein expresses the worry (in the *Grammar* and in the *Investigations*),

> If a proposition is conceived as a picture of the state of affairs it describes and a
> proposition is said to show just how things stand if it's true, and thus to show the
> possibility of the asserted state of affairs, still the most that the proposition can do is what
> a painting or relief does: and so it can at any rate not set forth what is just not the case.

> (1974:82, cf. 1953: 520)

A proposition shows the asserted state of affairs as possible, so as a possibility. If
the grammar tells us that, possibly, white chocolate really *is* best, then possibly it
is. So in telling us what propositions there are (on its understanding of a
proposition), a grammar tells us that certain things are possible. But if what a
proposition is is up to a grammar, or language, to decide, thus arbitrary, can
what is *possible* be arbitrary? Suppose a grammar tells us, in this way, that things
may be both red and green in the same place. Is this then possible? Surely what
such a grammar told us would be criticizable from without.

If a grammar is thus responsible to something outside it—if it can go right
or wrong as to what things are propositions—that is to say that there must be a
certain harmony between thought, or language, and the world if thought is to
be about the world at all; and that such harmony is a *substantial* requirement,
one a would-be proposition might fail. A version of this idea is reported in Lee
and King's notes of Wittgenstein's Cambridge lectures in Lent term 1930:

> But in order that propositions may be able to represent at all something further is needed
> which is the same both in language and reality. For example, a picture can represent a
> scene rightly or wrongly; but both in picture and scene pictured there will be colour and
> light and shade.

> (1980: 10)

But this is not the *Grammar* view. There Wittgenstein says two things. First, if a
grammar merely tells us that there are propositions that something is red and
green at the same spot, which are contingently either true or false, it has so far
told us nothing about how to operate with those propositions—when these
things are to count as true, when false, how they are to interact, for example,
inferentially, with others. So far, then, the grammar is not determinate enough
to count as having specified, or provided, any propositions at all.

The second thing Wittgenstein tells us is this:

> A construction may have a superficial resemblance to . . . an empirical proposition and
> play a somewhat similar role in a calculus without having an analogous application; and
> if it hasn't we won't be inclined to call it a proposition.

> (1974: §82)

A more perspicuous version of the point I want to focus on here is in the *Investigations* continuation of that passage beginning, 'If a proposition is conceived as a picture . . .':

It is not every sentence-like formation that we know how to do something with, not every technique has an application in our life.

(1953: §520)

So there is, after all, one sort of criticism that can be made of a grammar: what it presents as propositions are not things *we* are able to treat as propositions. A grammar can go wrong in that sense. This is the only sense Wittgenstein provides for the idea that a grammar may go wrong (still bracketing our proviso).

Note the crucial reference to *us*. Who the 'us' is may be somewhat negotiable. But something on the order of we humans: *not*, in any event, we thinkers. For where what a grammar may and may not do is fixed by what it is to be a thinker at all—by, as Frege puts it, 'The Mind, not minds' (Frege 1918: 74)—there *is* an external standpoint from which grammar is subject to criticism in just the way Wittgenstein says it is not. The grammar proposes such-and-such as a proposition. The question is then whether it is consistent with what thinking is *as such* that this should be allowed as a proposition. '*We* cannot treat that something is red and green at the same spot as a proposition', so reading 'we', then becomes, 'it is inconsistent with what thought is *as such* that this should count as a proposition'. So this is inconsistent, full stop, with the notion *proposition*. But this is precisely what was not supposed to be the case. That it is not is *the* main departure, in the *Grammar*, from the *Tractatus*.

So the point needs to be about an entirely parochial form of thought. We are thinkers of a particular kind, equipped by our nature with certain sensitivities, equipped to treat the world, in thought and deed, in certain ways. For thinkers *like us*, the proposition so far on offer, to the effect that something is red and green at the same spot, cannot, perhaps, be treated as a proposition. It is not one for us, by our lights. That, and nothing else, makes it correct, where it *is* correct, for us to say that what is on offer is not a proposition. It is *not* a possibility that something is red and green at the same spot. Insofar as there is something true to be said in saying this, we, a parochial form of thinker, are in some such way the measure of *what* it is true thus to say.

It can easily seem worrying to assign the parochial such work. Much of the *Investigations* is concerned with *why* this should seem worrying, and whether it really is.

2.5 A caveat

With Wittgenstein I have spoken of a grammar as telling us that it is possible that something is red and green in one place: it fixes a contingent proposition to that effect. This can seem to be putting things wrongly. This can introduce another conception of how it is that, in present matters, a grammar cannot be mistaken. I will explore it briefly.

On the alternative conception, my talk of being red and green at one spot was loose talk. What I should have said is this: the grammar provides a contingent proposition to the effect that an object is simultaneously a certain way, and a certain other way, at one spot. By virtue, perhaps, of other things it tells us, I have identified those ways as being red and being green. But perhaps wrongly. For, if the grammar has told us what it has, the thought would go, then for an object to be the first way in question is for it to be a way it might be, at a spot, while also being, there, the second way, and vice versa. To speak of ways for a thing to be of which this was not so would simply be not to speak of the ways the grammar specifies. So if this is not so of being red and being green, then the grammar was not speaking of red and green. A grammar cannot be *wrong* in what it tells us, because anything of which it was wrong would *ipso facto* not be what it was speaking of.

This is an incorrect idea, perhaps flirted with occasionally in the '30s, but definitely out of the picture in the *Investigations*. One development of a Tractarian idea might tempt one to it. That Tractarian idea is that there is no outer boundary around thought, or propositions:

We cannot . . . . . say in logic: This and this there is in the world, that there is not.

For that would apparently presuppose that we exclude certain possibilities, and this cannot be the case since otherwise logic must get outside the limits of the world: as if it could consider these limits from the other side also.

What we cannot think, we cannot think: thus we cannot *say* what it is we cannot think.

(1922: 5.61)

To think of thinkables (propositions) as inside a boundary, we would have to think of there being something on the other side of it. So we would have to be able to say what this might be. But this, of course, we cannot do. (If this is a problem, it is also one for our being able to think of ourselves as parochial thinkers, which can also be a way of seeing what is wrong with the idea.)

In the early '30s, a descendant of this idea returns as follows:

Can we give a description which will justify the rules of grammar? Can we say why we must use *these* rules? Our justification could only take the form of saying 'As reality is so and so, the rules must be such-and-such'. But this presupposes that I could say 'If reality were otherwise, then the rules of grammar would be otherwise'. But in order to describe a reality in which grammar was otherwise I would have to use the very combinations which grammar forbids. The rules of grammar distinguish sense and nonsense and if I use the forbidden combinations I talk nonsense.

(1980: 47)

So it is not that the notion *proposition* lacks the determinacy that might place a grammar's proposals within or without its extension, but rather that there is no saying a grammar to be wrong without lapsing into nonsense.

This idea meshes with that idea, occasionally floated in the early '30s, that to change grammar is to change topic. If a grammar provides for the possible truth of 'It's red and green just *there*', then what this could not be true of would not be what *those* words 'red' and 'green' spoke of—so not of red and green if what they are rules out such possibility.

The *Investigations* will show why these are bad ideas. Meanwhile, though, there is the following consideration. On the *Grammar* view, what a grammar may do is limited at most only by what logic dictates. It must be consistent; provide *consistently* for propositions. Suppose a grammar tells us that there is a contingent proposition, 'X is both A and B at the same spot', and, further, that 'X is A' is to speak of X being red, 'X is B' of X being green. It thus stipulates that it is *red* and *green* that the relevant propositions speak of. Why can it not do so? Logic does not forbid this. It is no principle of *logic* that something cannot be red and green at the same spot. Something extra-logical must prohibit *ever* taking being red and being green to be what might so behave. But *that* sort of criticism of grammar is just what there cannot be on the *Grammar* view.

So Wittgenstein is right to put the problem, as he does, as one of what goes wrong, or how anything could possibly go wrong, if a grammar tells us that something might be *red* and *green* at the same spot. And the only available answer seems to make reference to thinkers like *us,* and *our* capacities to think of things. We are now almost ready for the last step to the *Investigations*. But we need first to see what forces us out of the *Grammar*.

2.6 *Logical form*

Wittgenstein's earliest mention of Diderot may be October 27 1930:

A French politician once said that French was the most perfect language because in French sentences the words followed exactly the sequence of the thought. The fallacy here is to think that there are, as it were, two series, a thought series . . . and a words series, with some relation between them. A further fallacy is to suppose that 'thinking a proposition' means thinking its terms in a certain order.

(1980: 16)

Other occasions were *Grammar* §66 and *Investigations* §336. (See Chomsky 1965 for the relevant bits of Diderot.)

Suppose that in speaking English we express thoughts. Or even that (as the *Grammar* has it) English sentences are expressions of thoughts (or are propositions). Suppose that a *thought* is something essentially structured: built up from given parts in a given way (as per the *Tractatus*). Then an English sentence has three different sorts of structure, each defined by a different goal. There is, first, ordinary English syntactic structure. This is a device for building indefinitely many sentences from a *much* smaller number of parts. Mastering the syntax makes English sentences recognizable to us as such, even if never seen before. That is the goal of syntax. A language chooses one means among many possible for achieving this. There is considerable freedom of choice. Second, there is semantic structure: the way in which, in the language, the meaning of a whole expression depends on the meanings of its verbal parts. Syntax shapes what semantic structure must be. Suppose, now, that the sentence 'Sid grunts' expresses the thought that Sid grunts. On the *Tractatus* view, there is a structure (conceptual structure) essential to that thought. So English must assign that sentence that structure too. The structure in question is determined by what is so according to the thought expressed: that such-and-such things are *so* structured. For all of this the *semantic* structure of that sentence might be any of many things, depending on what English syntax is. That semantic structure might be isomorphic with the conceptual structure. Or, so far as the goals of syntax go, might be arbitrarily far from it. Thus Diderot's idea: in French, as it happens, semantic structure mirrors conceptual structure exactly. In other languages, perhaps not. It is this idea that Wittgenstein now mocks. To mock it is to reject his own Tractarian conception of what representing (as so) is.

On the *Tractatus* view, discovering conceptual structure is a project for analysis. Wittgenstein later confessed that he took Russell's method, as applied to definite descriptions, as the model of analysis. (See *Grammar*, part 1, appendix 4.) Russell deliberately ignored (ordinary) syntax, which he thought could be misleading. His central question was when given words would be *true*. That conception of analysis unfolds, in Wittgenstein, into the above idea, now rejected, of a triple of distinct structures—structurings of different things to meet different goals.

In the *Grammar*, a language embodies but two structures: an ordinary syntax, and a grammar. Grammar is here a more general affair than mere semantic structure. It gives rules for use. Such rules may operate entirely within the conceptual ('If it's red, then it isn't green'). Perhaps Wittgenstein also thought of them as connecting the conceptual to the non-conceptual ('*This*, e.g. (that lawn) is green.') Grammar makes an expression 'one position of an indicator, among others'. And the now crucial point is: the grammar of a language is as proprietary as its syntax. It represents *one* way, among others, of going about representing things as so, just as a syntax represents one way, among others, of making a large set of sentences recognizable to speakers.

Just here lies a problem. Pia and I are at the *Terminus du Nord*. The waiter announces, 'Les oursins sont arrivés.' Pia speaks no French. Can I tell her what he said? I would be inclined to say, 'The sea urchins have arrived.' *Does* this tell her what he said? The waiter expressed a proposition. That quoted English sentence does too. But, according to the *Grammar*, it is for a language to say what its propositions are. 'Les oursins sont arrivés' is, or expresses, a proposition in French. 'The sea urchins have arrived' expresses what is one in English. The notion *proposition*, aside from its application in a particular language, lacks content that might fix which things are propositions. So this leaves it undefined what it might be for a French proposition to be the *same* as an English one. No such notion of *the same* is yet available. It is undefined, that is, what saying the same thing inter-linguistically might be. Which shows that the *Grammar* is not quite the right thing to which to assign that role which the *Grammar* assigns it. This paves the way for our final step to the *Investigations*.

For Frege, a law of logic is a *thought*, so (since a law) true. It is as general as a thought could be. So it mentions nothing, not even thoughts. It has nothing but structure to make it true. How, then, can such a law speak to thoughts—saying how they are related inferentially? The idea, in brief, is that that structure which identifies the law reflects the most general structure of a system of thoughts to which the law belongs. Thoughts which are related inferentially thereby belong to a system. (And, for Frege, any two thoughts are related inferentially—e.g. from them their conjunction follows.) Their inferential relations are a part of the most general structure of the system they help form. A law identifies those relations in reflecting the structure of that system, to which it, too, belongs.

This conception of logic does not fit with the *Grammar* view. On that view, for a proposition to belong to a system is just for it to belong to a language. Any other proposition which cohabits the system with it, and which, in its structure reflects the structure of that system, would just be another proposition of that *language*. A law of logic, as Frege conceives it, is not a piece of French and German. There is no such thing as French logic, German logic, etc. A law of logic speaks to all propositions. Conceiving such a law as Frege does, there is, the *Grammar* tells us, no such thing as doing this.

Such need not be a *problem* for the *Grammar*. After all, its starting point was the idea that the notion *proposition* is not well enough defined for there to be such a thing as all propositions. What we do not yet have, though, is any alternative, non-Fregean, conception of what logic might be. This, too, is something the *Investigations* aims to provide.

3. The Final Step

We begin now on the *Investigations* view. The crucial final step is this: the role the *Grammar* assigns a language is now assigned to a language game (a notion hinted at in *Grammar* §36). This is not yet to say much. It remains to say what a language game is.

On the *Grammar* view, the notions *proposition* and *truth* admit of an indefinite variety of different understandings, where what they would apply to varies accordingly. In the *Investigations* the same goes for *any* notion. Language games will show us how.

The role of the parochial will also now expand, or come into greater prominence. In the *Grammar*, insofar as a language could go wrong in presenting such-and-such as a proposition, its going wrong would consist in the fact that it so presented something which *we* could not treat as a proposition. The problem with which the last section ended was: What would it be for the *same* proposition (or thought) to have been expressed, say, in English and in French? The form this answer will now take is this: there were two expressions of the same proposition—two instances of saying the same thing—where that is what we are prepared to recognize—as we might well be for what the waiter said and my translation at the *Terminus du Nord*. This illustrates and adumbrates the role the parochial will now assume. Such addresses the second of our initial questions. But the same idea operates in the *Investigations*' response to the first: When is something a *proposition*—the content of a judgement, something truth-evaluable? The main locus of this response is §136.

The *Tractatus* gave a picture of the essence of representing. So does the *Investigations*, though it may seem odd to say so. The *Investigations* opens with that picture. Our first task will be to extract it.

3.1 The proposition as fundamental

Frege begins with propositions (thoughts), not with smaller units out of which propositions may be built. So *being* a given proposition is not the same thing as being built, in such-and-such way, of such-and-such smaller units—just as, now, being a given proposition had better not be the same thing as being such-and-such bit of such-and-such language. *Investigations* Wittgenstein shares Frege's view of the primacy of the whole (the whole attitude, or, at the opening of the *Investigations*, the whole speech act). But then, by what *is* a given proposition, or whole, identified as the one it is?

A proposition is the content of a judgement. Frege tells us (1918): to judge is to expose oneself to risk of error. Wittgenstein's answer could start from this. We are all, constantly, exposed to risk of error; each of us, at a time, in all the ways he then is. I am in for a come-uppance if today's meeting is not in Stewart House. I will find myself standing in an empty room, counter to my expectations. Your plans, perhaps, will also go awry if there is no meeting there, but perhaps differently—as it may be, the circulars you have left there will be all for nought. Judging that the meeting will be in Stewart House is *a* way to expose *oneself* to error. It is, here, an element in my exposure to risk, and in yours. It is something we share in common: both our exposures so decompose. Now we can adapt Wittgenstein's 1930 point about elements of a proposition (in its weaker Fregean form): to say that something is an element in an exposure to risk is to say that there is a *range* of exposures to error which are the same in a certain respect. So to say that I think the meeting is in Stewart House is to say that there is an identifiable shape for an exposure to error to have, which is recognizable in my exposure, and would be recognizable in the exposures of a certain range of other thinkers at other times; something for different exposures to share in common. The proposition is then identified by what would be, recognizably, *someone's* being exposed to risk in this particular way. (This shareability of judgement—a point Frege insists on—already eliminates the possibility of private language.)

One risks error (as Frege also insists) in one's dealings with what there is for *one* to meet with, notably with things in that environment we cohabit. It is in those dealings that the shape of thinking such-and-such is found. What we judge is what can matter to what to do—how to treat things. Wittgenstein exploits this point.

3.2 'Im Anfang war die Tat'

Faust, translating the Bible's first line, was unimpressed by words. Power would be closer to a beginning. Its exercise—the act—would be closer still. Wittgenstein approved: action is the foundation of representation; representation is, essentially, by, and for, agents. A language game is a device—an artificial one—which we can use to connect content and action explicitly. For this, we can take such a game to be fixed entirely by how it is to be played, which, further, we can think of as fixed by explicit rules. For a given game there are the moves to be made in playing it. For each of these, there are the rules which govern it. Rules govern *whole* moves. So these are the basic units of the game, just as, for Frege, the proposition is basic for logic.

We can divide the rules governing a move into introduction and elimination rules. Introduction rules say when a move may be made; elimination rules what follows from its correct making—notably, what then is to be, or may be, done. As it may be, if, in the game, I say, 'My glass is empty', the elimination rule for that specifies that you are to fill my glass.

A language game can thus model particular connections between content and action. The content of given words 'My glass is empty' may consist, in part, in the way my glass is if they are correct; but also in part in what is to be done: you are to fill it. If in this first aspect a proposition is a picture of reality, this second suggests something else for it to be. In the *Grammar* Wittgenstein says,

> The role of a sentence in the calculus is its sense.
>
> (§84)

So a proposition might be identified by its role—by how it is eliminated, how to be acted on—rather than by the picture it provides. A language game furnishes a reading for this thought.

3.3 *The fundamental point: names and content*

The *Investigations* begins by using the notion *language game* to make a specific point as to what representing is. It is as follows.

Suppose a language game contains a move, 'My glass is empty.' What do that move's parts name? Following Frege, something *is* a part of this move only relative to an analysis. Further, to be a part is to play a logical role: to perform a subtask which, together with those performed by the move's other elements (on the relevant analysis), adds up to doing what the whole move does. We could say that 'My glass' was an element, and named my glass, if the correctness of the whole depended in some way on how my glass was (or, in the game, was to be treated)—if we then said suitable things as to what the remainder of that move did. Or, again, we could say this if the whole move required, or licensed, certain further moves (verbal or not), and if whether a move was what was thus licensed or required depended on how it related to, or treated, my glass. Similarly we could say that 'is empty' was an element and named being empty—that certain way for a glass to be—if the correctness of the move depended on something or other being empty, or if whether a further (putative) move was licensed or required by it turned on the credentials as a response to the thing(s) in question being empty.

In the opening part of the *Investigations* Wittgenstein takes over this much of Frege's view: there is nothing other than what the whole move does—hence nothing other than how the game is to be played (so, on our present idealization, its rules)—to determine what, in a move, names at all, and what any such thing does name. (See §10.) Saying that such-and-such is a part of a move and names such-and-such is nothing other than another way of saying part of what the rules of the whole game say as to what the move in question does.

Suppose, then, that 'My glass is empty' is a move in a game, such that 'My glass', in it, names a certain glass, and 'is empty' names (speaks of) being empty, *and* that the whole says my glass to be that way. Do these facts determine how that whole is to be treated? Of course not. What said a glass to be that way might require or license any of an indefinite variety of further moves, depending on the game. Do they determine when the move would be *correct* as to what it thus said (as to how my glass was)? Wittgenstein's answer is, 'No. Just as little as they determine how that whole is to be treated.' To see this consider two games, each containing such a move. In the one, saying 'My glass is empty' licenses you in opening the champagne. The move is correct only if my glass stands ready (or at least is in condition) to receive the bottle's upward welling contents. In the other, the move requires you to refill my glass with pellets of fish food, and is correct only where my glass requires such refilling. Suppose that, in both cases, my glass lies at the bottom of the fish tank, immersed in water. Then the move, as a move in the first game, was incorrect, as a move in the second was correct. Yet in both cases parts may be identified as suggested, and in both 'is empty' can be said to name (speak of) being empty. Being devoid of fish food *can* count as being empty for what deems being filled with it, the water it is immersed in notwithstanding. There are just various ways of speaking of a glass being empty, various language games accordingly. *What parts name, within a given whole, does not, as such, determine when that whole would be correct.* Where correctness would be truth, what parts name determines no unique truth condition. This goes for parts which name such things as my glass and being empty. The moral of the first part of the *Investigations* is that it goes for words which speak of any determinate way things may be or not (or any admitting of novel instances). Language games are but a convenient device for making this point.

Perhaps Frege is, unusually, a foil here. The culprit is captured in his idea (1891) that a concept is a function from objects to truth values (though this *is* a culprit only on a certain reading of that 'is'). Suppose that in 'Sid snores', 'Sid' names Sid, and 'snores' names being a snorer—thus, a function from objects to truth-values. Then the whole names the value of that function for the argument Sid. What these parts name thus does determine just when that whole would be true. The first point in the *Investigations* is that sense does not work like that. One must then explore *why* Frege spoke as if it did.

3.4 Languages

A move in a language game is made correctly or not. For a part of the move to name such-and-such would be for it to make some specific contribution to when the move would be correct. English is not a game. Nor are its sentences correct or not per se. As we have just seen, 'My glass is empty' may be used to say different things, correct under different conditions, of a given glass. English asserts nothing. So nor do its sentences, unless spoken. When spoken, a sentence may say any of many things. So, on a Fregean account of what it is for something to be named, no bit of English names anything. Nor will a Fregean account of *being* a part apply here. Intuitively, though, English sentences *have* parts, which name, or speak of, things. What sense is to be made of this?

The key is aspect. There is a switch on my wall which operates the dryer. This does not make me worry about what it is up to while I am away. It is *flipping* the switch that does the work. The English 'is on the rug' speaks of being on a rug, in something like the way the switch operates the dryer. There is something 'is on the rug' is *for* in speaking English. Use it speaking English, and so as to say something, and there is something you will thus speak of: being on a then-given rug. What precise contribution this made to what you thus said remains to be negotiated (the *Investigations'* opening point) thus depends on the occasion. In this sense, so in this aspect of 'speak', 'is on the rug' speaks of being on a rug.

There are indefinitely many different language games with moves in which 'is on the rug' speaks of being on the rug; in each of which, in so doing, it makes a different contribution to the proper treatment of the whole of which it is thus a part. Different such moves would be correct under different conditions, so on a different condition. The English 'is on the rug' is no more bound, by its role in English, to contribute to some one such condition than to contribute to any other. In meaning what it does, it is equally eligible to contribute to any. If this were not so, it would not speak of being on a rug, but rather of, say, being 'on' a rug, on some particular special understanding of 'on'. *It* speaks of being on a rug on a different understanding of *speaking* than that on which Pia is now speaking of this.

3.5 *Language games and what is said*

Language games link content to action. What one may do, or is to do, can be, in them, part of what it is for things to be as said. Propositions carve up exposures to risk of error in a particular way, confer particular understandings on *exposed in the same way*. Language games carve up such risk by their rules. There is the risk one runs, in taking wine to be on the rug, where wine on the rug would call for salt, and the different risk one runs where wine on the rug would call for a corkscrew. There is something one might think which would be running the one risk and not the other. They thus show how, *pace* Frege (on a reading), facts as to what parts name do not determine correctness conditions uniquely. This leads to a second departure from Frege.

What is the relation between saying something, in English, in saying, 'My glass is empty'—and playing a language game? *Not* that to speak of a glass as empty is to play such-and-such game. Wittgenstein stresses that language games are 'objects of comparison'. (See §§81, 130, 131.) Where I say 'My glass is empty', I may have said what would be so just where, or only where, those words would be a correct move in certain language games. Such games would be one sort of object of comparison. We could use 'play' so as to speak of me as playing them.

Pia says, 'My glass is empty.' Sid, abashed, reaches for the wine. But the glass is in the sink, immersed in soapy water. Are things as Pia said? To say which language games she was playing, on our present use of 'play', would be to answer that. Things are as she said if they are such as to make so speaking correct in those games—if things being as they are licensed introducing those words there. There *are* games in which such a move *is* correctly introduced. There are others in which it is not. In some it will do for Pia to have finished her wine. In others her glass must await a refill. A glass being empty admits of different understandings. Which games (if either sort) Pia played is a question of for what she is to be held responsible, to what she is hostage for things being as she said— whether, for example, to her glass being refillable. How is responsibility assigned?

A game's elimination rules say how a move must, or may, be responded to; its introduction rules under what circumstances it is correctly made. If a game has an object, then its elimination rules may show things as to what its introduction rules ought to be—if it is not to be just stupid, or pointless, or senseless. If, say, 'My glass is empty' is eliminated by a refill, then (depending on what the game pretends to be), it may be just stupid or senseless to allow that move unless the relevant glass is, in fact, fillable. It may take a certain sort of introduction rule for given elimination rules to make sense. This models something central to assigning responsibility to those who say things.

Where Pia said to Sid, 'My glass is empty', one would have supposed, in the circumstances, there was a certain point to doing so. *One* would have supposed: such was *to be* supposed. It may be part of what one would have supposed the point to be that reaching for the bottle was, *ceteris paribus*, responding as called for, or at least licensed. (To know what was in fact so, one would have to know Pia, Sid, and the course of the evening, better.) *If* this is so, then (again *ceteris paribus*) it would have been stupid, not sensible, *then* to say 'My glass is empty' unless the glass was then apt for filling. It would be stupid to allow such a move in a game with such elimination rules and with a certain object. This is to say that a sensible such game would have introduction rules permitting the move only where there was a glass in such condition. In the same way, in real life and real discourse, the stupidity of *then* speaking of a glass as empty when it is in the sink fixes Pia's responsibilities: to what, in *so* speaking, she has made herself hostage for things being as she said—inter alia, a refillable glass. (There *may* have been *no* point in Pia saying what she did. There may, by the same token, be no saying whether things as they are is things as she said.) In this way, language games can model the assignment of responsibility, and thus of sense, content, to the things we in fact say.

In the *Grammar*, the parochial—the particular form of thought *we* are endowed with—decides what a *language* may be. This is fixed by what we can treat as one. The parochial now fixes what language games are played when in our current sense of 'play'. What is stupid, what sensible, in the particular circumstances in which such thinkers as us in fact speak to one another is what would be stupid or sensible for us, by our lights. Which is to say: stupid, or sensible, for those engaging in conversation.

There are two things to be said in saying a glass to be empty, one true of the glass in the soapy water, the other not. Such is no threat to the Fregean idea of a concept as a *function*. It is just—so far—that some words, 'is empty', may name either of two of these. It is another matter when one assigns language games the role just given them. For now we have a new way of carving up exposure to risk of error. It gives us, for *any* concept—for either of the above supposed two—different things it *could* be to fit *it*, so different things to be said, on different occasions, in saying something to fit it—different language games one might be playing, on different such occasions, in so speaking. In the language game of §2, the builder calls 'Slab!' and the assistant is to bring a slab. Suppose the assistant brings a broken slab. Is he correct? Nothing said so far decides this. But there *are* games in which it is decided—where it is specified that a slab in halves will do, or that it will not. For any given game, further games may thus refine it. Exposure to risk, carved in this way, is always liable to be carved more finely.

For Frege, there must be a way to identify what words said which finishes the parochial's work: when things would be the way they were *thus* said to be simply cannot depend on more about the circumstances of so saying. With language games in the role now assigned them there is no such point. For *any* way things may be said to be—a way there is *for* them to be—there are always games one may or may not be playing in speaking of things as that way, differences always liable to matter to when things would be as said in so speaking. We thus arrive at a different picture of representing as so (in saying something). Whether things are as they were said to be on some given occasion is answered by the circumstances of so speaking, and our parochial perceptions of them. Nothing detachable from this, as for Frege a sense *for* words to have is detachable from an occasion of some words having it, answers all questions that could arise as to when things would be as they would thus be said to be.

Representation is *by* a certain sort of thinker *for* that sort. Its content is formed accordingly. Such is the *Investigations'* new conception of what representing is. It can be hard to see how the point could hold so generally. So far we have only discussed language. There is another important case.

3.6 Non-linguistic representing

The other principal case of representing things as so is representing things to oneself as so (taking them to be so, expecting them, noting them, etc.). If I am going to represent something to you as so, I need your attention. So I need something towards which attention can be directed, some perceivable vehicle which *bears* content. I do not need to attract my own attention to think something so. Nor could my representing to myself per vehicle (a note, say) be my thinking something so. Where there is no such vehicle, there is nothing to be *taken* in one way rather than another. It is so far obscure how the above idea of the work of the parochial can have any application in such a case. What is missing from the present story is thus an account of such attitudes as meaning, thinking, and understanding—a topic introduced in *Investigations* §81, and taken up seriously from §138 onwards. I cannot discuss that here (though see essays 8, 9, 11).

Here, though, is a hint. Propositions are *one* device for carving up exposure to risk. Language games are another. Such games are used in the *Investigations* to make a particular point, as above. This is not to banish the notion *proposition*. In suitable circumstances I may say to you, 'Pia said that there is wine on the rug', where this admits the response, 'And is there?'. We may then go on to discuss 'the proposition that there is wine on the rug'. What proposition is this? When would it be true? I mentioned it in words 'there is wine on the rug'. Things would be as they are according to that proposition when they would be as those words speak of things being; when that would be is fixed by the operation of parochial equipment on *my* words in just the way described, above, for Pia's. The above model of representing finds just this application here. Such a proposition, one might say, is what it is to us. Nor does it thereby speak of a way for things to be which admits of no divergent understandings. (Cf. §§429–465.)

4. The Limits of the Parochial

The idea of language games (and equally (§81) calculi) as objects of comparison gives the parochial a certain purchase on thought and its objects. Among other things, the parochial gains a role in how logic applies to thought. Which raises questions about Frege's conception of logic's distance from psychology. Here, I think, we encounter an unfinished area in Wittgenstein's thought. I will sketch a few issues.

4.1 Which things are propositions?

(The first of our three initial questions.) In the *Grammar*, it was for a language to tell us which things were propositions *in it*. A language could not tell us the *wrong* thing about this. There is no way it could be purporting that such-and-such were propositions where in fact they were not, with this caveat: a language cannot tell *us* that such-and-such is a proposition if we cannot grasp how such a thing could be a proposition (or if for us it just plainly is not one). A language which simply says that there is a contingent proposition that something is red and green at the same spot, Wittgenstein suggests, so far has not told us anything. One might say: what fits *our* notion *proposition* is what we are prepared to recognize as doing so. Here is what this idea has become in the *Investigations*:

> What a proposition is is in one sense determined by the rules of sentence formation (in English, for example), and in another sense by the use of the sign in the language game. And the use of the words 'true' and 'false' may be among the constituent parts of this game; and if so it *belongs* to our concept 'proposition' but does not 'fit' it. As we might also say, check *belongs* to our concept of the king in chess (as so to speak a constituent part of it). To say that check did not *fit* our concept of the pawns, would mean that a game in which pawns were checked, in which, say, the players who lost their pawns lost, would be uninteresting or stupid or too complicated or something of the kind.
>
> (1953: §136)

Here a role of a language, in the *Grammar*, has been taken over by language games. The rules of English present us with things which *look* like propositions, sentences in some sense apt for stating them. But something *is* a proposition just where it functions as one in the language games where it occurs.

Language games, again, are objects of comparison. Pia said, 'My glass is empty.' Did she thus express a proposition? This is a question answered by finding the language games she counts as thus having played. In those games do her words function as a proposition would? Are they truth-evaluable? Pia's words count as a proposition (or as stating one) just in case the answer to that question is yes. Again, the games she counts as playing are those the right sort of parochial thinker would be prepared to recognize as such. So, in this now-familiar way, the parochial informs the answer to this question.

In the *Grammar*, a *language* fixed an understanding of being a proposition on which it could be true or false to say that such-and-such was a proposition. The language fixed what it was one said in saying so. This function is now assumed by language games, and, through them, by the parochial. Pia says, 'The room is dark'. There are the games she was thus playing (in our present sense). There are the moves she thus made (in this sense). These moves may be, or not (or express, or not) what we are prepared to recognize as truth-evaluable: in those games, the correctness of 'The room is dark' is to be settled in certain ways; these may or may not be, recognizably for us, ways for the *world* to decide the correctness of a stance as it would in deciding a question of truth. In speaking of a *proposition* that the room is dark, thus expressed by Pia, we say what would be correct or not accordingly. It is on *such* understandings of *proposition* that it may be true or false that such-and-such is one.

The point blocks one reading of §136. Imagine people who seriously supposed that it is either true or false that vanilla tastes better than chocolate, or that there is an understanding of a glass being empty on which the matter is decided by an oracle. Some have seen in Wittgenstein the view that, in such a case, all there is to say is, 'Such is the way of their people. For them, there *are* such propositions.' Such is not the present reading. Pia's words may be rightly understood to be purporting to say what is either true or false, and not merely to express sentiment. This may well militate, even heavily, in favour of so taking them. For all of which, if the words tell us that vanilla tastes better than chocolate, it may be wrong so to take them: there is not here a recognizable way for the *world* to speak on correctness. Pia's words cannot be so understood, so they are not to be: they are not, in fact, truth-evaluable. The ways of her people, the language she speaks, are not what is most central to giving *proposition* the understanding on which *we* speak of it. Perhaps the *Grammar* contains a suggestion to the contrary. Such is not the *Investigations'* view.

The *Grammar* left us with a problem: if a proposition belongs to a language, how can the same proposition be, or be expressed, in different ones? We now have an answer. The waiter's 'Les oursins sont arrivés', and my 'They have sea urchins' would be one proposition here if (so far as matters) for things to be as the waiter said is for them to be as I said, and vice versa. This would be so if, so far as mattered, the games the waiter counted as thus playing made the same demands on the correctness of his words (and their treatment) as the ones I counted as playing made on mine. There is indefinite variety in the occasions there may be for raising, and speaking to, the question whether the waiter and

I said the same (to be so). On a given one, there is what one who thought parochially as we do would then be prepared to recognize as to when things would be as he said, when as I did, and then as to whether it would be the same thing for things to be as he said and for things to be as I did. What a thinker of our sort would be prepared to recognize (whether this is *realizing* or *acknowledging*) is what one *would* suppose, thus what *is* to be. Propositions are to be counted, as one twice or two once, in different ways on different occasions, and on each according to what those who are to do the counting—thinkers of a particular sort—would (are prepared to) perceive as the same.

An issue remains. Suppose Pia says, 'That sculpture is both red and green just *there*' (pointing to a spot). Could she be counted as expressing a (possibly true) proposition while also counting as using 'red' to speak of red, and 'green' of green? If she expressed (or produced) a proposition, it is recognizable how things, in being as they are, may decide its truth or falsity—may instance the zero-place concept her words expressed. Perhaps that spot does not behave so as to count as red as opposed to green, or vice versa, on any understanding we can muster of it doing so. It may look, sometimes red to an observer, sometimes green, and otherwise behave sometimes as a red thing, sometimes as a green thing, would. But its total behaviour adds up neither to being red rather than green, nor to the reverse. Might its behaviour nonetheless add up to its looking red, but not rather than green, and, equally, green, but not rather than red? If so, might this be the behaviour Pia ascribed it? Perhaps (there are sculptures like this) *one* can, by staring for a moment, both see it looking red and see it looking green (though not quite simultaneously). Might this not count as seeing, in one observation, both its being red and its being green? Can we talk this way? Could one so understand being red and being green? Such would supply the right sort of thing *for* Pia to say. The answer now is: there is such an understanding of being red and being green if we (thinkers of our sort) are prepared, in the circumstances, to recognize this as an understanding of that. If so, then, depending on how one would perceive Pia, she may have performed the feat in question. Nothing external to the perceptions we are thus prepared to have can dictate what they here must be.

4.2 The harmony of thought and reality

A proposition makes a demand on the world: to decide, in being as it is, the proposition's fate—true or false. The proposition fixes a way for the world to decide this—if the proposition is that the setting sun is red, then what about the world would make this so or not. Whether deciding things in that way would be deciding *truth* depends on parochial perceptions of what truth might be. But might the way thus fixed not fail to be a way for the world to decide anything at all? The proposition's way, say, supposes that there are such things as colours. Perhaps there just are not. If there is no such failure, we may say that proposition and world are in harmony. Where there is *room* for such failure, harmony is a substantial accomplishment on the part of the proposition. True propositions, of course, are in harmony with the world. But there is then something substantial a proposition must first accomplish to be so much as false. In what ways, if any, might harmony be substantial.

In *Investigations* §429 Wittgenstein says,

The agreement, the harmony, of thought and reality lies in the fact that if I say falsely that something is *red*, still, for all that, it isn't *red*. And when I want to explain the word 'red' to someone, in the sentence 'That is not red', I do it by pointing to something red.

There is such a thing as (something) being red. So if a proposition demands that its truth be decided by something being red or not, there is (*ceteris paribus*) a way for the world to oblige. So there is harmony. Suppose there were no such thing as being red. Then if a proposition demanded that its truth be decided in that way, it would be out of harmony with the world. So if it could do such a thing, then there is the possibility of disharmony, and harmony is a substantial accomplishment. But could it? If there were no such thing as being red, how would a proposition impose such a demand?

If propositions cannot do such things, this is not to say that it is decided, independent of how the world is, which demands are harmonious. It is not yet to say that one can raise questions of truth so formulated that the world *could* do no other than answer them. Frege sometimes speaks as if there were such questions. The *Grammar*'s idea of the arbitrariness of grammar *could* be read so as to suggest this: there is no external standpoint from which a grammar can be held to generate propositions *wrongly*, because, whatever it dictates as to how the world is to decide their fate, there is no such thing as the world failing to comply. Modulo logical consistency, one can stipulate just anything.

This sits ill with the *Investigations*' conception of what representing is. Max has knocked over a glass again. Wine spills. Pia says to Sid, 'There is wine on the rug.' But *this* rug is covered with an invisible, removable, film. No molecule of wine reaches any fibre of it. Is there wine on it on the understanding on which Pia said so? Pia raised a question of truth. The world might have been such as to answer it. There might not have been the film. But the world *is* such as to answer it only if Pia's words are one of two ways: such that she is to be held responsible for no more than what is so, or that she is responsible for more (for wine reaching fibres, say). They are the first way just if one (a thinker of a certain sort) would so perceive them. The same goes for their being the second. But a thinker of the right sort *need* not be such as to perceive them either in the one way or the other. Faced with the facts, one may be at a loss. More generally, there need be nothing that one (of the right sort) would find. Correspondingly, it need not be that the world answers the question of truth that Pia raised.

It is one thing for there to be such a thing as something being red. It is another for the world in fact to decide whether such-and-such is red. If there is such a thing as being red, then a *proposition* can, intelligibly, ask the world to decide its fate according to whether such-and-such is red, on some understanding or other of what its being red would be. The world need not oblige. There is that much room at least for disharmony between the way a proposition asks its fate to be decided and the deciding in fact done by things being as they are. That the world does what a proposition asks it to, is not achieved by stipulation.

For Wittgenstein, the sense to be made of an explanation *explaining* or failing to is such that some do explain and some do not; and that one is or not 'is no longer a philosophical proposition, but an empirical one' (1953: §85). Similarly, the sense (so far) to be made of disharmony is such that some propositions are in harmony with things and some are not; and that one is or not is an empirical matter. Here is another key idea in later Wittgenstein. Austin had it too, and expressed it thus:

The feelings of royalty . . . or fakirs or bushmen or Wykehamists or simple eccentrics—these may be very hard to divine.

(1946: 104)

Can we know the mind of another? Sometimes not. This supposes there are two kinds of case. A Salopian, perhaps, can never know what *he*, a Wykehamist, was thinking when he said *that*: you would need the Winchester experience. So there is such a thing as knowing. This contrasts with what the philosopher says in saying that one can never know the mind of another. Here there is no such thing as knowing this. On inspection we also lose our grip on what knowing it is meant to be. The philosopher produces something which *looks* like the empirical proposition, but which, Austin suggests, is in fact senseless. The empirical ones capture all the sense there *is* in the idea of knowing, or not, the mind of another. Similarly, for Wittgenstein, that *this* explanation failed to explain, as opposed to *this* one, which succeeded, captures all the sense there is in the idea of an explanation explaining or failing to; that *this* proposition was not in harmony with reality as opposed to *this* one which was, captures all the sense there is to the idea of harmony. And so on.

And so on. For some practical ends or other I want, on occasion, to speak as if I knew, or *might* know what Pia was thinking. For those purposes I accordingly understand knowing to be such-and-such achievable status—an interesting status for the ends in view. For some practical ends or other I speak, and think, as though Pia had spoken truth, or, at worst, falsehood—as though in harmony with how things are. I thus understand harmony as though it were such-and-such achievable condition. To achieve the generality he wants, the philosopher prescinds from practical ends. In this sense he aims for a perspective on the relevant phenomenon. What is it to *know* the mind of another, full stop—independent of any practical use to talk of knowing this or not? Similarly for thought being harmonious. Wittgenstein's point, and Austin's, is that when a philosopher makes this move he stops making sense. From a transcendental standpoint there is nothing to be said.

In the *Investigations* this is a point of principle. It is a corollary to the view there of what representing in words is. Words are to have a point, ends to serve. They are by given thinkers, for thinkers of a given sort. This setting is to give them such point. Point's role is to fix how things are according to the words: *how* the world is to speak to things being as thus said or not. This role is substantial. The world does speak only where it has been played adequately. Such is a substantial requirement on the harmony of words and world. Such is the idea of the essence of representation elaborated in section 3. The abstraction the philosopher aims for precisely blocks the playing of any such role. It thereby blocks making sense. This entirely general point applies in particular to the philosopher who tries to see our ordinary perceptions of truth and falsity as leaving open some further question as to whether our thought is 'really' in harmony with things.

Would-be transcendental propositions, in the present sense, fail to express thoughts in just the way that private language (as per (1953: §§243–308)) does. What would instance a way for things to be transcendentally, just as what would instance a way for things to be privately, is beyond the reach of the parochial— of what *one*, a thinker of a certain sort, would recognize. On the *Investigations'* view, the parochial gives Frege's fundamental logical relation its purchase: allows for facts as which ways for things to be are instanced by the ways things are, and which are the instances of given ways there are for things to be. The parochial's involvement is a condition on the satisfaction of concepts by the non-conceptual, so on representations according to which such-and-such is so—a condition failed equally by would-be private, and by would-be transcendental, thought.

Frege stresses intersubjectivity—availability to *one*—as a condition for being a thought at all. As he notes, this rules out private thought. But it may seem—and may have seemed to him—to leave room for transcendental thought in the present sense: (zero-place) concepts instanced or not full stop, quite apart from any transient point in taking them to be, quite apart from any parochial perception. This last 'one', read widely enough, may even seem to require this. Thinking through, with Wittgenstein, this idea of availability to *one*—of the *same* thought to many—exposes such appearances as mere illusion (if he is right). For, on inspection, it takes the parochial to make good sense of 'same thought'. Such different diagnoses of the incoherence of the idea of private thought mark perhaps the greatest divergence between Frege and later Wittgenstein.

4.3 The Hardest Thing

A law of logic, Frege tells us, cannot be *explained*, except, perhaps, by other laws of logic. There is nothing (other than more logic) in virtue of which it holds. What brooks no explaining is what *could* not be otherwise—there is no such thing. So it is, on Frege's view, with logic: the *hardest* sort of necessity. What sort is that?

I invite you onto my balcony. You fear it will collapse. I tell you, 'Don't worry. It can't collapse.' Momentarily, you feel relieved. Then I explain: 'Whatever happens, it won't count as my balcony collapsing. It's part of what collapsing is that nothing counts as a *balcony* doing it.' Your relief vanishes. If I am right, the balcony cannot *collapse*. For all of which it might *shmollapse*—like collapsing, except done by a balcony: equally injurious to health. If it really is part of the concept of collapsing that balconies cannot do it, then there is, really, no such thing as a balcony doing it. That my balcony will not holds with that kind of necessity. But such necessity is, as a rule, cold comfort.

Perhaps it is, similarly, part of the concept *proposition* that nothing is one unless governed by Frege's laws of logic. This leaves open that there might be gropositions, equally useful guides to exposure to error in dealings with the world, equally central to a cognitive economy as rich as ours, but governed by other laws. This is not what Frege had in mind.

Descartes (1637: 92–94) pointed to ways our abilities to solve problems, and to communicate, are qualitatively different from those of other animals (as he saw them): a plasticity, and versatility in our dealings with the world which other creatures lack. He called that qualitative difference *intelligence*. Stances in which we risk error at the world's hands are central to such plasticity. If there were a sort of stance which could play this role, while not subject to Frege's laws, intelligence, then thought in any sense that mattered, might be otherwise than those laws prescribe. Logic would not be necessary for thought in the sense Frege had in mind. The *hardest* necessity is not bought on the cheap.

Wittgenstein's view of same-saying does not, anyway, allow *part of the concept* to do the work to which it has just been put. Perhaps, in *some* good sense, it is part of the concept *red* that nothing can be red and green at the same point.

Such *can* be put by saying, 'There is no such thing as that.' What we cannot rule out is that, confronted with the unexpected, we will *learn* how to make sense of it—that there will turn out to be something for *this* to be. If someone claims to have discovered such a thing, we (may) need to *look*. Whether he has, is a verdict to be given by our *parochial* sensitivities. Such is doubtfully the hardness Frege had in mind.

For Frege, it is part of what judging, so what a proposition, is that for every proposition there is another true just where it is false, and vice versa, for every two propositions there is one true just where both are, and so on. Suppose, confronting the unexpected, we come to speak of 'propositions' which do not always form conjunctions. Would we be speaking of *propositions*? Or of truth? The usual story about speaking of the same thing applies. There are different ways of reading Frege. But his conception of logical necessity *seems* to call for something outside the parochial dictating the verdict it must on such a point. It would be *wrong* if it allowed propositions which did not form conjunctions: there is *absolutely* no such thing as that.

What logic is, Frege *rightly* held, should not be hostage to chemistry, or geology. Nor should it be hostage to psychology. So, he held, it should not be shaped by anything parochial. *Empirical* psychology does not study what *any* thinker must be. That is not an empirical issue. It only investigates ways we are *different* from what a creature might be. But the parochial is precisely what a thinker need not be. Might psychology not study that—say, what *we* would recognize as a proposition when? Is it not then studying what logic might be?

(Human) psychology studies a particular form of thought. A law of logic should apply to *all* thought—to thought by any thinker. If there are Martians, then if a Martian holds a certain *proposition true*, the same laws of logic apply to him as to us. Nor do laws of logic change. 'From *that A &B*, that *A* follows up until 2050, but afterwards not always' is shaped wrongly to be a law of logic.

For later Wittgenstein, the above conception of hardness misunderstands such truisms. Just as, in the *Grammar*, there is no *independent* standard by which a language might be found to say wrongly what its propositions are, so, in the *Investigations*, there is no external standard by which our parochial equipment might say the wrong things as to how propositions might behave. The misunderstanding makes this seem to threaten the very idea of logic. As Wittgenstein puts it,

But what becomes of logic now? Its rigour seems to be giving way here.—But in that case doesn't logic altogether disappear?—For how can it lose its rigour?

(1953: §108)

The objection comes to this. Logic fixes a way *any* proposition must behave, independent of how anyone is parochially equipped. So the parochial equips us to recognize the *right* things only if it equips us to acknowledge just this as the behaviour of any proposition. (One might even—inadvisedly by Wittgenstein's lights—hold there to be no such thing as acknowledging the *wrong* things.) So for a proposition to behave *thusly* is *not* just for us to be equipped to acknowledge this. There *is* a standard independent of us which decides, so far as logic reaches, what a proposition *really* is.

A way of working towards what the misunderstanding is here is to see just how much of Frege's good motives can be honoured while holding to the *Investigations'* view of the autonomy of the parochial—that development of the *Grammar* idea of the autonomy of language. A preliminary: on a Fregean conception of logic, a law of logic forms a system with all other thoughts; its structure (so its place in it) mirrors the most general structure of that system. That notion of 'all other thoughts' became inadmissible in the *Grammar* and remains inadmissible in the *Investigations*. So we need a new idea of how it is that logic speaks to the things we in fact think. The *Investigations'* new idea is hardly unfamiliar nowadays. It is in §§81, 130, 131. A logical calculus is now an object of comparison in just the way a language game is. I introduced, above, a notion of playing a language game: on it, Pia, in saying, 'Wine is on the rug', is playing a language game in which one says that if, in the circumstances of her speaking, those words (of hers) are subject to the standards of correctness fixed by the rules governing that move in that game.

A (familiar) logical calculus does not have moves in it which consist of words: no moves such as 'Wine is on the rug.' It has formulae, consisting of variables, or place-holders, and proprietary signs for logical constants. Such a formula is a possible move in constructions the calculus designates as 'proof-structures'. As such it is subject to a standard of correctness given by the introduction and elimination rules governing its main connective. Suppose we assign each of some list of thoughts—things said—in some 'The room is dark', in some 'There's wine on the rug', etc.—a formula. Then we might say this assignment to *model*, jointly, those respective things said just in case they are jointly subject to those standards of correctness fixed by the rules governing those formulae in the calculus.

A familiar calculus is an expression of some laws of logic. By the laws, propositions analysable as of certain forms behave in certain ways. What is analysable as a conjunction, for example, entails each of its conjuncts so analysed. To model an item by a formula with a certain main connective is to analyse it as a conjunction. Where, and insofar as, the item is correctly so modelled, it counts as so behaving. The calculus spells out what that behaviour is. On the *Investigations'* view it is thus that logic speaks through a calculus to thought.

A law of logic is a generalization: *any* conjunction, behaves thus and so. That generalization seems about all propositions. We now have a new way of understanding that idea. For now the law need not (and cannot) be understood in terms of some domain over which it extends. Rather, we can think of the law as an instruction, somewhat along these lines. Suppose you are treating some given things as propositions. You must, for any two things you so treat, recognize a third, true precisely when they both are. Suppose you treat some further item as such a third thing. Refer to a calculus which thus models what you are doing (on the above notion of modelling) to see to what you are thus committed.

There is a point in this way of thinking of how logic speaks. For a start, it allows us the idea that how a given proposition *is* correctly modelled—so how logic says it must behave—may depend on the occasion for asking what standards of correctness in fact govern it—notably, what standards logic in fact imposes. In particular, it may depend on where—in the context of which propositions—this one is so to behave or not. Pia says, 'If Sid is already on the motorway, then he will get here on time.' She has expressed a proposition which may be modelled, for some purposes, as a conditional in that proprietary sense of familiar calculi. Logic speaks accordingly. Similarly if Zoë says, 'If Sid has an accident, he will not be on time.' But this does not mean that it follows from the truth of what each said that if Sid is on the motorway he will not have an accident. Sometimes-correct modellings of each proposition do not jointly form a correct modelling of the pair, do not model the one in the suggested way in the context of so modelling the other. What is sometimes a good modelling need not always be. We have gained that much.

But, it seems, there must be more than this that logic says to thought, or at least more to say to honour Frege's worthy intuitions. So far, logic, as expressed through a calculus, lays down standards of correctness to which given propositions *may* be subject—if correctly modelled in such-and-such ways. This does not capture the Fregean idea that any proposition (thought) *must* be subject to logic's laws—that one cannot think, because there is no such thing as thinking, *illogically*—not that one cannot make logical mistakes, but that one cannot think so as to be governed by standards of correctness at odds with logic's. Nor does it capture for him the absolutely central idea that a law of logic admits of no extra-logical explanation—that, where such a law is concerned, there *cannot* be anything to be explained extra-logically.

We can start from this idea: for what really is a law of logic, no modelling in our present sense which contravened it—which assigned some proposition a standard of correctness inconsistent with it—could be correct. So, since on our present notion of modelling, a proposition, on one, is assigned properties of some formula in a calculus, no calculus which assigned a formula properties inconsistent with the law (e.g. through ill-matched introduction and elimination rules) could model anything. Such things are, literally, inconceivable, as, on Frege's view, they must be.

This bears on our second question. If it is inconceivable that a law of logic—say, a law capturing conjunction elimination—should not hold, that is one reason, perhaps among several, why the law does not admit of chemical explanation. Nothing explains why things cannot be otherwise where there is no such thing as their being otherwise (except, perhaps, that fact). It is not that if chemistry were different, things here might be otherwise. So nor, equally, does its being as it is explain their not. And where otherwise is inconceivable, there is no such thing as being it. If there is anything specially inept about chemistry here, equally so for psychology. For if there were a psychological explanation of a law of logic, there could, in principle, be a chemical one too. As Frege says, whether we *had* the right psychology for the law to be a law might *then* turn out to depend on the level of phosphorous in the cerebral cortex. (See 1897: 148.)

We cannot recognize any modelling as correct if it violates what really is a law of logic. We could not correctly model Pia's thoughts, or talk, that way. Nor, equally, a Martian's. If we can ascribe to a Martian the property of thinking such-and-such (so), then what we ascribe to him is thinking one of the things we can recognize there is to think—one of the things, thus, there is for *us* to think—a fortiori, something with the logical features that something there is for us to think would have. As a special case, this is so of the modelling of thought we can ascribe to a Martian—the logical features we can take him to take a thought to have.

We cannot recognize a modelling as correct if it assigns to thoughts features logic says they cannot have. Nor could such a modelling *be* correct. Such is inconceivable. But is it good fortune that what we are prepared to recognize as possible and impossible assignments of logical features to the thoughts we model, just happen to be the combinations of what really are, respectively, conceivable and inconceivable? Should we give thanks for this? Or is it that what is conceivable, what inconceivable, just *is* what we are prepared to recognize as such? And if the latter—no thanks due, on this score, to a deity—then is this not just our parochial capacities shaping what there is for logic to say?

Wittgenstein says, in a slightly different connection,

'There is another solution as well' means: there is something else that I am also prepared to call a 'solution'; to which I am prepared to apply such-and-such a picture . . . and so on.

(1953: §140)

For 'there is another solution' one might say, 'there is this combination of logical features', or 'there is this modelling'. So 'logic permits thoughts which behave *thus*, but not ones which behave *so*' means 'I am prepared to recognize thoughts which behave *thus*, but not *so*.' This, Wittgenstein tells us, 'We might also be inclined to express . . . like this: we are at most under a psychological, not a logical compulsion.' (Ibid.) Logic, that is, places us at most under pyschological compulsion. To which Wittgenstein responds, 'And now it looks quite as if we knew of two kinds of case' (ibid.).

These two kinds of case correspond to two notions of recognizing, marked in Dutch and German by different verbs ('herkennen' and 'erkennen'; 'erkennen' and 'anerkennen'). 'Herkennen' (Dutch), or 'erkennen' (German), speaks of a cognitive accomplishment—re-cognition, or identification of something as what it *is*. (Kamagurka: 'Een mooie vrouw herken je aan haar uiterlijk.') 'Erkennen' (Dutch) or 'anerkennen' (German) is being prepared, or committed, to treat something as with a certain status, granting or accepting credentials. 'For me, in my books, she is a leading philosopher' ('She is what *I* call a leading philosopher') versus 'She *is* a leading philosopher', invoking, or presupposing, an agreed standard for being one.

The one sort of recognition is not in general the other. But the two are not *always* to be distinguished. To be prepared as one is to grant credentials—to *call* something a case of such-and-such—may be to be prepared to grant credentials where they are due. This may be to be able to recognize cases where they are due—cases which do, in fact, count as that such-and-such. It may be to be *equipped* for cognitive *achievements*. A fluent Dutch speaker would *recognize* a certain difference between 'herkennen' and 'erkennen'. On what notion of *recognize*? What would doing the one thing rather than the other come to here? Do we know of two kinds of case—two ways for the fluent speaker to be? A fluent speaker bestows credentials just where they are earned. We accept the sun as it is on the horizon as something its being red might be. What more is needed for there to be this to be *identified* as something its being red might be, and then for us to be equipped to make such identifications? We are prepared to accept (in the end) certain modellings of thoughts as possible, others not. Is there any more question of two kinds of cases here—mere acceptance, short of recognition—than in those others? For Frege, logic, recognizably (by us), dictates such-and-such. Is there really room here for *different* applications for our two notions of 'recognize'?

This question begins, rather than ending, a story. The above sketches some of the material Wittgenstein has given us for dealing with it. Having gone on too long, I stop here.

8

Truth and Merit

The traditional 'statement' is an abstraction, an ideal, and so is its traditional truth or falsity.

(Austin: 1962a, p. 147)

Frege and Austin present two deep and compelling, but starkly contrasting, pictures of truth. One must, it may seem, choose. *Perhaps* it would so seem to the authors. But there is no choosing between *insights*. We need to see how to fit together what each has right. I aim to say how. I will first set out three elements in Frege's picture, then three elements in Austin's. I will then look for the context in which truth is to be treated in Frege's way, and that in which it calls for Austin's treatment. We can then see both as true pictures of one phenomenon.

1. Frege

1.1 Invisibility

'Invisible' is here shorthand for invisible, intangible, inaudible, etc. It refers to what is not, even in an instance, geometrically, or acoustically, or physically, some certain way; moreover, what need not be—and in the cases at hand is not—so much as apt for having instances. The letter A is, geometrically, a certain way. So is an instance of it—*this* letter A on the billboard. The thought that time is now short is not geometrically any way. Nor does it have instances—even if there are instances of someone thinking it.

The invisible, on present use, is thus opposed to what we might call, still on a slightly stretched use, 'the perceivable'. Frege starts on his point about the perceivable as follows:

One finds truth predicated of pictures, presentations (ideas), sentences and thoughts. It is striking that here visible and audible things occur together with items which cannot be perceived by the senses. This indicates that shifts have occurred in its sense. Indeed! So is a picture, as pure visible, tangible, thing really true? And a stone, a leaf, not true? Clearly one wouldn't call the picture true if an intention did not attached to it. The picture is *meant* to represent something.

(1918: 59)

Imagine Monet painting Kölner Dom. Consider the canvas he produced: one covered in a certain way with paint. If it is to be true or false, there must be a way things are according to it. For sake of argument, suppose that there needs to be a way Kölner Dom is according to it. What way? There is a region of the canvas which is rather like an image of a stone wall with flying buttress attached. Positioned within that region is a patch of blue paint. Such a canvas *could* be an image of a stone wall with a patch of blue stone in it, or of a stone wall defaced by a crude graffito. Or an image of a stone wall with shadow cast on it in late morning light. *If* the canvas further represents Kölner Dom as being as thus depicted, then there would be different things it would be for Kölner Dom to be as represented, depending on what it is that blue patch depicts: on how it does its representing, thus how it represents the cathedral to be. Paint patterns cannot teach us how a canvas represents things. If they needed to fix that, there would be no way a canvas depicted things. Thus it is that the painting, considered as mere painted canvas, represents nothing as so. Hence no question as to truth yet arises.

What, to begin, must we add to a painting to make it depict something as so—for example Kölner Dom as looking thus and so (or thus and so on a certain occasion, or at a certain time of day, or after a planned remodelling). Frege's answer is: an intention. The painting is meant to depict *in* a certain way, thereby what it depicts (Kölner Dom) *as* a certain way. 'Intention' can stand in for whatever exactly plays the role an intention thus might. What matters is that the painting is to be taken in a certain way. This may be because the artist meant it so to be taken. Or there may be a more complex story to tell.

Intentions are always liable to leave issues undecided. In the painting, a saint's effigy above the entrance is depicted as blue. The effigy has blue projected on it by lasers at certain times of day. There is an understanding of it being as thus depicted on which, thanks to the lasers, it is that, and another on which the lasers merely make it look that way. If that is how things are, then how the painting is to be taken is liable to leave it undecided whether things are as thus depicted. The intention was to depict the effigy as blue. Whether it is as *thus* depicted depends on what you count as an effigy being blue. There may be no further intention towards the depicting which decides what one *ought* to count for purposes of being as thus intended to depict.

One attitude towards raising a question of truth would be that one has not done this if truth is liable to depend on whether things were represented as this way or that, and nothing about the would-be representation decides in which way it in fact represented things. But one need not take such an attitude. If I represented an effigy as blue, whether it is as represented *could* depend on what you count as an effigy being blue. But then again, it may not. There *may* be a question of truth which is decided by just that much as to how I represented things. We *could* thus think of me as having raised a question of truth. If it so happens that truth is not decided by this much (an odd effigy, as in the case of the laser), then the question I raised happens to have no answer. So, as it happens, my representation is neither true nor false.

One *might* resist the idea that a representation of something as so could be in that position. Perhaps Frege wanted to. But one need not. And he need not have. There is a difference between a canvas with no intention attaching to it, and one with an intention attaching to represent things in such-and-such way, where that intention *may* prove inadequate to decide whether things are as represented. There is a difference between a Delvaux fantasy, say, and a painting of a flying buttress where there turns out to be just a clever fake. Still, one *could* insist that truth has not come into question unless the representation is such that the world could not but make it either true, or, at worst, false. To ask whether Frege insisted on this is to adumbrate the topic of the last section of this essay.

So it is by an intention attaching to it—or what does the work an intention would—that a picture represents in a certain way, and thus things as a certain way. It is thus at least by means of an intention (or its like) that a representation raises a question of truth, namely, whether representing in *that* way is representing truly. An intention—that things be represented thus and so—is, in some sense invisible, even if someone's holding an intention need not be. That things be represented thus and so is not a visible, tangible, thing. What matters about this? For Frege, it is the intention itself—thus, an invisible thing—which raises the question of truth. This is not to say that the intention need be intelligible, or need determine the question of truth it does, independent of visible things. An intention attaching to a painting may be that it should represent the colour of the wall in this way: the colour of the paint in the image of the wall should *be* the colour of the wall (this being an idea which, of course, admits of understandings). Or, again, it should be the colour a photo would have if made with such-and-such film and such-and-such colour filter, at such-and-such hour. Then how the painting represents the wall, given that it is so to be taken, depends on how the artist mixed his paints when making that image. If he chose pigment badly, then, with that intention attaching to the picture, he misrepresented it, even if the colour of the image is not what he meant it to be.

On Frege's view, though, only the invisible *can* raise a question of truth. What he has in mind here emerges in a further discussion of invisibility. Considering an objection to the view that it is the invisible which raises questions of truth, he says,

> But don't we see that the sun has set? And don't we thus also see that this is true? That the sun has set is no object which emits rays which arrive in my eyes, is no visible thing like the sun itself. we *recognise* it as true that the sun has set on the basis of sense impressions.

(1918: 61, italics mine. See also 1897: 149)

That the sun has set is a circumstance which now obtains. It does not represent anything as so. A fortiori it requires neither an intention nor anything else to fix a *way* it represents things. But that the sun has set bears on representing: if it has, then there is a particular way to represent things which will be representing truly. Such is the fact one captures in saying that it is true that the sun has set. Frege insists that, in a sense in which the sun itself (or its afterglow) is visible, that it has set is not.

A distinction can help us understand this point. I begin with a related one, crucial for Frege. He speaks of an *object* falling under what *he* calls 'a concept' as the fundamental logical relation. (See 1892–1895: 128.) As he speaks of it, a concept is a function from (sequences of) objects to truth-values. Fundamental as this relation is for logic, another underlies it which is fundamental for our cognitive engagement with the world, notably, in judging. Suppose we so speak that the function *being empty* is the one which maps precisely the empty things into the value true. If a function is what a function does—is known by what it maps into what—which function holds this title? That depends on how things are. If the way my cup is—its being as it is—is a cup being empty, then it is a function which maps my cup into the true; if not, not.

Judging is engaging with the world precisely so as to be right or wrong about it according to how it is. A thought is the content of a judgement. It is, that is, a particular way of making one's fate—being right or wrong—depend on how the world is. It decides how the way things are *matters* to thus being right or wrong, how the world is to speak to that. It does that in fixing when things being as they are would be one's being right. The thought is that things are such that P; one is right just where things being as they are *is* things being such that P. The role of the thought is to fix when this would be.

Departing from Frege, we might think of a concept as intrinsically of a way for an object, or sequence of them, to be—of being wooden, or square, or an iguana, say. For a given concept to be the one it is, on this way of thinking, would be for it to be *of* the way it is. So any concept is the concept of being an iguana just in case it is of being an iguana. There is, then, that way which a given concept is of. What this way is fixes when something (or some sequence of things) would count as being that way—when, say, something would count as an iguana, or as wooden. The way some things are—their being as they are—is, inter alia, something being an iguana, or wooden. The way other things are is not something being that. What is that way might still be if it were different in some ways. If Sid gives Pia an iguana for Christmas, it is still an iguana after it comes to belong to her. It would still be if she dyed it puce. Anything different from it in other ways—as that orange is, say—would not be an iguana. So what way for a thing to be being an iguana is, fixes that range of cases of something being as it is which would be something being an iguana, and that range which would be something not being one. So, in particular, it fixes which actual cases of things being as they are are ones of those things being iguanas. So it fixes which concept in Frege's sense—which function from objects to truth values—is, in fact, the concept *iguana* (in Frege's sense). Had things been other than they are, it would still fix which concept in Frege's sense would be the concept of an iguana. But that might turn out to be a different concept. For different things might turn out to be the iguanas were the world different enough.

A concept in our present sense thus, as Frege says of a thought, 'always contains something which reaches out beyond the particular case, by which this is presented to consciousness as falling under something general' (1882: *Kernsatz* 4). The particular case is presented as belonging to a *range* of possible cases. The concept in this sense thus has a particular sort of generality which concepts in Frege's sense lack (though they are general in other senses). By this particular sort of generality that attaches to it, it does what concepts in Frege's sense cannot. It imposes that demand on title, satisfaction of which qualifies some one of Frege's concepts as the concept *iguana*, say, and satisfaction of which would have qualified other Fregean concepts for that title had the world been suitably different.

It is time to note two uses, or senses, of 'thing'. It may be a count noun. Or it may bear, as I will call it, a catholic reading. If there are, on the first use, ways for a thing to be, there is, on the second, ways for things to be, where it is inept to ask 'Which ones?'—as it would be if I said, 'Things have been slow around here lately.' If being wooden is a way for a box to be, then that box being wooden is a way for things (catholic use) to be. If we speak so that, for every way for things to be, there is its concept, then in addition to the concept of something being an iguana—a way for an object to be, so a one-place concept—there is also the concept of that iguana sunning itself. It is satisfied, as what it is of is instanced, not by some object or other being as it is, but rather by *things* (catholic use) being as they are. So we might call it a zero-place concept. So speaking underlines its having *just* that particular sort of generality that marks positive place concepts. So it is apt for the same roles in identifying the way a given judging is hostage to the world—with the obvious difference that the lot of positive-place concepts is to play sub-roles in the role which, so speaking, a zero-place concept plays. The generality in question belongs, for Frege, to a thought. If we think of a thought as, for example, the thought of that iguana sunning itself, then a zero-place concept just is a thought. If we think of the thought as *that* the iguana is sunning itself, then the thought is of a zero-place concept as satisfied.

Another feature goes with the above sort of generality. A way for things to be, as we are now conceiving this, is, for any case of things being that way, an identifiable way there would still be for things to be, even where things were not *just* as in that case. Had that sunning iguana, startled, hidden under the rock, there would remain, for all that, such a thing as something being an iguana sunning, and nothing would change in what mattered to being one, in when something's being as it was *was* its being an iguana. One could still have thoughts as to one thing or another being precisely *that*. *Mutatis mutandis* for zero-place concepts, once recognized. I will take these two features, to identify what I will call the conceptual.

What contrasts with the conceptual is that which instances what concepts, on present use, are concepts of. That iguana's being as it is just *is* something sunning itself. Things being as they are just is that iguana sunning. Things being as they are admits no range of instances. It fixes no distinction between what matters, or would matter, and what does (would) not, in how things are, or were (subjunctively, or in the past) to being *it*. If we were to speak of mattering at all here, *everything* matters to being it—as everything matters, too, to some object, or sequence of them, being just as it is. So, too, one could not have thought of things as precisely what they in fact are, had things not been precisely as they in fact are. No way one could then think things would qualify as that: there would then have been no such thing as qualifying. Something being as an object (that iguana, say) is is not, on present understanding, a way *for* a thing to be; things being as they are not a way for *things* to be. Such things lack the marks of the conceptual, in present sense. I will call them *non-conceptual*.

One might, perhaps, speak of recognizing how things are, perhaps even of recognizing things being as they are. One might also recognize that an iguana is sunning on that rock. But there is a great gulf between these two sorts of recognition. Recognizing how things are is, if anything, just being aware (well enough) of how things are. It is such things as awareness of the iguana, sunning. Recognizing that there is an iguana sunning on that rock is, as Frege insists, recognizing things being as they are as an iguana sunning on that rock, recognizing the way things are as instancing a certain generality, of that particular sort that marks the conceptual. It is recognizing the place of actual circumstances in that range of cases which would be ones of an iguana sunning. This was the point of Frege's remark about the setting sun. It is the distinction he had in mind when, in a similar remark (1897: 149), he says that if we speak of seeing 'that this flower has five petals . . . we mean by that something connected with thought and judging'. We recognize the way that flower is as a flower having five petals. We can factor that generality out of its being as it is. We recognize the flower, being as it is, as connecting to the conceptual in a particular way, as what would (so does) satisfy a certain concept. Frege goes on to suggest a non-perceptual understanding of 'see that' in such cases, the same sort of non-perceptual understanding it bears in 'I see that the banks have decided to undermine the pound'.

The main point, for *present* purposes, of speaking of concepts as per above, and thus stressing the distinction between the non-conceptual and the conceptual as this does, is that very much of Frege's and Austin's concerns with truth are about how the non-conceptual relates to the conceptual. Where they do differ, it is precisely here that the difference lies. The above is not only a good way of framing Frege's concerns, but an even better way of framing a comparison between these two.

Frege concludes his case for the invisibility of what 'brings truth into question at all' with this:

Without meaning to give a definition, I call thoughts something for which truth can come in question at all. . . . The thought, non-perceivable in itself, clothes itself in the vestments of a sentence and is thus graspable. We say, the sentence expresses a thought.

The thought is something non-perceivable, and all perceptually observable things are excluded from the domain of that for which truth can come into question at all.

(1918: 60–61)

A thought, as he also tells us, is marked by that special sort of generality which is the mark of the conceptual. So it is the conceptual which 'brings truth into question at all'. And it is what is invisible, in the present sense, which does this: a sort of generality, a demand on membership in a range by which certain ranges of cases belong to it—recognizably so, but not in a sense of recognition, if there is one, in which it is a *perceptual* accomplishment—mere awareness of what is, visibly, there.

The generality of the conceptual might *attach* to visible, tangible things. I pass yet another sign which reads, 'Vous n'avez pas la priorité.' In French this says: you do not have right of way. I feel accordingly belittled. That French sentence is a visible thing. There is a certain way it is written. It is the, or an, expression in

French of a certain concept: that of one not having right of way. That instance of it I just passed surely expresses the concept of one who then passes it not then (or at the impending roundabout) having the right of way. I am sure that the French traffic code makes more explicit the understanding on which I do not have this.

The generality attaching to the sign is not a visible thing. Frege also tells us that the sign, being visible, is 'excluded from the domain of things for which truth can come into question at all'. I do not think Frege means to tell us that signs (*panneaux*) are not the sorts of things which can state truth or falsehood. Rather, the idea would be: a *panneau* does so only in attaching to (expressing) something *invisible* which raises the question it raises. Knowing which question of truth is raised is knowing which invisible bearer of truth raises it. There is thus a certain priority attaching to the invisible in matters of truth.

There is this much reason. A visible truth-bearer, such as the *panneau*, is identifiable as the truth bearer it is, independent of identifying the question of truth it raises, that is, independent of identifying just that generality of the conceptual which belongs to what the sign expresses, so *what* question of truth is raised. This means that, in principle, just what generality attaches to the question the sign raises is negotiable. One may ask just how the sign ought to be taken, in particular, whether this or that instance of things being as they are belongs to the range of cases which would be ones of things being as the sign says. The answer to the question one thus raises is liable to depend on all sorts of factors—for example on what the reasonable French driver would be prepared to recognize as instancing the generality properly taken to attach to that sign, whereas an invisible bit of the conceptual is identified as the bit it is by nothing other than that generality which in fact is its (and, perhaps, its relations to other bits of the conceptual, also so identified). So, it may seem, what generality *it* has can depend on nothing. One *could* take this to mean: for any candidate for instancing it (for bearing the fundamental logical relation to it), whether that candidate does instance it can depend on nothing other than the candidate being the candidate it is, and that bit of the conceptual being the bit it is. So whether a *thought* is true can depend on none of those factors which *may* bear on whether something visible or audible expressed what is, in fact, truth.

Monet's canvas is meant to show how Kölner Dom looks. Neither the canvas nor its looking as it does shows how to go from it to instances of things (or of the Dom) so looking. That depends on how the canvas is to be taken as representing—not itself something visible. This banal point models a more general one about the non-conceptual. If the sun has just set, then things being as they now are, a bit of the non-conceptual, instances the sun just having set, a bit of the conceptual. That bit of the non-conceptual, things being as they are, does not show us how to get to those bits of the conceptual it instances—to, for example, the sun just having set. It does not decide anything as to what else would be an instance, even given the fact that *it* is one. For that we need, so to speak, a technique for classifying things as instances or not, a way in which things being as they were would matter to their instancing, or not, the sun just having set. To see that the sun has just set is to recognize in things being as they are what matters to this, so to be sensitive to what thus does matter. A technique of classifying, what *matters* to classifying in one way or another— that certain way of looking beyond the particular case which belongs to this bit of the conceptual, *the sun just having set*, is not something visible. It is what is thus invisible that raises questions of truth. The first part of Frege's discourse ends here.

1.2 Identity Under Predication

The second point of Frege's I will consider here is that predicating truth of a thought does not yield a thought with a different content, hence does not yield a new thought. I express this, somewhat picturesquely, as: truth is identity under predication. Frege expresses the idea this way:

> One can anyway observe that we cannot recognise a property of a thing without at the same time finding the thought that this thing has that property true. So for each property of a thing there is a connected property of a thought, namely, that of truth. It is also noteworthy that the sentence, 'I smell the scent of violets', has, clearly, the same content as the sentence 'It is true that I smell the scent of violets.' So it seems that nothing is added to the thought by attaching the property of truth to it.
>
> (1918: 61)

Nothing is added to a thought by predicating truth of it. This is not because truth is somehow an insubstantial notion, or not a condition for a thought to be in (though Frege flirts with that idea). Rather, the stated reason for it here is that to recognize a property of a thing is already to be thinking of truth—of the thought that that thing has that property as *true*. Truth enters the picture, so to speak, at the ground level. We think of it in thinking of anything as so—for example, in thinking that the sun has set. If I now try to inject it anew into the picture by mentioning its being true that the sun has set, I assign truth no role that it did not play already. So I add nothing new to the thought in question. This is to say nothing as to how rich the role was which truth played already.

The underlying point here is about judging (though one can think of things as a certain way without taking them to be). Judging is, as Frege tells us, exposing oneself to risk of error. (In 'Der Gedanke' (1918), this is in two stages: first, 'by the step with which I win myself an environment I expose myself to risk of error' (1918: 73.) Second, to judge is to judge of an environment.) In judgement, what *one* may think of—what one may think to instance such-and-such—is the limit of what there is for anyone to judge of (where there is no one one must be to do what *one* might do). This, and this, alone holds sway over whether one has succumbed to, or escaped, any error risked in judging. One *judges* only what others might. The ways one may judge things to be are only those others can. This is so just where others, too, can take that which in fact instances those ways, or which instances things being otherwise, to do so. Only against this background can it be a mark of the sway of *things* that someone judges correctly only where anyone who so judged would.

Truth is that particular correctness for which judging is eligible. This eligibility is the mark of judgement. To judge, Frege tells us, is to pursue the goal truth. Pursuit here takes a special form. If I play poker, I play to win. To do that, I play the odds: raise or fold, depending on what I think my chances are. Whatever I do, I thus reckon with the possibility that it was not, in fact, the winning move. If I judge that the sun has set then, of course, as a rational person, I recognize that there is such a thing as my turning out to be wrong about this. It is just in that sense that in judging I inevitably expose myself to risk of error. But suppose that, as with the poker, I see myself as perhaps holding, perhaps not, the winning hand: it might turn out that the sun has set, or, again, it might not. To see myself in that way is per se not to judge—to take it to be so—that the sun has set. It is to take it to be so that the sun might have set, or might not have. So to judge that the sun has set is to see myself as with the winning hand, in a way that I need not see myself in seeing and raising you in poker. It is to see *so* judging as the only thing which, as to what I judge of, would be, for me, pursuing the goal truth. So to judge that the sun has set is *ipso facto* to see my so judging (myself in doing so) as judging truly. So to judge that the sun has set, and further, that this is true, would be redundant. This is Frege's underlying point.

That truth is thus an identity under predication can be formulated in seductive, and possibly misleading, ways. One *can* capture the idea in saying things of the form, 'It is true that the sun has set iff the sun has set.' One thus exploits a feature of normal discourse. Those two instances of 'the sun has set' demand to be read as saying the same thing of the sun, or, more generally, to speak of the same way for things to be. Where I say how things must be for it to be true that the sun has set, I speak of that very way for things to be which I judge them in judging that the sun has set, so which I mention in speaking of its being true so to judge. Formulas of this form, read as thus mentioning twice just one way for things to be, express truisms. This speaks in favour of no form of insubstantiality of truth. This shows up in one way where we speak of the truth of what someone said on some occasion in speaking of the sun having set where what he said is not what *we* would in speaking in those terms. When my friend in Sydney texts me, 'The sun has set', I would be unlikely to express truth in saying, 'What he said is true iff the sun has set.' One might ask when, in *such* a case, I should take him to have expressed truth. But this adumbrates Austin.

1.3 Definability

The third element I will note in Frege's picture is the (supposed) indefinability of truth. The main part of the argument is as follows:

Truth admits no more or less. Or perhaps it does? Can one not establish that truth consists in the occurrence of a correspondence in a certain respect? But in which? What would we then need to do to decide if something was true? We would need to investigate whether it was true that—say, an idea and something real—corresponded in the relevant respect. And with that we would face a question of the same kind, and the game could begin anew. This attempt to explain truth as a correspondence thus fails. And so too would any other attempt to define truth. For in a definition one presents certain characteristics of truth. And in applying them to a particular case it would always be a matter of whether it was true that these characteristics occurred. So one would turn in circles.

(1918: 60)

I take this point out of order. Frege argues for it in the midst of his case for invisibility, before broaching the idea of truth as identity under predication. But I think one cannot see the point of Frege's argument (if argument it is) without first having on board the idea of truth as identity under predication. For the point is: definability of truth (as Frege conceives this) clashes with this feature.

There are two notable oddities in Frege's argument. First, if Frege wants to make a case that truth is indefinable, one would expect him to do it for things which bring truth into question, hence might be true—so, for him, invisible things. Instead, Frege considers defining the truth of a picture, or an idea (something which presents things as thus and so). These are precisely things he thinks do not bring truth into question, so cannot be true or false—unless their truth is just that of some invisible item attaching to them. One might, for example, call a statement (an *Aussage*) true iff it expresses a true thought. But then one *has* defined a statement's truth in terms of a thought's. What one needs to see is why one cannot say, in other terms, what it is for something to be true, where its truth is *not* a matter of the truth of something else. One *might* best do this by reference to something whose truth is not that.

The second oddity is the way Frege concludes this argument. He says,

From this it is probable that the content of the word 'true' is entirely singular and indefinable.

(1918: 60)

It could only be sarcasm if I produced for you a standard proof of the Pythagorean theorem and concluded it with, 'This makes it highly probable that the square of the hypotenuse is the sum of the square of the other sides.' For Frege, of all people, this is a strange way to conclude a *proof*. One can only conclude that he did not think he had one.

In any event, the definability of truth seems to clash with its status as identity under predication. Conversely, that truth *is* such an identity, is a case against *some* forms of definition. Consider this maxim: Whatever you hear three times is true*. Take that as a definition. Now consider the thought that the sun has set. This thought is hostage to a particular aspect of the way the world is: whether the sun has set. Now consider the thought that it is true* that the sun has set. This thought is also hostage to a particular aspect of how things are: by the definition, to whether you have heard three times that the sun has set. But then this can hardly be the same thought as the thought that the sun has set. So truth* is not an identity under predication.

One might generalize: suppose that for something (of the right sort) to be true is for it to be F. The thought that the sun has set remains hostage to the world in the way described above. The thought that it is true that the sun has set, by contrast, is hostage to whether the thought that the sun has set is F. As above, these being two different things for one's fate to turn on, these must be two different thoughts.

The thought that the sun has set and the thought that it is true that it has are one for this reason. To be a thought is to be the content of some judgement. To be a given thought is to fix how one is exposed to error in some given judgement there is for one to make. To be the thought that the sun has set is to fix that particular way of thus exposing oneself. But to judge *anything* is to see oneself as, so to speak, holding the winning hand in a game of being hostage to the world, as judging what one *must* to achieve the goal *truth* in the matter at hand. Things not being as one *thus* sees them is already part of the risk one runs in standing towards the sun's having set as one does in judging it to have. So the thought that one holds the winning hand—that one achieves truth in so judging—fixes no new way of exposing oneself to error, no way one was not exposed already merely in judging the sun to have set. So it is no new content for a judgement to have. So it is no new thought.

So the above argument breaks down wherever one substitutes for 'F' something which is part of what it *is* for something to be true, which is, accordingly, such that, whatever thought one judges, one *ipso facto* exposes oneself to the risk of error if that thought is not that way. The laws of truth (logic), Frege tells us (1918: 59), unfold the content of the concept truth. For a thought to be true is for it to be what it must to fall under a concept with that content. It is, for example, to have a negation, and for all of its negations to be false. But to judge it is already to treat it as fitting that bill.

Truth *is* indefinable in this sense. It could not be defined in terms of what one did not need to grasp already to be judging at all. It could not be defined in a way that might inform one who did not already grasp what truth was. Judging truly is holding a winning hand in a certain kind of game. But one cannot know what this comes to except in knowing what truth is. Truth could not be reduced to something else. What could? In truth's case, given its special role in judging, one could not get so far as an attempt.

Frege ends his discussion of identity under predication as follows:

The meaning of the word 'true' appears to be entirely singular. Might we here have to do with something which cannot be called a property in the usual sense at all? Despite this doubt I will for the present, following usual usage, express myself as though truth were a property, until something more suitable is found.

(1918: 61–62)

One cannot, Frege tells us, take any thing to have any property without thereby taking a certain thought to be true. So truth, if a property, is an unusual one. Being an identity under predication is unusual. Still, in taking the sun to have set I must *take* a certain thought to *be* true—a definite way for a thought to be, or not; a definite sort of success for a thought to enjoy. What more need a property be?

2. Austin

2.1 History

The starkest contrast between Frege and Austin on truth is their choice of what 'brings truth into question at all'. For Frege this is something invisible. It is that generality of the conceptual embodied in some particular identifiable bit of it—a thought, in his terms, or zero-place concept in mine. For Austin it is an historical event, or something produced in one, an exemplary case of something visible and tangible in our present sense. For Austin, it is a statement so conceived, as for Frege it is a thought, which brings truth into question:

A statement is made and its making is an historic event, the utterance by a certain speaker or writer of certain words (a sentence) to an audience with reference to an historic situation, event or what not.

(1950: 119–120)

What truth is is then seen in what it would be to state truly; or, again, for what one said in speaking to be what is true. Truth is brought into question by someone stating something.

Now it need not be that what was said is identifiable independent of what it would be for its sayer thus to have spoken truth. It need not be that, anyway, the speaker said things to be such-and-such way; now the question is whether *that* is true—whether things *are* that way. *What* way things were said to be may depend on what speaking truly in speaking as, and when, this speaker spoke would be. This locates an *apparent* stark contrast with Frege. For Frege, if words are (an *Aussage* is) true, that is because they (it) expressed such-and-such thought, where that thought is true. If, as Frege suggests, truth reduces to the truth of a thought, then which thought the *Aussage* expressed does not depend on what truth is. It is not as if expressing one thought rather than another is part of the *Aussage*'s satisfying *truth's* demands. Austin's shifted perspective thus leaves room at the outset for an interesting new idea.

In the central case, Austin means, in speaking of a 'statement', to speak of 'the historic use of a sentence by an utterer'. But, as he himself recognizes, 'statement' has other good uses too. To avoid ambiguity, I will use the inelegant nominalization 'stating' when I mean to speak of what Austin thus takes as this central case.

For Frege, truth comes in a package with a kind of attitude: what he calls *judging*. It is that success to which judging is uniquely liable. Some linguistic activity is also liable to such success. But it is the attitude which is fundamental to understanding what truth is. For Austin there is *something* fundamental about communication, or at least something fundamental about what truth is which it takes that case to make perspicuous. In judging something so, I represent things to myself as thus and so. This does not require, as communication does, something identifiable anyway, other than by its representing—say, by a geometric, or acoustic, form—which *is to be taken* in one way or another. (Nor *could* it be thus effected.) One might call representing to myself *autorepresenting*, and communicating *allorepresenting*. For Frege autorepresenting has a central role in truth in way that allorepresenting does not. It is the reverse for Austin. One might expect this to be a very fundamental difference between them as to what truth is. But, as I will argue, the difference can be considerably slighter than it first seems.

Frege and Austin differ in their choice of central case. Neither denies that there are others. Austin (1950) lists some others as follows:

> I suggest that the following are the primary forms of expression:
> It is true (to say) that the cat is on the mat.
> That statement (of his, etc.) is true.
> The statement that the cat is on the mat is true.

(1950: 118)

If it is true to say that the cat is on the mat, this is not just about what it is true for so-and-so to do on such-and-such occasion. (Further, what it is true to say it is also true to judge.) That the cat is on the mat may be stated by different people on different occasions. (A sentence 'may be used on two occasions or by two persons in making the *same* statement' (1950: 120)). But for Austin, such uses of 'true' are to be understood in terms of what he chooses as the central case, just as for Frege other uses of 'true' are to be understood in terms of his candidate for centrality. The next section will be dedicated to seeing just how such less central cases look, given Austin's choice for centrality.

The contrast between Frege and Austin must lie in the *point* of each one's choice of central case. Austin states the point of his choice most clearly as follows:

If you just take a bunch of sentences... impeccably formulated in some language or other, there can be no question of sorting them out into those that are true and those that are false; for... the question of truth and falsehood does not turn only on what a sentence *is*, nor yet on what it *means*, but on, speaking very broadly, the circumstances in which it is uttered.

(1962b: 110)

How do questions of truth depend on circumstance? What someone said on an occasion is true just in case things are as he thus said them to be. Suppose he said, 'There is red meat on the white rug', speaking of the rug in Pia's salon, at a given time, using all words to mean (speak of) what they do speak of in English. He thus spoke of there then being red meat on that rug, and of that as the way things were. Which *might* make one think that whether he thus spoke truth turns precisely on whether there was then red meat on that rug.

So let us set about so settling it. Returning from the market, Sid crosses the white rug, heading for the kitchen. As he does so, the bottom of his recycled-paper bag breaks, and the kidneys he has bought for the mixed grill fall in their butcher paper to the rug. Is there, now, red meat on the white rug? One question is whether kidneys count as meat. Though one would not offer them to vegetarians, their usual rubric (at any rate, in Sid's parts) is *offal*. Meat, on one understanding of the term, is flesh. And flesh, as one typically would understand that, is muscle. Thinking in this way, one should say that, however unenviable the condition of the rug, it does not, at any rate, have meat on it. On the other hand, what Sid dropped is, in fact, the meat course for Sunday brunch. So meat *can* be understood to be something which those kidneys are. Then there is the matter of being on the rug. The meat is still wrapped in its butcher paper. So, on one way of understanding things, it is (so far) only the paper that is on the rug. On the other hand, if Sid, now missing the kidneys, asks where they are, telling him, 'On the rug', *may* be saying no less than *where they are*.

How, then, *should* we settle the question whether there is meat on the rug? There *could* be an answer to that question. But there need not be. As I now speak (in this essay) nothing dictates counting kidneys as meat, nor counting their place in the surroundings as being on the rug. What it is to be meat, and to be on a rug, does not as such determine any one right answer. So if there is an answer, the circumstances in which to give it must play some role in fixing what that answer is. The present circumstances of this essay highlight that fact precisely by failing to do so.

But, if there is no unique right answer to the question whether the situation at hand counts as there being meat on the rug, there *can* be a unique right answer to the question whether things are as Pia said in so describing it. *That* is the point of historicism. Pia, noticing the ruined eco-bag, says, 'Sid, there's meat on the rug.' What now matters is not how *we* should settle the question whether there is meat on the rug, but rather how that question ought to be settled in the circumstances of Pia's speaking to it. Pia does so in particular circumstances which, unlike those of this essay, may call for an answer. Pia is, say, chiding Sid for being oblivious to the quotidian. In which case, kidneys may well do for meat; being wrapped in paper will do for being on the rug. That is how to answer the question in her circumstances. It is *that* fact, rather than how the question is to be answered in ours, which determines whether she spoke truth.

What our words speak of—being meat, being on a rug—admits of under-standings. There are different things being on a rug may, sometimes rightly, be taken to be, each with its own results for when things would be that way. Thus for *all* the ways for things to be our words speak of. Do I speak truth in saying that the cat is on the mat if its paws are off it? For a start, what would be the point (if any) of my saying so now, in these circumstances? With no answers to such questions, there is no answer to this one. What it is as such to be on a mat provides none. Circumstances must matter if there is to be either truth or falsehood to tell in so speaking. So history matters. The historical event of my saying such-and-such to be such-and-such way may be my saying what is true, or it may be my saying what is false. But we must refer to history—to what I was doing in speaking as I did—to see whether it is the one or the other (or neither).

We begin to get at that deeper possibility which Austin's shift in perspective makes room for. I described the cat as on the mat. What did I thus say to be so? Something so if its paws hang off? Or something not so in that case? Well, for what ought *I*, in so speaking, be held responsible? What treatment of the world is licensed if *my* words are true? I am held responsible for what *ought* to be demanded for speaking truly, in my circumstances, in describing things in the terms I did. What I said to be so is thus fixed (in part) by what speaking truly (then) would be. Just what Austin foresees.

The point's present linguistic cast *could* make one underestimate it. Frege suggests, in passing, that some things which appear as closed sentences may really be open ones:

Often . . . the mere form of words which can be fixed by writing or the phonograph is insufficient for the expression of the thought. . . . If the present tense is used to indicate a time, one needs to know when the sentence was uttered in order to grasp the thought correctly . . . In all such cases, the mere string of words, as is fixed in writing, is not the complete expression of the thought, but to grasp it correctly one still needs knowledge of certain circumstances accompanying its speaking.

(1918: 64)

The English string of words, 'The cat is on the mat', say, might be an open sentence, closed by reference to time: one made by the speaking of it, and *to* that speaking's time. So the English predicate, '__ is on the mat' is really a two-place predicate, true or false of an object such as a cat, and a time. Other predicates, on their surface, mere one, or two (or etc.) ones, may actually have many more places to be filled by times, places, speakers, indicated objects, and so on. Frege's suggestion shows that Austin's underlying point should really be understood as about open sentences. Let an English open sentence—say, '__ is on the rug'—have n places to be filled, for any n you like. So it is true, or false, of n-tuples of given sorts—an object, a time, a place, what have you. It thus speaks of a way for such an n-tuple to be. Then Austin's point is: the way it thus speaks of admits of understandings. There are various things it may be understood to be for an object to be on a rug at a time, for it to be on a rug at a time at a place, if that is relevant, for it to be on a rug at a time relative to any other set of parameters you think relevant. It is ways for n-tuples to be, or those our words speak of, which, intrinsically, admit of understandings.

The underlying point can take non-linguistic form. Frege tells us (in my terms) that a zero-place concept, and equally for any n, has a generality which looks out in a particular way beyond the particular case: for any concept there is a *range* of cases which would be ones of being that which the concept is a concept of. This is just to say: if it is a concept that is in question at all, then there is a determinate way things being as they are (or a thing being as it is) is to *matter* to the concept's being satisfied. For it to be a concept of a way *for* things to be, not *everything* can matter. Things need not be *just* as they are to be that way. What Frege calls a 'concept' is a function from (n-tuples of) objects to truth-values. But seeing such a function as what captures a particular generality of (an element of) a thought can mislead.

Suppose, on different usage, we take a concept to be identifiable by that which it is a concept of—some determinate way for things to be. Then Austin's point takes this form. A concept does, as Frege tells us, look beyond the particular case in some particular, determinate, way. But that way of looking outward leaves it negotiable which particular cases are to be classified within the range of cases of satisfying that concept (instancing the relevant way for things to be). The proper outcome of such negotiation is fixed by circumstances for engaging in it, or for treating one or another outcome as proper. Whether the cat's being as it is is its being on the mat, may depend on the circumstances in which, or the point for which, one is to treat it as that or not. If the generality of a thought-element (say, of something being on a mat) were captured by some function from objects to truth-values, then the cat, being as it is, must map onto the value true, or not, full stop. (Though such a function could no more capture it than it could that of a whole thought (say, that the cat is on the mat).) For Austin, however, it may *count*, or be to be counted, as a case of something being on the mat for some purposes, on some occasions, but not so count on others. If a concept is intrinsically one *of* being thus and so, then the link between concepts and what satisfies them is, Austin holds, via such a notion of counting, in given circumstances, as such-and-such, rather than just being *tout court*. Concepts, if they look beyond the particular case as Austin says they do in the zero-place case (a thought, or what *it* is of—the cat being on the mat), cannot be identified by any function from objects to truth-values (even if, for particular purposes, they may be treated as so identifiable).

This last point brings out the deep sense in which, for Austin, truth is a historical matter, and the deep change which Austin's change of perspective brings with it. Frege's argument for the invisibility of what raises questions of truth was, as I have read it, primarily a case for bringing the conceptual into the picture: no truth except of the conceptual (by its standing, I have argued, towards the non-conceptual)—an abstraction from the simple idea: no truth without representation. Nothing in Austin challenges *that* idea. For Frege, though, that idea appears to go with an ahistorical view of what being true is. For Austin, such ahistoricism obscures crucial aspects of what truth is. The difference comes out neatly in the above contrast between the views of each towards the way in which the conceptual looks out beyond the particular case. Austin's departure from Frege, such as it is, is elaborated within the framework Frege himself provides.

2.2 Ahistorical Truth

We have now dealt with Austin's central case. In my saying something to be so, the words I use invoke a particular bit of the conceptual. To just what cases— what bits of the non-conceptual—this bit of the conceptual reaches *so used* depends on the circumstances of its invocation. These decide for what work, in them, that bit of the conceptual ought to be held responsible, what is to be expected if it has *here* been deployed *truly*. They thereby decid (where it is decided) whether *this* (things being as they are) is any other than things are according to the invocation, any other than for what was invoked to do the work expected of it. What of other cases of truth-bearing?

What, for a start, would it be true to say? Perhaps that the cat is on the mat. This may just mean: it would be true for me, now, to say that cat to be on that mat. What it would now be true to say is what, if now said, would be said truly. Historicism for the central case already tells us when this would be. But if I tell you it is, or would be, true to say that the cat is on the mat, what I say need not be confined to saying something now. I may tell you something it would be true to say *wherever* it might be said, no particular occasion required for the saying. How should that idea be understood?

To identify something it would be true to say, I must invoke some bit of the conceptual, some zero-place concept. If occasions matter as they do on Austin's historicism, one would not always say the same thing to be so in invoking that bit of the conceptual to state something. Nor, more generally, would one always speak of the same thing being so in invoking it—here in mentioning something it would be true to say. I may mention something it would be true to say in invoking the concept of the cat being on the mat. I thus speak of a way which, according to me, it would be true to say things. Things would be the way I say it would be true to say things just where they would be as said, where I speak, in saying the cat to be on the mat. Historicism has already said where that would be. A zero-place concept need not be deployed assertively in order for the occasion of its deployment to do its work. (A caveat: saying that such-and-such need not always be saying such-and-such to be so. I am concerned here only with understandings on which it is that.)

When, in general, would one say what I thus said it would be true to say? When, in general, would one say things to be the way I thus spoke of? The

248 OBJECTIVITY AND THE PAROCHIAL

point of historicism is that one would not always say the same thing to be so in invoking a given bit of the conceptual. In particular, one would not always speak of the way I mentioned in, or by, invoking the concept of the cat being on the mat. Paws off the mat may matter to whether things are the way I so spoke of, but not to whether they are the way you now thus would, or vice versa. Where one would not speak of the right thing in invoking the concept I did, one would have to say what I said it would be true to say in another way, by invoking some other concept—if this could be said at all. What *other* concept might then do this job?

Austin tells us: 'a state of affairs which makes [a statement] true' can only be specified '*in words* (either the same, or, with luck, others)' (1950: 123). Sometimes the words *must* be others. When may they be? On occasion I may say what I want to say, or at least say to be so what I want to, equally well in different ways. I might say, 'There is meat on the rug', or, archly, 'There are edible animal parts on the carpet.' I can tell you what I think Frege's argument for *Sinn* is in any of several ways. My being right in this conspicuously does not depend on stating it in precisely the way Frege did. Kidneys instance the concept *meat* on some invocations of it, but not on others—on some, but not other, understandings of what being meat might be. So, normally, I could do this only where invoking the concept meat would be invoking it on an understanding on which kidneys would do. Even so, I could not reasonably expect that just *any* (sometimes) conceivable thing which would instance that one zero-place concept (there being meat on the rug) would, *ipso facto*, instance the other (there being edible animal parts on the carpet). Had beasts grown edible fur, things might have instanced the second of these without instancing the first. (That edible fur need not be meat on any plausible understanding of being meat.) So *this* cannot be a condition on there being different ways for me to say the thing I want to, or to say the same thing to be so—on that perfectly good notion of this on which the above may be doing it.

Not everything which would satisfy the concept *rug* (*moquette*, e.g.) would satisfy the concept *carpet* (as opposed to *carpeting*). Yet invoking either may be speaking of the same thing—that carpet. Similarly, not everything which satisfied *there being edible animal parts on the carpet* would satisfy *there being meat on the rug*. Yet invoking either may be speaking of the same way things are or not, on that good understanding of speaking of a way things are or not just canvassed. How so?

The conceivability of edible fur, or that just mentioned, need not bear on whether the above two ways of saying something are ways, on an occasion, for me to say the same thing—the thing I wanted to—or the same thing to be so. Why not? To start with, there is a good sense (if it is not more than that) in which, in the circumstances, there being edible fur does not count, is not to be treated, as a way things might be. (The world would belie this if there in fact were edible fur in reasonable proximity.) Edible fur—something on the order of candy floss—is, I think, conceivable. Genetic engineers may envisage it already for all I know. But it need not, for all that, count as possible.

That thought expands here along these lines. In the circumstances, treating edible fur as what there might be is not the way to guide one's treatment of things. It is not, at least, when it comes to engaging in those projects, or pursuing those aims to which, in the circumstances, I would speak—for whose guidance I am to be held responsible—in saying what I wanted to. This last remark condenses historicism's story of what it is for things being as they are to make for my having spoken truly—said what is true—in invoking, in my circumstances, some particular bit of the conceptual. So if edible fur is not, in the circumstances, to be treated as what there might be, then it does not bear on whether I would then have spoken truly in invoking the one of those above two zero-place concepts just where I would have done so in invoking the other—on that understanding of *just where* relevant to whether I would then count as having spoken of the same thing each time.

Stating something is, as said, offering a guide to treating things. Against this background, stating something in either of the two ways just mentioned may, in the circumstances, be offering the same guide. Against that background, each may say the same—may be to be held responsible for just the same—as to how to treat things. This can just be what it is for these to be two ways for me to say just what I wanted to, and to say the *same* thing to be so.

Suppose, now, that on one occasion I mention something it would be true to say to be so, and on another you are to say just *that* to be so. When would you count as having done so? I mention what I do in invoking the concept *there being meat on the rug*. You say what you do in invoking the concept *there being edible animal parts on the carpet*. Under what conditions would that be a success? The short answer is: just where invoking the first of these concepts on my occasion, and the second on yours, each time in saying something so, would be offering the same guide to treating things: the difference the guide you give makes, on yours, to how things are to be treated matches (nearly enough) the difference the guide given in invoking the concept I did would make to this. If there is meat on the rug, on the understanding on which I spoke of this, then there is urgent call for stain remover. Equally so if there are edible animal parts on the carpet, on the understanding on which you spoke of that. And so on. Along these lines, Austinian historicism makes sense of a notion of saying the same thing, so, too, of the same thing being so, which is both crucial to our cognitive economy and, without historicism, deeply mysterious.

There is one more notable case: that of (thinking) something it would be true to think. Here we deal in things necessarily ahistorical. For, as Frege showed, what *I* may think is what there is for *one* to think: there is no one one must be to think it. To see what truth comes to in this case, we might ask what I say of someone in saying him to believe that such-and-such. In doing this, I mention a thing there is to think. I do so by invoking some zero-place concept—say, that of meat being on the rug. In my invoking of it, I identify a way for things to be, where the circumstances of my invocation contribute to fixing just what way this would be. And I say the person to judge that things are—to take them to be—*that* way. The way I thus identify is the way things would be where there was meat on the rug on the understanding on which, in the circumstances, I spoke of this. It is a way things could be said to be, on my occasion, in speaking of there being meat on the rug, and a way things could be said to be on others—perhaps on mine too—by thus invoking different zero-place concepts. It is not (in general) tied specifically to any given one. As we have just seen, the 'where' in the above 'would be where there was meat on the rug . . .' must be understood accordingly. Historicism, in what has already been said about it, thus tells us what it is that I might say someone to think, and by what its features are fixed.

There is then the matter of someone thinking such a thing. Here we can follow Frege. Judging something, he tells us, is exposing oneself to risk of error. Something there is to think is a particular way of doing this, a particular way for the world to matter to whether one succumbs or escapes. What the thing is is fixed by when, if so exposed, one would succumb, when escape. Any thinker at a time exposes himself to risk of error. He is exposed to the error he is. He sets his course, or is prepared to, as he does, or is; there are countless ways for him to go awry. One arrives at the lecture hall at four o'clock to discover that the lecture was at three, or is in the basement, or is not the lecture one expected—had one but known, he would have stayed in bed. Such are among the myriad disappointments a given thinker, at a time, exposes himself to suffering.

For a thinker to think a particular thing there is to think—that things are such-and-such way—is for his exposure to error to articulate in a particular way, for there to be a certain discernible pattern in the way he is liable to disappointment, or to escaping it. (Something there is to think is thus a way for *a thinker's* exposure to error to articulate, not merely for this or that thinker's exposure to do so.) That a thing to think (a thought, in Frege's terms) is so identifiable is part of what it is for whole thoughts, as Frege puts it, to enjoy pride of place (relative to anything that might be an element in one). (See (1919a: 253).) The thought is that things are such-and-such way; there is a discernible way in which the thinker succumbing to or escaping error turns, or may turn, on whether things are that way. There is more to the story. One thinks what is a guide to conducting one's life, to treating things. So for one to think that such-and-such is for one to be suitably sensitive, in the way one is prepared to conduct his life, to the distinction between things being the way in question and their not, sensitive to it in a way such that that distinction can enter rationally into what one is prepared to do, and how one arrives at such preparedness.

So to credit someone with thinking such-and-such is to credit him with thinking things such-and-such way, which is to credit him with suitable sensitivity to whether things are that way. There are many things, any of which suitable sensitivity might sometimes come to. It need not involve, nor is generally confined to, sensitivity to the instancing of some particular zero-place concept which, on one occasion or another, might be invoked in *saying* things to be this way. So much is part of the ahistorical nature of objects of thought. Someone suitably sensitive to the instancing of meat being on the rug may or may not *thereby* be suitably sensitive to the instancing of edible animal parts being there, partly depending on how he is, but partly depending on what would count, for the purpose, as *suitable* sensitivity to this. So if I credit someone with thinking such-and-such—say, that there is meat on the rug—I credit him with some such suitable sensitivity, but what exactly I thus say of him depends on the circumstances of my saying it, in just the way that what I say of the rug in saying there to be meat on it does. Historicism speaks here as it speaks throughout.

That meat is on the rug on one understanding of this being so, and that meat is on the rug on another are, or may be, two different ways for things to be. There are, accordingly, or may be, two different things for one to think. Sensitivity, moreover suitable sensitivity, to whether things are the one way *need* not be sensitivity to whether they are the other. Thinking the one thing and thinking the other are, thus, two different ways for a thinker to be. This *can* suggest a picture on which what someone 'really' thinks is fixed uniquely, and precisely, just by how *he* is. So a given thinker may think one, or the other, or both, of the above things according to the precise nature of his sensitivity to things. Where it may be tempting to apply this picture, historicism has a reminder for us. What would be thinking such-and-such on some invocations of that concept would not be on others. Thinking such-and-such is something one may count as doing on some occasions for the counting, but not on others. Before looking for that precise understanding of meat being on a rug on which *that* is the way Pia thinks things, one should recall that whether she thinks this on any given such understanding is liable to depend on what one understands by her so doing. Austinian historicism contributes in this way, among others, to our understanding of the mind.

Someone *could* say, 'It is true that there is meat on the rug just in case there is meat on the rug.' If he thus said anything at all, it seems, whatever it was would be true. What could make that right? Just this (if it is so). *One* way for things to be, there being meat on the rug, is mentioned twice: the first time in identifying a way for it that would be true to say things to be, the second in identifying the way things would be if it *were* true to say so. Such a double-mention, in the context of *one* statement, will speak of that way for things to be, both times, on the same understanding of things being that way. Where this is so, the upshot is a truism. All of which, we now see, says nothing as to just *what* truism one would express in these words on a given occasion. Such depends on how one ought to understand, on that occasion, meat being on a rug. This points to why it is that the existence of such truisms has *no* implications as to the richness, or not, the concept truth is.

Is truth identity under predication? The core of that idea was: to judge that there is meat on the rug is already to judge that this is true—that so judging is a winning way of exposing oneself to risk of error. That idea survives historicism. To set out historicism, one needs to say quite a bit as to what it would be to be speaking, or thinking, truly, for something to be true to say, and so on. To say this is just to elaborate what one sees oneself as doing in taking something to be true, or true to say. As I have urged, that idea of identity under predication cuts against saying what it is for something to be true, or done truly, only where what one thus says is *not* part of what this is.

2.3 Merit

Austin's final word on truth is the set of lectures *How To Do Things With Words*. These aim for the demise of two closely related dichotomies (or 'fetishes'): one between that which is either true or false and that which is not, and one between fact and value. The procedure, in both cases, is to exhibit what is in common between evaluations as to truth or falsity, and evaluations as to the particular sorts of success or failure, goodness, or badness, to which other sorts of things we say—for example, commendations—are liable. Truth, Austin stresses, calls for the same sorts of virtues as does, say, fitting advice or a just verdict. It, like them, is the sort of thing which is *merited* or not.

The lectures are meant to bring us to see that:

Truth and falsity are . . . names for . . . a dimension of assessment—how the words stand in respect of satisfactoriness to the facts, events, situations, etc., to which they refer.

(1962a: 148)

But adequacy to what words represent as so

depends not merely on [their] meanings . . . but on what act you were performing in what circumstances.

(1962a: 144)

Which makes truth and falsity

a general dimension of being a right or proper thing to say as opposed to a wrong thing, in these circumstances, to this audience, for these purposes, and with these intentions.

(Ibid.)

Stating truly may thus prove not a (very) 'different *class* of assessment from arguing soundly, advising well, judging fairly, and blaming justifiably', 'the good reasons . . . for stating' not 'so very different from the good reasons . . . for . . . arguing, warning, and judging'(1962a: 141).

When a constative is confronted with the facts, we in fact appraise it in ways involving the employment of a vast array of terms which overlap with those that we use in the appraisal of performatives.

(1962a: 141–142)

Thinking of the rug as having meat on it may be a good, or adequate, way to think for the purposes of an occasion. *This* may be the rug being truly so describable. It being true so to describe the rug thus assimilates to it being right to call Sid mean for tipping as he did, or boorish for offering one at all to whom he did.

A fact-value dichotomy collapses because questions of truth do not *contrast* with questions of value as they would have to for the dichotomy in question. Whether it was true for Pia to say there was meat on the rug depends on whether the way the rug was *ought* to be so counted. Such is liable to depend on the value, to us, of counting this as meat being on the rug or not—recognizing it as instancing that way for things to be, where this is *Anerkennung*, and not the pure cognitive achievement which 'Erkennung' speaks of. Frege's fundamental relation is not one that either holds, or fails to hold, per se, between the rug in that condition, and something having meat on it. Meat being on a rug admits of understandings. One speaks truth in meeting one's responsibilities—those one incurs in purporting to do so (purporting to say how things are). Things must be as one is to be held responsible for their being, given the description one gave of things—is to be held responsible, that is, so far as *truth* is concerned. Truth is, in part, a matter of for what, in the circumstances, one ought to be held responsible.

What speaking truth would be on an occasion is fixed in part by what images are then apt for treating current matters—which, thus, *ought* to be employed. This *ought* resembles that in 'Ought Sid to be deemed rude or merely gauche?' Should I put things by saying that there is meat on the rug? One *could* put it that way if one counted Mary's lamb, for whom we have certain weekend plans, or Sid standing there, his belly full of sirloin, as meat on the rug. There *could* be occasions for so speaking. Is this one? Suppose that, eyeing the doomed lamb, I so speak. Do I thus commit myself to more than is so? I do if counting the lamb as meat is not a sufficiently good way of thinking of meat in the circumstances in which I speak—if, say, all attention is focused on what happened to Sid's steak. Truth—things being as I said—depends both on how the world is *and* on how, in what terms, it is *then* well thought of. The question is which bits of the non-conceptual are to be counted, for this purpose, as instancing this bit of the conceptual. It is a question of *Anerkennung*, where there is *no* question of pure *Erkennung*.

Sid is standing on the rug, belly full of sirloin. Should that count as meat being on the rug? It is, in ways, *like* things which surely would so count. Sid's belly surrounds the sirloin topologically speaking as butcher paper would. We can see how we would have to think of meat being on a rug to think of this as an instance of it. So one sometimes might. Here is a discernible way one *might* fit the non-conceptual to the conceptual—discern ranges of instances. But is this a way to do it in the kitchen, as we begin to search for what has fallen from the broken bag? Are the similarities here helpful, useful? Or is the better course here to exploit the dissimilarities? The concept of meat on a rug does not decide this. This occasion for exploitation must tell us if anything can. It can do so only given what the goal *truth* here demands.

To hold words *satisfactory* for a given situation is not just to hold a view as to how the things described are, but also one as to the right way of thinking of that which the concepts thus expressed are concepts of—for example, of meat being on a rug. Austin's point is: the right way of thinking of being such-and-such is always the right way for, or on, given occasions for so thinking. Truth is *thus* the name of a general dimension of assessment of the suitability of words both for the specific situations they are used to speak of, *and* for agents who, in the circumstances of their speaking, are to take them in one way or another.

In speaking of there being meat on the rug I commit myself to the *suitability* of a way of thinking of the rug in its current condition. We are all staring at Sid's ruined eco-bag, wondering what happened to the meat. There is nothing on the rug but Mary's lamb. 'There is meat on the rug' is hardly suitable for that. The way the rug is *might* be described, for *some* purposes, as there being meat on it. But not for these. Meat on the rug should not *so* be understood here. It is thanks to such facts that I can speak truth, or falsehood, at all in using this description. If I take myself to be speaking truth in giving it, there are thus two ways I might be wrong. The world might be other than I think. I may be shocked to find no sirloin on the rug. Or I may be wrong as to the sort of rug which, here, is aptly so described. If the first is failure to appreciate the world's condition, the second is failure to appreciate the circumstances in which I speak. Those two different things to be wrong about correspond to two different things to say in using the words in question: that *this* is meat being on a rug, or, given what meat on it would be, that such is the way the rug is.

Which descriptions it would be true to give of things depends on the occasion for the giving. Whether a given instance of saying something is truly describable as speaking truly also so depends. Pia said there to be meat on the rug. Did *she* speak truth? Only if she met the responsibilities she ought to have in so speaking on that occasion; only if she ought to be held responsible for no more than things as they are. What responsibilities were these? The answer to that question, as to any other, is liable to depend on the occasion for giving it. On the rug, Sid has displayed his new work of art: a ribeye in a block of perspex. There may be two ways of viewing the circumstances of Pia's speaking, neither incorrect as such. On one the circumstances demanded more of Pia's speaking truth than the world delivered. On the other they did not. There may then be occasions for viewing things in the first way, while there can be others for viewing things in the second. In the first sort, Pia may truly be said not to have spoken truth; in the second to have done so.

On Austin's view, representing in, or by, descriptions articulates into identifiable sub-tasks: suiting one's way of representing to the work it ought to do on its occasion, and then suiting it to the world it represents as a certain way. Applied to what we say, can truth then be an identity under predication? In judging, truth is at work at ground level. To judge that there is meat on the rug is to see this as what judging *truly* would be. It is, *ipso facto*, to see oneself as doing all that judging truly would be. It is for that reason and no other that judging it to be true that there is meat on the rug is judging no more than what one does in judging there to be meat on the rug. A similar point holds of stating. This, too, is aiming at truth, or so representing oneself. So if to arrive at that goal is to do such-and-such—fit words, say, to the work expected of them—then in stating, say, that there is meat on the rug, one represents oneself as doing that. If one were to *say* oneself to be doing precisely what one thus represents oneself as doing—in, say, saying it now to be true to say that there is meat on the rug— one would thus thereby represent nothing as so that one had not already represented as so in simply saying there to be meat on the rug. So, for the same reason as in judging, if one were to say oneself to be saying *truly* that there was meat on the rug just in case there was meat on the rug, one would state a truism. Which is no sign that there is any less to being true than Austin points to.

Frege tells us,

We express recognition (Anerkennung) of truth in a statement's form. We do not use the word 'true' for this. And even if we do use it, the true assertive force does not lie there, but in the form of the statement, and where this loses its assertive force, the word 'true' cannot restore it.

(1918: 63)

We represent ourselves as recognizing *truth* in stating what we do merely in stating what we do. Truth need not be mentioned. If we substitute 'act' for 'form', the point holds on Austin's view. To say there to be meat on the rug, or just to speak of there so being, is to speak of the condition of the rug, whereas to speak of it being true to describe the rug as having meat on it is to speak of the fate of a particular description. On the face of it, there are two different topics here. But one says there to be meat on the rug in using a particular description—either of the rug as having meat on it, or some other which would suffer the same fate. In using this description in the act of stating, one represents it as a way of telling truth, whereas in so representing it by *mentioning* it as a way of speaking truth, one represents what it would thus speak of—the condition of the rug—as what it needs to be for this to *be,* to instance, speaking truly. So one speaks truth in the first of these ways just in case one does in the second—just so long as in both cases one speaks of there being meat on the rug on the same understanding of there so being. For all of which, speaking truth may depend on all those factors Austin calls to our attention.

If I describe the rug as having meat on it, I am right just in case counting the rug's being as it is as its having meat on it is a right way of fitting the non-conceptual to the conceptual on the occasion of my so describing things. If I describe *that there is meat on the rug* as something it would be true to say, I am, again, right on that same condition. If I did both things at once—for example, in the context of one statement—I would be right in both, or in neither. But suppose I do each thing on a different occasion. I say, 'There is meat on the rug', say, where so counting things is a *wrong* way of fitting the non-conceptual to the conceptual. So I speak falsely. I say, 'It would be true to say that there is meat on the rug', or 'Describing the rug as having meat on it would be speaking truly' on an occasion on which so counting the condition of the rug would be a right way of fitting the non-conceptual to the conceptual. So I speak truly. Does this truth not entail that I spoke truly on that occasion where, as we have said already, I in fact spoke falsely? No. For what I say it would be true to say where I speak of this is not what I did say on the first: what is so according to the one thing is not that which is so according to the other.

I may, on an occasion, say what counts, on some further one as having spoken truly, and on some yet further one as not having done so. But I cannot, on any occasion, count as having done what would have counted as speaking truly on the occasion on which I did it, but which, on this further occasion, does not. For that would be for me to count as having fitted the non-conceptual to the conceptual, on my occasion, in what was then a right way—as it then did count as fitting—while, simultaneously, counting as not having done so. There is no occasion for counting me as having done all that.

Austin's view of truth takes this form. The conceptual—the general—does not alone decide how it relates to the non-conceptual—the particular case. It alone does not decide which pairs, to which it contributes but one member, belong to the extension of that fundamental relation, *instancing*. More positively put, it allows for different ways of allocating particular cases to the ranges of generality it marks out, so as to be flexible as to the work done by assigning a case to a given range—the sort of guide such an assignment may be to one's dealings with the world. So it is the work that would be done by a given assignment, the kind of guidance this would be, that must decide how the conceptual is to be taken as relating to the particular for the purposes of given representing. In general, such can give no determinate results apart from a particular occasion on which such an allocation is to be put to work.

As he tells this story, Austin places great stress on a feature I have so far suppressed: a statement is not always true or false. But *so* much was in the cards as soon as our starting point was in view. What meat being on a rug is does not, as such, decide what does and does not instance this. There are, after all, Mary's lamb, and Sid's belly. There are various ways of thinking about such things. The *point*, on an occasion, of classifying Mary's lamb as meat on the rug, or as not, may decide how we should then speak of things. It *may*; but it need not. If (the concept of) meat being on a rug does not as such do the needed work, nothing else is *guaranteed* to do it either. Is France a hexagon? Just what are you prepared to call a hexagon? Tell me what is to follow, on an occasion, from my calling France one and I *might* have an answer for you. But I might not. It might still be all the same whether you so call France or not.

Austin's view of truth is, he tells us, meant as an attack on a dichotomy between fact and value: what to do in saying how things are is just a particular question as to what to do, continuous with others in the relation of its answer to what matters, or ought to matter to us. There seems room here for conflict with Frege, who is most concerned to stress that questions of truth arise for stances as to how things *are*, their truth settled (if at all) solely by things being as they are, no matter how that matters to us. But we must here recall the difference, on Austin's view, between the question whether things are such-and-such way and, where someone spoke of things as being that way, the question whether things are as he thus said (or spoke of their being). To settle the question what to do, on an occasion, to say how things are, and to settle it in favour of speaking of things as being such-and-such way is to settle for what one is held responsible in then so speaking—for example, whether for more than the presence of Mary's lamb on the carpet would make so. It is for that that what matters (or ought to matter) to us matters. As to whether the world is as one is thus responsible for it being, that is as much purely a question of how things are as it is on Frege's view. The difference is just that, on Austin's view, how what matters for us in our dealings with the world matters to for what one makes himself responsible in speaking of things as some given way is, as much as anything else, part of what being true is. This idea can fit with Frege's conception of the objectivity of judgement. The demise of a fact-value distinction is not the demise of fact.

3. Reconciliation

A question of truth arises just where something is *represented* as so: that things are a certain way. For such a question to arise, there must be, on the one hand, how things *were* thus represented, so what they need to be to be that way, and, on the other, how things, or the things so represented, in fact are. There is truth just where things being as they are is their being as represented. So one raises a question of truth in representing only where one's representing makes for such a thing as how things must be to be as represented, so only where it distinguishes what matters to things so being from what does not.

Frege stresses this. Austinian historicism acknowledges it. So far, Frege and Austin are one. Each, though, develops this idea differently. Frege thinks in terms of identifiable questions of truth—ones there are for *one* to raise. Representing, so speaking, truly or falsely is raising some specific one of these. One speaks truly just where *that* question has a positive answer. For Austin, speaking truly is satisfying the demands of an occasion. To speak truth is, to be sure, to say things to be as they are and not otherwise. But for any question of truth there is for *one* to raise, what would be doing this in raising any *given* such question on an occasion is liable to vary not just with what the question is, but also with the occasion of its raising. An occasion may add to, or modify, what a given question anyway demands. If whether there is meat on the rug is such a question, then whether the meat may be unwrapped will depend on the occasion of its raising. And so it would be for any other such question we know to ask. When things would be as I represented them is not settled by the mere fact of my having raised such-and-such question, though, depending on what the question is, and how the world is, such may—or may not—decide whether I in fact spoke truth.

Truth is a point at which the conceptual and the non-conceptual meet. What questions arise at that point as to *when* something would be true depend on how things are. I may ask of the way the rug in fact is whether just this is things being as represented on some occasion in speaking of there being meat on it; I can think that just this *is* that. I could not have had that thought—thought just *that* to be things being as represented—were the rug not just as it is. Such would not change how things were represented in what raised that question, on any reasonable understanding of this. This points to a way in which a way for *one* to represent things cannot foresee all such questions which *may* arise, so how reference, after the fact, to the circumstances of a representing of things as that way is always liable to be called for. Such lies at the core of Austin's view.

On the other hand, it is absolutely central to the notions of truth, and of judgement, that to think, or speak, truly or falsely is to represent things as a way there is for *one* to think them. Any one of us may judge, or say, only what there is for *one*—no particular one—to represent (to himself, or to others) as so. As Frege stresses, thoughts—the contents of a truth-evaluable stance—are *essentially* sharable. They must be so to be thoughts at all. So if on one occasion I say something to be so, others may say, or think, just that to be so on others. Austin's account of truth-telling must be true to this idea. It is so on the right (the needed) understanding of same-saying. It was the burden of section 2.2 to set out just what this understanding is.

Frege and Austin stress different strands in the notion truth. But there is not much on which they need divide. Each of their ways of portraying truth is a correct way, and, each, the right one for the purposes each philosopher envisages. For each spoke to different questions about truth's role. Seeing the concerns of just one thinker as the only ones in which truth figures can make them seem at odds where they need not be. Frege's central concern was, in his own picturesque terms, for truth to be something whose content would be unfolded in laws of logic. Truth was to be that by which logic got a grip on thought. This leads him to say—rightly for his purpose:

A concept that is not sharply defined is wrongly termed a concept. Such quasi-conceptual constructions cannot be recognised as concepts by logic; it is impossible to lay down precise laws for them. The law of excluded middle is really just another form of the requirement that the concept should have a sharp boundary. Any object $\varDelta$ that you choose to take either falls under the concept $\varPhi$ or does not fall under it, *tertium non datur*.

(Frege, 1903, §56)

Suppose there is on the rug one rack of ribs and one clump of *ris d'agneau*. Suppose that the concept *meat* is undefined for the case of *ris d'agneau*, or the concept *piece*, in the context *piece of meat*, for the case of *racks* of ribs, or *clumps* of *ris d'agneau*. Then the thought that there are two pieces of meat on the rug lacks a truth-value. And the rot spreads. For now what of the concept *equinumerous with the concept* either zero or one? Is the concept *piece of meat on the rug* in its extension? There is no saying. Arithmetic is in trouble. This might seem to exclude Austin's role for occasions: specify an object and a (genuine) concept; then of what conditions of things it could be said truly that that object falls under that concept cannot depend on the occasion of saying this.

Frege's problem, given his concern, is that, as he says, logic does not apply to what he calls 'quasi-conceptual constructions'. Nor, he adds, could any precise laws do so. Logic, though, is concerned, *au fond*, with what is so or not: with what follows from something's being so, and what entails that it is. If we think of thoughts as identified by what is so according to them, then logic describes the most general ways the truth of some thoughts may depend on that of others—the most general structure of dependencies that would be found in any, or any large enough, system of thoughts. There is no place in such a system for what would behave as a quasi-conceptual construction would. That such is excluded is, as Frege notes, reflected, in classical logic, in the law of excluded middle. A zero-place quasi-conceptual construction is liable to be neither true nor false, a possibility excluded by this law—and excluded equally by intuitionist logic, even without generating this law.

Logic does not describe the behaviour of quasi-conceptual constructions. Its concern is with what is *so*, and what not, with what else would be so or not if such-and-such. It is concerned with that in whose obtaining a judgement is correct or not. So to see logic as speaking to a thought is already, *ipso facto*, to see that thought as of what is so, or what is not, that *that* is so or not. So, it may seem, a thought must be of what would be so or not no matter how things were. This may seem at odds with Austin's view of what it is to represent as so.

But if logic does not apply to quasi-conceptual constructions, this just means that we must apply logic only to what is *treatable* as a conceptual construction in Frege's sense—so treatable, that is, for purposes of the application we want to make. Pia said there to be meat on the rug. If it turned out that the rug was empty but for a ribeye encased in perspex, nothing to be understood as to how things were according to her might then decide whether things were as she thus said. In this case, she would have spoken neither truth nor falsehood. This is compatible with there being no problem as to whether what she said *is* true or false, or would be under those circumstances which matter, for present purposes, in considering what follows from what. In this case, we can treat Pia as having expressed a thought by Frege's standards, something treatable as a zero-place *concept*, and no mere quasi-conceptual construction. To count Pia as having said something true (or false), we must count things as flatly being as she said (or not), independent of how one thinks of this. So we count her as having expressed a thought—one we can then mention as *the thought that there is meat on the rug*—which, just in being the thought it is, decides wherever need be what makes it true and what makes it false. It can be correct, on occasion, so to view her. What she did may then count as doing that.

At the same time, it may be considerations of the merit, in the circumstances, of describing the condition of the rug in those terms, where there *are* two ways of viewing this, which make it right so to view her. Truth enters at this point, too, in pointing to how we may rightly regard one another. Both Frege's and Austin's views of truth thus find their place.

One applies logic to quasi-conceptual constructions on a premise: so far as it matters for our current inferential ends, those constructions will behave like concepts in Frege's sense. The world *may* always let us down in this. In which case we may discover that logic does not quite have the import it seemed to. That ribeye encased in perspex may show this. But that the world *may* let us down does not mean it *will*. Logic can have just the import it would on our application. Such is something we can sometimes know. Austin's view of truth makes room for logic's application. Where it applies, it applies just as Frege's view of truth requires.

9

The Shape of the Conceptual

The human intellect and senses are, indeed, *inherently* fallible and delusive, but not by any means *inveterately* so....Being aware that you may be mistaken doesn't mean merely being aware that you are a fallible human being.

(J. L. Austin (1946: 98))

Kant raised a problem for philosophy. It may be part of someone seeing something—part of what it would be for it to be *seeing* we are discussing— that someone *sees* only what comes before his eyes. But that there is such a thing as seeing so conceived—that for someone to see (or even not see) something is, so conceived, a way for things to be—can admit of, and then need, showing. There is room for *showing* our concepts, or forms of thought, to fit the world (what there is to think about)—though Kant did not quite see just *what* such room there is. So, it can seem, that we see (some of but) only what comes before our eyes cannot follow merely from what seeing is to be supposed to be. Kant's plan for showing our concepts to fit the world cannot work. Frege, and early Wittgenstein, worked to show how no such proof is needed. Their plan for showing this does not work either, which has made some despair of there being such things as truths which follow merely from which concepts are in question. Such despair would be a draconian way with thought itself. It is Putnam who showed us the true nature and significance of the worries Kant saw room for; and who thus was able to find the right way with those problems Kant could not solve and Frege and early Wittgenstein could not dissolve. This is a synopsis of a story I will now begin to tell.

1. Preliminaries

Kant aimed to make philosophy (or metaphysics) respectable. He faced a problem about the credentials of what we can see (or seem to see) of the conceptual. We can frame the problem in terms of a posture towards the world which Kant, and Frege, called *judging* (*urteilen*). On this usage, judging is a posture for *one* to hold towards things (where it is a solecism to ask *which* things). It is identified by one central ambition: to be held in a world it would be right for. Where there is such a posture, a world it was right for would be a certain sort of world; there is something it would be for the world to be this. The posture identifies *what* this would be. The posture is for holding in a world which is thus and so. Holding it is thus committing to the world so being, a commitment correct or incorrect (if at all) *solely* by virtue of the *world* so being, or not. Where there is such a posture, there is, accordingly, a *thought*—that the world is thus and so, a thought true or false according as that posture would be one correctly held. A thought is thus, as per Frege (1918: 60) that which raises some particular question of truth.

What there is to judge depends, for one thing, on how the world is. Had evolution omitted sloths, there would be no such thing as judging that sloths like bananas. Had cuisine omitted *torresmos*, there would be no such thing as judging that *torresmos* are fried. A complementary thought: for any opportunity the world affords for judging, one would need the means to recognize it to be able so to judge. One would need to be suitably endowed. In general, though perhaps not always, a thinker *need* not be so positioned.

A converse thought is: how one is endowed as thinker determines what it is that one can judge: which opportunities, afforded by the world, are open to him. Or, on second thought, it would do that insofar as what it equips one to see as opportunities really are that, really are afforded by the world. And now a worry. If I am able to judge things a certain way—able to hold just that posture—this must be through a cooperation between mind and world. The, or my, mind must equip me for opportunities the world in fact provides. But if, or where, co-operation is genuinely called for, how could we know whether it existed?

This is one version of the most general form of Kant's problem. Another version exploits a distinction which starts from this idea:

A thought always contains something which reaches beyond the particular case, by means of which this is presented to consciousness as falling under something general.

(Frege: 1882b, *Kernsatz* 4)

A thought—the content of a judgement—fixes when the world *would be* right for the holding of that posture: what is required for it being so. What it thus requires of the world cannot be merely that things be as they are. Such a judgement could only be what would be expressed in answering, 'Thus!' to the question, 'How are things?' It would not be *judging* things to be some way at all. A thought, to be a thought at all, must fix what *matters* to things being as they are according to it, what measure things being as they are comes up to if the thought is true. If the thought is that red meat is on the white rug, it is of a way things might have been had the meat been drier, or from a different species, had Pia's eyes been green, had Sid not grunted. But not if the rug were bare. The thought represents the particular case, things being as they are, as *one* way, within a range of ways, in which things being as they were would be things being as they are according to it. It *reaches* to a range of what would thus instance it. Such is its intrinsic generality.

What a thought represents as instancing its generality is things being as they are. Things of a sort to instance—fall under—such generality do not themselves have it. There is no *range* reached to by things being as they are, nothing *it* asks for making some posture right. Nothing *else* could instance it.

The generality intrinsic to a thought is shared by other things. If we decompose a thought into parts, we will always, Frege tells us, arrive at some part which has it. What the thought that Sid grunts requires of the world *can* be decomposed into requiring that *Sid* be some way, and that *being a grunter* be that way. This last demand might be met in a variety of ways—for example with or without torn T-shirts—all the ways there are for someone to be a grunter. So this element in a thought reaches to a range of cases just as a thought does. So, too, for that way for someone to be—being a grunter—and so too for a way for things to be, for example for Sid to be a grunter. By contrast, Sid's being as he is lacks the reach in just the same way as things being as they now are does. Nothing in the way he is fixes what any given posture asks for being right.

Henceforth, I will call what has this distinctive generality *conceptual*, and what lacks it *nonconceptual*. We might speak of what is conceptual, collectively, as *the* conceptual. If we permit ourselves to think of this collectivity as a domain, we can also think of the conceptual as having a *shape*, formed by all the bearings instancing some bits of it have on instancing others. Bearing *may* be entailing, as (one case) for something to instance being red is *ipso facto* for it to instance being coloured. But it may also take more subtle, less easily formulated, forms. Being red, say, if it does not strictly *entail* not being green, may still be something such that being red always counts, so far as it goes, against counting as being green. Or perhaps being red (and, in its own way, being a pig) is the sort of thing to be, generally, *visible*. And so on. On the other side of the distinction, the nonconceptual (things being as they are) just is whatever the world supplies by way of it. What instances any bit of the conceptual is none other than whatever the world supplies to do so. So now Kant's problem in a different form. What assurance is there that the world supplies anything to instance (or counter-instance) any bit of the conceptual which our endowment as thinkers—our equipment to think—brings, or seems to bring, into view?

2. Kant: Engagement

Kant thought that where our mental equipment saddles us with thinking in given terms, there needs to be assurance of adequate cooperation between mind and world: a substantive demand is made on the *world*. Demonstrating such cooperation, where the conceptual concerns philosophy, he saw as *crucial* to respectable philosophy. It is not clear how *pressing* he thought the task in general, though if it is pressing where he thinks it is, it *should* be pressing throughout. Kant marks the *crucial* area thus:

> Among the manifold concepts which form the highly complicated web of human knowledge, there are some which are marked out for pure *a priori* employment, in complete independence of all experience; and their right to be so employed always demands a deduction. For since empirical proofs do not suffice to justify this kind of employment, we are faced by the problem how these concepts can relate to objects which they yet do not obtain from any experience.
>
> (1781/1787: A85/B117)

So begins the 'deduction of the categories'.

Kant has this much right: if assurance is needed that the world permits of being thought of in some given way, such assurance had better come from how the *world* is. Our way of thinking of the world is all right only if the world provides those opportunities for judging one would exploit if judging in so thinking. It is for the *world* to provide the opportunities or not. Kant's plan for showing that it does, in matters which concern him, is to locate some tract of reality necessarily so shaped as to provide the opportunities there would thus have to be. Kant thinks this is the only possible plan.

By 'tract of reality' I mean something on which the truth of a judgement might turn, something a thought might represent as a certain way. Such talk simply prescinds from questions of whether Kant needs special *objects* to judge to be ways for *a thing* to be.

The tract Kant wants would permit judgements of *all* the most general shapes ours might take. It would also, while not the only tract, be all *we* ever genuinely *judged* of. For *any* (finite) sentient thinker, he thinks, there would be some tract so shaped. Necessarily, he thinks, there is such a tract if we experience at all. Necessarily, it contains the requisite shapes.

What tract might play the role Kant assigns it: first, to be that which we *judge* to be, and experience being, thus and so; second to be, by nature, incapable of failing to give those 'pure *a priori*' concepts which concern Kant, those employments he sees them as marked out for? How could both these demands be satisfied at once?

Kant's tract consists of what he calls 'appearances'. These 'have no independent existence outside our thoughts' (A491/B519). They 'do not exist in themselves but only relatively to the subject in which, so far as it has senses, they inhere' (B164). Their career is exhausted by our sensory awareness of them. 'Nature' he tells us, our habitat, 'is merely an aggregate of appearances, so many presentations of the mind.' The trick is to be: those very faculties which saddle us with *judging* things of the forms we do are what enable us to experience appearances (or to experience at all); they thus shape *what* we experience—give it forms exactly corresponding to our forms of judgement. So those general principles which hold, *ipso facto*, of judgements of the forms our mind makes available to us must also hold of that which we experience. Given, but only given, our mind's role in providing these objects of experience, things could not be otherwise in this respect.

The point of Frege's *Kernsatz* 4 applies here. A judgement (or its content) presents the particular case as falling under a certain generality, in bringing it within a certain range of cases. The judgement belongs to the conceptual. It reaches to, and thus is *of*, the nonconceptual. It is things being as they are which is, or is not, things being as judged. So if we take Kant's idea seriously we must see our minds as forming the nonconceptual itself, or that tract of it of which we judge. Those very faculties by which we experience it as we must must also work to make *it* just as we thus experience it. (It is difficult, as Frege notes (e.g., 1918: 70–72) to take this idea entirely at face value, which may explain talk of 'transcendental' and 'empirical' things to say.)

Appearances *have* been conceived as what must be as experienced—a conception rife in Kant's time, and still extant. Kant may have *wanted* no part of it (see B275–276), though wanting is not always having. On this notion, appearances are contents of someone's consciousness in Frege's sense: for any given one, there is someone one must be to be aware of, or experience, it; its career is coeval with that awareness of it. Nothing beyond what someone is aware of in experiencing such an appearance bears on whether it is thus and so, for it has no career beyond its experiencing which could make something bear. So one could not *mistakenly* take it to be thus and so. But, as Frege showed (1918) this is because one could not really *take* it to be thus and so at all. For, with a career so attenuated, it would not be an object of *judgement*: it could not, in being as it is, instance *things* being some way they might be judged to be. Such appearances cannot guarantee any concept employments, a fortiori not those Kant sees as marked out for those concepts he calls 'categories'. They are useless for Kant's purpose. They do not provide opportunities for *judgements* of any form, hence not for those of the forms our faculties provide for us. We must hope this is *not* Kant's notion. But I begin with it.

As Frege notes, it is a solecism to speak of *perceiving* (seeing, tasting, etc.) contents of consciousness (1918: 67). A core idea has driven many philosophers to just this gaffe. Suppose that my experience on an occasion is such that, for a certain way there is for things to be, if things were that way, that experience would provide no means for me to tell that I was not experiencing, or in, the presence of F, but I would not in fact, be experiencing, or in the presence of F, but rather in the presence of, or experiencing, some ringer for that, G. For example, if I were in the presence of a very clever wax lemon, rather than a lemon, I could not tell from my visual, or auditory, or etc., experience on that occasion that this was so. Then, the idea is, I then experience something which I would be experiencing either way—whether in the presence of (or experiencing) F or G. (A possible addition: I *directly* experience at most that. But this goes beyond the present point.)

Call some such thing *H*. Suppose that there are circumstances which, if they obtained, would be ones in which, on the occasion now in question, I would not be experiencing H, but such that my (current) experience would provide no means for me to tell this. Then the argument repeats itself: there is something I would then be experiencing whether I were then experiencing H, or what I would be in these other circumstances. Call that *J*. Now the rest of the core idea: in experiencing what I do on that occasion—in the presence of F, say—I experience something, call it *K*, for which there are *no* circumstances in which, if they obtained, I would not be experiencing *that*.

Nothing which bore on whether, on that occasion, I was experiencing F rather than G (or vice versa), and which was not then manifestly (for me) present in my experiencing what I then did bears on whether I am then experiencing H. By parallel, *nothing* not then, for me, manifestly (recognizably) present in my experiencing what I then did bears on whether I was then experiencing K. Such a terminus for this core idea is one notion of (an) appearance. *Such* a terminus is a content of consciousness in Frege's sense: whenever I perceptually experience *anything*, I experience (visually, aurally, etc.) some content of consciousness: nothing bears on whether *it* is present other than my experience being, for me, manifestly as it is; so it can *have* no career extensive enough to allow for such bearing.

Frege's brief is that where this line of thought terminates, so, too, does any possibility of *judgement*: there is *no* way *such* appearances might or might not be, and might be judged to be. In *very* brief synopsis, it is part of our ordinary understanding of *truth* that what would be what a judgement was true of—what would be things being as they are according to it—is what *one* could see to be this; what bore on, or was borne on by, a judgement's truth is what *one* could see to do this (where bearing always extends beyond our present ken). *One* could not grasp what it would be for a (would-be) judgement about a content of consciousness to be true: for that one would need to see how that 'judgement' reached to relevant cases of the nonconceptual; for a content of consciousness, there is someone one would need to be to do this. So 'true' could apply to such a would-be judgement only on some new understanding of truth. But a new understanding of a concept is an understanding of what it would be *true* of. So there is no means for introducing what is needed here. So there can be no such judgements. (See Travis: 2005.)

Appearances as per above thus cannot validate what Kant wants validated. So he had better seek another notion. It needs to be one which makes appearances independent enough of what anyone is aware of in any experience of them to make room for judgement. As Frege put it, judging of an environment is exposing oneself to risk of error. Judging about appearances in the needed sense had better be exposing oneself to risk of error—except, perhaps, in those special cases in which what is judged is just what must be so for those concepts of concern to Kant to have those employments he sees marked out for them. At the same time, it must be that appearances, in this sense, could not be other than they must be for those concepts to have those employments. How is this to work?

To get judgement into the picture at all, a Kantian appearance must be something for *one* to experience (as *one* may experience Sid's sallow appearance) so as to be able to think the conceptual to reach *thusly* to them. They must have careers independent enough of us for them to bear, and be borne on, by things beyond our ken, so that a judgement that they are thus and so may be correct or not independent of our awareness, or acknowledgement, of its so being. If I judge that *this* berry is red, then, for Kant, for things to be as I judge is none other than for appearances to be a certain way. And, he tells us, appearances exist 'only relative to a subject' in whom, thanks to his senses, they 'inhere'. But, however that may *sound*, whether appearances are as I thus judge them is independent of what any, or all, of us is aware of, and of any attitudes we may have towards appearances. Such allows my posture towards (as it were) that berry to be a *judgement*.

But now we come to the second demand. For those concepts which concern Kant to have application to the objects of our experience—for those objects to admit of judgements of the forms we are saddled with—is for certain general temporal, locational, causal, principles to be true. However independent of us appearances' careers may be, they must not be *so* independent as to leave room for the possibility that *these* principles are false. Now the question is: if they are independent enough of us to leave room for the berry *not* being red, even if everyone insists it is, what stops their independence at just this point?

One answer might be: whether *these* principles hold does not depend in any way on what a world is like. They do not say the world we judge of to be one way rather than another. They would hold no matter what. That would be to deny the antecedent in Kant's good idea. *If* a guarantee were needed that the world we inhabit is one of those admitting of judgements of those forms ours are bound to take, rather than one of those which do not, it would need to be the *world* that supplied that guarantee. But no such guarantee is needed. Frege and Tractarian Wittgenstein had this idea. It is not Kant's. For him it is *only* because we judge only of appearances that there are the guarantees he seeks. These supply the needed guarantee because of the special sort of career they lead. They are the right sort of thing to validate the principles Kant wants validated.

What then? One such principle might be (roughly): everything has a cause. This entails: that berry's being red has a cause. The career of some appearances (or, if one allows oneself the conceit, of the berry) is independent enough of us to allow for the berry not being red, even though it may seem patent to us that it is. Why is it not independent enough of us to allow for its turning out that the berry's being red lacks a cause? In which case, since its having one follows from the principle, the principle is false. In outline, the story is supposed to go like this. We could not *experience* unless our faculties shaped, organized, our experience in a certain way. So *what* we experience—that on which the truth of our judgements turn—*is* so shaped. We experience *that berry* as *being red*. We might do that even if that berry were not red. It might just so seem to us. But not if that *object* were not a certain *way* for an object to be.

The idea seems a fundamental mistake. *Perhaps* we could not experience at all without experiencing what we do *as* given objects having given properties, or participating in causal networks, or whatever. It is another thing to say that what we experience *is*, in fact, all that. Those faculties shape *experiencing*. They are thus meant to give form to *what* we experience; just that form which those same faculties impose, ineluctably, on our thought. *Such* a form belongs to the conceptual—membership captured here by that 'as' after experience. The form reaches to a *range* of cases. Recall now *Kernsatz* 4. The form reaches in representing (or here presenting) the *particular* case—something nonconceptual as falling under a certain generality—falling within some particular range of cases. What does that does not provide, nor change, the nonconceptual itself. It merely stands in a particular way towards the nonconceptual anyway provided. What imposes form on a bit of the conceptual—its place within the conceptual as a whole—imposes nothing on the nonconceptual itself. At best it makes some bit of the conceptual something which the nonconceptual recognizably instances. So if our faculties condemn us to experiencing the nonconceptual—as much of it as we do experience in experiencing Kantian appearances—as though it instanced such-and-such in the conceptual, that is without effect on whether what we thus experience in fact does so—particularly not if what I experience of the nonconceptual on an occasion—things appearing as they then do—is something there is for *one* to experience, if appearances thus belong to things. (Notions of appearance which do not allow this have been dealt with already.) So if there ever was a question as to whether the objects of our experience provide those employments to our (most general) concepts which were marked out for them, it *cannot* be answered by pointing to what shapes our experiencing of them.

Verificationism may seem to offer hope. Since we cannot but experience appearances as just what the categories call for, nothing we could ever learn from experience could count against the (now *thesis*) that appearances *are* just what is called for. But this, as we now know, is simply false. Perhaps no single experience could give evidence that all was not right with the categories. But experiences must all add up. Experiences in one area may show that all is not what it seems in another. Even given Kant's assumption about forms of experience, one may be unable to make experience as a whole coherent without supposing, even when it comes to categories, that what we experience things *as* is not always what they are, no matter how convincing a ringer for it it may be. If there is any way space and time seemed (globally) to be, such has proven so in their case.

So the point remains. A tract of reality is something nonconceptual, some tract of things being as they are. Our engagement with it may rest (necessarily) on capacities which present it to us, visually, aurally, etc., as shaped thus and so (if we can make sense of that idea). If an appearance were, necessarily, coeval with someone's awareness of it, if nothing beyond that could bear on whether the appearance were thus and so—*and* if, for all that, an appearance, in being as it was might, in fact, *be* thus and so, then perhaps the work of such capacities might per se force an answer to the question how an appearance really was. But once we give up those ideas, such remarks about the work of our capacities are without force for how things really are.

Those most general principles which must hold of the world we inhabit if there are to be just those opportunities for judgement Kant wants there to be, cannot, it seems, be secured in the way Kant thought they could: by the mind's supplying the *nonconceptual* they would apply to. The most general shape of the judgement that Sid grunts makes its truth turn on a certain *object* being a certain *way*. So if there is to be such a thing to judge, either truly or falsely, then there had better be objects and ways for them to be. If that is for the world to be a particular way, then capacities which bring the world in view cannot guarantee this. A deduction of the categories cannot take this route. There remains what Kant is right about: insofar as, or where, there is space for mind and world to fail to mesh in providing opportunity for judgements, the world we experience must show what opportunities there are. It remains to see what to make of this.

3. Kant: Generality

Kant worries about the most *general* shape of the conceptual on *some* notion of comparative generality. Kant's worries differ from Frege's. Their questions differ accordingly. A concept, for Kant, is a contribution to the shape thoughts within some particular region of thought take. The concept *grunts*, for example, contributes to the shape of such thoughts as that Sid grunts. It makes the truth of these thoughts turn, somehow, on who grunts. Kant's conception of relative generality is Cartesian. Most general concepts, for him, are most general forms of contribution a concept might make.

Descartes (21 May 1643) saw concepts as forming classes, each marked by a member with the following features: every concept in the class applies to anything this concept applies to; anything which fits any concept in the class fits this one. Here **a** *fits* C (C applies to **a**) means: it is an (intelligible) thought that **a** is C. So, for example, for Descartes the concept *extension* defines a class of concepts which apply to material bodies (or spatial things). So, for Kant, for example, there are the notions *object* (substance) and *property* (accident). These are, as Kant conceives them, most general ways of playing the role in a thought that the concept *grunts* does in the thought that Sid grunts, or the concept *man* in the thought that some men do. *Object* and *concept* are (for Kant) most general ways of forming that unity found in a certain kind of thought: of (a) particular object(s) that it is/they are such-and-such. They mark, in the Cartesian way, classes to which all less general ways of doing this belong. Most general concepts in this sense are what Kant calls *categories*. Categories thus form thoughts of the same kind (most general shape) as thoughts formed by concepts belonging to the classes they mark.

Frege thought differently about generality. He first gave 'pride of place' to the whole thought. So it is a thought which is more or less general than other thoughts. Starting from the thought that Sid grunts, we reach higher levels of generality by quantifying. There is, say, the thought that someone grunts, then the thought that someone does something, and, perhaps, so on, until eventually there is nothing left over which to quantify. We have then reached a most general thought. Kant lacked a clear notion of quantifying. For him, a thought in which the function performed by the concept *grunts* was performed in the most general way would still have the same form as one in which that function was performed by the less general concept *grunts*, whereas for Frege a most general thought is of a different form than less general ones. Quantifiers make for that. For Frege, there is the question what most general thoughts 'say', that is, what is so according to them. That is for the next section. Kant does not quite ask that. His focus is on *concepts* rather than thoughts. Despite these differences, Kant and Frege agree on much about the most general.

Kant notices that a most general form of a thought is one some thoughts would have, with or without any given more specific version of that form. If evolution had omitted sloths, there would be no thought that sloths eat leaves. There would still be thoughts to the effect that some object is some way. Conversely, evolution might have graced us with thoughts of that form which, in fact, there are not, which he takes to mean that whether there are thoughts of this general form can depend in no way on how the world *happens* to be. Further, he supposes, the world could not have taught us that there are such thoughts; nor conferred on us the ability to think them. Nor could it have taught us anything so simply by virtue of there being *some* such thoughts. Nor could the truth of such principles in any way turn on *what* the world provides to make thoughts true or false.

Kant thinks it needs to be shown that these most general forms of the conceptual (or the conceptual our mental equipment saddles us with) actually engage with the nonconceptual the world provides—that there are those opportunities for (forms of) judgement there thus would be. But such proof could not rest on anything that *need* not have been so. It certainly can, and had better, depend on how the world is. That was Kant's correct insight. But then this must be on how the world could not but be. This is what led Kant to look for that tract of reality which, we saw, there could not be. From which it already follows that there is *something* amiss with Kant's conception of the significance of maximal generality.

G. E. Moore noticed something wrong, though in discussing a somewhat different question: what it might be to *prove* there was an 'external world' (a response to a footnote in the first *Critique* (B xl)). In that context he considers a sample argument, from premises expressed in saying 'Here is a hand' (gesturing), and 'Here is another' (gesturing again) to the conclusion, 'There are (some) hands.' To make his discussion bear on what it might be to prove the 'objective validity' of the categories, we might change the sample, so that it begins from premises expressed in 'This hand is dirty' and 'So is this one' (same gestures) to the conclusion, 'Some hands are dirty.' This bears on a deduction of the categories in the same way Moore's actual sample bears on proving there is an 'external world'. *If* it is a good argument—if it *proves* its conclusion—then it has been established that some objects have some properties—there are *some* ways things are which consist of some things (objects) being some given ways. So there are true things to think of the form formed by the categories *object* and *property*. Which is just what was to be proved in proving their objective validity.

Is the sample proof good? Again adapting Moore, it certainly is *if* we are entitled to start an argument from its premises—if *they* can be used to prove things. *This*, Moore tells us, is an occasion-sensitive affair. *Sometimes*, that *that* (demonstrated) hand is dirty may need, and then admit, of proof. Sometimes it does neither. All depends on the occasion on which question as to it might (or might not) arise—notably, here, on the occasion on which proving that some hands are dirty might be called for. But, Moore further insists, if, on an occasion such a premise cannot be proved—perhaps because it does not then admit of proof, because nothing would count as a proof of it—this does not per se mean that we are not entitled to start what would be a perfectly good proof from it.

Kant is explicit that our sample premises could not be ones on which to rest a proof of what he wants proved (B 118/A 85–86). So, for purposes of giving that proof, we are not entitled to suppose what was stated in that 'This hand is dirty', or that 'So is this one'. Nor is the problem about *those* hands in particular, or about being dirty. We would be equally not entitled to suppose, for these purposes, that that sloth is asleep, or that that crisp is greasy, and so on ad infinitum. Where there was any question of giving the proof that Kant wanted, *nothing* would be to be supposed as to the condition of any object. And/or nothing would be to be supposed as to whether sloths are objects, or crisps are objects, or hands are objects, and so on.

Such strictures, though, face a severe problem. If I am asked to prove that (at least some) crisps are greasy, I might produce an adequate sample of crisps, perhaps distribute them across the pages of your essay, and let you see for yourself. You could see that this, that, and the next, crisp are all greasy. Proof done. But suppose I am not allowed to suppose of any of these things that these are crisps, or of any of the ways they are that *this* is a greasy crisp. Suppose no such 'assumption' could, for our purpose, appear in a proof. Such may well rob me of proof. But it also may well leave us wondering just what it would be for something to be a crisp, or greasy—just what our question is a question about. If *this* is not a greasy crisp, what is? Now a parallel thing might be said of Kant's proof in circumstances that would call for, or permit it. If nothing 'empirical' bears (conclusively) on what he wants shown, then just what would it be for there to be objects which were given ways? What Moore saw (however clearly) is that the right answer might be: we no longer know what this would be. At which point proof is out of the question.

Moore has cast the insight in epistemological form. In that form it is about the occasion-sensitivity of proof, which he expresses in terms like these:

Some people would feel... not merely that they want a proof of something which I haven't proved, but that they think that, if I cannot give such extra proofs, then the proofs that I have given are not conclusive proofs at all. And this, I think, is a definite mistake.... Such a view can be shown to be wrong—though shown only by the use of premises which are not known to be true, unless we do know of the existence of external things. I can know things which I cannot prove.

(1939: 148)

What they really want is... something like a general statement as to how *any* propositions of this sort ['Here is a hand'] may be proved. This, of course, I haven't given, and I do not believe it can be given: if this is what is meant by proof of the existence of external things, I do not believe that any proof of the existence of external things is possible.

(1939: 147)

If there is a proof that (some of) Kant's categories have application to the world we experience, it will be on the model of Moore's sample. It will start from premises available as such where it is given, but liable to need proof on other occasions. Kant wants proof to be something else, starting from what does not rely on the right occasion for its status as a legitimate starting point. This, Moore tells us, is Kant's mistake; his misunderstanding of maximal generality. There *are* no such absolutely secure starting points. On the contrary, it is none too easy a thing to raise an intelligible question as to whether there are objects and properties. Moore's point is made in that conditional above. It is fine, for that purpose, if his sample does *not* prove what Kant wanted proved. It is idle, for his purpose, to debate that. Perhaps there is no such thing as a proof of that. Such would be fine by Moore's lights.

The insight, so cast, can strike the hard-nosed as concerning some mere liberal-arts notion of proof. Frege shows how it is far from that. We can start here:

The fundamental logical relation is that of an object falling under a concept; all relations between concepts can be reduced to this.

(1892–1895: 25)

In present terms, any bit of the conceptual stands in two sorts of relations. It relates to the rest of the conceptual in given ways; and it relates (reaches) to the nonconceptual in a given way. Being red bears on being green and on being opaque in given ways. One might think of such things as assigning it a location within the conceptual. It also reaches to particular cases in given ways: *this* cabriolet, *this* tomato, are red. Frege's idea, in translation, is: for bits of the conceptual to bear on each other in given ways is for them each to reach in a given way to the nonconceptual.

Relations between bits of the conceptual are intrinsically between things each with a determinate reach to the nonconceptual. Structures independent of those reaches do not by themselves bring *any* bit of the conceptual into view. No bit, or region, of it is identified until enough is given, both as to the internal structure of the conceptual and as to the reach of the things so structured. *That* is the deep point behind Moore's insight. That a whole range of related concepts reach to the nonconceptual as they do may constrain significantly just what *red* reaches to. Any fix on the structure of that range which leaves the reach of those other concepts open fixes nothing about the reach of *red*. So we will not have brought any bit of the conceptual into question—there is nothing as to whose features we will be askng—unless enough facts are fixed as to which cases are, or would be, ones to which this, or related, bits of the conceptual in fact reach. This is Wittgenstein's point about rule-following. Putnam makes the same point, cast as about interpreting (oxymoronically) an 'uninterpreted language'. (See (1977: 24), (1999: 14).)

The nonconceptual for the conceptual to reach to is just that which the world supplies. So it may matter crucially to *what* bit of the conceptual we speak of that, for example *this* (say, this cherry, or cabriolet, being as it is) is a case of it—of, say, something being *red*. When it comes to proving the objective validity of the categories, Kant deprives us of *so* many such fixed points that we no longer know what is *meant* by a claim that there are objects with properties. Such is Moore's point in a more Fregean context.

Kant's project of showing the 'objective validity' of the categories starts by prising the conceptual off the nonconceptual more than one can while still having any of the conceptual to ask about. To ask Kant's questions, one would have to suppose it 'up for grabs' how being a crisp, being a hand, being a sloth, and so on ad infinitum, reach to the nonconceptual. With that much 'up for grabs', none of the conceptual is in view. One *cannot* ask the question Kant meant to. That is what Moore says when he tells us there is no such thing as the sort of proof Kant had in mind. This is not to say that one cannot ask questions about the objective validity of even the most general concepts, questions as to whether they correspond to any genuine opportunities for judging. But those questions will need to come into view differently than as Kant envisaged. Maximal generality does not mean what Kant thought it did. What he did not get right is how the structure of the conceptual bears on how the world bears on the structure of the conceptual. Frege (once again) will help us see just what that problem is.

4. Frege: Autonomy

Assurance of cooperation between the world and a given region of the conceptual with which we find ourselves saddled—that things admit of being thought of in the terms we apply—must appeal to *things*, to what there is to think about. So far, Kant was right. He failed to find anything thus to appeal to, which *might* seem inevitable. What would provide assurance, it would seem, would need to be that the world is thus and so. That the world is thus and so belongs to the conceptual. If it assures us, then it belongs to the conceptual within our reach. But what we needed assurance of (at the most general level) was that the conceptual within our reach in fact applies to the world. So—it would *seem*—the most we could learn is that it applies if it applies. This may make one ask anew whether such cooperation actually does need showing, or even whether we can even make sense of that idea. Perhaps no cooperation is called for. Frege thought this of maximally general structure.

The maximally general, for Frege, was a type of *thought*. His focus was on certain true ones: those he saw as unfolding the concept *true* (1918: 59). Quantification in mind, we might amend this to: the concepts *true* and *object*. The question whether the concepts *true* and *object* have 'objective validity'— whether the most general shapes of the conceptual have application to things— can be cast as ones as to the truth of these thoughts. Frege's answer to the questions so formulated is:

> The question why, and with what right, we acknowledge a law of logic to be true, logic can answer only by reducing it to another law of logic. Where that is not possible, logic can give no answer. If we step away from logic, we may say: we are compelled to make judgements by our own nature and by external circumstances; and if we do so, we cannot reject this law—of Identity, for example; we must acknowledge it unless we wish to reduce our thought to confusion and finally renounce all judgement whatever. . . . What is [thus] given is not a reason for something's being true, but for our taking it to be true.
>
> (1893: 15)

The idea is: the truth of *these* thoughts could turn *only* on the shape of the conceptual itself. Since these thoughts are *most* general, bits of the conceptual which *reached* to the nonconceptual—to particular cases—would have no place in them. So it matters not at all to *their* truth what it does or does not reach. So whether the world admits of judgements of the shapes these truths reflect can depend in no way on how things are. So nor can whether the conceptual which *is* so shaped, or contributes to such shapes, reaches (and (or) counter-reaches) all the way to the nonconceptual. Here there is *no such thing* as things being otherwise. So there is no call for (nor could there be) the substantive assurance Kant sought. Such, for Frege, are the fruits of maximal generality.

What is maximal generality? Start with the thought that Sid grunts. Its task is to fix how the world matters to a certain posture towards it. That task can be decomposed into subtasks. On one such decomposition, truth turns on how *Sid* is (in a particular way), and on how *grunting* is distributed. One can use 'about' to say this: the thought is about Sid and about grunting. We might now move to a new thought by replacing being about Sid, in this decomposition, with some quantification, moving, say, to the thought that someone grunts. The resulting thought would be more general. Another quantification, deleting another aboutness, might move us to yet higher generality—say, the thought that someone does something. And so on until (on this decomposition) there is no more aboutness to remove.

As Frege insists, a thought is decomposable in many ways, structured only relative to an analysis (1892b: 199). Any decomposition of the thought that Sid grunts provides some way of moving to greater generality. A most general thought, by contrast, admits a decomposition which provides *no* route to greater generality. On that decomposition, there is nothing the thought is about, in the way that the thought that Sid grunts is about Sid, or is about grunting. The thought might be, say, that everything is something.

A way a thought is structured out of elements (on some decomposition) is a way its truth depends on how things are. For the thought that Sid grunts to decompose as per above is for its truth to turn on how things stand with Sid. A most general thought, decomposed as only such generality allows, has no elements: no objects, or ways to be it is about. It has only structure, so only this to make it true. How can *structure* do that? To coin a phrase, the structure of each thought reflects the structure of the whole system of thoughts (of the conceptual) from its own point of view. For the thought that Sid grunts to decompose as per above is for it to share something in common with a range of other thoughts—that Sid snores, that Sid drinks, that Sid wears torn T-shirts— and with a range of thoughts that Ed grunts, that Ted does, etc. Dividing into such ranges is one way the realm of thought is structured (again, on *a* way of decomposing it).

Now the idea is: a thought of maximal generality reflects, through, and solely through, its structure, the most general structure of the realm of thoughts as a whole. In being structured as it is it represents that realm as structured thus and so; it is true just in case that realm *is* so structured. A law of logic, say, is expressible as: *If A&B then A*. Decomposed so as to exhibit its maximal generality, its structure would reflect the conceptual's being so shaped that for any two thoughts there is a (weakest) third, entailed by both and entailing each.

Its structure would thus limn certain truth-preserving paths through the conceptual, from certain items to certain others.

(Perhaps thoughts cannot be thought of as forming some one definite totality. A most general thought might then reflect the structure of any large enough totality. Further, if a thought is structured only relative to a decomposition, so, too, in the same sense, for a realm of thoughts. So, too, perhaps, for *what* elements—thoughts—it decomposes into (what differences there are between one thought and another; how thoughts are to be counted as two once, or one twice). Most general thoughts might then be thought of as reflecting a structure a realm of thoughts would have on any decomposition, thinking of that structure as identified independent of what stands at its nodes.)

A law of logic is a most general truth. So its truth turns on nothing other than the conceptual itself being structured as it is. It turns on nothing external to the conceptual, so on nothing as to what nonconceptual there is. Since it depends on no such thing, there is no such thing as the world other than so as for the law to be true. Thus with most general truths in general. Nothing is asked of the world for their truth, so there is thus no such thing as things being other than they state. In Kantian terms, there is nothing the world (the nonconceptual) need do in order to provide opportunities for judgements shaped in the way the law reflects. There is no way for it not to provide such opportunity.

There is a simple way in which maximal generality itself may seem to make for such insulation from the course of events. Take a thought not so insulated— say, the thought that Sid's face is red. Decomposing one way, it is (in shorthand) about Sid's face and about being red. Being red reaches to particular cases (something's being as it is) in a particular way. Its participation in Frege's fundamental relation thus locates it within the conceptual. Conversely, its location there reflects its reach. Does it, in so reaching, reach Sid's face? By this location, the conceptual speaks to how the nonconceptual matters to this. (Other decompositions may speak in other, but harmonious, ways with this.) Its location in the conceptual speaks equally to how the nonconceptual matters to the truth of a most general thought. Here, though, what it says is that *no* way is a way this matters. So, the thought is, there is no way the nonconceptual *could* matter to the truth of any most general thought. *If* so, Kant was mistaken: we need (and could have) *no* assurance from the *world* that thought's most general shape is fit for representing what we encounter.

We started from the thought that the availability of things for us to judge was a cooperative enterprise: the world provided things of which to judge; our minds equipped (or saddled) us with preparedness to see them—*if* they but exist. We are such as for our thought about things to take a certain shape: at the most general, a shape it could not but take. *Judgement* can take that shape if, *but only if*, the world cooperates in providing things so shaped to judge. Kant sought assurance that it did. Frege's idea is that, at the most general level, there is no work for the world to do. What of the mind's part of the bargain? Frege's thought is: if the world mattered to the most general shape of the conceptual, the conceptual itself would have to tell us *how* it did; *what* it tells us (and could not but) is, 'In *no* way', so there is no such thing as the conceptual having any other most general shape than what it does. We may still think of ourselves as saddled, by our design, with thinking of this shape. But now this is a matter of psychology, or design, making us one thing or another only so far as it makes us *thinkers* rather than, say, vegetables. Whatever, if anything, we may thank for being thinkers, as for the most general shape of our thought, there is only *one* thing to be in being that. Such is *one* way of reading this idea:

> Anyone who has once acknowledged a law of truth has by the same token acknowledged a law that prescribes the way in which one ought to judge, no matter where, or when, or by whom the judgement is made.

> (1893: 15)

If Frege is right, Kant's problem about maximal generality disappears. But I will argue that, though Frege is right about much of the above, this last consequence is not right. Neither the world (the nonconceptual) nor our minds cancels out in this way.

5. Having Structure

A most general thought, on our present notion, is so by virtue of the decomposition it admits of. As Frege conceives things, it belongs to a particular structured realm, to which *all* thoughts belong. Its structure reflects a specific structure in that realm; one permeating every region: part of all things there are to think, no matter what about. Such a thought has nothing but its structure to make it true. So, the idea is, for it to be true is nothing other than for its structure to reflect the most general structure that realm has. So, the thought goes, its truth is hostage to nothing but that structure being the structure that it is. So if it is true, there is no more such a thing as it not being than there is such a thing as that structure being other than the structure that it is. On this way of thinking, one might equally say: for such a thought to be *false* would be for this realm to be structured other than it is, which would just be for it to be a different realm, but such a thought is hostage to no more than the structure of that realm to which it does belong. A thought that if A and B, then A might be such a thought. Call it G. By this line, there is no such thing as things being other than as G represents them.

The thought that Sid grunts occupies this realm. There would have been no such occupant had Sid's parents been stranded on the tarmac rather than conjugally engaged that fateful night. The structure of the realm would then have been different. But, the idea is, its most general structure would remain untouched. It would still have been the realm of all the thoughts there would have been. But, the idea is, no realm without that most general structure could possibly have been the realm of all the thoughts there were, no matter what. Why should this be?

There seems a confusion in the above line of thought. The structure a domain *has*—some structure *for* a domain to have—would not be *that* structure while structuring things differently than it does. There is no such thing as that. Trivially, *if* a domain has a given structure, then no domain structured differently *is* that one. But, as the thought that Sid grunts shows, this is not yet to say that a domain could not have been structured differently (or turn out to be differently structured than we take it to be) while, for all that, remaining *that* domain. The domain of all thoughts includes, but might not have, the thought that Sid grunts. This is one way of identifying domains. It is, presumably, the way of interest if the question is what thought could not but have been.

Just what is a most general thought committed to? A Euclidean parallel postulate defines, in part, the structure of Euclidean geometry. There is no such thing as Euclidean geometry being such that that postulate does not hold. The postulate *can* be understood to say something about the geometry of space, or of certain paths present in space. So understood, there is such a thing as it being false. Understood one way, there is no such thing; understood another, there is. Now, to just what is a most general law of thought committed?

We might think of a sub-region of thought as having a most general proprietary structure. Think of a sub-region as consisting of all thoughts about being one or more of some specified set of ways there are for something to be. (A sub-region may be relative to a way of decomposing thoughts, or may consist of all thoughts decomposable as about these things.) Then the most general proprietary structure of the region would be what was reflected in all thoughts (decomposable as) about nothing other than those specified ways for something to be. Suppose that space just flatly is Euclidean. Then that parallel postulate may reflect the most general proprietary structure of that region of thought—thoughts about paths in space. Now recall the idea that the location of a thought within the conceptual dictates how the world (the nonconceptual) may speak to—what bears on—its truth. For a most general thought, what it says is that there is *no* way. So, too, for most general proprietary thoughts. If the parallel postulate reflects this most general proprietary structure, then its position in the conceptual tells us that nothing in the nonconceptual speaks to its truth. But, we know, the nonconceptual *can* speak to the truth of the postulate, understood as a proposition about paths in space. What we thus need to ask is what the conceptual tells us in telling us that no way is the way the nonconceptual speaks to the truth of some (locally) most general thought.

The conceptual is made up of all ways there are of reaching to the nonconceptual so as to bring the particular case (things, or some thing(s), being as they are) under some particular generality; bringing it within some range of cases. The realm of thoughts is that part of the conceptual made up of things of the form of a thought. For a realm to be the realm of thoughts would be for it to encompass precisely all the things there are to think (if that is a determinate notion). It would encompass all, and no more than, all those opportunities for judging that the world in fact supplies (if there is such a thing as doing that). Kant's worry was whether such-and-such structure for a domain to have was in fact the structure of that realm. Frege's answer is that nothing could qualify as that realm—as what encompassed precisely what that realm would—unless it had that structure (or Frege's reworked version of it). The idea was that Kant's worry should, on reflection, be seen as bogus: there is no substantive question as to whether the relevant realm has the relevant structure. But that what would encompass precisely the above has that structure for a realm to have seems a substantive claim. Nothing so far shows it not to be. So Kant's anxiety has not yet been allayed.

Moreover, we have seen room for a confusion. Whatever the most general structure of the relevant realm would be, it would tell us that there is no way which is the way the nonconceptual bears on whether that *is* the most general structure of that realm. But that cannot mean that there is no such thing as the nonconceptual so bearing. If this seems a paradox (as well it might), that simply means that we have yet to learn how to understand what structure says (or how it speaks).

The *Tractatus* adapts Frege's idea to particular sub-regions of thought—with the explicit aim of allaying one sort of Kantian anxiety. The exemplary sub-region is mechanics. The adaptation starts from this Kantian theme:

All propositions such as the law of causation, the law of continuity in nature, the law of least expenditure in nature, etc., etc., all these are a priori intuitions of possible forms of the propositions of science.

(6.34)

A priori intuitions are what we are saddled with. To be so saddled is to see one's thought as structured in a particular way. Does the world admit of being so thought of? Does it articulate into events such that to be one just *is* to have a cause? Wittgenstein's idea is: there is no such thing as it failing to, nothing it must be so to admit. This just adapts Frege's idea to most general proprietary structures. His aim is to still a Pyrrhonian worry Kant sometimes suffers—as here:

Since we cannot treat the special conditions of sensibility as conditions of the possibility of things, but only of their appearances, we can indeed say that space comprehends all things that appear to us as external, but not all things in themselves, by whatever subject they are intuited, or whether they be intuited or not. For we cannot judge in regard to the intuitions of other thinking beings, whether they are bound by the same conditions as those which limit our intuition and which for us are universally valid.

(A27/B43)

Grass *appears* green to us. But who knows, Sextus asks, how it appears to a cow? Best avoid commitment as to its *being* green. The world *appears* to articulate into events, each with a cause. But who knows how it appears to other thinkers? Best avoid commitment as to how it really is (or as to how anything other than appearances really is). Kant's worry, the *Tractatus* tells us, is bogus. No cause to confine commitment to any special tract of reality.

The *Tractatus* views a sub-region of thought as a particular system for describing the world—something which generates a particular range of structurally related descriptions to give of it. Its most general proprietary structure is what gives each of those descriptions the particular content it has: makes the world matter to its truth in a particular way. What merely reflects the structure of that system has no such content. There is no way the world matters to it. It says nothing about the world.

Wittgenstein offers a comparison. Suppose we stretch a net over a white canvas with black spots on it. We can then describe the canvas by describing what each cell in the net covers either as black or as white. If the net is coarse enough, some cells may be part black, part white. Call them that. A finer net would then allow us more exact descriptions. For some degree of fineness, each cell will be either entirely black or entirely white. Such a net provides a *complete* description of the canvas. (See 6.341.) The cells may be triangular, or square, or hexagonal, or etc. Saying so says nothing about the canvas. The truth of what one *thus* says does not depend on how the canvas is. Similarly, the thoughts which define a system, as above, concern only the shape of that system, say nothing about the world. So there is no such thing as things being other than they represent it.

So Kant's Pyrrhonian moment is defusable. A parochial design for *thinking* makes certain systems of descriptions available. Other thinkers may have different systems available than we do. But any system there is to be endowed with is shaped as it is, independent of *anyone's* psychology. So whether *our* systems exploit genuine opportunities for judging does not depend on whether our psychology happens to be benevolent. There is no such thing here as malevolence. So long as some coherent system is available to us, the *only* way of our going wrong in judging is in judging something it generates which, in fact, is just not so.

Now, though, the *Tractatus* story takes a peculiar twist. At 6.34 Wittgenstein calls the law of causation a *proposition*—oddly, since he has just told us (6.32), 'The law of causality is not a law but the form of a law' (in a note, 'any law of a certain sort.'), and is about to tell us,

> If there were a law of causality, it might run: 'There are natural laws.'
> But that clearly cannot be said: it shows itself.
>
> (6.36)

So a law of causality, though an a priori intuition reflecting the most general structure of mechanics, is *not* a relatively most general true thought—since not a thought at all. To adapt *Frege's* idea, Wittgenstein thus shifts to talk of Newtonian mechanics. It is this of which he says,

> Mechanics determines a form of description by saying: All propositions in the description of the world must be obtained in a given way from a number of given propositions—the mechanical axioms. It thus provides the bricks for building the edifice of science, and says: Whatever building you want to build, do it, somehow, with these, and only these, bricks.
>
> (6.341)

> The fact that it can be described by Newtonian mechanics asserts nothing about the world.
>
> (6.342)

But Newtonian mechanics is a theory, not a region. For it to *contain* a thought is for *it* to represent things to be as they are according to that thought—to commit. For a *region* to contain a thought is simply for there to be such a thing to think. A region defined by *mass* and *velocity*—mechanics—contains all thoughts, both true and false, about mass and velocity. *It* commits to the truth of none. It is the wrong sort of thing for that. It has two different senses of 'contain'. Nothing *could* be Newtonian mechanics which did not commit to what Newtonian mechanics does. No region would have contained the thought that Sid is gaining mass rapidly around the midsection but for that circumstance on that fateful night. Some region would still have been mechanics. That Newtonian mechanics contains a certain law is not enough for that law to be true. Mechanics contains some most general proprietary thoughts. Some of these may count as laws of Newtonian mechanics (which might, after all, count as still expressible, even though *not* true).

For a region to contain a most general thought is not enough for the thought to be true. That thought must, further, reflect the region's most general structure—as the thought G does for the whole realm of thought: its truth reflects certain truth-preserving paths within that realm. Whether a thought reflects a region's most general proprietary structure depends on what that structure is. As we know from the case of Newtonian mechanics, what that structure is *is* liable to depend on how things are. Counter to what the *Tractatus* suggests, that it is such-and-such *does* say something about the world. For the structure of a region to make a thought true is *not* just for that thought to reflect such-and-such structure there is for a region to have. We may share Wittgenstein's sense that Kant's Pyrrhonian worry is bogus. But we have not yet seen how to identify what makes it so.

So Wittgenstein's adaptation of Frege's idea collapses, as he was soon to realize. Pressing two of Frege's own ideas also yields collapse. The first is that a thought is structured only relative to an analysis. A maximally general thought is one which *admits* of an analysis on which it is not about any object or way for one to be. Such does not exclude it also admitting of analyses on which it *is* about such things. The second is: laws of logic unfold the concept *true*. That concept forms a packet with *judging* and *thought*: truth is success at judging's central aim; a thought a particular way for the world to decide such success or failure. So, for all its maximal generality, a law of logic *can* be seen as about this packet, or its bits. These bits reach to the conceptual in substantive ways. *What* they reach depends on what there *is* for them, or their contraries, to reach to. (The concept) *judging* reaches just that range of cases which would be ones of someone judging such-and-such. For each such case, there is a bit of the conceptual: that which someone thus judged. That this concept thus populates the realm (the conceptual) it itself inhabits is a special feature of it; just that which permits thoughts about its most general status—allows them to be seen as about nothing. But would it, *whatever* there was for it to reach to, thus populate the conceptual with items which gave the whole realm of thoughts that structure reflected in those thoughts we recognize as laws of logic?

Frege sees all propositional logic as contained in a particular aspect of what a posture must be to count as judging: hostage *solely* to things being as they are. The idea is: if one is hostage in that way, there are only two ways for the world to speak. One may *escape* error (the world may *be* one the posture is right for), or one may succumb to it. For any such posture, his idea is, there is another, which would succumb to error just where that first would escape it, escape it just where that first would succumb. And so on through all the truth-functional ways thoughts might relate. Which imposes a structure in the realm of thought which the laws of truth (propositional logic) reflect.

By this idea, if there is the thought that Sid grunts and the thought that Pia snores, then there is a third, true just where each of those two is, entailing both, and entailed by any other with these properties. So if one can be hostage solely to the world in the first way, and can be hostage solely to it in the second, then one can also be hostage to it in the third. Is there simply no such thing as things being otherwise in this respect? Could there not have been (such a thing as) two ways of being hostage to the world, such that the one could be (or count as) open to a thinker only where the other was (or counted as) not? As it were, we can think of the world as dividing into the grunters and the not, or as dividing into the snorers and the not, but we cannot make sense of it dividing up both ways at once. Perhaps no such thing could have been. But if not, that cannot be simply because the laws of truth reflect such-and-such structure *for* a domain to have, nor even *just* because they reflect that structure which, in point of fact, the domain does have.

Frege's tactic thus does not silence Kant's worry. Rather, it calls a new problem to our attention. If Frege's laws of truth do reflect the most general structure of the conceptual—we have no reason to think otherwise—then there is something that structure says as to what might bear on them: no way for the nonconceptual to be is a way which would. But we cannot conclude simply from this that this would have been the most general structure of the conceptual no matter what. To make sense of this situation, we need to turn to Putnam.

6. Putnam's Master Insight

As Kant saw, mind and world *jointly* make judgements available to us. So where assurance was needed that some judgements we *take* to be available—part of the way we think of things—really *are* available, that assurance must come from the world. Kant just did not see what would be the *world's* bearing on this.

Frege saw that a most general structure of the conceptual (or of thoughts) makes no provision for the world (the nonconceptual) to bear on whether the conceptual *has* that structure. It provides no *way* for the nonconceptual to bear on this. Whatever such structure might be, there are thoughts which are no more than its reflection, which require no more for their truth than that the conceptual be so structured. These, then, would be true no matter which ways

for things to be were instanced by things being as they are—insofar as it was
open to the nonconceptual either to instance them or not. This just is what it
would be for them to *be* most general. A location within the conceptual shows
how, if at all, what occupies it depends, for being instanced, on how things are.
The structure of the conceptual as a whole, whatever it may be, concedes no
bearing on any most general truth. Tractarian Wittgenstein extended this point
to most general structures of particular domains of thought—for example,
thoughts about mechanics, or colours.

Frege read his correct point as meaning that the nonconceptual simply could
have *no* bearing on whether the conceptual was structured this way or that.
Conversely, on this reading, that the conceptual is structured as it is says *nothing*
about the world (nothing as to *what* nonconceptual there is). For most general
structure of the conceptual, as Frege understood this, there is no such thing as
things being otherwise; nothing it ever *could* be for the conceptual not to be so
structured. The *Tractatus* extended this understanding to more specialized
domains of discourse. Such, if right, would mean there could *never* be call for
the kind of assurance Kant sought (nor any prospect of providing it).

But we need not read Frege's good point that way. Putnam shows why it
would be wrong to. He shows, too, how else to read it. To begin, if the
conceptual *is* structured thus and so, then for no way there *is* for things to be (or
not) does its being so structured turn on whether things *are* that way. So if the
world *were* to bear on whether the conceptual is structured *thus* or rather *so*, we
would have to look elsewhere to find *how* it thus bears.

We can find a place to look starting with Moore's good idea and developing
it as Putnam does. The good idea: there is no conceptual about which you are
asking whether it is this way or that—no question being asked at all—unless
enough is fixed about the *reach*, as well as the location, of enough of its denizens.
What does *being red* reach to? Well, what *is* something being red? An available
answer had better be, '*This*, for example.'

Developing this point we can insist, for a start, that here enough is not
(usually) *everything*. It is enough for it to be *being red* that is in question, that,
anyway, it reaches to *these* cases, and (presumably) relates in *these* ways to other
ways for a thing to be. (The ways need not just be entailments. Whether
something is red *bears* on whether it is green, even if being red does not,
absolutely, exclude being green.) Now there is a sort of question one can ask
about the conceptual. Given that it is, anyway, such-and-such that is in
question—endowed with whatever identifies it as that which is in question—
what else would be so of it? How would concepts which, anyway, reached *thus*
be located within the conceptual? How would concepts which, anyway, were
recognizable as ones of, say, being red, or moving at a certain rate, reach to what

emerges as what there is to reach to—to that which there is in fact to instance something being red, or not red, say? The questions would be ones of what *fits* with what, what else would rightly join with reaching, or being located, thus and so.

This much points already to the deep point Putnam makes as follows:

The distinction between statements necessary relative to a body of knowledge and statements contingent relative to that body of knowledge is an important methodological distinction. . . . For the difference between statements that can be overthrown by merely conceiving of suitable experiments and statements that can be overthrown only by conceiving of whole new theoretical structures . . . is of logical and methodological significance, and not just of psychological interest.

(1962: 248–249)

[In (1962)] I argued that to identify 'empirical' and 'synthetic' is to lose a useful distinction . . . which I proposed to draw . . . as follows: call a statement *empirical relative to a body of knowledge B* if [then-] possible observations . . . would [then] be *known* to disconfirm the statement . . .

If I were writing (1962) today, I would alter the terminology. . . . Since a 'body of knowledge', in the sense in which I used the term, can contain . . . false statements, I would replace 'body of knowledge' with 'conceptual scheme.' And I would further emphasize the nonpsychological character of the distinction by pointing out that the question is not a *mere* question of what some people can imagine . . . it is a question of what, given a conceptual scheme, one *knows* how to . . . disconfirm.

(1994: 251)

With this we can fill in our present schema. Different occasions provide different opportunities for identifying the conceptual, or regions of it—different ways of doing this. (Just so that the conceptual itself does not provide the wanted guidance here.) Correspondingly, they provide different questions to be raised as to whether what is so identified is, furthermore, thus and so; different thoughts to the effect that it *is*, or is not, so shaped, thus different questions of the general form just sketched, on each of which the world (things being as they *are*) is liable to bear, differently according as the questions differ. With opportunity comes limits. No occasion provides opportunities for raising such questions for *every* feature the conceptual may or may not have. Something must remain fixed in order for there to be possibility for other things to vary (for them to come into question at all).

It is a familiar idea that in order to think of such-and-such that it is thus and so, one needs acquaintance with that of which one thinks this, whatever such acquaintance might be. Our acquaintance with the nonconceptual, on an occasion for thinking of the shape of the conceptual, provides what is thus needed. The conceptual reaches, not to *objects*—the participants in Frege's fundamental relation of falling under—but rather to particular cases of things being as they are, or some thing as it is—to that which is, for example, Sid's being a grunter, or that rose's being red. Our acquaintance with *how* things are in being as they are may vary from occasion to occasion (usually in a temporally progressive way). Such acquaintance brings a particular grasp of what there is *for* the conceptual to reach, or counter-reach, to; thus particular ways of identifying what *might* reach (or counter-reach) to this; thus particular questions to raise, and thoughts to think, as to what else would belong, by way of reach, or location, to that which is so identified. On different such acquaintance there would be different such thoughts for us to think. Pending suitable acquaintance, *these* thoughts are not available to us; pending some such suitable acquaintance, no thoughts to that effect at all. But for that with which we would thus be acquainted, there would be no such thoughts full stop. Given the nonconceptual we come to see there is, we can ask how what was recognizably a notion of velocity, or mass (or of having velocity V, or mass M) might reach to *this*, and then how what so reached would be located within the general structure of thought about mechanics—how reach and shape could fit together here. There would not *be* this question but for what we thus see there is for thought to reach.

For any structure for the conceptual to have, there is a range of thoughts whose truth turns on nothing other than whether the conceptual is so structured. If it is, then their truth does no more than reflect that fact. One way to understand necessity would be such that a proposition is necessary if it merely reflects the structure the conceptual in fact has. For a proposition to have this status is for there to be no other proposition, not itself a mere reflection of that structure, on whose truth its truth turns. So there is no way for things to be instanced or not according to how things are, which bears on this proposition's truth, given the way things are, so no such thing as the way the nonconceptual matters to its truth. Such is how things are; which is not to say that there is no such thing as things having been otherwise.

There is also, Putnam shows us, another possible understanding of necessity. A given acquaintance with the world makes only certain questions available as to how the conceptual is organized, and as to how it relates to the nonconceptual. For some features of the conceptual, that acquaintance makes no thought available as to the presence or absence of that feature, whose truth turns, in any determinate way, on how things are—on what nonconceptual the world provides. A given acquaintance, say, provides no way for a thought to be about *being red* on which being red may or may not be being coloured. Equally, it may provide no way for a thought to be about *being red* on which being red may or may not be what is instanced by *this* (towel, say) being as it is. From the vantage point of such a notion of necessity we can get a view of how, for all of what is so of the first notion, still, how things are may matter to whether the conceptual is structured *thus*, or rather *so*.

We thus gain a new understanding of Kant's problem. First, mind and world *may* fail to cooperate in providing the opportunities for judgement there had seemed to be (on a certain acquaintance with the world). But *our* minds endow us with *flexible* members of the partnership: forms of thought which give the world a say in how the conceptual within *our* reach is, in fact, organized, and where it reaches. There is no *one* form of judgement to which the world must be receptive if our concepts are to have the employments in fact marked out for them. The point holds at any level of generality.

Second, there is something it takes to make for an *intelligible* question (that is, a question at all) as to whether the world is hospitable to this or that form of judgement. It takes special conditions for there to be something one is asking in asking whether being red excludes being green (or at least thus asking something to which how the world is, matters). Enough must be fixed as to how enough concepts anyway reach—not just most general concepts, but those less general ones which are their specializations (not just, e.g. being coloured, but being red). If we think of the problem as Kant did, it can seem that what we want assurances for is, of ways in which we could not but think, so to which we could not but take the world to be hospitable, that these are forms of judgement to whose correctness the world is, in fact, equipped to speak. Here I see Putnam as lining up with Moore: if we reflect on what it would be for there to be an intelligible question as to whether this is so, we can see that there is none.

If the question is whether this rose is red, the conceptual itself—the shape it in fact has—is our guide to when an answer would be correct. *It* fixes how the world matters to correctness here. Such is its role. If the question is what *else* would be so of the conceptual if, anyway, such-and-such is—that sort of question which can make the conceptual's shape itself negotiable—the conceptual itself provides no such guidance. Newtonian mechanics does not tell us what bears on whether its most general shape is the most general shape of mechanics. *Mutatis mutandis* for whatever the most general shape of mechanics may be. What, then, does fix how questions of this form are to be answered? The standard of correctness for answers to such questions is, Putnam tells us, no more than is to be found in what a reasonable person would think. (This is clear in 1962. See also 1975: 235, and 2002, especially I.2, II.7.) We share a sense for what the right answer to such a question would be. The right answer is what, to such a sensibility, would be correct. One *could* insist that it is not gold if it is not yellow. But—as Leibniz also insisted—for most purposes, at least, that would not be a reasonable view of what we were talking about all along when we identified certain items in the world as gold.

Guidance by the conceptual—standards imposed by its shape itself—can seem comforting, as opposed to mere guidance by some sensibility we share (perhaps in being the sort of thinker we are), since the former guidance seems guidance entirely independent of anything to do with our psychologies, in comparison to which the latter is *mere* guidance by our inclinations, which, as such, subverts that very objectivity which makes judgement *judgement*—thus subverts the very idea that there is a *fact* as to, for example, whether to be gold is to be yellow.

The illusion is unmasked in a point already made. The rose is red only if its being as it is is something being red; only if *being red* reaches to particular cases in a particular way. If we conceive of the conceptual as with a shape which remains constant no matter how its denizens which reach at all reach the nonconceptual there is, such shape determines *nothing* as to where *being red* reaches. Perhaps if it is red, then it is not green. Perhaps a host of other things of that sort. But, independent of where being green reaches, this ties our hands not at all when it comes to whether to call the way that rose is, red. The conceptual is our guide to what would count as something being *red* only insofar as bits of it have given reaches. As to the reach of that bit, *being red*, there is what we would (or would be prepared to) count as something being red. There is no other standard by which what would *really* count as that—as being that very way I have just identified—might diverge from this. The concepts *we* identify reach just where one who shared our sense for such things would see them reaching. Putnam (1977, 1999) has this point in view in dismantling the (illusory) project of interpreting an (oxymoronically) uninterpreted language. In (1999), commenting on (1977), he says,

I went on to say, 'to speak as if *this* were my problem, I know how to use my language, but, now, how shall I single out an interpretation' is nonsense. Either the use of the language *already* fixes the 'interpretation' or *nothing* can.

I still agree with those *words*. But I would say them in a rather different spirit now. The difference has to do with how one hears what is involved in an appeal to 'use.' . . . On [the] alternative picture . . . [i]f one wants to describe the use of the sentence 'There is a coffee table in front of me,' one has to take for granted its internal relations to . . . facts such as that one perceives coffee tables . . . [in] the sense in which to see a coffee table is to see that it is a coffee table.

(1999: 14)

For talk to be about *coffee tables*, there being a coffee table before one must be the sort of thing one suitably au fait with things can recognize (e.g.) by sight, the sort of thing a case of which one of us could recognize. I return to this in section 8. (See, too, essay 10.) What we *say* of a rose in calling it red is fixed by no less than our sense for what particular cases would be ones of *being red* being instanced.

Our minds are accommodating. We can *see* how the world could be hospitable or not to thought of a given shape. We are prepared to learn from the world how to shape our thought to fit it. We can recognize such lessons. What we *can* see here—room for gaps between how it seems we can, or must, think of things, and how they may, in fact, be thought of—is just what can make Kant's problem *seem* to arise. At which point we need to note: what we can see is how the world might, *recognizably*, cooperate other than we thought it did in providing opportunities for judgement.

It takes special conditions—conditions of *acquaintance* with the world—to provide intelligible questions as to whether the world admits of being thought of in thoughts of such-and-such shape. Intelligible questions: that is, any questions at all. There is not, always, and automatically, such a *question* for just any form of thought—for example as to whether the world admits of thoughts governed by conjunction elimination. For to understand such a question—to identify what question it is—one must see how the relevant region of the conceptual—that of which the question is asked—is to be identified. The *world*—the nonconceptual—must furnish the opportunities for such identification that there are. Without them there is no more such a question than there would be thoughts about *Frege* without Frege. Such is Putnam's unfolding of what Moore began.

In asking for a 'deduction', Kant meant to raise a question asked from no perspective on the world; a question there would be to ask independent of whatever acquaintance one might have with it. Such is a *transcendental* question, answered by some special transcendental thing to say. Putnam helps us see why there are no such questions.

Frege cast that point in one way: from no perspective, there is just the conceptual there in fact is (after the world has had its say). *That* provides no way for the world to bear on whether it *is* the conceptual there is, so it provides no way for a Kantian question to arise. Putnam gives the right form to Frege's insight. The trouble lies in the idea of the transcendental, not in the unintelligibility of the very idea of the conceptual having been shaped otherwise. Neither the nonconceptual, nor our minds, are *simply* irrelevant to the conceptual having those shapes we can identify in it.

Moore glimpsed that same point in a different form. A transcendental perspective on the world cancels out that very acquaintance with it which allows thinking about any given bit of the conceptual at all. It deprives us of the possibility of saying of *what* we are asking whether it has 'employments marked out for it'. Acquaintance with the nonconceptual is needed for bringing the conceptual in view. Putnam shows us the essential role of such acquaintance in a cognitive economy.

Putnam's way with Kant's problem leaves distinct sorts of questions to be asked, not of each thought, but each, sometimes, of some. For it is not as though the conceptual is *unstructured*. We cannot so think of it. Nothing requires us to. So there will always be questions as to some thoughts' truth, or what bears on that, which are answered simply in unfolding concepts (to borrow Frege's term) as we can see them to unfold. For any shape the conceptual may have, there will be thoughts which reflect it: their truth demands no more than that the conceptual *be* so shaped. Correspondingly, in given circumstances, the truth of *some* thoughts is settled just by what we can *see* the shape of the conceptual to be. Does a thought expressing conjunction elimination reflect the shape of the conceptual? What would it be like for it not to? *Is* there a question which brings into question the conceptual's having *that* shape? Not at present. (There is, of course, such a thing as merely *thinking* one sees such things; as one may only *think* he sees a lemon on the sideboard.)

Second, there are also sometimes questions as to some thought's truth, or what bears on it, which are only answered by what decides whether the conceptual *does* have such-and-such structure rather than some other. No given structure for the conceptual to have, supplies an answer to them. Here it is for the nonconceptual—or what we can see there is of it—to speak, through the bearing on such questions we could recognize it to have. For all of which, where the nonconceptual provides us with such questions, there remain those of the first sort.

Finally, as the conceptual is fixed on an occasion, there are questions as to whether this or that bit of it—the rose being red, say—is instanced by the nonconceptual there is; where it is for the conceptual which is in view on that occasion to show how the nonconceptual—things being as they are—bears on whether this is so.

That the nonconceptual may bear on how the conceptual itself *is* shaped leaves genuine projects of unfolding concepts: plenty for a *philosopher* to do. Putnam shows how to conceive such bearing. Projects of unfolding concepts are left standing (within their proper bounds).

7. Putnam: Logic

The conceptual *has* structure: thoughts which reflect it ask no more for their truth. That is one sense in which how things are has no bearing on them. But this is not the only sense in which the world may or may not bear on what is so. Structure the conceptual *has* need not be structure it would have had no matter what.

If, with Frege, we view laws of logic as *thoughts*, then they are true (absolutely) most general ones, hence reflect the most general structure in any structuring of a domain of thoughts. They have nothing but their structure to make them true—that is, as noted, on some decomposition they admit of—what could not be so if their truth turned essentially on whether things were *thus*, or rather *so*. So the conceptual, structured as it is, leaves no way for the nonconceptual to bear on them. But, by the master thought, this does not mean that there could be no such thing as the nonconceptual having such bearing.

Nor, by that thought, does this mean that the nonconceptual *does* bear (so bear *thus*) on whether some such most general thought is true. There can be such bearing only where there is enough conceptual to hold fixed while leaving open whether *such* conceptual would form (part of) a system of which that most general thought—say, an expression of conjunction elimination—would hold. As things stand, we can find no such thing to hold fixed. So there is simply no question for us to raise as to the truth of conjunction elimination, or thought for us to think in thinking the conceptual to be so structured, on which the nonconceptual would bear. We cannot say that the future *could* not make such thoughts available. But nor could we say what they might be. Thus Putnam tells us,

What I *am* inclined to keep . . . is the idea that logical truths do not have negations that we (presently) understand. It is not . . . that we can say that the theorems of classical logic are 'unrevisable'; it is that the question 'Are they revisable?' is one which we have not yet succeeded in giving a sense.

(1994: 256)

Saying that logic or arithmetic may be 'revised' does not have a sense, and will never have a sense, unless some concrete piece of theory building and applying *gives* it a sense. . . . Knowing the 'sense' of a statement (or a question) is knowing how the words are used in a particular context; this may turn out to be knowing that the words had a 'different meaning' but this is relatively rare. . . . I may know the meaning of words, in the sense of knowing their 'literal meaning' and not understand what is said on a particular occasion of the use of those words.

(Ibid.)

Making sense, in some loose liberal-arts sense of 'sense', might require saying what is *reasonable*, rather than simply saying something to be so. Putnam is, here, no liberal-artist. Making sense is simply saying something liable either to be so or not, something with a tolerably determinate condition for its truth. Nor does adding a modal to a non-thought yield a thought. A question (on which the world might bear) as to whether conjunction elimination holds would demand new understandings of such things as *being a judgement*, or *being true*: a monumentally ambitious project whose execution we cannot so much as yet imagine.

The only thought we could presently think in thinking conjunction to distribute (or not to) across disjunction is the sort expressed in logic classes, answerable simply by appeal to the conceptual's recognizable shape. Different acquaintance with the world might provide other things to think. It is not that there could never be, or have been, sense to be made of the idea that conjunction does not so distribute. It is just that there is not now any sense for us to make of that—so nor even in holding that it might not.

We can ask about the conceptual at all only in asking of what, anyway, reaches (or is to be supposed to reach) to such-and-such, from such-and-such locations within it. So we must see it as structured. On any occasion for asking after its features, there will be features, among them structural features, which we simply, literally, *cannot* inquire into in a way such as for the world to bear on their presence. That is one reason why we cannot but see the conceptual as something for logic to reflect. Which is not the same as seeing it with features which say nothing about the world.

For there to be the assurances Kant sought would be for certain very general facts to hold. As both Kant and Frege conceived such generality, nothing the world might or might not have provided for instancing ways for things to be could ever bear on whether those facts held, no matter what. There *could* be no such thing as such bearing. In which case, as Frege pointed out (in one way, Moore in another), there cannot *be* the assurances Kant sought. Not that those very general facts admit of 'mere empirical proof'. Not, for that matter, that *anything* is proof of them occasion-independently. Rather, both Kant and Frege missed something about what necessity might be. Putnam, rethinking mathematics, shows us the *hardest* necessity there is.

8. Anxieties

Kant and Frege shared a conception of the conceptual which issues in an impasse. Putnam showed the way out. It turns crucially on a role for the parochial in giving the conceptual its shape—not *just* in reaching to some sub-regions and not others. Such a role for the parochial can awaken anxieties.

If for something to be gold is for it to have atomic number 79, rather than for it to be heavy, yellow, and malleable, such is the price of preserving the thought that gold is a familiar sort of metal. If it is a fact that the metal with atomic number 79 is what gold is, then it is a fact that that price *is to be paid*. Quine thought, in effect, that there could be no such fact as that such-and-such is the thing to do. He thought, accordingly, that if we *do* identify gold with that metal, there is no more to be said for that than that such is the way of our people. But suppose that, as per above, *what* way for something to be *being gold* is, is identified by what we would understand it to be—by what we are prepared to recognize as to its reach to the nonconceptual, and the place it thus assumes within the conceptual: that there is nothing in it to make it diverge, in these respects, from what we are equipped to see in it. Then there is more to say. It is part of what it would be for something to be gold that, as things turned out, being that is having a certain atomic number, rather than having a certain colour, weight, and malleability. If this means that there are facts about the thing to do—here what price to pay—then so there are.

No shape we took the conceptual to have prescribes any way for the world to bear (as, by the above it does) on what way for stuff to be being gold is. But the conceptual, at work as above, *can* make the world bear on this. If the shape of the conceptual were all that *could* prescribe such things, Quine would be right: choosing the one option, above, is merely the way of our people. Neither the shape we supposed the conceptual to have, nor that we now see it to, prescribes any such thing. It may still seem paradoxical that a sense for what is fitting can be an ability to see what is just *so*.

If there is such a thing as the world bearing on how the conceptual is shaped—for example on which way for something to be, at what location, being gold is—then there had better be possibilities for *judging* that the way things are bears thus and so. There had better be *facts* as to how it bears. If what gold is is all a matter of what you choose to *call* gold, then whether the ring on my finger is gold is all a matter of what you choose to call gold. The threat is to the possibility of judgement *überhaupt*.

Just here, though, is the rub. There is a *judgement* only where the world holds *sole* authority over its correctness. On the present story, we are imbued with a sense for how the world ought to be seen to matter to, for example, what it would be for something to be gold. Without the workings of this sense in our responses to things being as they are (or what we see of this), it now seems, being gold could not *be* some one way for things to be, as opposed to others. The worry is: how can *this* be the world holding sole sway over what being gold in fact is—the sort of sway needed for that to be something to *judge* of?

Behind Wittgenstein's failed attempt to defuse Kant's Pyrrhonian worry there was this idea: there is the system which generates descriptions for the way things are, and then there is our having that system at our disposal. Our psychology may work ad lib. in putting that system at our disposal. It is the system's task to give those descriptions their content, to make the world matter to each in the particular way it does. Our psychology, the thought was, has no bearing on how any given system does its work. The world's sway over the fate of any given judgement—here taking the world to be as it is according to some given description within the system—is thereby insulated from any compromise by our psychology. Abstracting from the details of the Tractarian view of judgement, the crucial point here is this: psychology can play whatever role one likes in providing opportunities for judgement, so long as all it does in that role is fix what it is that is thus judged; how the world is to matter to that judgement's fate. Kant transgressed that stricture: for him psychology shaped the very thing our judgements represent as one way or another. It would also be transgressed if, somehow, psychology worked to make the correctness of some posture depend not just on what it represented as such-and-such, but also on our feelings towards that. But so long as the stricture is not transgressed, judgement is not threatened.

A sunset over the Atlantic provides opportunities for judging. One may judge the sun to be sinking rapidly below the horizon. Galileo showed us an understanding of *sinking* on which one could not thus be judging truly. But there are others, on some of which, in so judging, one may be exactly right. Psychology may work ad lib. in the identifying of some such understanding. A sense for what *sinking* would reach on that understanding might fully identify that reach, so far as it matters to the present worry. The understanding once fixed, there remains the question whether the sun is sinking rapidly on that understanding of its doing so—a substantive question over which nothing so far threatens the world's sole sway. (Even if whether things being as they are (over the Atlantic) is the sun sinking on that understanding of it doing so is decided by what we are prepared to recognize, one can still be wrong as to whether the sun is sinking (on that understanding) in being wrong as to how things are—failing to think anything at all of the way things in fact are.)

Such was the *Tractatus*' idea. A system for describing fixes what each of its elements *says* about the world: how it represents things. Whether the world then obliges in being as represented is left, for all that, entirely the world's affair. Hence, too, whatever the role of our psychology in getting us to think within some particular system: so long as *that*, and just that, is what it does, the world's role is in no way compromised. Tractarian Wittgenstein did not worry much about how a *system* could get its elements to reach to just some *one* range of particular cases. He supposed it did so somehow. Such still would not compromise the world's role. He did not envisage what he later stressed: what we are prepared to recognize works to shape what we have in mind, all the way down to particular cases of things being as we find them. But that unfolding of that 'somehow' leaves the general point intact.

What the *Tractatus* missed is that the world also must play a role in how an element in a system represents things to be—what is so according to it—even when the system to which it belongs makes no provision for this. To grant the world such a role is to admit the possibility of judging it to have been played, in a particular case, in one way or another. If there is that possibility, then there is the concept *showing when stuff would count as gold*, which, if the world has a role in showing such things, reaches to a range of particular cases, among which cases in which what is shown is that for something to be gold is for it to have atomic number 79. What is that reach? The answer depends on *what* it is that is thus asked about: a particular thing there is for stuff to be, inhabiting a particular stretch of the conceptual. Which thing that is, which region it inhabits, is not fixed apart from what we are prepared to recognize it to be, so not apart from what we could recognize as something being that. What the reach is of a concept of the form *showing such-and-such as to what would count as stuff being gold* is, similarly, not fixed apart from what we are prepared to recognize, in given circumstances, as a case of *showing* such a thing.

Sid *could* say, 'The sun is sinking', where *nothing* decides what is to be understood by *sinking*. Such would be to say *nothing* to be so. Quine makes that the position we are always in in saying anything. For, for Quine, there is never any judging as to how the world, in fact, speaks to the truth of what we say. We are pushed to that position by his view of the special case: as to how the world bears on the shape of the conceptual, there is nothing but *choices* to be made according to the way of our people. Putnam saves us from that fate. His path to salvation no more threatens judgement than the *Tractatus'* path. On the contrary, judgement perishes precisely in rejecting what he offers.

Judging is *essentially* felt as forced from us by the world. If, as I see things, I could as well think that the sun has set as that it has not, I thereby do *not* to judge that it has set. Judging that is seeing myself as *not* in that position. It is also seeing it as not just *me* who, exposed to things as I am, would be so forced. I cannot help suspecting Pia of peccadillos. But that is just me: racked by jealousy. For me so to see things just is for me not to *judge* her guilty. Where the world could force me into postures *only* by exploiting what is, in this sense, 'just me', not by extracting reactions *one* would have, there is no judging to be done. One might also think: where the world could force a posture on me only in exploiting some way I am, but a thinker might not be, that posture would be just like my jealous suspicions of Pia—not just with no real foundation, but no real judgement at all. But, we have seen, if we are to have any judgement—any stretch of the conceptual—available to us at all, this cannot be right.

There is, though, a different worry as to whether the parochial—our sense for what to acknowledge—could really play the role here seen for it. *We* could not but take the world to admit of certain forms of thought. We are so designed. But if our design really plays a role, other thinkers might think differently about this. Then Kant's Pyrrhonian worry arises. It is, it seems, always a substantive, even if unknowable, fact that the world is as we cannot but suppose it. Frege seems to have raised this spectre:

> We may say: we are compelled to make judgements by our own nature and by external circumstances; and if we do so, we cannot reject this law ... this impossibility of our rejecting the law in question hinders us not at all in supposing beings who do reject it; where it hinders us is in supposing that these beings are right in doing so; it hinders us in having doubts as to whether we or they are right.

> (1893: 15)

Barry Stroud has stressed the same idea. (See, e.g. 1999.)

To disarm it we need only recall what judging is. Just as a thought that such-and-such is so may be articulated into components (its task separated into intelligible sub-tasks), so an agent's being exposed to error as he is may be articulated into particular components: one can carve out of it particular shapes of (preparedness) to assume risk. A judgement just is some such component, a shape for an agent's posture towards the world to take, liable to be found in a range of agents. An agent commits error where (inter alia) there is that which would surprise, or disappoint him, where the ways he is prepared to deal with things would thereby go awry. The spectre is that there is such a thing as the *real* shapes thus to be carved out of *our* postures towards the world, and that we are somehow congenitally blind to error as to what these real shapes are. We *think* the world can speak to such shapes; but it is in fact so constituted that it cannot. Undiscoverably, the opportunities we *see* for judging are not really there. To which one might ask: How would things be different if we saw opportunities there really were? The answer can only be: in no way that would surprise or disappoint us, or that would be any reason for us to engage, or be prepared, to engage differently with things. Which is just to say: we commit *no* error in seeing our postures towards the world as articulating into constituent postures, judgements, in the way we do.

Wittgenstein's response to Kant's Pyrrhonian moment, for all its faults, still undoes that moment. Let Martians be thinkers as different from us as a *thinker* might be. Their postures towards the world would differ from ours. They might see theirs, or *ours*, as carving up differently into constituent postures with the ambitions of a judgement, over which the world holds sole sway. The things they saw there were to think would thus belong to different systems of thoughts—systems for describing things—than any we could envision. Such has precisely no bearing on whether the systems we see and use are ones for describing the world as ways it is, or, at worst, is not. *That* is just between us and the nonconceptual.

Putnam's insights, on present ground, come from careful attention to the details of particular cases—in the first instance, cases of scientific discovery—and a keen sense for the deep principles of thought at work in them. He offers a new way of understanding Kant and Frege, and with it the means for moving beyond their own understandings of the problems they engaged with. He removes for us a problem Kant could not solve, nor Frege dissolve. He gives us a new view of maximal generality, thus removing the need Kant saw for the mind to shape reality itself, and the illusion Frege harboured that, at some level, the conceptual is not open to being shaped at all. He thus limned the limits of what there is to ask intelligibly about the cooperation of mind and world.

In all this Putnam leaves philosophers—first of all, himself—with a distinctive sort of problem to approach and grapple with. Philosophic questions remain different in kind from scientific ones, though, as Putnam shows, seeing them clearly may draw on scientific knowledge. Philosophy is not a kind of armchair science. There is that activity which Frege called 'unfolding' a concept: seeing what there is for us to see, as things stand, of how the conceptual is shaped—*what* might require, for example, that a thinker be an agent. There is work enough for a philosopher, without either denying the world bearing on the conceptual's shape, or abandoning the methods which are his own.

10

Thought's Social Nature

> Not just agreement in definition, but also (strange as it may sound) agreement in judgements, is part of what an understanding *is*.
>
> (*Philosophical Investigations* §242)

It is not hard, and not *always* wrong, to see Frege and later Wittgenstein as opponents. But it is often more productive to see Frege as bequeathing deep and seminal insights which Wittgenstein then adopts, unfolds, and brings to full fruition. This essay concerns a case in point. Frege's insights, in this case, are, first and foremost, two ideas about thoughts: one about a thought's essentially social character, one about a sort of generality which is intrinsic to being a thought. Wittgenstein's main idea here is contained in the motto above. It is thus the main moral of the rule-following discussion of the *Investigations*. It is an idea he is already working towards in the *Blue Book* when he says,

> What one wishes to say is: 'Every sign is capable of interpretation; but the *meaning* mustn't be capable of interpretation. It is the last interpretation.'
>
> (1958: 34)

It is an idea of how to conceive our meaning our words as we thus must. It is an idea Wittgenstein also is working towards in the *Investigations* from about §§429–464, for example in this passage:

> We say: 'The order orders *this* —' and do it; but we also say: 'The order orders this: I am to . . .' Sometimes we translate the order into a proposition, other times into a demonstration, other times into action.
>
> (1953: §459)

It is an idea of what it is for such a translation to be correct, a response to something which *may* make the idea of correctness here seem problematic. The idea is also in view in that area of the *Investigations* in which Wittgenstein tells us,

> 'But how can a rule show me what I have to do in *this* case? Whatever I do is reconcilable with the rule on some interpretation.'—No, we should not so put it. But

rather: Every interpretation hangs in the air, together with what it interprets; it cannot serve as support.

(1953: §198)

What this shows it that there is an understanding of a rule which is not an interpretation.

(1953: §201)

So cast, it is an idea of what an understanding which is not an interpretation might be.

1. The Social

In 'Der Gedanke' Frege raises the question whether a thought could be an 'idea' ('Vorstellung') (Frege 1918: 66). He answers in the negative. The core of the idea that thoughts are intrinsically social lies in that answer. The words 'idea' and 'Vorstellung' both have a (related) notorious philosophical past. But Frege is careful to say what *he* means by 'Vorstellung'. A *Vorstellung* needs a bearer: there is someone such that for that *Vorstellung* to be, is for him to be aware (or conscious) of it. There is nothing it would be for me to *fail* to be aware of the very *Vorstellung* I now have. Correlatively, a *Vorstellung* admits no two bearers. There is nothing it would be for you and me to have the same *Vorstellung*—nothing such trans-bearer identity of *Vorstellung* might consist in. (We cannot both be aware of something such that, for each of us, there would be no such thing were *he* not aware of it.) A *Vorstellung* is *anything* which, in this sense, needs a bearer.

A *Vorstellung* need not be an object of *sensory* awareness. Whether one can *sense* thoughts is orthogonal to the question Frege means to raise here. Nor, if thoughts are not *Vorstellungen*, does this mean they do not represent. Rather, it means that a thought represents *things* as a certain way, where *things* so being is what *one* might encounter, (rationally) investigate, debate—thus the way in question one that *one* might get in mind. Here 'one may do this' means: for any given thinkers who can do this, there could be more. So a thought's truth could turn on nothing extra to how things are in one's shared environment. Minimally, then, a negative answer to Frege's question will mean that anything *I* can think, *one* can think (or doubt, deny, dispute, investigate)—'one' as per above. It is intrinsic to a thought to be shareable—in that minimal, perhaps unexciting, sense social. (The slogan, 'thought is social', may conjure up more exciting visions—of thought as something undertaken jointly, or shaped by social forces, or etc., whatever such might come to. But the excitement in Frege's minimal point is, perhaps, as much as is *philosophy's* lot.)

Frege's argument for his negative answer is, in effect, an argument against the possibility of private language. It is a neat argument, which I will not try to spell out here. (See, though, Travis 2005.) But I will give a brief synopsis of the strategy. The argument proceeds in two stages. At the first stage, Frege argues that if a predicate—'is red' is his example—were to be applicable to a *Vorstellung* (in the example, one which *is* meant to be an object of sensory awareness), it would need, for this, a different sense than it would have in application to some item in our shared environment (that is, as he also argues, a sense different from the sort of sense we usually take 'is red' to bear). The reason for this, in brief, is that it is part of what it is for something to be red, in the usual sense of that word, for it to participate in networks of factive meaning: other aspects of the environment bear on whether a given item is red, as its being red bears on other aspects of the environment. For example (again Frege's example), it matters to whether a strawberry is red what will happen when you compare it with (hold it next to) a standard sample of the colour red, whereas *Vorstellungen* are not the sorts of things which could have a place in (such) a network of factive meaning. In the second stage of the argument, Frege notes that if a thought were a *Vorstellung*, then, by the conclusion of the first stage, 'is true', as applied to it, would have to have a different sense from that which we usually take that predicate to have—one on which it would apply to, and only to, *Vorstellungen*. Here is a very brief statement of the problem with that. A thought was meant to be *precisely* the sort of thing which is liable to be true or false, according to how things are. Being *truth*-evaluable (bringing truth into question) is the central mark of a thought. Our question was whether a *thought* could be a *Vorstellung*; to respond by pointing to *Vorstellungen* which can be true only in some new sense of 'true' is just to change the subject. (Again, this is meant only as the outline of an argument.)

So far, the point is that any thought is shareable: anything anyone might think is what others might think (or dispute, debate, investigate)—for any list of others, still others. (Henceforth, what *one* might think (etc.).) Frege describes what failure of such minimal shareability would be like:

I might have my science, namely the totality of thoughts whose bearer I am, another his science. Each of us would occupy himself with the contents of his consciousness. A contradiction between both bodies of knowledge is then not possible; and it is really silly to dispute about truth, as silly, in fact nearly ridiculous, as it would be if two people disputed whether a hundred mark note was genuine, where each meant the one he had in his own pocket, and understood the word 'genuine' in his own special sense. If someone held thoughts to be ideas, what he thereby recognised as true would, on his own account, belong to the contents of his consciousness and would not concern anyone else at all. And if he heard the opinion from me that thoughts were not ideas, he could not dispute it; for it would surely not concern him at all.

(1918: 69)

One cannot disagree, or dispute, with someone as to whether such-and-such— there cannot be even that minimal shareability on which Frege insists—unless there is enough else which both parties agree to. If I call copper tresses red and you do not, then if I would call Pia's hair red and you would not, we are not yet expressing disagreement as to how Pia's hair is coloured; no disagreement settled by its being coloured as it is. (Not implausibly, we may disagree as to how Pia's hair is where I would call it red, you not, only if we would agree, of the way Pia's hair is in fact coloured, as to whether *that* is being coloured red.) This leaves room for honest disagreement: one (or both) of us may be ignorant of something significant as to how Pia's hair is in fact coloured. We *may* disagree as to what is to be called *red*. But it is *red* that we thus disagree about only if we both have being *red* in mind, so only if we agree on enough as to when something *would* be that. We disagree on what colour copper tresses are to be called only in agreeing, for example on whether ripe tomatoes, or certain sunsets, or fresh pools of blood, or whatever, are (of) the colour thus in question. We both have some one way for hair to be in mind only if we agree on *enough*, not necessarily everything, as to when hair would be that way. We can both have *red* in mind while disagreeing on copper tresses. We both have *red* in mind only if we both agree to enough (again, not necessarily all) of what there *is* to agree to as to what being *red* is (so what would count as a case of it).

Thought's social nature means: *I* think things to be some given way only where some extendible range of thinkers would agree (and agree with me) sufficiently as to what would count as things *being* that way; only where, so to speak, there is a (potential) community of agreement (or of ones who agree). But now, this idea, however Fregean, must be squared with the second half of Frege's denial that a thought could be a *Vorstellung*. Frege states that second half in these words:

Thus, for example, the thought which we express in the' Pythagorean theorem is timelessly true, true independent of whether anyone holds it true. It needs no bearer. Like a planet, which has been interacting with other planets before anyone has seen it, it is not true only after it has been discovered.

(1918: 69)

Fix a way for things to be—say, such that the sum of the squares of the sides equals the square of the hypotenuse, or such that the rug is white. Now whether things are *that* way depends in no way on what thinkers would agree to: not on what we, or any thinkers, would *count* as what; not on how we *stand* towards the sides of triangles relating as they do, or towards the rug's being coloured as it is. Such is built into Frege's conception of the objectivity (or, equivalently, truth-evaluability) of judgement: the idea that a judgement is correct or incorrect *solely* by virtue of things being as they are, and *not* by virtue of anyone's attitude towards the bearing of that on the correctness of the judgement. It bears stressing that nothing to follow—so nothing in Wittgenstein—disputes, or is in conflict with, that idea.

In the *Blue Book* Wittgenstein reminds us:

Words have those meanings which we have given them . . . a word hasn't got a meaning given to it, as it were, by a power independent of us.

(1958: 27–28)

The *Investigations* expands this thought into §242, my present working motto, and, just before that, with this:

'So you hold that it is agreement among people which decides what is true and what is false?'—It is what people say that is true or false; and it is in language that people agree. This is not about agreement of opinions but about forms of life.

(1953: §241)

This is not to deny Frege's last point. It does point to a reverse side to his coin. By Frege's side of the coin, for any way for things to be, there is that which is to be recognized (that which is so) as to what it would be for things to be that way—what would count, what not, as a case of that. Suppose, now, that there is a community of thinkers who, jointly, have a given way for things to be in mind—who can, perhaps sometimes do, think, and speak, in terms of things being that way or not. So, by Frege's point about the importance of agreement, there is that to which they would agree (or are prepared to) as to what would count, and what not, as things being the way in question. Then, the idea is, to identify what way it is that they have in mind, look for a way for things to be such that there is (sufficiently nearly) just that to be recognized as to when things would count, when not, as things being that way. Bracketing complications where there are several such ways, if you find such a way, you will have found, or identified, what it is they have in mind. What *they* would agree would be a case of being some way *they* have in mind—what they call being such-and-such—is, in fact, say, what *would* count as a case of something being red. Again bracketing those complications, such just is their having being red in mind. The community in question might be us. So, by the reverse side of the coin, where there is a question as to which way for things to be *we* speak of in speaking of things being such-and-such, one can find an answer to that question in looking to what we would agree to as to what is to be called 'being such-and-such'.

Without care in stating, and applying, this reverse side of Frege's coin, it *can* look as if it is in conflict with Frege's side. Hence Wittgenstein's persistent concern to insist that it is not. He says, for example,

You say, '*That* is red.' But how is it decided if you are right? Doesn't human agreement decide?

(1967: §429)

Colour words are explained like this: 'That's red' e.g.—Our language game only works, of course, when a certain agreement prevails. But the concept of agreement does not enter into the language game.

(1967: §430)

Does human agreement *decide* what is red? Is it decided by appeal to the majority? Were we taught to determine colour in *that* way?

(1967: §431)

Frege's coin *has* two sides. If there is a problem, it is to reconcile them.

2. The Conceptual

Frege remarked,

A thought always contains something which reaches beyond the particular case, by means of which this is presented to consciousness as falling under something general.

(1882: *Kernsatz* 4)

A thought represents the particular case as a certain way. For it to do that is for it to reach to a range of cases: just those in which things being as they were would be their being that way. For there to be a range is just for not everything to matter to things being as the thought represents them. If the thought is true, then things being as they are *is* things being that way. This is *one* way for things so to be. But there is always an indefinitely extendable variety of others. If the thought is that red meat is on the white rug, the meat might be venison or mutton, Angus or Charolais, the rug shag or broadloom; Pia might be sleeping or surfing, or might not have been. And so on ad infinitum. But it could not be tofu on the rug, or plastic 'meat'. So this thought reaches to an indefinitely large range of cases. Equally for things *not* being as it represents them—the cases it does not reach. The generality intrinsic to a thought demands, for *any* thought, at least one such range.

If a thought reached to just one case, this would have to be that very particular case which it represented as falling under some generality. *Everything* in things being as they thus were would matter to that thought's truth. Or else more cases would be reached. So the thought would not really bring anything under a generality at all. It would, as it were, gesture at what it was to represent, but then do no representing of it. As Leibniz saw, it would not even be some very long conjunction, each conjunct reaching to many cases, the whole narrowing these down to one. There are no such conjunctions. To grasp how things would be in being this way, one would need to grasp no less than *all* of how things were. Thoughts are guides to the conduct of a life. A given one has specific bearing on what to think and do. A thought true of just *this* case—things being as they (in fact) are—would have all the bearing one could wish—if one could but grasp it. But, for a finite thinker, there could be no such thing as seeing the bearing *this* thought would have; nor as the bearing one would see in grasping it. So no such thing as (as Frege puts it) the way one exposes oneself to error in so judging, which, again, makes this not really a thought at all.

The particular case is what the thought represents as a certain way. What it so represents is: things being as they are. *Another* case for the thought to reach would be things being, somehow, other than they are—for example things being as they will be tomorrow. One can decompose a thought, in one way or another, into elements—some set of partial contributions which jointly add up, in one way or another, to what the whole thought does. When we do this, Frege tells us, no matter how, we always find at least one element with the same sort of generality a thought has. If the thought is that the meat is turning brown, one element one might find—on *some* decomposition—is: (being about) something turning brown. There are a multitude of ways for something's being as it is to be it turning brown, and for something's being as it is *not* to be this. All the above applies. Here different cases of something turning brown might be found in different *things* being as they are. Further cases need not merely be what might have been. Finally, if the thought is *that* the meat is turning brown, then the meat's turning brown is a way for *things* to be, just as (something) turning brown is a way for *a* thing to be. A way for things, or for a thing, to be again shares a thought's generality.

The particular case—what a thought represents as thus and so—precisely lacks a thought's intrinsic generality. A thought is tied to the ambitions of a certain posture; the way things are is not. The thought's reach lies in those ambitions. Nothing gives the way things are a reach at all. There are no *two* cases of things being as they are. Things might have been just the same *on some understanding* of *same*, while then not the same on others. Things being as they are confers no understanding on *same*.

I will call what has a thought's intrinsic generality *conceptual*, the domain of such things (if we permit ourselves the conceit) *the conceptual*; what lacks that generality *nonconceptual*, or, again, *the nonconceptual*. A bit of the conceptual— things, or something, being such-and-such way, or what presents (or makes a thought about) this—reaches to just those particular cases which are (or would be) ones in which things (or something's) being as they are (or were) would be things (or that thing) being *that* way. I will also speak of what some bit of the conceptual reaches to as *instancing* it.

This first idea of Frege's fits together with another. He writes,

> The fundamental logical relation is that of an object falling under a concept: all relations between concepts reduce to this.

> (1892–1895: 128)

Objects, for Frege, are what *are* thus and so, not what instances *being* thus and so. Concepts, in his sense, are not ways of presenting something, not elements in a thought's way of doing it which make it *about* some way for something to be. Nor are they a *way* for things to be. Nor are they any more than *contingently* of being such-and-such (in whatever sense they might be this at all). Concepts (his sense) are what some parts of an *expression* of a thought *refer* to. I will say no more here about what *this* is. In any case, the relation between an object and a concept is not the same as that between a particular case—the nonconceptual— and some bit of the conceptual. *Falling under* is not *instancing*.

There are, for all that, parallels. A Fregean concept is the sort of thing under which an object falls. An object is not. The distinction between objects and concepts is, for Frege, absolute and fundamental. The same thing cannot be, sometimes an object, sometimes a concept. A Fregean concept thus connects with a range of cases: those objects which fall under it; and another range, those objects which do not. An object falls under concepts. It is an object's being as it is that *instances* ways for things to be. Still, what instances here is not what is itself instanced. It is fundamentally different from that. Nor can something some- times belong to the nonconceptual, sometimes to the conceptual. Relations between concepts, Frege tells us, reduce to one between concepts and objects: falling under. I will not speak of reduction. But I can say: relations within the conceptual cannot really be brought in view at all, are not the ones they are, and do not give the conceptual any reach at all, independent of the fundamental relation between the conceptual and the nonconceptual: *instancing* (or its converse, *reaching*). The conceptual-nonconceptual distinction is the key to understanding those initial *Blue Book* passages.

3. Instancing

I turn now to Wittgenstein's unfolding of those Fregean ideas just scouted. The core response to Frege's first idea was the reverse side of Frege's coin. The core response to the second—developed here into a conceptual-nonconceptual distinction—is to see something conceptual as participating in two sorts of relations. There are relations entirely within the conceptual, between some of its bits and others. Something being red, for example, participates in one such in bearing as it does on something being green. Then there are relations in which the conceptual reaches outside of itself to participate in relations with things nonconceptual. Instancing is the central case. Now the main idea can be put this way: the internal shape of the conceptual—that structure imposed on it simply by those relations within it—cannot, purely on its own, impose *any* shape on relations between the conceptual and what lies outside it; notably, cannot give any bit of the conceptual any particular reach to the nonconceptual.

What makes being red reach where, or as, it does? One might see this in terms of being red's position in a system of ways to be coloured. For example (say), where being green reaches, being red does not. This *may* help us see where being red reaches—insofar as, but only insofar as, we see where being green reaches. But without the reaches of other ways to be coloured already fixed, a place within a system of them fixes nothing as to reach.

Often, in particular circumstances, for particular purposes, we can, and *do*, say how some less familiar bit of the conceptual reaches by connecting it to more familiar bits. It sometimes helps to identify the reach of *being a chair* to point out that a chair is a seat for one. Or if you want to see how my present notion of *way for things to be* reaches, you may look to what I have said in introducing it, which consists almost entirely of linking it to other bits of the conceptual. But suppose what we wanted was an explanation of the instancing relation's being, as a whole, as it is rather than otherwise—an answer to the question what *makes* it as a whole relate just those things to one another that it does, rather than relating these things in some other way. Or, to ask the question differently, suppose we wanted an answer to the question what makes the conceptual as a whole reach as it does (or, for that matter, reach at all), rather than in some other way. Then the point is: there *is* no answer to such questions. Nothing *makes* the conceptual as a whole reach as it does. Nothing, for that matter, makes *being red* reach as it does. Reaching as *being red* does is just part of what it is for a way for a thing to be to be *that* one, being red; is intrinsic to what *being red* is, to which way for a thing to be it is. It is a misunderstanding to think that something else *makes* being red reach as it does, or, in the *Blue Book*'s terms, justifies its so reaching. This will be the main point.

Now let us return to that *Blue Book* idea: signs may admit of interpretation, but someone's meaning must not. There is a simple point of grammar here. If I say, 'The sails were red', you may ask whether those words are to be understood in a way such as to be true if the sails' red look was just the work of a sunset, or such as then to be untrue. Either answer might be right, depending on the circumstances in which I spoke. The words I used, as such, might be interpreted in either way. In that sense, *they* admit of interpretation. I, too, might be interpreted in either way, though rightly or wrongly depending on how I meant them (or was to be taken to have). I may have *meant* my words so as to be true of sails red only in the sunset, or so as not to be. Or I may have meant them such as for them to be true, or false, of such sails only on an interpretation, thus not in a way on which they would be true or false (outright, pleonastically) at all. But it cannot be that I meant them in one such way only on a certain interpretation of my meaning (which, if this means anything, would be for me *not* to have meant them in that way); nor that I meant them in a certain way only if a certain interpretation of my meaning is correct. For an interpretation of my meaning to be correct, if this meant anything, would just be for that to be the way I meant it; which would be for my meaning *not* to call for interpretation.

The application of this grammatical point in the context of our present main point is just this. For me to have meant (to say) that the sails were *red* (forget for the moment any fine points as to what would count as their being red), I must have had, at the time I spoke, their being *red* in mind. But, reflecting on the main point, it can seem problematic that I, or anyone, could do such a thing as having being red in mind. Similarly for any other way for a thing to be in terms of which we (think we) think. For, for it to be *being red* that I had in mind, what I had in mind would have to reach—participate in the instancing relation— (nearly enough) as *being red* does reach. (The reverse side of Frege's coin.) And this can now seem impossible. To see why, I will make a comparison.

A man in Ulan Bator is now standing before his yurt, sipping tea. (Make it ten o'clock his time.) I cannot think a thought, of *him*, that he is doing that—a thought which presents *him* as the one who must be some way for the thought to be true, and sipping tea before his yurt at ten as what he must be doing. I cannot do this, since I neither know, nor know of, anyone in Ulan Bator (though I am sure some people live there). I can, to be sure, think that everyone in Ulan Bator stands before his yurt at 10 and sips tea. What I thus think will be false if this man does not do that. The thought I thus think has a certain kind of generality which allows it to be true, or false, in this way. But as Frege points out (1914: 108–109, different example), that man falsifies my statement only given that he is in Ulan Bator—in present terms, only given that his being as he is participates in the instancing relation with that way for a thing to be. And it is just this last that I am not in a position to think—a corollary of not being able to think of him at all. Thinking a thought which is false, given his being as he is, is not the same thing as thinking a thought of *him*.

Now consider those sails, or rather, that particular bit of history which is their being as they will be tomorrow (at ten o'clock). This is something which may well either bear the instancing relation to *something being red*, or fail to (but rather bear it to something *not* being red). Which is to say that *something being red* is the sort of thing which has such reach: if it does not participate in the instancing relation with the particular item just mentioned, it will with others of that sort—say, those currently white sheets being as they will be after coming out of the wash tomorrow. So to have *being red* in mind, I must have in mind something with that sort of reach. But items of this sort—things being *just* that which they will be—are items I cannot yet get in mind at all. I can as little, now, think thoughts *of them* that they are thus and so as I can think thoughts of that man before his yurt. In particular, I cannot think thoughts *of them* that they bear the instancing relation to some way for things to be—say, to *being red*. I can, of course, think that those sails will be a way tomorrow which will be (inter alia) their being red. (Just that, in fact, is the problem.) But I cannot now think of just that which they will, in fact, be tomorrow in being as they then will be that *that* is a case of something being red. There is as yet no such thing to think about. So the problem is: How can I have in mind a way for things to be which reaches to something when the thought that it reaches to *that* is not one that I can as yet so much as entertain?

This is the problem Wittgenstein points to in *Investigations* §459. You give the order. I translate it into action. That is, I do what I then do. But that very thing, my doing of what I then do—that particular episode in world history—is not something you could have had in mind, had thoughts about, at all, at the time you gave the order. So, whatever I do, how can *that* be either what you meant me to do, or not what you meant me to do—carrying out the order as you meant it, or not?

It can be tempting to try to answer this question by looking for something else I could have in mind which would require that just those cases of something bearing the instancing relation to *being red* which I cannot yet get in mind be ones of bearing the instancing relation to what I do now have in mind. Frege (1904) considers, and rejects for the role of *function*, the sort of thing which might seem to do the trick. It is what he there calls a *Gesetz der Zuordnung*—a *law*, specifically, a law of association: something which spells out, somehow, what is required, *in general*, for something to be a case of what I have in mind. But a law belongs to the conceptual. It is thus clearly useless for the present purpose. It only postpones the worry. For how do I get in mind a *law* which dictates just that reach for what I have in mind which goes with *being red*? This is no easier a question than the one with which we started. So if we approach the apparent problem in this way, we are only spinning gears, engaged with nothing. There is no solution along such lines.

We can get traction in applying Frege's idea of thought as social. Here I will only sketch the main ingredients. I start with thinking. First, where there is something I think so, I belong to a range of thinkers who might think just *that* so, or not so. These thinkers form a community of agreement as to what would count, what not, as this being so. I think, say, that there are truffles beneath the oak; the agreement is as to what, *in particular*, would, and what would not, count as there being truffles beneath that oak. 'Community' here does not refer to some social, or geographical, entity. Membership is gained simply in ability to think the thing in question (e.g. that meat is on the rug); hence in (sufficient) agreement as to what would count as a case, and as not a case, of that thing (e.g. of meat being on the rug).

Second, agreement here will be extendable in the same sense as the community is: for any given cases of community agreement (*this* would count as things being the way for things to be in question, *this* as things not so being), further cases can be made or found on which the community would also agree. The community will, recognizably, share a sense for what to count as a case of this way for things to be—a sense which (to count as a *sense* for something at all) reaches to novel cases. Agreement then consists, not in unmitigated, or majority, consent, but in there being such a thing as that which someone with the sense in question *would* find (such a thing as what the sense in question dictates).

To make the third point, I appeal to a distinction between two notions of *recognize*: recognition as acknowledgement, and recognition as pure cognitive achievement (of one of several sorts). That distinction is marked, nearly enough, in German and Dutch by different verbs—in German by *anerkennen* and *erkennen* respectively. Thus, for Frege, to see that the sun has set is to *erkennen* a truth; to *judge* that the sun has set to *anerkennen* its truth (1918: 61–62). To *erkennen*—see—that the sun has set is to judge—so *anerkennen*—that it has. Conversely, one's *Anerkennung*—judging—that the sun has set, for example, as one sees it sink over the horizon, may well be *Erkennung*—seeing that the sun has set. Similarly, where I think something—say, that the sun has set—for the relevant community to share its sense of *Anerkennung*—of what to count as a case of things being that way which I thus thought them—may be for it to enjoy a capacity for *Erkennung*—a capacity to tell what *is* (*does* count as) a case of things being that way.

Where there is a community of agreement, there is anyway *some* distinction to be drawn between two sorts of particular case: cases that this community would *count* as a case of being such-and-such way, and cases which it would count as *not* that. This is a familiar point. Now the idea is: if this community is the community of those thinkers with just *that* way for things to be in mind, then what they would *count* as a particular case of things being that way *is* that.

Now the conclusion: since I belong to that community, I can, sometimes would, have in mind just that way for things to be which is the object of that capacity of *Erkennung*. I can think, in given circumstances would be thinking, thoughts to the effect that things are that way. Since, by definition, a capacity extends to novel cases, I thus have in mind a way for things to be—am thinking things to be a way—which is instanced by, and *not* instanced by, particular cases of which I cannot yet think. My membership in the community thus permits me thoughts which reach to cases of which I cannot think.

But all this is in the form of a conditional. This may lead to an objection, as follows. Granted, *if* I am thinking something so, then the above three conditions are met, so that, indeed, I have in mind what reaches to cases of which I cannot think. But that I have such a thing in mind *if* I am thinking something so, we knew already. Could these conditions not *seem* to be met where they are not? Could I not seem (inter alia, to myself) to be thinking something so, where there is no such thing for *one* to think? (What about witches, e.g.? I *think* being a witch is a way for someone to be; but there is no such way to be at all.) If there could merely seem to be something to think where there is not, then (what seemed) our original problem just returns in a new form: What would it be for something to be a case where the above conditions were actually met, as opposed, notably, to its being a case where they (at best) merely seemed to be?

This worry will not be answered here in the detail it deserves. I confine myself to two remarks. First, we can (let us suppose) find an understanding of being a witch on which there is really no such thing as that. (Let us call this the sixteenth-century understanding.) Holding such an understanding, I might 'think that Pia is a witch', but could not be thinking that Pia is a witch: since there is no such way for things to be, I could not be thinking things to be that way. Were I living in the sixteenth century, I would be surrounded by others who thought there was such a way, and that they could distinguish between those particular cases (those bits of the nonconceptual) which did instance someone being a witch (count as a case of that) and those which did not. Do

314 OBJECTIVITY AND THE PAROCHIAL

they form a community—in the present sense of 'community'—which, through their shared sense of what to acknowledge as a case, were at least drawing *some* distinction—one between cases which they would *count* as ones of someone being a witch, and ones which they would not? Probably not. Not, for example, if, from case to case, they were just moved by some contagious hysteria, or someone with a way with words. If things were like that, there would be no fact as to how the distinction they might *seem* to be drawing would extend to novel cases. This would make it no distinction at all. (On the other hand, if they really were drawing some distinction, it might be, as one bio-chemist once suggested, one between women with, and those without, such-and-such a hormonal imbalance, which points to one perfectly good thing being a witch *might* be.)

This points to a more important point. If I have the sixteenth-century understanding of being a witch, and do what I call 'thinking Pia to be a witch', I do not thereby think anything to the effect that Pia is a witch: there is nothing to think which would be thinking *that*. But there are some relevant things I still do think, notably that there is such a thing as someone being a witch, and that Pia's being as she is instances (is a case of) someone being this way. If I do think that, it follows that I belong to a community of thinkers who can think thoughts about there being such a thing as someone being a witch (on the sixteenth-century understanding), and thus who can have in mind a certain way for things to be, namely such that there *is* such a way for someone to be, and thus a certain way for things to be, namely, that there is such a way, and someone *thinks* so-and-so to be that way (a way which, in fact, never obtains). This community—to which, hypothetically, I belong—will share a sense for what to count as a case of there being such a way for someone to be, and there being such a way for things to be, a sense which (to wax pleonastic) extends to novel cases. *We* share such a sense, and are thus able to recognize, of *any* case of someone's being as he is that *that* does not count as a case of someone being a witch (sixteenth-century understanding), so, too, of any case of someone being as he is that *that* does not count as a case of someone thinking someone to be a witch. This is to say: insofar as there is such a thing as someone merely seeming to think things to be some particular way, where there is really no such way to think things, we can also recognize such a case for what it is (given, of course, sufficient access to how things in fact are). Naturally, insofar as there is such a thing, we may make mistakes—if not as to what would *count* as a case of such *schein*-thinking, then, anyway, as to whether such-and-such *is* such a case.

This introduces my second, and more important, remark. There is one more element in Wittgenstein's way with the problem which concerns him so much: how one can have in mind what reaches to what one cannot (then) think of. It is, perhaps, the most crucial element of all. The objection just raised starts from the premise (granted here) that there is such a thing as there seeming to be a way for things to be, and hence a thought for one to have, where there is not. So, it adds, there is such a thing as those three above-stated conditions seeming to be satisfied when they are not. This is also granted here. It then asks for a mark, or test, by which one could see where there is genuine, where only spurious, satisfaction of these three conditions—a way of deciding such questions which itself begs no questions. No such answer is in the offing, either here, or in Wittgenstein. This is for principled reasons, which begin (but only begin) with a way of finessing the question.

The suggestion is that we turn our problem around. The objector supposes that there are two kinds of case: cases of genuine ways for (say) something to be—on a rug, say; and cases of *schein*-ways for something to be—a witch, say. Wittgenstein's suggestion (found, e.g. in *Investigations* §136) comes to this. Suppose there *are* these two kinds of case. Now ask what, in particular, you would be prepared to count as a case of the first sort, what as a case of the second. On present knowledge, at least, unless physics yet holds surprises, I would count being on a rug as of the first sort, and being a witch, or a Euclidean straight path in space, as of the second. I am fairly confident that you would too. But in each case I am receptive to correction in the light of empirical fact. En route to his case against private language, Frege suggests a case of the second sort:

Is that linden tree an idea? Inasmuch as I use the expression, 'that linden tree' in posing the question, I already anticipate the answer; for I mean this expression to designate something which I see, and which can also concern and be touched by others. Now there are two possibilities. If my intention is achieved, if I do designate something with the expression, 'that linden tree', then the thought expressed in the sentence, 'That linden is my idea' is obviously to be denied. But if I fail in my intention, if I only think I see, without actually seeing, if, accordingly, the designation of 'that linden' is empty, then, without realising it or wanting to, I have strayed into fiction. Then neither the content of the sentence, 'That linden is my idea', nor that of the sentence, 'That linden is not my idea', is true, for then in both cases I have a predication which lacks an object.

(1918: 68)

Either 'That linden' refers to a tree, or 'That linden is my idea' is only the *schein*-expression of a thought. I am with Frege here. In any case, let us suppose that, when we engage in this exercise, we prove to agree well enough, often enough, on what we *would* call genuine, and what we *would* call spurious, given that there *are* those two types of case. We are not regularly unable to agree; and what we do agree on leads us into no intolerable messes. Then there *is* such a distinction; and it *is* to be drawn (nearly enough) as we are prepared to draw it.

On the one hand, this story re-invokes agreement, in at most only a slightly different form. We agree on what one *would* call *something being on a rug*, given that we are going to call some such things that at all; and we agree on whether *so* treating the nonconceptual (the historical unfolding of the world) lands us in intolerable messes—forces us to say, or commit to doing, things which are, as Wittgenstein puts it, 'uninteresting or stupid, or too complicated, or something of the sort.' On the other, Wittgenstein's point here is that there is no *other* way for there to be *schein*-thoughts, or *schein*-ways for things to be—so, in particular, for there to be *schein*-agreement—than for there to be agreement as to what would count as a case of a *schein*-way for things to be (or etc.)—which, he suggests, as to when it would be too stupid, or etc., to suppose otherwise.

The core point can be put in terms of stating. Where I state something, agreement decides what is to be expected of the world if I am right—what is to be expected of the world's unfolding, that is, of the nonconceptual, on pain of my not having said things to be as they are. Those expectations might be disappointed, or satisfied, by the unfolding world. If disappointed, then at the least, I have not said what is so. If *such* expectations are disappointed systematically, and profoundly, enough, then, perhaps, there is no way for things to be of which I spoke. It is not just that *Pia* is not a witch (sixteenth-century understanding): disappointment of this sort is endemic to calling anyone one. But suppose there is no disappointment. The world unfolds just as we agree one would expect it to if I am right; none other than what *we* agree I thus committed to. Then, the idea is, there is no *other* way for me to be speaking of a mere *schein*-way for things to be; nothing more to being a genuine way for things to be than for the world to satisfy *our* expectations aroused in, and by, so treating it.

I have unfolded these ideas in terms of thinking, rather than meaning. But a story about meaning can now begin here: Where, in given words, I mean to say that such-and-such is so, I mean to express a thought in Frege's sense, thus to say what a community of thinkers can think, dispute, investigate, etc. Agreement within this community allows my meaning to extend to cases I cannot then get in mind just as per the above story. Not that the only way I can mean words is to say something to be so. There is anyway more to be said about meaning in particular. But I will not say it here.

What, then, is the importance of communities of thinkers, in our present non-geographical, non-ethnic, non-historical (and hence very minimal) sense? A community of agreement, with its sense for acknowledgement, makes at least for a distinction between particular cases which are what it would acknowledge as instancing such-and-such, and ones which it would not so acknowledge (or acknowledge as not doing that). But why cannot I, on my own, no thanks to a community, make for a parallel distinction? The idea would be: N now has some way for things (or a thing) to be in mind; he cannot now think, of novel particular cases (relative to now), that they instance that way, or that they fail to. But when they come along, in the future, he can find them to do the one thing or the other. Why cannot this evince a sense—*N's* sense—for acknowledgement; for what, in general, to count as a case of something (or of things) being that way? If it can, why is there not a distinction, among particular cases, between those which are what N would count as a case of something being A, and those which are not that?

The quickest way with this idea, I think, is to invoke Frege's private language argument. If having a sense for what to acknowledge as such-and-such is a way N may count as being, then it is a way for *one* to be; N's, or anyone's, being that way is something *one* can get in mind. The thought that N is that way cannot be an idea (since no thought can). So *that* N is that way cannot be an idea either. Acknowledgement, and senses for it, in such connections, are what *one* can get in mind, and what *we* have in mind in asking whether N could have such a sense. Its participation in the instancing relation (or that of those ways for things to be we thus ask about) is fixed by the particular cases *we* would be prepared (so equipped) to acknowledge as within its reach. If, given that, there is a distinction between what N would so count and what he would not, this is to say that *we* can recognize when a case is what N would count as something being A, which is to say that *we* can recognize what it is that N is counting as something being A. If N thus identifies a way for things to be, then what *he* would so count identifies what would count as something being A. So we, too, can get something being A in mind. And now we form a community with N, to which all above remarks apply.

Suppose that only N could apply the notion *what, by N's sense for what to acknowledge, would be a case of something being A.* Then that would not be a notion of what to *acknowledge* as such-and-such. The subject would have changed, just as you change the subject of whether a thought can be an idea when you stop talking about ideas being *true* and start talking about their being 'true' in some new sense. On this supposition, what a community can be said to do in saying it to acknowledge something, or exercise a sense for this, is not something which N, apart from a community, can be said to do at all. Neither this, nor anything in this section, is meant as a private language argument. That came (in outline) in section 1, its result assumed thenceforth and throughout. This last point simply applies Frege's conclusion.

Our minds cannot change the nonconceptual—what there is for the conceptual to reach to—excepting, at most, that part of it which just is their being as they are. This, in essence, is what Frege's side of his coin says. But they can furnish our ways of articulating the nonconceptual. How we carve up the *way* things are into particular ways *for* things to be may depend on the means thus supplied. The way *our* minds work can thus matter to what bits of the conceptual we can get in mind—what there is within our grasp with reach to the nonconceptual. This is Wittgenstein's reverse side of Frege's coin. Minds can do this working jointly, forming a community of thinkers. Following Wittgenstein's unfolding of Frege's core ideas, I have just argued that there is no other way for them to do so.

4. Shadows

That remark in the *Blue Book* from which we started, about someone's meaning not admitting of interpretation, occurs in a longer discussion of what Wittgenstein there calls shadows. This discussion, particularly as it concerns intention, asks to be read as a commentary on Frege. It is critical of an idea one *might* find in Frege if one read him in a certain way. Again it concerns a misunderstanding of an idea of not admitting of interpretation, this time as applied to thoughts.

Misunderstanding how certain expressions work, the *Blue Book* tells us, can create a seeming puzzle—to which shadows may seem to offer a solution:

How can one think what is not the case? If I think that King's College is on fire when it is not on fire, the fact of its being on fire does not exist. Then how can I think it?

The next step we are inclined to take is to think that as the object of our thought isn't the fact it is a shadow of the fact. There are different names for this shadow, e.g., 'proposition', 'sense of the sentence'.

But this doesn't remove our difficulty. For the question now is: 'How can something be the shadow of a fact which doesn't exist?' . . . 'How can we know what the shadow is a shadow of?'

(1958: 32)

In present terms, if King's College is not (now) burning, then nothing in the actual unfolding of the world instances that bit of the conceptual, King's College (now) burning—what a thought that King's College is now burning would be of. So there is nothing of which one could think, '*This* is things being as thus thought.' There is simply *no* thought to such effect. So there is no *such* way of identifying how things would be if they *were* as thus thought. So we posit some other way of identifying this. Wittgenstein calls it a shadow. When I think that King's College is burning, this other thing, the shadow, is the 'object of my thought'. If King's College *is* burning, then King's College's being as it is will exactly match the shadow—in present terms, instance it. If King's College is *not* burning, then King's College's being as it is will exactly fail to match. The shadow provides for both possibilities. On the one hand, if it did not, it would not be the object of the thought that King's College is on fire. But, on the other, if there is such a shadow, and if, say, King's College is not on fire, then there is *nothing* (in the unfolding of the world) of which to think truly that *this* matches it. So how can there be such a thing as the envisioned matching at all?

In our present terms, the problem is how a thought can have the sort of reach that a thought would have to have in order to be the thought that King's College is on fire. What could make it reach? So far, at least, the idea of a shadow does not seem to help. Wittgenstein suggests, though, that we can see how a thought can have such reach—we can solve, or dissolve, our puzzle—if we can see how a portrait can be a portrait of so-and-so:

> I can restate our problem by asking: 'What makes a portrait a portrait of Mr. N?'
>
> (1958: 31)

I remark that this is not obviously correct. Standardly, at least, one needs to sit for a portrait. (There is deferred sitting, as in sending a photo.) So there can only be portraits of people there *are*. They require the artist's acquaintance with the person (again, perhaps deferred). Acquaintance matters to what thoughts the artist can think. Perhaps Wittgenstein himself is making a mistake here. For his first response to the question how one can think what is not the case is:

> How can we hang a thief who doesn't exist? Our answer could be . . . : 'I can't hang him when he doesn't exist; but I can look for him when he doesn't exist.'
>
> (1958: 31)

But surely one cannot look for a thief who doesn't exist. (In the *Investigations* (1953: §462), this is changed to: 'I can look for someone when he isn't there, but not hang him when he isn't there'; which is correct.) The best one could do is think he is looking for someone when he is not. To devote my life to 'looking for the thief of Baghdad' is just to suffer an illusion. (See my (forthcoming) for elaboration on why it is an illusion to think otherwise.)

Bracketing this point, though, let us see how Wittgenstein thinks the question about portraits can be answered. We can then work out how this answer is meant to apply to the problem shadows were meant to (but cannot) solve. About portraits, he says this:

> An obvious, and correct, answer to the question 'What makes a portrait the portrait of so-and-so?' is that it is the *intention*. But if we wish to know what it means 'intending this to be a portrait of so-and-so' let's see what actually happens when we intend this.
>
> (1958: 32)

This reference to portraits and intentions also reads as reference to Frege's introduction, in 'Der Gedanke', of the notion of a thought, on which the discussion of shadows thus becomes commentary.

Frege compares thoughts and pictures as follows:

So is a picture, as mere visible, tangible thing really true? And a stone, or leaf, not true? Clearly one would not call a picture true, if an intention did not attach to it.

(1918: 59)

Think of a picture as painted canvas. Now what, if anything, does it depict? Frege's point is that there is no answer to that question unless there is an answer to the question how it is to be taken (to be depicting)—for example what manner, or style, of depiction it is to be taken to be engaging in. Frege refers to an intention attaching to the picture as what (if anything) answers this. Perhaps that is not quite right. But it will do for present purposes. It may be, given such an answer, that the picture depicts Cologne Cathedral. It may then be further to be taken to depict it as looking a certain way, and then, further, perhaps, as looking the way it looks. All that may leave further questions to be answered. Does that patch on the canvas depict early morning shadow or a graffito? Is the church really fuzzy around the edges, or is that meant as morning mist? Are those flying buttresses intentionally distorted for some effect, or to capture a particular perspective? Is the picture meant to depict the cathedral as it will look after renovation, or as the artist remembers it from childhood, or as it did look on a particular morning, or simply as it looks—in which last case, what would count as looking as it looks? And so on. If the picture is to be taken to represent the cathedral as it looks, then we *might*, intelligibly, view it as truth-evaluable. But only if there are answers to enough such questions as to in which way it is to be taken, enough for us to see, of the cathedral's being as it is that this *is* its being as depicted, or that it is not.

This states half of Frege's point. The other half is that there is always *substantive* work for intention to do. A painted canvas, no matter how painted, *could* represent in any of many ways, or in none, depending on how it is to be taken (on what intention attaches to it). Painted canvases always admit of representing in any of many ways; always admit, so far as they go, of any of many intentions attaching to them.

Frege's first point, then, is that a question of truth arises—something so or not has been represented as so—only where an intention, or what does that work, has settled enough such issues. He then goes on to argue:

Accordingly, the sense of a sentence emerges as the only thing with which being true can come into question at all.

Without meaning by this to give a definition, I call something a thought by which truth can come into question at all.

(1918: 60)

So intentions, in providing answers to enough questions of interpretation, can make a definite question of truth arise—can bring truth into question. They can do this, notably, for words to which they attach. For them to do this is for them to make an identifiable something attach to those words: a given sense of a particular sort (the sort that goes with saying something so or not). Such a sense answers all the questions of interpretation which need answers in order to see when what was thus said would be true, when false. It fixes a reach for what was said. It itself is not open to interpretation. That is, it cannot be that whether it answers those questions in one way or another depends on whether one thing or another attaches to it—or, for that matter, on anything. It is, in this respect, like a canvas so painted that it admitted only one intention to attach—so called for none. We already know, from Frege's initial point, that no painted canvas could do this. Which explains (from one perspective) why Frege insists that thoughts must be invisible and intangible.

So far, Frege has said nothing one, or Wittgenstein, need disagree with, if it is read right. What would that reading be? Wittgenstein's commentary on this picture of what an intention might do for words begins with this remark:

We imagine the shadow to be a picture the intention of which *cannot be questioned*, that is, a picture which we don't interpret in order to understand it, but which we understand without interpreting it.

(1958: 36)

And it ends with this one:

If we keep in mind the possibility of a picture which, though correct, has no similarity with its object, the interpolation of a shadow between the sentence and reality loses all point. For now the sentence itself can serve as such a shadow. The sentence is just such a picture.

(1958: 37)

How might these connect?

Here is one way of conceiving a picture the intention of which cannot be questioned: it would be a canvas so painted that only one intention could attach to it, which is to say that no intention is needed for it to represent in that one and only way in which something so painted could. One simply *could* not make such a canvas represent in either of two different ways by attaching either of two different intentions to it. This idea is, as Frege saw, incoherent. But

Wittgenstein's shadows, like Frege's thoughts, are meant to be invisible and intangible (not objects of sensory awareness). In that respect, they are not like a canvas. And they are meant to be things which need no intention attaching to them in order to occupy a given place within the conceptual, hence in order to reach to the nonconceptual just as, and where, they do. This entails that no intention (nor anything else) attaching to them could make them reach in one way rather than another. So they admit of no interpretation in the sense that they could not *correctly* be understood in either of two ways, depending on further factors in some occasion for identifying, or understanding, them. Which also suggests that all this may be just a piece of grammar.

We might conceive a picture on the model of a painted canvas; something which is what it is anyway, independent of any intention that might attach to it. It takes up space, or is mostly yellow, say, regardless of how you understand it, or what intention attaches to it. Nor could any *intention*, or understanding, attaching to it change all that. With respect to such features of it—those which make it the canvas that it is—it is like Fregean thoughts. On the other hand, such a canvas needs something else to be so of it—if we follow Frege, then some intention attaching to it—before it can represent, or depict, at all; but not before some central square in it can be yellow. In that it is unlike Fregean thoughts. We might also conceive a picture on the model of a portrait—say, a portrait of Goethe's mother, or a picture of her sitting, or a depiction of quiet desperation. It would not be *that* portrait unless it portrayed Goethe's mother. It admits of no interpretation: you could not *correctly* understand it to do other than portray Goethe's mother, no matter in what circumstances you did this, no matter what *else* was so of the portrait. So the portrait needs no intention attaching to *it* in order to portray Goethe's mother: it needs no *further* intention attaching to it. An intention already attaches to the canvas, which makes that canvas, and thus this portrait, a portrait of Goethe's mother. Nor could any further intention attaching to *it* make it portray otherwise than it already does. Perhaps I can see a portrait of Goethe's mother as a picture of quiet desperation, while you, with equal right, see it as a picture of self-satisfaction. But if so, *it* neither represents her in the one way or the other. In these respects it, too, is like a Fregean thought, and like a shadow. But a Fregean thought does not represent as it does because something else, such as an intention, attaching to something else, makes that into the thought.

Thoughts are thus neither canvases nor portraits. They are not things to which an intention might attach, thus making them represent in one way or another. They already represent in the only way they could. But nor is there something else which, canvas-like, by dint of an intention attaching to it, might be a thought. So they are not like portraits either. No intention, and nothing like one, no matter where attached, makes *them* represent as they do. A *thought* brooks no interpretation. It *answers* questions as to the reach of representations; it does not pose them. All of which is just the grammar which fits a certain notion—that notion which Frege labels 'a thought'. Thoughts just *are* what answer, but do not pose, a certain sort of question. It is inept to seek explanations for how they are *able* to do such a thing, as if there were something else which *could* be enabled to do this. If you have not identified what fits the grammar which goes with *thought*—what reaches without, and admits of no, interpretation—then what you have identified (if anything) is just *not* a thought. (It would be equally inept to think of a thought as a kind of cognitive prosthetic which, once we had somehow installed it in our thinking, allowed this to reach where it could not reach already. To repeat the main moral of this essay, there would be no way for such installation to be achieved.)

Something fitting the grammar of *thought* is required, as Frege saw, by the social nature of our postures towards the world: insofar as they articulate into (truth-evaluable) postures towards particular ways *for* it to be or not, they must be postures for *ranges* of thinkers to adopt (or reject), hence ones whose reach rests on a background of agreement, in the way sketched above. So if Pia said, 'The meat is on the rug', and thereby said something to be so—something towards which one may hold a posture of thinking it to be the way things are (or are not)—then we can say such things as, 'What Pia said is true', and 'Sid thinks so too'. In doing this we identify something which fits the grammar of a thought—something with a definite, non-negotiable, reach: *just* that which thought would have in assuming just that posture. We thus identify some *one* thing over which to agree or disagree. Or we can also do all this in saying, say, 'Many think that the meat is on the rug', or, 'It is true that the meat is on the rug', and so on.

One has not identified a thought unless one has identified what fits the grammar just set out—what reaches just *so*, independent of interpretation, or of any form of agreement as to its reach. This *might* make one wonder how we ever manage to do all that. But if we drop the idea of a thought as a cognitive prosthetic, there is nothing extraordinary about this. This is the point of Wittgenstein's concluding remark that, insofar as a thought is a shadow of a fact, words themselves may be such a shadow—perhaps not the English sentence, 'There is meat on the rug' (or 'Fawns gambol'), but words for which agreement does the work of deciding when they would be true, when false. Where Sid said, 'The meat is on the rug', there is (if he said anything at all) a notion *things being as Sid said*, where the reach of that notion is the reach of Sid's words. And there is a range of thinkers who can get that notion in mind. These form a community of agreement as to just where (to what particular cases) that

notion would reach. By Wittgenstein's reverse side of Frege's coin, this identifies where that notion reaches, which is to identify where Sid's words reach.
By the same token, this is to identify a thought: one which reaches just *so*, and
thus which fits that seemingly demanding grammar for the notion *thought*. In
just the same way, if I purport to speak of a thought, in saying, say, 'Many think
that there is meat on the rug', or 'If it is true that there is meat on the rug, then
we need a carpet cleaner', and if I speak intelligibly (as I may or may not do),
there is again a range of thinkers who, in the same way, identify the reach of the
notion I express in my words 'that there is meat on the rug'—again thereby
identifying something which fits the grammar that goes with the notion *thought*.
If a thought is not a cognitive prosthetic, there is no more to identifying one
than there is to identifying the reach of given words.

An asymmetry. From *someone's* words—as from someone's posture towards
the world—we can abstract things shareable: things *defined* by their reach, so
brooking no interpretation; things on which different thinkers may agree or
disagree. Suppose we locate some such thing in the words of different speakers.
Do we thereby settle when the words of each would be true? Perhaps not.
A thought—something to commit to—admits of no interpretation. A way for
things to be—something for a thought to be of—does so admit. Meat being on
the rug is a way for things to be. Different understandings of things so being are
possible. Is calf's brains on the rug, or ribeye separated from the rug by butcher
paper, things being that way or not? In each case there is an understanding of
things so being on which it is, and an understanding on which it is not. Calf's
brains (offal in general) sometimes would, sometimes would not, count as meat.
Sid and Pia may agree as to there being meat on the rug. Each may have said
things to be that way. We may see such agreement in what each said as
agreement on a thought which each expressed, to which each thus committed.
The ribeye, perhaps, makes both right. But might one have been right, the
other wrong, had there been calf's brain on the rug (and might it depend on in
just what form this happened)? Nothing in the grammar that fits *thought* rules
this possibility out. Such is the point of Wittgenstein's commentary on Frege in
Investigations §22. But it is a point to be developed elsewhere.

Wittgenstein, thinking through Frege's most central ideas, leads us to such
points. Frege emerges, not as target, but as inspiration.

11

Faust's Way

> Geschrieben steht: Im Anfang war das Wort! . . .
> Ich kann das Wort so hoch unmöglich schätzen . . .
> Wenn ich vom Geiste recht erleuchtet bin.
> Geschrieben steht: Im Anfang war der Sinn . . .
> Ist es der Sinn, der alles wirkt und schafft? . . .
> Mir hilft der Geist! Auf einmal seh ich Rat
> Und schreibe getrost: Im Anfang war die Tat!
>
> (*Faust* Part I)

Any irony in pacted Faust's intimations of enlightenment is lost here with the rhyme. A suggestive path remains from Frege to later Wittgenstein. For Frege, not word, but *Sinn*, comes first—something invisible and intangible which words clothe, and which, alone, can bring truth into question. It is *that* in which the shape of our rational relating to the world is woven. *Sinn*, for Wittgenstein, is abstracted from our deeds. In some sense, it is those deeds which come first. But in *what* sense? *Investigations* §22, I think, points to Faust's way. Exploiting its images, I will develop one, perhaps not the only, answer to that question.

There are two cases of representing something to be so. One is representing something to oneself as so: *taking* something to be so; judging it on that philosophical use of 'judge'. The other is an *act* of representing—which *is* that only in making its representing recognizable to *one* (for any ones, perhaps to another)—for example stating, or asserting, something. Such an act needs, for *recognizable* representing, a *vehicle*—something recognizable as what *it* is independent of recognizing, or identifying, any representing as being done. For example, in stating we speak words which might also be spoken (present) without anything thus being represented to be so. Philosophers often speak of acts of *judging*—inspired, I think, by an ordinary use of 'judge'—'casting an experienced eye, the Condestavel judged there to be about 200 French cavalry'. But judging in philosophical usage is just taking something to be so (for Frege, acknowledging the truth of something): a certain posture towards the world.

A thought, in Frege's sense, is what brings truth into question. So it has a role in judgement. A judgement aims for a particular sort of success: one such that the world, and the world alone, just in being as it is may oblige, or frustrate, it. Any obliging world would oblige in just one of the indefinitely many ways this might be done. If the judgement is that Sid snores, a world might oblige with, or without, Pia indulging in macramé, or Sarkozy inhabiting the Élysée. There is what matters and what does not. For any judgement, there is the thought which identifies what matters, which thus fixes when the world would be obliging, when not—a condition on obligingness. Words, or a picture—specimens of that second sort of representing—are true, or false, only given that they bear a certain understanding (or, perhaps, the understanding that they do). For Frege, for them to bear some such understanding is for a thought to attach to them (since thoughts alone raise questions of truth). Frege suggests (1918) that for a thought to attach to them is for an intention to attach to them. The intention would be that they say (or depict) such-and-such to be so. So we say what they say, or represent, to be so in mentioning some thought. A statement, Frege tells us, is the making public (*Kundgebung*) of a purported posture towards the world—the acknowledging of the truth of some thought. This suggests, at least, a certain picture of the sort of content a statement has.

In some sense, the start of the *Investigations* moves in an opposite direction. The starting point, for this direction, is historical, concrete, speech acts. A given speech act aims at given successes, even if its author need not. To understand some words, 'Sid snores', as an assertion is to understand them as making themselves liable to truth, or falsity, thus as that particular sort of failure if Sid does not snore—even if their speaker meant to lie. Similarly, to understand some words as an order is to understand them as obliged by the world just where the order is carried out—even if the speaker meant to be disobeyed. The initial, fundamental, question on this alternative route I mean to trace is what it would be for the world to oblige, or disoblige, an historical speech act with the successes it represents itself as aiming at—in the assertive case, truth. The task is then to move from there to an understanding of what it is we say of, say, an assertive speech act in saying that what was said in it was that such-and-such. One moves from *there* to seeing what it is for someone's posture towards the world to instance judging such-and-such. Such is a way of challenging a picture Frege *suggests*, though may or may not have held. What follows identifies a picture thus under challenge.

1. *Investigations* §22

On Frege §22 comments:

Frege's thesis that every assertion contains a supposition, which is that which is affirmed, is in fact based on the possibility which exists in our language of writing an assertoric sentence in the form, 'It is affirmed that such-and-such is the case.'—But 'that such-and-such is the case' is not in fact a sentence of our language—not yet a *move* in the language game. And if I write an instance of 'it is affirmed that ...', 'It is affirmed: such-and-such is the case', then the words 'It is affirmed' are simply redundant.

Of course we have the right to use an assertion sign in contrast with, for example, a question mark ... It is only a mistake to think of an assertion as consisting in two acts, one of considering and one of affirming (attributing the value *true*, or something analogous), and that we perform two acts in accord with the propositional symbol, more or less as when one sings from a score.

(footnote) Think of an image representing a boxer in a certain fighting posture. This image might be used to show someone how it must be done, how he must hold himself; or how not to hold himself, or how a certain man was in this or that position, and so on. One could call this image (in chemical terms) a propositional radical. Frege conceived 'suppositions' analogously.

Wittgenstein warns against a bad idea—Frege's, or a misreading of him. It is not evident *what* idea.

This becomes, if anything, still less evident when we examine Frege's own statements of the idea that a thought is detachable from any force with which it might be expressed:

In a declarative sentence two things are customarily closely bound up with each other: the thought expressed and the assertion of its truth. And thus it happens that these are often not clearly distinguished. But one can also express a thought without thereby portraying it as true. A scientist who makes a scientific discovery usually first only grasps the thought, and wonders whether it is to be acknowledged as true; and only after investigation has come out in favour of the hypothesis does he venture to present it as true. In the question, 'Is oxygen condensable?', and in the sentence, 'Oxygen is condensable', we have the same thought expressed, once connected with a request, the other time with an assertion.

(1897: 150)

Judging does not alter the thought judged true. Where there is judging, one can always cull out the thought thus judged true, and the judging does not belong to this. If I attach the word 'saline' predicatively to the words, 'sea water', I construct a sentence which expresses a thought. In order to make clearer that the thought was only expressed, but not asserted, I convert the sentence into dependent form: 'That sea water is saline'. Instead of this I could also let it be spoken on the stage by an actor in his role; since one knows that an actor playing a role only appears to speak with assertive force.

(1915: 271)

In poetry we have the case where thoughts are expressed, even though in the form of an assertion, without their really being presented as true.... Thus also with that whose form presents it as an assertive move, there is always the question whether it really contains an assertion. And this is to be denied if the seriousness needed for that is absent.

(1918: 63)

So a thought is detachable from—may occur independent of—any particular occurrence of it. It is detachable from any *historical* occurrence—from anyone's expressing of it, or attitude towards it. It is detachable from any occurrence of it in the context of something *to* be said, or towards which to hold an attitude. Hence it is detachable from any force with which it might occur. (This is not yet to say that it can occur with *no* force, or *no* stance taken towards it.) A given thought is the arbiter of success for a given judgement. What can measure that success can also measure others. Pia may judge Sid to have made chillidogs for dinner. There is a thought which fixes when the world would oblige *so* judging with success. That same thought can also measure the success (of a different sort) aimed at by some request for chillidogs (by Sid) for dinner. Or, again, it may measure when the world would oblige in fulfilling a certain condition— that Sid made chillidogs—on which, in some judgement, a young Beaune is called for.

As Wittgenstein himself remarks:

If an order runs 'Do such-and-such' then executing the order is called 'doing such-and-such'.

(1953: §458)

The very same thing which is success at fulfilling an order to do such-and-such is the success of a judgement that such-and-such was done. What else? How else for anyone, ever, to get what he wanted? How could Wittgenstein (or anyone) object to the idea of the detachability of a thought from some particular instance of its expression? Thoughts are precisely *for* that.

Might §22 nonetheless object? A superficial problem: its grounds would then be, by and large, the very same considerations Frege uses to call the idea to our attention. 'That such-and-such' is not a move in the language game. Indeed not. Which is why Frege puts thoughts in that form—to call our attention to their detachability from their occurrence in any such move. 'It is asserted that' is redundant. A fundamental point in Frege: forms of words (notably, 'is true') cannot impose assertive force when the needed seriousness is absent. Any form of words can be put in the mouth of an actor in a role. If these points ought to be taken as counting against Frege's idea rather than for it, it remains to say why.

Frege's deeper reasons raise a deeper problem. One reason concerns the needs of logic. If the same thought could not recur in different surroundings, for example in different lines of a given proof, there could not be such a thing as logic. A second is to preserve the objectivity of judgement. For Frege, this requires judgements, so thoughts, to be essentially social: anything *anyone* can think, *one* can think; one can agree or disagree with, investigate, dispute. *That* thought can thus be part of different attitudes, each aiming for different success. So *it* can be held, or expressed, with different forces. For Pia to think that Sid made chillidogs is for her posture towards the world to include a certain shape for *a* posture for the world to have. It is for her being as she is to be *one* case falling under a given generalization, in just one of the indefinitely many different ways this may be done. (As a red balloon may instance something being red while filled with air, or with helium, or empty.)

For Frege, any thought is an object for agreement, disagreement, dispute, investigation, by communities of thinkers. In "Der Gedanke" he raises the question whether things might be otherwise—whether a thought could be an 'idea' (*Vorstellung*). An idea, in Frege's sense, satisfies two main criteria. First, it needs a bearer: there is that idea just so long as it belongs to someone's consciousness (is something he is conscious of). Second, no idea admits of two bearers: if you now have an idea, and I also have one, then yours is not mine. Frege argues elegantly (1918: 67–69) for a negative answer to his question, thus that any thought is public in the sense just made out. (For elaboration see my 2005 and essays 3, 10.) In effect, he argues the senselessness of the idea of private language. This is hardly something Wittgenstein would dispute. But it requires any thought expressed by anyone to be detachable from that expression of it; and, if open to *dispute*, then from any force attaching to it in that expression. Wittgenstein *cannot* disagree with this.

We could not see ourselves (or others) as thinkers, nor our postures as standing in logical relations to others there are to take, without that idea of detachability of thoughts from force, or from occurrence, which Frege calls to our attention. The idea would be less innocent if read to mean: for any (historical) speech act, there is *the* thought, identifiable independent of that expression of it, which is *the* one thus expressed. (So that saying something to be so is just, for some thought thus identifiable, somehow to get *that* one to attach to one's act as thus expressed; and what one says to be so is *just* what *is* so according to that thought.) Again, it would be less innocent if read to mean: a thought can occur (be expressed, be a content *borne*) with no force at all, and still, independent of force, be evaluable per se as what is true, or what is false. §22 helps us see what is less innocent about those ideas.

2. Language Games

Wittgenstein begins the *Investigations* with a notion, *language game*. As he explains in §7, he uses this term in several different ways. But the initial notion—what is of concern for present purposes—is of a language game as, like a logical calculus, an object of comparison (§§130–131). On this notion, we can think of a game as constituted by: a set of roles (player A, player B, etc.), for each role a set of moves, for each move a rule stating when it may, or must, be made. So in a given state of play, and for a given role, there is what the player in that role may, or must, then do according to the rules. Moving correctly will be doing all that he must, no more than he may. For example, the assistant, in §2, after the builder has called 'Slab!', will move correctly just in case he brings a slab. I will abbreviate 'all that must and no more than may, be done' to: 'what is to be done'.

We are not saddled with some fixed repertoire of language games to play. English, for example, is no such repertoire. But where there is a condition on some success a given speech act aims for, that may also be a condition on the correctness of a move in some language game. In that sense, the game may model something we do (or which someone once did) in speaking. Sid, reclining languidly, seeing Pia afoot, asks, 'As long as you're up, could you get me an Aberfeldy?' There is a condition on Pia doing what was asked. Satisfying it involves pouring Aberfeldy into a whisky glass, adding a drop of branch, and so on. There is, correspondingly, the game in which when player S speaks as above, player P is to pour Aberfeldy, etc. Such models modelling.

The *Investigations* starts from a picture, suggested by Augustine, against which, it seems, some sort of complaint is made. Language games are used to make the basic point; §22 elaborates. The offending picture is:

The words of the language name objects—sentences are connections of such names.— In this picture of language we find the roots of the idea that every word has a meaning: this meaning is associated with the word. It is the object for which the word stands.

(1953: §1)

It may be (briefly) tempting to take the counter to this picture to be: there are words which do not name objects—prepositions, say. Wittgenstein scotches such a reading when he insists,

If we say, 'every word designates (*bezeichnet*) something', we have thus said *nothing at all*; unless we have explained precisely *which* distinction we wish to make.

(1953: §13)

Nothing at all; so, inter alia, nothing false.

We get closer to the intended complaint (or warning) in passages like these:

Only someone who knows something of what to do with it can sensibly ask what something names

(1953: §31)

Much in language must already be prepared for it if a bare naming of something is to have a sense

(1953: §257)

Wittgenstein's specific concern here is with ostensive definition. In the first case someone points to the king on a chessboard and says, 'That's the king.' What he means to be explaining is what it is for a piece to be the king in chess. The piece pointed to is just one case of something being the king in chess. One instance of some *general* way (or thing) for a thing to be cannot decide, or fix, what another case of that generality might be. What is to be defined is the generality, not this or that particular case. There is nothing it would be to define a particular case, though one might define that generality, *being one*. Unless something else fixes how *this* particular case is to be taken to bear on what *a* particular case might be—what being the *same* thing as this might be—the ostensive definition is impotent. In the second example, the supposed intended definition is to be a private one. Here Wittgenstein gives reason for thinking that *nothing* could give the requisite further understanding.

The point thus becomes: one can *say* that each well-formed expression of a language names, or stands for, something, compatibly with indefinite variation in the ways different expressions work towards fixing what would count as *instancing* that of which they speak—for example, *when* something would count as a case of being the king in chess, when something would count as a case of being a charitable donation, when something would count as a case of being a *sauce mousseline*. To insist that, for every meaningful word, its meaning is that for which it stands is merely to opt for a form in which to cast an account of what it means. It is not to *discover* something in which meaning always consists.

What *do* words (of human language) name, or speak of? This is not a question about Frege's very special notion of *Bedeutung*, nor would it be to the point here to explain that notion. One might say, for example, that 'whisky' speaks of whisky, 'to aquaplane' speaks of aquaplaning. Such might be the beginning of an answer. One might also say that, roughly, for 'whisky' to speak of whisky is for its use as meaning what it does, in saying what was said in a given speech act, to make the success aimed at by that act turn in some specifiable way on how things stand with whisky. It is on such an idea of speaking of, or naming, that Wittgenstein responds thus to the question what words of a language game speak of:

What is to show what they designate, unless the manner of their use? And we have already described that.

(1953: §10)

On the present notion *language game,* the (proper) use of words in a game is fixed by its rules. These fix what a correct move would be in any given state of play. If this, in turn, fixes what words designate in the game, then what a given word designates is fixed by its contribution to the correctness of moves in which it occurs, and to their bearing on the correctness of moves in resultant states of play. Such need not fix *unique* designata for meaningful words in the game. The correctness of a given move, or its contribution to the correctness of further ones, may be decomposable in many ways into particular contributions of its parts. As Frege holds of thoughts, a word may designate something in a game only after a scheme for decomposition has been chosen. I now remark: if it is in this way that 'slab' may be said to name slabs in §2, then it may be said to do this in many games, in each of which it contributes differently to conditions on correctness.

What of English—'king', say, (used of chess), or 'whisky'? Their contribution, used as meaning what they do, to what is said in speaking English is to make what is said somehow about, respectively, kings in chess, or whisky. 'About' here means: the success (or correctness) aimed at by what is thus said turns, in one way or another, on what is, or is not, a (chess) king, or whisky. 'In one way or another': for a start, in one way in 'Whisky is flammable', in another in 'If whisky is flammable, one could make *haggis flambé.*' For a start. But now, being whisky is a general way for something to be: for any case of something being it, there could be more; *mutatis mutandis* for any case of something *failing* to be it. A given use of 'whisky', for example in saying whisky to be flammable, contributes in one way or another to deciding when there would be a case of something whose being as it is would bear on whether what was *thus* said in calling whisky flammable is correct. What work is done here?

Consider a question Wittgenstein actually raises about the king in chess. Suppose we changed the rules of chess. Or, less tendentiously, suppose we began to play a game with rules much like those of present chess, but not quite the same. Suppose, for example, that we disallowed castling, or allowed bishops to jump pawns. Would there still be a piece in this game which counted as a *king in chess*? The answer, he suggests, is that this all depends on what we are prepared to recognize as what we were speaking of, or had in mind, all along, when we spoke, or thought, of being a king in chess. Some changed games, perhaps, would still simply count as *chess*, full stop. Someone who used 'king' to speak of the relevant piece in them would, recognizably, thus be speaking of kings in chess (or being one). Others would simply *not* count as chess, full stop. Someone who used 'king' to speak of a piece in them would *not* be speaking of kings in chess. But what of the game where bishops jump pawns? Would someone who used 'king' for the relevant piece in it be speaking of *kings in chess*? An answer (what we are here prepared to recognize) is liable to depend on the occasion of his so using it, or, again, on the occasion for asking us.

What of whisky? What turns for truth on how things stand with being whisky—which things are that, which things not—certainly turns on how things stand with Aberfeldy—whether, for example, it is flammable. Or so I will suppose. But suppose you take some perfectly good product of a Highland still and mix it, about 1 to 4, with neutral grain spirits. Is that whisky? Custom has militated towards making us often so speak. One might reasonably resist. Suppose Alf said, 'Pia is pouring whisky', using all those words to speak of what they do, while Pia is pouring such a blend. Has Alf spoken *truth* (given that he used 'whisky' to mean *whisky*? Such may well depend on the circles, or circumstances, in which Alf does his speaking (or in which we are asked to judge him). On some occasions, the blend would pass for whisky. On others, not. Neither sort of occasion is convincingly stigmatizable as one on which 'whisky' was *not* used to mean what it means in English.

We thus come to the first main point of the *Investigations*. What words of a *language* speak of (*bezeichnen*) underdetermines what contribution they make to the truth (or, more generally, success) conditions of what is said in using them (as meaning what they do). Perhaps they always make truth turn, *in some way or other*, on how things stand *in re* instancing the generality they speak of. But there is not just one way for things thus to turn (within a given syntactically fixed whole). What words of a language game speak of is fixed by the conditions on correctness of moves of which they are a part (or on responses to these). But games which thus fix that 'W' names G may, for all that, differ in their conditions on correctness. In some games, perhaps, slabs may be hexagonal, in others not; in some games, made of iron, or boiled sugar, in some games not.

That feature of language games models a feature of our language. That feature of our language reflects a feature of our thought: we think of the world in terms of ways for things to be which admit of understandings: there are different things it might be understood to be for something *to be whisky*; for different understandings, different cases which would count as ones of something being that.

3. What To Do

An assertion aims, even if its maker does not, at a certain success: being made in what is, anyway, a world right for it, one anyway such as to oblige in being as thus represented. It is rightly understood so to aim. To aim at this success just is to have assertive force. Other forces—for example, imperative, optative, interrogative—are similarly defined by some success per se aimed at in having them. One might say: to have a force is to aim at some success; the force a speech act has is fixed by the success it aims at—a notion of force which, on its face, applies to both acts and attitudes. (The idea that what *has* no force may, as such, be either true or false is now bound up with the idea that, where things are represented *being* (not necessarily *to be*) some given way, force can have no bearing on when things would be as *thereby* represented.)

We may now note that an assertion may aim at more parochial successes. Itself an act, it may represent itself (be to be taken) as part, or what would be part, of some larger project(s). It may represent itself as a contribution to such projects. As it represents itself, if things are as thus asserted, there is a way those projects would be to be carried out. Or, more cautiously, a way the world would bear on how they are to be carried out. So it is the success it aims to be only if the world does so bear on the thing to do. The assertion may also speak of some way for things to be as the way things are—say, being such that Sid snores. If there were *no* way of understanding things *being* that way on which things so being *would* so bear on what to do, that speech act would be *one* sort of failure. (I will not stop to consider here whether speech acts *might* bear such an unhappy understanding.) But if the project in question were choosing bunkmates for a trip on the Trans-Siberian, there *might* be such an understanding, in which case those more local ambitions *this* speech act was to be understood to harbour may point to what is to be understood by *snoring* as that was thus spoken of.

Sid, morning paper before face, remarks, 'The toast is burning.' There is an understanding of *toast burning* on which the thing to do might be to fetch a fire blanket, or raise an alarm. Sid is not to be so understood. His remark is to be understood as having a different sort of bearing on the thing to do. If that intended bearing were acted on, Pia would remove the toast. Such would be the thing to do in execution of the project he would like her to carry out: the provision, for him, of a happy breakfast. If toast burning can be understood to be what happens in certain cases of surface carbonizing, then Sid can have said what will have the bearing he represented what he said to have. Which, in the circumstances, points to what *he*, on *that* occasion, is to be understood to have said to be so in speaking of the toast as burning.

Zoë, in telling Pia, 'There's Aberfeldy in the cupboard', may be to be taken to be speaking to getting Sid his Aberfeldy, and in such a way that things are as she said only if the world bears in a certain way on how to do this. If things are as she said, perhaps, opening the cupboard would be the thing to do. If the cupboard is bare but for a rag still damp from mopping up spilled Aberfeldy, then, perhaps, the world is not as Zoë represented it. One *might* still macerate the rag in grain neutral spirits. The resultant facsimile might fool Sid. In the circumstances, this might even be the thing to do. Such would neither make things as Zoë represented them, so, given that there *is* an understanding of whisky in the cupboard on which the damp rag does not instance this, nor as she said.

Suppose there is a full bottle of Aberfeldy in the cupboard. Opening the cupboard might still not be the thing for Pia to do. It might trigger an explosion. Or cause an anxiety attack which makes her spill all the whisky. Or etc. ad infinitum. But if some such extraordinary circumstance obtained, this need mean neither that things were not as Zoë represented them, nor that they were not as she said. She need not have been to be taken as speaking to such eventualities. The world might still have had that certain bearing she represented it as having on the thing to do in getting Sid his Aberfeldy. Its having just that bearing is not cashable, occasion-independently as its meaning, do *this*, do *that*, for some specified set of things to do. The notion *certain bearing* cannot be so understood.

Such more special successes an assertion aims at define a force, *its* force, just as that success all assertion aims at defines assertion. Assertive force now appears as a generic; the forces of particular assertive speech acts are potentially complex affairs, and ones which bear on what their truth-evaluable content is. Such is one path along which one might try to see action as the origin of content. It is only one such path. But it will prove *some* help in understanding the images of §22.

4. Pugilism

If Pia said, 'There's Aberfeldy in the cupboard', and thus said something to be so, there is, accordingly, a certain way for things to be: things being as she said (or such that they *are* as she said). If she spoke of there being Aberfeldy in the cupboard, *that* is a way for things to be, perhaps a way things are, or are not, depending on how things are: two different *mentions* of a way for things to be; perhaps two different such ways. The first way is what figures in Aristotle's account of truth: saying of what is that it is, or of what is not that it is not (things being as said). The second way is fit for answering a question as to *what* way Pia said things to be. It shows the sort of thing an *answer* to such a question might look like; the sort of thing we *expect* an answer to be. 'She said things to be as she said' would misrepresent what she said (she was not speaking of her own reliability); 'She said things to be just that way they would be precisely when they were as she said' would be no answer at all. To *know* what way Pia said things to be is to know when things would be as she said. So if, or where, 'such that there is Aberfeldy in the cupboard' *answers* the question how she said things to be, knowing what is thus stated is knowing when things would be as she said, so, by Aristotle, knowing when she would have spoken truth; §22 can be read as warning against a misreading of the above, specifically, of the relation between things being as she said, and things being thus and so, where that answers the question what she said. On the misreading, if Pia said something to be so, then there is *one* answer to the question *what* way she thus said things to be, such that for things to be as she said is just for things to be that way. What follows works out why, or how, this is a misreading. To adumbrate, the problem starts in ignoring the role of occasions in fixing what we ask in asking what it is that Pia said.

I will expand this by unpacking two images in the footnote to §22. The first involves a picture of a boxer in a stance, which might be used to show any of many things, each in some act of representing. To stress, the picture is *of a boxer in a stance*. It is not just some lines on paper. It *depicts*. It represents something as a certain way (the boxer as in a certain stance)—though, perhaps, it does not, as such, represent anything *to be* a certain way. In Wittgenstein's analogy, it thus plays the role of a thought, conceived as something which may be expressed with any of many forces.

The point here concerns *exhaustion*. The same thought, expressed with different forces (put to different uses in the way Wittgenstein suggests) may contribute to historical speech acts which differ substantively in the conditions on their correctness, specifically, in things being as said. So if one would speak truth, on some occasion, in saying of some given such act that what was said was that such-and-such, thus mentioning a thought which contributes to whole acts as the picture of the boxer does, still, for all that, things may thus be left unsaid as to *just* when things would be as said to be in that act. Or at least, there is room for there to be, on some other occasion, more to be said, and more that needs saying, as to this. So what we say in answering an ordinary question as to what was said in some given act cannot, so does not, claim to exhaust all there might be to be said as to how things were according to the act, or under just what conditions it would be one of speaking truly.

The second image models Frege's 'assumption' (or thought entertained) as a propositional radical, on the model of a chemical radical. Here there is a clear suggestion. A chemical radical is, so to speak, a few atoms short of a molecule. It has electrons to bond to. An OH radical, for example, might be made into CH_3OH, C_2H_5OH, C_3H_7OH or H_2O ('zero-degree alcohol'). A molecule decomposes (into radicals and their mates) in a *unique* way. If, with Frege, we think of an assertion as decomposing into a force (assertive force), and some thought expressed (what Wittgenstein refers to as an 'assumption' ('Annahme')), then we must not think of it as having some one true decomposition in the sense in which a molecule does. To borrow a word from Frege, an assertion would not be built up of *Bausteinen* as a chemical compound is.

That pointed borrowing puts us immediately in mind of what Frege says about the composition of a thought. For a start, he advises us that we must never forget that the same thought can be expressed in very different sentences. Each sentence organizes it into some structured predicating of things of things (an *Aussage*). But different such sentences might organize it into different such structures, predicating different things of different things. In his words,

A thought can be decomposed in many ways and . . . through this now this, now that appears as subject and predicate. The thought itself does not yet determine what is to be perceived as subject. If one says, 'The subject of this judgement', one thus designates something determinate only if he at the same time indicates a given manner of decomposition. Usually one does that in relation to a given wording. But one must never forget that different sentences can express the same thought.

(1892: 199)

All this is a consequence of what Frege depicts as *most* central theme in his approach to logic:

What distinguishes my conception of logic is first of all recognisable by the fact that I place the content of the word 'true' to the fore, and then by the fact that I immediately proceed to *thoughts* as the things by which truth can come into question at all. Thus I do not begin from concepts, and build up thoughts, or judgements, out of these, but I obtain parts of thoughts by decomposing thoughts.

(1919: 273)

Thoughts are decompos*able* into parts. But they are not built up out of parts. Their unity is not thus conjured out of other things. A thought performs a certain definite task in judgement. A judgement aims at a sort of success granted or withheld entirely in the world being as it is. It is intrinsic to judgement that where the world obliges, or disobliges, it does so in only one of indefinitely many ways it might. It might, for example, oblige a judgement that Sid snores whether or not Sid wears boaters in the spring, or Pia garlands her tresses with early hyacinths. A thought fixes, for some judgement, when the world will have obliged. Such is its central task. Like any other task—say, cleaning the kitchen—this task may be divided into sub-tasks. For example, in the case at hand, a sub-task might be making the success of this judgement turn somehow or other on how Sid is. Another might then be: making success turn, somehow, on who snores. As with cleaning the kitchen, a set of sub-tasks is a decomposition of the whole task only if their joint successful performance just is the performance of the whole task. If the subtasks, jointly performed, leave the sink stained, there *is*, so far, no structuring of the task, cleaning the kitchen.

So if a decomposition *is* a decomposition at all, then the elements of the thought, on it, add up to the whole thought. The thought awaits no further unifying. Thoughts thus contrast with, say, English sentences. An English sentence is formed out of some string of words. But, even strung together in the order that they are, they form *that* sentence, rather than some other, or none at all, only given that they are structured syntactically in some given way. There is always, 'Flying planes can be dangerous.' Thoughts are *not* like that. They have no visible surface form, as sentences do. A fortiori they call for nothing to be added to such a form. More importantly, if all it is for something to be a decomposition of a thought is for it to add up to the whole thought, on above lines, then there can be no guarantee that any particular decomposition of the thought is *unique* in any interesting sense. Again thoughts differ here from sentences; also from statements, and from *Aussagen*. An *Aussage* articulates the thought it expresses in one particular way, among the many that thought may admit of. The thought itself is not tied to any one particular *Aussage* or statement.

The second image thus concerns *uniqueness*: to decompose an assertion in the way Frege suggests—correct as this may be—is to do this in only one of the perhaps indefinitely many ways it might be done. This point is not entirely separable from the point of the first image. After all, if a decomposition of an assertion is not exhaustive, then, presumably, there might be more to say. To say some of it would be to offer a new decomposition. Such is *one* way, but only one, that one correct decomposition of a given assertion might differ from another.

Articulation into force and content *might* fail to be unique because what belongs to force on one decomposition belongs to content on another. In some 'It looks like it will be a hard winter', or 'I think I locked the door', the 'It looks like', or 'I think', might be understood as particular weakenings of assertive force, or rather as contributing to the circumstance thus asserted to obtain. More pertinent to present issues, though, is what we have already seen about assertive force: this is a generic which admits of coming in more specific forms, corresponding to the specifics of the bearing the assertion is to be understood to have. So understanding *force*, the point can be: what one needs to say about the force of Zoë's assertion as to the whereabouts of Aberfeldy—about the uses of what is said for which this assertion is to be held liable—in order to say with *what* force what was said was said, may vary with the occasion for saying this. Given such particulars may change the understanding of a given specification of what Zoë *said*—of what she would be said to have said, for example in saying Aberfeldy to be in the cupboard—so may call for different specifications of what it is she said.

Such is an idea about force. There is a parallel for content. If the boxer in a stance is the model for identifying thought expressed, no such identification can claim exhaustiveness, for different uses of *that* picture, on which it depicts what *it*, anyway, does, can impose different conditions on things being as said. The picture is used to show me how to stand when fighting an enraged bald naturalist, or for a photo shoot. *When* will I be standing as shown? So when will standing as shown be standing the right way? It shows a certain distance between the boxer's feet, and a certain ratio between that distance and the width of his shoulders. Which, if either, of these values matters to whether I am standing as shown? If the point is a photo shoot, perhaps only the snarl matters. If either matters, how close must I be to the depicted value to be standing as shown? (Unless I am the boxer's spitting image, not both of these can matter equally.) Answers to such questions await further details of what was being done in so using the picture. Different questions arise where the picture is used to show how the boxer did stand. The picture, in depicting what *it* does, does not answer them. Again we need more fine detail of the sort of representing with the picture being done. So the *picture* cannot claim to exhaust the truth-evaluable content of any use of it. If thoughts are like that, no thought can claim to exhaust the truth-evaluable content of an act in which it was expressed.

Suppose one identified the thought expressed in a given assertion merely in identifying that of which the words used speak. So, for example, where Pia said, 'Sid snores', the identification might be: the thought that Sid snores. The picture of the boxer really would model the way in which such answers to the question what was said could not claim exhaustiveness. For *our* words speak of ways for things to be which admit of understandings. Sid's congenital defect means that he *would* rattle the windows every time he slept. But thanks to those adhesive strips which hold nostrils wide, religiously used, no snoring sound ever escapes him. Does Sid snore? There is an understanding of what it would be for one to be that way on which he does, and another on which he does not. The first is likely to be to the point in dealing with his medical condition—for example when passing out (scarce) adhesive strips. So it is likely to be borne by assertions which purport to bear on that. The last is to the point when it comes to a decision as to whether to bunk with him on the Trans-Siberian. So it is likely to be borne by what purports to bear on *that*. What has been said so far, in identifying the thought expressed in Pia's assertion as the thought that Sid snores, leaves room for more to say as to just when what she thus said would be true.

5. Understandings

A concrete speech act affords an understanding which exploits, so requires, acquaintance with that historical happening, the act's being as it was—as in witnessing, seeing, its so being. I will call thus understanding a speech act through acquaintance, *act-understanding*. In a speech act things are spoken of as being such-and-such ways. The whole act speaks of (is one of speaking of) things being some given way. It thus speaks of what would be so in (instanced by) certain cases, not so in others. In asserting things to be the way in question, it would say what was *true* of those first cases, false of those second ones. As we have seen, there is more than this to the way a speech act represents things. For example, it may represent what it says as bearing in a certain way on certain projects, without *saying* things to be that way. But for the moment I want to focus attention on features of the sort just mentioned. So, artificially, and with an artificial word to mark that, I will call them *contentual* features, and a set of them a *content*. A speech act bears just that understanding, so has just that content, which it would be ascribed correctly on acquaintance with it.

Within this frame, the suspect misreading of the idea of detachability can be put thus: for any (historical) assertion, there is a contentual feature which it has, such that *all* of its content follows from this: to have *this* feature is to have all the features it does have of being true of *this*, not true of *that*, and any other *contentual* feature it might happen to have. *Nothing* could have this feature without having precisely and only all the rest. (Force, e.g. remains negotiable.) This is just what would be false if the picture of the boxer models the role of a thought in a decomposition of an act. Accepting it, one might then hold, first, that once an act-understander sees the act to have one such feature, there is no further need for his understanding to rest on acquaintance—he need only reflect on what features *an* act would have in having that one—and, second, that all Zoë need do to get her assertion to have just the content it does is to get *that* (or some such) feature to attach to her act—for example, following Frege, in intending it to. (This second idea makes plausible a quite wrong role for intention in fixing what was said—a point which concerned Wittgenstein greatly. (See essay 10 and Wittgenstein 1958: 31–37.)

It will help here to ask how, in general, seeing *that* such-and-such may rest on acquaintance. Frege points the way in writing,

A thought always contains something which reaches beyond the particular case, whereby this is presented to consciousness as falling under some given generality.

(1882: 189)

Two pieces are in play. The first is a particular sort of generality intrinsic to any thought—be it, in another sense, general or singular. The second is the particular case: that which a thought *represents* as instancing some one or another generality. As for the first, a thought is the arbiter of success (truth) for some particular judgement. If a judgement is true (false), it is so in just *one* of indefinitely many ways it might be. The thought tells us what such variations on the actual case are thus compatible with being as represented. So it reaches to a *range* of cases, of ways of being the relevant way. This is what it is for a thought to present something as falling under a given generality. It is what its generality, in the present sense of generality, consists in. A thought—say, that Sid snores— presents a particular way for things to be—such that Sid snores—as a way things are. Its generality is that of that way for things to be. Being such that Sid snores (or simply *Sid snoring*) reaches to a range of cases: those which would be ones of things being such that Sid snores. I will call something with this generality *conceptual*; imagistically, the domain of things conceptual *the conceptual*.

Now the second piece. The particular case is what the thought represents as falling under some generality—as a case of things being some particular way there is for things to be. What I represent as a particular way in thinking that Sid snores is: things being as they are (the *way* things are, as opposed to some collection, or totality, of *ways* things are, each a way *for* things to be). *That* is what is such that Sid snores. One can also say: I represent Sid's being as he is as a case of someone snoring. One could say more. Such things are historical, parts of the world's unfolding. As such they lack the generality of thoughts. They reach to no range of cases. The sun now sets over Cádiz bay. Examine its setting as closely as you like. You will not see there what it would be for something to be another sunset, or anything else that setting is. You must look elsewhere to find the *generalities* under which things fall. (Frege makes this point in (1897: 149) and (1918: 61). It is Wittgenstein's point about ostensive definition.)

Watching the sun set gains acquaintance with a particular case—things being as they then are, the sun's doing what it then does. Acquaintance is opportunity to exercise capacities for recognition. You may recognize that case—things being as they are as *one* case of the sun setting, one cases of a sky reddening: one thing which would so count. What you see *instances* those generalities. You *recognize* this in *seeing* enough of that in this case which *makes* it one of the generality in question.

Acquaintance with the nonconceptual is needed for seeing its connections to the conceptual. Frege suggests the importance of this in writing,

The fundamental logical relation is that of an object falling under a concept; all relations between concepts can be reduced to this.

(1892–1895: 128)

Frege's *Begriffe* are not conceptual. They lack *that* generality. They are *Bedeutungen*, not *Sinne*. Nor are his objects particular cases which might instance some generality. Their being as they are is that. But a parallel holds. It might be put: the fundamental *conceptual* relation is that of a particular case *instancing* (being a case of) something conceptual, a relation between the conceptual and the world. All relations within the conceptual rest on this. That what is red is not green, or that a chair is an artefact for sitting on, *may*, on occasion, help me see whether it is true that such-and-such is red, or a chair. But only if I have a suitable grip on this fundamental relation. That what is A is not B is no help in seeing what *being B* reaches to unless one already grasps enough of how, and to what, being A reaches. If one could so much as think that being *green* excludes being *red*, without already grasping how being green and being red each reach to particular cases of items being as they are, then, in that position, knowing that however being 'green' reaches, it excludes something being 'red', however that reaches, would get one nowhere in identifying the reach of either.

Not all nonconceptual participants in the instancing relation are things with which one *could* now be acquainted. Pia's being as she will be tomorrow at midnight is a particular case which may, or may not, instance someone snoring. To think of precisely the way she then will be that *that* is someone snoring is to think a singular thought, just as to think precisely of Frege that he was bearded is. Before 1848 no one could think this last thought. But for his birth there would be no such thought. Equally, what one would need to think of to think *it* to be a case of someone snoring, where that is Pia's being as she will tomorrow, is not yet there to be thought of.

Grasp of the reach of something conceptual is a *capacity* to recognize the right things of its reach on acquaintance (when available) with that which *might* instance it or not. Exercising such capacity on a particular case—recognizing that conceptual item as instanced, or not, by *this* case—demands acquaintance with the case: seeing enough of how things are in it. Acquaintance is what distinguishes *seeing* such-and-such to be (count as) a case of someone snoring from merely supposing, or inferring, it to be. No mere ability to navigate one's way about within the conceptual permits this. The connections to be made here are *not* within the conceptual. They are between what *has* its distinguishing generality and what does not: the nonconceptual.

For any historical speech act, there is its being as it was. That is a particular case, ripe for instancing all sorts of ways for things to be. Pia's act of saying, 'Sid snores', in being as it was, may, for example, be a case of someone speaking loudly, or in a fit of pique. It may instance the having of various representational properties—saying someone to snore, saying what would be true of such-and-such cases of Sid rattling windows, or, of Sid, what would be so of someone in such-and-such cases of his rattling windows, saying, say, what *is* false of Sid as he has come to sleep of late, but would be true of Vic. A speech act's content is those representational features it instances. It is an act-understander who is suitably equipped for seeing it to have those features—on sufficient acquaintance with those particular cases, if any, there must be for there to be that feature (e.g. being true of *this*).

No particular case which falls under some generality of itself identifies what that generality is (or what its reach is). Nor does any proper part of the whole range of that generality's instances. (Again, Wittgenstein's point about ostensive definitions, and about following a rule.) One who grasps the reach of the generality, *things being as said in Pia's speech act*, who grasps when something would fall under this generality, is thus one able to recognize the right things of particular cases he cannot yet get in mind, on adequate acquaintance with them. Only one who, in this sense, can recognize when things *would be* as said can count as grasping this much. The point of act-understanding—what presupposes acquaintance with the act which is thus to reach to cases—is to permit such grasp—to see, for example, of Vic's sleeping as he will tomorrow, that that is a case of someone being as Pia said Sid to be in saying, 'Sid snores'.

Suppose that Sid, a physiological anomaly, makes snoring sounds, while sleeping, through his ears, or only thanks to Pia's remote manipulation of his larynx. Is he then as Pia said? An act-understander may have no answer to that question. The fault may be his: in the face of such things, his mind goes blank. Or there may just *be* nothing to say: nothing about Pia's act makes its being as it was instance either saying what would be true of this case, or saying what would be false of it (just as Pia's act of chewing on her glasses instances neither of these things).

Suppose that Zoë tells Pia, 'There are slabs in Sid's cellar', but the only slabs there are the marble cladding the walls of his home *hamam*. Are things as Zoë said? She was to be understood as making a certain contribution to Pia's project of building a patio; as thus saying what would bear in a certain way on the thing thus to do. There is a way in which those slabs of Sid's *might* be supposed to bear on this—if one wanted a marble patio, if one were prepared to relieve Sid of his cladding. Not, one might have thought, a very reasonable view of the thing for Pia to do. Is this, nonetheless, the sort of bearing Zoë's act is to be understood to have? If so, things might be as she is to be taken to have represented them, then, further, as she said. If not, not. But perhaps neither 'It is' nor 'It's not' state what there is to recognize.

Someone acquainted with Zoë's performing of her act might be equipped to evaluate such issues: to see just what sort of thing Zoë was proposing as to the thing to do. Suppose someone unacquainted with the act were simply told, reliably, that what was said was that such-and-such (that such-and-such thought was expressed). This would not position him to see how it is that her act ought to be taken in the one way or the other. Still, might such a one—one who grasped the thought he was *told* was expressed—thereby know all that was so as to when (of what) what Zoë said would be true, so all there is to know as to its content? If so, then knowing Zoë to have said that, would relieve him of all need for *acquaintance* with her performance in order to see just *what* content the act had. If there is such a position to be in, then, reversing direction, all Zoë need have done for her act to have the content it did was to intend to say just *that*, and get herself to be *to be* understood accordingly.

Suppose I say that Pia said that Sid snores, and thereby speak of a certain way for things to be: such that Sid snores (just the way those words speak of). To grasp that mentioned bit of the conceptual is, inter alia, to grasp how it reaches to particular cases. One would rely on such grasp in seeing, from what *I* said how *Pia's* speech act reaches. The way I said her to have said things is, like any other we might mention, one which admits of understandings. Suppose that Sid is a congenital snorer, but, thanks to adhesive strips, always sleeps silently. Are things the mentioned way or not? They are on one understanding of being such as to snore, not on another. That is *all* there is to say here. So, so far, things neither count as being that way, nor as being not that way. So far, there is nothing in what I said Pia to say to make her either a speaker of truth, or a speaker of falsehood. On the other hand, Pia may have done all I thus said her to, and done that in speaking of Sid snoring on some particular understanding of his doing so—say, one on which, by virtue of the work of the adhesive strips, what she said is false. So for all I said as to what she said, her act might have instanced saying what would be true of Sid as just imagined, or, again, as saying what would be false. There may be more to say as to what it is she said. Such is the model of failure of exhaustiveness.

Suppose, now, that I say Pia to have said that Sid snores, but *I* speak on some particular understanding of things being such that Sid snores—perhaps one on which, thanks to the adhesive strips, he does not. Let us call snoring, on the understanding on which I spoke of this, *snoring**. To grasp what (someone) snoring* is is to grasp how it reaches to particular cases. To grasp this is, perhaps, to grasp of some cases which, as such, neither instance, nor counter-instance, snoring *simpliciter*—for example, some cases involving adhesive strips—that they do (do not) instance someone snoring*. But, keeping in mind all there *is* to get in mind as to what I was speaking of in speaking of snoring on the understanding on which I spoke of this, might there not be two contrasting cases of someone speaking of a way for things to be, in each of which the way spoken of reached differently than it did in the other, both of which were recognizable to us as cases of speaking of someone snoring*? If Wittgenstein's general point about a word naming such-and-such in a language game is correct (many games, each with different conditions on correctness, in which a given word names *N*), then the answer must be 'yes'; or at least that everything there is to understand as to what I was speaking of in speaking of snoring* leaves room for this. This is to say: *any* way for things to be which we can speak—or think—of admits of understandings. This leaves room for par-ticular cases to encounter such that whether *they* instance things being as Pia said is not settled by her having spoken of Sid as snoring*, even if she in fact did that. With which what has already been said about speaking of Sid snoring goes for Sid snoring*, and for any other way for things to be which someone may be said to have spoken of in saying things to be that way. So substitute snoring* for snoring in our first case, and the model still applies intact. Exhaustion fails in just the same way.

But suppose I say, not just that Pia said that Sid snores*, but, further, that she said what would be true *just* where things were that way, no matter what. So if nothing settles whether a given case is, as such, one of things being *that* way, then nothing settles either that Pia spoke truly, or that she spoke falsely. Well, how are we to understand that claim, or my making it—how to understand that 'no matter what' so that I can be understood as so much as purporting to transmit knowledge? Minimally this: snoring* admits of understandings. It remains to see what particular cases the world might furnish which would be ones of snoring* on one such understanding, not on another. For any given such case (to which my claim's truth is hostage), I am right only if there is nothing in Pia's act which would settle whether it is true of that case. One can settle whether I *am* right, given this case, only from the position of an act-understander: from adequate acquaintance recognizing whether there is anything in Pia's performing as she did which settles whether things, in that case, would be as she said. It is hard to see what (sensible) to make of a claim that there is no such thing as a case for which the answer to that question would be 'Yes'.

What *matters* to instancing *things being such that Sid snores** differs profoundly from what matters to instancing *things being as Pia said*. One looks in very different places for what settles whether each was done. Even where Pia said that Sid snores*, there is room for such different searches to turn up different answers. Somewhere in history, we may have settled the question whether some stuff was gold in one way, whether it had atomic number 79 in another. We may have looked in different places for an answer to each question. The world taught us not to do this, or, at any rate, that, for most purposes, doing so would not be reasonable. But where whether Pia spoke truth is settled by the fact that she said Sid to snore*, it is settled merely by the fact of her doing what she then did falling under a certain generality—instancing a certain way for an act to be. Where the fact that she said Sid to snore* would not settle whether she spoke truth, we can, anyway, as things stand, make no sense of the idea that the world might teach us *not* to look at the particular case which instances *someone saying Sid to snore** to see what else it might also instance.

Faust's way thus might be read: *in Sinn's beginning was the deed*. *Sinn* begins, Wittgenstein suggests, in historical acts of representing. *Sinn* provides generalities for such particular cases to fall under. We carve out of the act shapes of saying such-and-such—discernible there in the context of a given scheme for decomposition. (Similarly, historical postures—someone's standing as he now does towards the world—in linking to action as they do, are the beginnings from which we carve such recurrent postures as *judging that such-and-such*. But this is a story for another occasion.) For a particular case to bear, in someone's thinking, on what he is to do, or think, is for it to be presented to him as falling under some generality—as a case of a cup about to run over, say. A *Sinn*, where a whole thought, is a way of thus presenting things. We could not regard others—or ourselves—as thinkers without bringing our own posture, or those of others, under such generalities as *someone who thinks (or said) that such-and-such*. We thus *give* a sense to *same*, on which two postures, or two speech acts, may be the same—same in a particular respect. We thus abstract away from features well worth abstracting from in order to see patterns which are patterns of *thought*, but well worth attending to when it comes to grasping *just* how thinkers, agents, make themselves hostage to the world; just how they depict it in representing as they do.

6. Radicals

The second image, in terms of the chemical radical, suggests the non-uniqueness of decomposition of a speech act into force and thought expressed. The point *might* take several forms. It might be expanded as a point that there is (in general) no *unique* right way of distributing a speech act's representing between some force and what is then said with that force. Non-exhaustiveness suggests a different elaboration: if there is such a thing as saying what it is that Pia said, then what would count as having said this, in given circumstances for the saying, might leave more to be said in other circumstances. That point might generalize. Perhaps, on a given occasion for saying what someone said in some given act, there are different, non-synonymous, correct, and equally correct, ways of saying this, which might further suggest that, on an occasion for saying something, there are equally good, but non-synonymous, ways of doing what would then count as saying *that*. Perhaps, further, what would count, on one occasion, as saying the *same* thing would not so count on another. This section explores these ideas.

Where Pia spoke of *snoring* as what Sid does, all an act-understander need do to see when things would be as she said, one might well think, is to grasp that understanding of snoring on which she said Sid to do this. But *what* would one thus grasp? Well, one might say, all one need do is to recognize something attaching to her words which requires what she said to reach *just* where it does. What might require this? Wittgenstein often raises this question, for example,

A wish seems already to know what will, or would, satisfy it; a proposition, a thought, what makes it true, even when that thing is not there at all! From where does this determining of what is not yet there come? (The hardness of the logical must.)

(1953: §437.)

Perhaps grasping what makes a speech act true is recognizing some rule for, or condition on, being as thus said to attach to the act—something like what Frege at least once referred to as a 'law of association' (see 1904). But this means: one knows when things would be as Pia said in knowing that they would be that just when they satisfied such-and-such condition. One sees how one bit of the conceptual reaches by seeing that it reaches as another does. And how does one see this? If we are to avoid homunculus explanation, all we can say is this. To grasp how what Pia said reaches—just where, to what particular cases, it would reach—is to have a capacity to recognize the right things of particular cases on gaining acquaintance with them. To recognize how (to what cases) a particular condition (or satisfying it) reaches is, again, to have such a capacity. *If* one can find a condition, identifiable independent of her act of speaking, which reaches just as being as she thus said does, then that condition might furnish a kind of prosthetic for grasping the latter's reach: one may have the capacity to see how the condition reaches, and, knowing that this is just as the act does, reach knowledgeable verdicts as to her act's reach, without grasping what it is about her act that makes it do so—without seeing what an act-understander would.

To say what it is that Pia said can be to do no more than offer such prosthetic—or, perhaps, what will do as such so far as it matters (on an occasion), if that is the best that can be done. Three ways of saying what Pia said now suggest themselves. One might say: 'She said that Sid snores', himself thus speaking of Sid snoring (as what Pia said him to do) on the same understanding as Pia did (or on the same understanding so far as it matters, if this is the best to be expected). Speaking on that understanding is not, of course, *saying* what that understanding is. So, second, if, or where, such is needed, one might identify the understanding by examples. For example, if Sid used those adhesive strips religiously (and effectively) he would not be as Pia said. For examples to identify the right understanding, they must be taken (and to be taken) in the right way. To repeat, no proper part of the reach of some bit of the conceptual requires anything as to its further reach. Third, one might spell out the relevant understanding, using words other than Pia's. For example, he might speak of regularly, or frequently, or often, or habitually, producing, while sleeping, a certain sort of sound (describing the sound, or its aetiology).

For present purposes I focus on the third tactic. For the moment I note only that it is one we do, and need to, resort to on occasion, so do, and need to, count as, where successful, means for *saying* what it is that Pia said. In what is already on the table I have suggested a number of *different* ways of saying on what understanding Pia spoke of *snoring. Frequently*, for example, is not *in general* quite the same thing as *habitually*; nor as *regularly*. Sid *could* snore frequently, though not habitually, through a bad run of cosmic accidents, or, again, frequently, but irregularly. A sound identified by aetiology need not have quite the same instances as one identified by acoustic features. That vibration of the uvula (if such it is), when done on helium, might produce a sound too high-pitched to count as that identified by those acoustic features (depending on what one counts as *same sound*). Or, again, a sound produced from Sid's regular normal breathing, through a miniature pick-up in his throat connected to a voice distortion box, may be just right acoustically, but not exactly snoring.

Thus far, the means at hand are non-equivalent. So if there is such a thing as *the* (really) correct way (even on an occasion) of saying what it is that Pia said, which is it? Two points. First, nothing in Pia's speaking as she did may choose between these options—for example dictate specifying the sound in terms of aetiology rather than acoustics, or vice-versa. Or it may dictate choices only given more specifics of how they matter to deciding whether what she said is true, or where it would be. If this is not so of aetiology versus acoustic features, it surely will be for other choices one could conjure up. Second, all the means so far on hand were for speaking to a particular issue which calls for under-standing snoring in one way rather than another—the sort of issue raised by those adhesive strips. Other issues—for example how high-pitched, or harmo-nious, a snore may be—would, to be addressed, call for yet different ways of saying what it is that Pia said.

On the other hand, choice between alternatives on view so far would matter to whether Pia spoke truth only in what are, so far, far-fetched circumstances. If one were correct *as opposed to* another, that would matter somehow to just when what she said *would* be true. But, as it may be, whether what she said *is* true is not liable to turn on whether one choice rather than the other is correct. Whether Sid snores, for example, is not *in fact* liable to turn on whether falsetto 'snoring' counts as snoring in the meaning of Pia's act.

In the perfectly ordinary circumstances in which Pia, over *apéros*, spoke of Sid as snoring, *choice* between snoring identified by aetiology and snoring identified by acoustic features is not an issue an understanding of her words would be expected to address. Or so we may suppose. In which case, nothing in the understanding her words bear would choose between these different ways of understanding *snoring* where they mattered to whether things were as she said. In which case, if to say, really and literally, what it was that Pia said, or, again, strictly speaking, to say again to be so the very thing she did, required producing what diverged *nowhere* in its reach from her words, then none of the means scouted so far would do for this—even if any of them would satisfy us perfectly well for our ordinary, less exigent, purposes. One would need means which were neutral between aetiology and acoustics in identifying what sound Sid was said to produce, and so on for any other issue that might arise as to whether such-and-such would be a case of Sid snoring in the meaning of the act. At this point one might quite reasonably despair of ever finding means for, strictly speaking, saying what it is that Pia said—if such a means must answer '*the*' question on *what* understanding of someone snoring she spoke of this.

At this point one might become suspicious of such a notion of, strictly speaking, saying what was said. At this point one might ask what the point is of speaking of *what N said* in the way we ordinarily do. Frege (once again) suggests an answer to this question. For Frege, as noted (see also essay 10), where there is a thought, there is a point of agreement or disagreement among different thinkers. It is fair to reverse the point: where there is a point of agreement or disagreement among thinkers, there is a thought. (Frege tells us only a thought brings truth into question, so where truth *is* in question, there is a thought.) Suppose that Pia says Sid to snore, and Zoë says Sid to snore. Each speaks on a different understanding of snoring—on much the same understanding, but such that what Pia says to be so would not be so if Sid produced those sounds through his ears, while what Zoë said would be (aetiology matters just that much more to what Pia said). Not that anyone ever has, or will, produce such sounds from his ears. Then there is something—rather important—on which Pia and Zoë agree, something they may both correctly be said to have said, so, on Frege's conception of a thought, a thought each expressed. That they agree on what they do may matter. It may be just that which convinces Vic to bunk with someone else on the Trans-Siberian. It may matter much more to any projects of ours than that on which they have not yet agreed. That each asserted what she did thus represents *one* correct way of decomposing the speech act of each—a correct decomposition on, but only on, the supposition that there may be others. Reason enough for us to speak as we do.

Frege insisted (1892) that the *same* thought may be expressed in quite different sentences. Wittgenstein's image now endorses this point, extending it, perhaps, beyond what Frege foresaw: two different *uses* of a sentence to say something may express the same thought—may say the same thing—even where there is room in those acts of thought-expression for divergence *somewhere* in conceptual space in where things would be as each said.

In *Investigations* §81, Wittgenstein stresses the idea that using language— saying things—is not like calculating in a calculus:

In philosophy we often compare the use of words with games, calculating according to fixed rules, but we cannot say that someone who uses language *must* be playing such a game.

A language furnishes a stock of means for making one's representing recognizable—for example a sentence, 'Sid snores', which makes it recognizable to one fluent in that language that one is speaking of someone, being called 'Sid', snoring. A syntax generates the stock. What is thus generated is something over which one *might* calculate—according to some rules or other, each of which permits replacing some string of such structures with another. Such is a model for calculating over thoughts. Fix some set of thoughts—things there are for *one* to think—and one can associate each with some syntactic structure in some system over which one can then calculate, as per above. There may be interesting such systems, and interesting rules by which to calculate within them—for example rules which would preserve truth. But thoughts are not *themselves* structures over which one might calculate. Their divergence from chemical radicals, as per above, brings this point home forcefully. And what a sentence of a language as such makes recognizable as to the representing done in speaking it in some historic act—*when used as meaning what it does*—is only the beginning of the picture thus offered in the representing thus done.

Pia represented Sid as snoring. But on what understanding of someone snoring, in incurring just what responsibilities for how things are (e.g. how the world bears on what to do)? And so on. What one cannot insist, nor even yet say sensibly, is that there are rules for calculating from what a *sentence* does to how one represents things in using it in given circumstances. Nor is the way one thus represents things to be yet something over which one might calculate. For that one needs the sorts of abstractions from the concrete speech act contained in decomposing it into force and thought expressed. The images of the footnote to §22 gain us understanding of what sort of abstraction that involves, hence of some of the point of saying, with §81, that someone who represents in language is not calculating by fixed rules.

7. Thought and Deed

What takes the place of the historical in attitudes, postures of representing— what corresponds there to the historic speech act, or its representing as it did, in *acts* of representing, is the *person*, or his standing towards things as he does. The person represents things to himself as he does; his doing that may be, inter alia, his taking things to be such-and-such way, for example thinking that Sid snores. What here parallel the points made by the picture of the pugilist, and the idea of the chemical radical, would be these. First, someone's standing towards things as he does is decomposable in no unique right way into his judging this, that, and the other; and in different ways for different purposes, or on different occasions. In more Fregean vocabulary, it is only relative to some particular scheme for decomposing that someone's picture of things is correctly articulated into his judging that such-and-such. Such is correct only within a particular conception of how thinkers are to be organized into same-thinkers; of what points there are on which for thinkers to agree or disagree; only according to some particular way of answering such questions as whether that Sid snores and that he regularly emits snoring sounds in sleep are one thing for one to think, or two. Second, if there is no one such privileged decomposition, so, too, no given decomposition can claim exhaustiveness. Just this is overlooked in such philosophical fantasies as the Representational Theory of Mind (see, notably, Fodor 1978, 1998: 6–12).

In *The Blue Book* Wittgenstein considered this idea: if a speech act admits of interpretation, there must always be a *last* interpretation, something not itself open to interpretation. Thoughts, conceived as Frege does, are designed to fit that bill. For someone to think that Sid snores is for his standing as he does towards things to instance a certain generality: someone being such as to think that Sid snores. For him to instance just *that* generality is for his stance towards things to have a certain reach: to think what would be so of such-and-such cases, *not* so of such-and-such others. The reach his thinking *thereby* has is just that of the way for things to be he thus relates to: things being such that Sid snores. *That* is not open to interpretation. If Sid snores on one understanding of this, but not on another, then that particular generality, *things being such that Sid snores*, neither *as such* reaches, nor counter-reaches, to Sid's being as he is. Similarly, if a speech act expressed the thought that Sid snores (assertively), then where it *thereby* reaches is not open to interpretation. Such is, so to speak, the grammar of the notion *thought*.

On the other hand, a thought is of some given way for things to be (that things are that way). Ways for things to be *do* admit of understandings. Things *are* such that Sid snores if you understand their so being in one way, not if you understand it in another. There are, for example, those adhesive strips. There is room in a person's posture towards the world for one who thinks that Sid snores also to do so on some understanding of this. To say that Pia thinks that Sid snores need not be to *exhaust* her view on that topic. Such just instances a general point about the nonconceptual and the conceptual. If my pet frog, Sapo, is green, no more is thus true of him than is contained in what it is for something to be green. But if his being as he is instances something being green, then, like any instancing of a generality, it does this in only one of the indefinitely many ways it might be done. Sapo, as it happens, is matte green (when dry). He might have instanced being green without that. Still, in *his* instancing being green, he also instances being matte green. Similarly for taking Sid to snore.

Here historic speech acts parallel historic whole postures. If Pia's saying what she did was (inter alia) her saying Sid to snore, and if, *thereby* the truth of what she said was made hostage to no more than speaking of Sid snoring can, per se, make it, still, there may be more to be said as to the understanding of snoring on which she so spoke, and *thus* more to be said as to just when things would be as she said, so as to *just* when she would have spoken truth. Such is involved in the non-exhaustiveness of decompositions. *This* point is what is missed by deflationists about truth.

Such are some of the directions in which the early work of the *Investigations* points; some ways in which §22, in summing up that work, adumbrates themes for more elaborate treatment later in that work. *This* exploration of the work ends here.

Bibliography

Austin, J. L., 1946: 'Other Minds', *Proceedings of the Aristotelian Society*, supp. vol. 20 (1946); reprinted in *Philosophical Papers*, 3rd edition, Oxford: Oxford University Press, 1979, pp. 76–116.

—— 1950: 'Truth', *Philosophical Papers*, 3rd edition, Oxford: Oxford University Press, 1979, pp. 117–133.

—— 1962a: *Sense and Sensibilia*, Oxford: The Clarendon Press.

—— 1962b: *How To Do Things With Words*, Oxford: The Clarendon Press.

Ayer, A. J., 1940: *The Foundations of Empirical Knowledge*, London: The Macmillan Press.

Chomsky, Noam, 1965: *Aspects of the Theory of Syntax*, Cambridge MA: The MIT Press.

Clarke, T., 1972: 'The Legacy of Skepticism', *The Journal of Philosophy*, vol. 69, n. 20, November 1972, pp. 754–769.

Davidson, Donald, 1974: 'On the Very Idea of a Conceptual Scheme', *Proceedings and Addresses of the American Philosophical Association* 47 (1974); reprinted in *Inquiries Into Truth And Interpretation*, Oxford: Oxford University Press, 1984, pp. 183–198.

Descartes, René, 1637 (2000): *Discours de la Méthode*, Paris: Flammarion.

—— 1643: Letter to Princess Elisabeth, May 21, 1643, *Descartes: Philosophical Writings*, G. E. M. Anscombe and P. T. Geach, eds., Edinburgh: Thomas Nelson and Sons, 1954, pp. 275–277.

Dummett, M. A. E., 1993: 'What is a Theory of Meaning?' (I and II), in *The Seas of Language*, Oxford: Oxford University Press, pp. 1–93.

Feyerabend, Paul, 1962: 'Explanation, Reduction, and Empiricism', *Minnesota Studies in the Philosophy of Science,* vol. 3, H. Feigl and G. Maxwell, eds., Minneapolis: University of Minnesota Press, pp. 28–97.

Fodor, Jerry, 1978: 'Propositional Attitudes', The Monist, vol. 61, n. 4, 1978; reprinted in Fodor 1981, pp. 177–203.

—— 1980: *RePresentations*, Cambridge, MA: The MIT Press, 1981.

—— 1998: *Concepts: Where Cognitive Science Went Wrong*, Oxford: Oxford University Press.

Frege, Gottlob, 1882a: Letter to Anton Marty, *Gottlob Freges Briefwechsel* (Frege: 1980), pp. 117–119.

—— 1882b: '17 Kernsätze zur Logik', *Nachgelassene Schriften*.

—— 1884: *The Foundations of Arithmetic*, J. L. Austin, translator, Oxford: Basil Blackwell, 1978, p. x.

—— 1891: 'Funktion und Begriff', *Funktion, Begriff, Bedeutung*, G. Patzig, ed., Göttingen: Vandenhoeck und Ruprecht, 1962.

—— 1892a: 'Über Sinn und Bedeutung', *Funktion, Begriff, Bedeutung*, G. Patzig, ed., Göttingen: Vandenhoeck und Ruprecht, 1962.

Frege, Gottlob, 1892b: 'Über Begriff und Gegenstand', *Funktion, Begriff, Bedeutung*, Göttingen: Vandenhoeck und Ruprecht, 1986, pp. 66–80.

—— 1892–1895: 'Ausfuhrungen über Sinn und Bedeutung', *Nachgelassene Schriften*, 128–136.

—— 1893: *Grundgesetze der Arithmetik*, translated as *The Basic Laws of Arithmetic*, M. Furth, trans. and ed., Berkeley and Los Angeles: The University of California Press, 1967.

—— 1897: *Logik*, Frege 1983, pp. 137–163.

—— 1903: *Grundgesetze der Arithmetik*, v. II, Jena: H. Pohl, 1903. Selections in translation in *Translations from the Philosophical Writings of Gottlob Frege*, P. Geach and M. Black, eds., Oxford: Basil Blackwell, 1960.

—— 1904: 'Was ist eine Funktion?', *Festschrift für Ludwig Boltzmann*, pp. 656–666; reprinted in *Funktion, Begriff, Bedeutung*.

—— 1906: 'Einleitung in die Logik', *Nachgelassene Schriften* (Frege: 1983), pp. 201–212.

—— 1914: 'Logik in der Mathematik', *Nachgelassene Schriften* (Frege: 1983), pp. 219–270.

—— 1915: 'Meine grundlegenen logischen Einsichten', (Frege: 1983), pp. 271–272.

—— 1918: 'Der Gedanke', *Beiträge zur deutschen Idealismus* 2, 1918–1919, pp. 58–77; reprinted in *Logische Untersuchungen*, Göttingen: Vandenhoeck und Ruprecht, 1966.

—— 1919a: 'Aufzeichnungen für Ludwig Darmstaedter', *Nachgelassene Schriften*, 273–275.

—— 1919b: Letter to Paul F. Linke, *Gottlob Freges Briefwechsel* (Frege: 1980), pp. 113–116.

—— 1980: *Gottlob Freges Briefwechsel mit D. Hilbert, E. Husserl, B. Russell, sowie ausgewählte Einzelbriefe Freges*, Hamburg: Felix Meiner Verlag.

—— 1983: *Nachgelassene Schriften*, H. Hermes, F. Kambartel, F. Kaulbach, eds., Hamburg: Felix Meiner Verlag, 1983 (2nd, expanded, edition).

Hume, David, 1739: *A Treatise of Human Nature*, L. A. Selby-Bigge, ed., Oxford: The Clarendon Press, 1888.

Kant, Immanuel, 1781/1787: *Kritik der reinen Vernunft*, Frankfurt am Mein: Insel Verlag, 1956.

Leibniz, Gottfried, 1696: 'On Locke's Essay on Human Understanding' (1696), *New Essays on Human Understanding*, A. G. Langley, trans., La Salle, Illinois: Open Court, 1949.

—— 1753: *Nouveaux Essais sur l'Entendement Humain*, J. Brunschwig, ed., Paris: Garnier-Flammarion, 1966.

McDowell, John, 1977: 'On The Sense and Reference of a Proper Name', *Mind* v. 86, 1977, pp. 159–185; reprinted in (McDowell 1998a), pp. 171–198.

—— 1979: 'Virtue and Reason', *The Monist*, v. 62 (1979), pp. 331–350; reprinted in (McDowell: 1998b), pp. 50–73.

—— 1980: 'The Role of *Eudaimonia*, in Aristotle's Ethics', *Proceedings of the African Classical Associations*, v. 15 (1980), pp. 1–14; reprinted in (McDowell: 1998b), pp. 3–22.

—— 1987: 'In Defence of Modesty', *Michael Dummett: Contributions to Philosophy*, Barry Taylor, ed., Dordrecht: Martinus Nijhoff, 1987; reprinted in (McDowell: 1998a), pp. 87–107.

—— 1998a: *Meaning, Knowledge and Reality*, Cambridge, MA: Harvard University Press.

—— 1998b: *Mind, Value and Reality*, Cambridge, MA: Harvard University Press.

Moore, G. E., 1939: 'Proof of an External World', *Philosophical Papers*, London: George Allen and Unwin, 1959, pp. 126–148.

Peacocke, C. A. P., 1992: 'Truth, Activation Vectors and Possession Conditions for Concepts', *Philosophy and Phenomenological Research*, v. 52, n. 2, June 1992, pp. 431–447.

Putnam, Hilary, 1962a: 'The Analytic and the Synthetic', *Minnesota Studies in the Philosophy of Science*, v. 3, H. Feigl and G. Maxwell, eds., Minneapolis: University of Minnesota Press, 1962; reprinted in (Putnam: 1975b), pp. 33–69.

—— 1962b: 'It Ain't Necessarily So', *The Journal of Philosophy*, v. LIX, n. 22 (25 October 1962); reprinted in (Putnam: 1975a), pp. 237–249.

—— 1975a: *Mathematics, Matter and Method: Philosophical Papers volume 1*, Cambridge: Cambridge University Press.

—— 1975b: *Mind, Language and Reality: Philosophical Papers volume 2*, Cambridge: Cambridge University Press.

—— 1975c: 'The Meaning of "Meaning"', *Mind, Language and Reality, Philosophical Papers volume 2*, Cambridge: Cambridge University Press.

—— 1977: 'Models and Reality', presidential address to the Association for Symbolic Logic, 29 December 1977; reprinted in (Putnam: 1983).

—— 1983: *Realism and Reason: Philosophical Papers volume 3*, Cambridge: Cambridge University Press.

—— 1994: 'Rethinking Mathematical Necessity', *Words and Life* (edited by J. Conant), Cambridge, MA: Harvard University Press, 1994, pp. 245–263.

—— 1999: *The Threefold Cord*, New York: Columbia University Press.

—— 2002: *The Collapse of the Fact/Value Dichotomy and Other Essays*, Cambridge MA: Harvard University Press.

—— 2004: *Ethics Without Ontology*, Cambridge, MA: Harvard University Press.

Quine, W. V. O., 1950: 'Two Dogmas of Empiricism', in his *From a Logical Point of View*, New York: Harper and Row, 1953, pp. 20–46.

—— 1987: 'Indeterminacy of Translation Again', *The Journal of Philosophy*, vol. 84, n. 1, January 1987, pp. 5–10.

Russell, B., 1918: 'The Philosophy of Logical Atomism', *Logic and Knowledge* (R. C. Marsh, ed.), New York, G. P. Putnam's Sons, 1956.

Stroud, Barry, 1984: 'The Allure of Idealism', *Proceedings of the Aristotelian Society*, supp. vol. 58 (1984); reprinted in (Stroud, 2000), pp. 83–98.

—— 1994: 'Kantian Argument, Conceptual Capacities, and Invulnerability', *Kant and Contemporary Epistemology*, P. Parrini, ed., Dordrecht: Reidel, 1994; reprinted in (Stroud, 2000), pp. 155–176.

—— 1999: 'The Goal of Transcendental Arguments', *Transcendental Arguments: Problems and Prospects*, Oxford: Oxford University Press, 2000; reprinted in (Stroud, 2000), pp. 203–223.

—— 2000: *Understanding Human Knowledge*, Oxford: Oxford University Press, 2000.

Travis, Charles, 2005: 'Frege, Father of Disjunctivism', *Philosophical Topics*, v. 33, n. 1, Spring, 2005, pp. 307–334.

—— 2006: *Thought's Footing: A Theme in Wittgenstein's Philosophical Investigations*, Oxford: Oxford University Press.

—— 2008: *Occasion-Sensitivity: Selected Essays*, Oxford: Oxford University Press.

—— forthcoming: 'Is Seeing Intentional?', *Philosophie du Langage Ordinaire*, B. Ambroise and S. Laugier, eds., Hildesheim: Georg Olms.

Waismann, Friedrich, 1979: *Wittgenstein and the Vienna Circle*, Oxford: Basil Blackwell.

Williams, B., 1978: *Descartes: The Project of Pure Enquiry*, Harmondsworth: Penguin Books.

Wittgenstein, Ludwig, 1922: *Tractatus Logico-Philosophicus*, London: Routledge and Kegan Paul.

—— 1929: 'Some Remarks On Logical Form', *Proceedings of the Aristotelian Society*, supp. vol. 9 (1929), pp. 162–171; reprinted in *Philosophical Occasions*, J. Klagge and A. Nordmann, eds., Indianapolis: Hackett, 1993, pp. 29–35.

—— 1953: *Philosophical Investigations*, Oxford: Basil Blackwell.

—— 1958: *The Blue and Brown Books*, Oxford: Basil Blackwell.

—— 1967: *On Certainty*, Oxford: Basil Blackwell.

—— 1974: *Philosophical Grammar*, Oxford: Basil Blackwell.

—— 1980: *Wittgenstein's Lectures: Cambridge, 1930–1932*, D. Lee, ed., Chicago: The University of Chicago Press.

Index